Victorian Ludlow

Edited for

The Ludlow Historical Research Group

By

David Lloyd, Roy Payne,
Christopher Train & Derek Williams

Scenesetters

First Published: 2004

Publishers: Scenesetters, Ash-Leys, Bucknell, Shropshire, SY7 0AL. Tel: 01547 530660.

ISBN: 1 874200 14 9 (softback); **1 874200 15 7** (hardback)

Printed by: The Cromwell Press, Trowbridge, Wiltshire.

Illustration credits: Photographs and illustrations, except where otherwise indicated, are taken from the collections of the authors. Every effort has been made to trace other copyright holders and apologies are extended to any copyright holders whose rights have been unwittingly infringed.

Cover illustration: Ludlow in the 1870s as painted by Edward Phipson.

Victorian Ludlow

The Setting...

A view of Ludlow from Whitcliffe common in the 1880s by local photographer Thomas Jones, showing a compact historic town, with expanding suburbs beyond.

...and the people

The Queen's diamond jubilee, 1897. The numbers on parade exceed the onlookers, as various organisations process down Old Street, headed by the Town Crier and the local police, then the Mayor, the four Aldermen, and the Borough councillors.

CONTENTS

PREFACE

The town of Ludlow has inspired much historical writing and research. Since 1976 the Ludlow Historical Research Group, under the guidance at various times of David Lloyd and Martin Speight, has played a major part in this work. Interest has focussed on Ludlow's more distant and visibly glamorous past – the prosperous medieval wool town, the "lost capital of Wales", the Georgian town of resort. The Victorian period has attracted little attention, Ludlow's nineteenth century history tending to be regarded as a somewhat dowdy postscript to a glorious past, characterised by a disastrous municipal lawsuit, electoral corruption of Eatanswill proportions and a Market Hall, which Pevsner called "Ludlow's bad luck".

That was always a questionable view, and a number of factors has conspired to suggest that, at last, the time is right for a more detailed survey of the life and times of Ludlow and its inhabitants during Victoria's reign. First, the interests of several members of the Research Group have of late led them to turn their attention to nineteenth century studies, for example the effects of the 1834 Poor Law on Ludlow and district, the place of servants in the life and economy of the town, and analysis of the Ludlow and Ludford censuses. Secondly, the letters of Anna Maria Fay, an acute American observer of the Ludlow scene in the 1850s, have recently been republished. Thirdly, the mid-nineteenth century diaries of a Broad Street solicitor, Francis Southern, were spontaneously and generously made available to the Group by his great-granddaughter, Rachel Millard.

It was as work began on examining and collating the information and gossip contained in the letters and diaries that the Research Group Committee decided to offer the Friends of Shropshire Archives a history day in the autumn of 2004 on the theme of Victorian Ludlow. Out of this proposal the idea for the present volume seemed naturally to grow, and specific chapters on topics not already being researched were commissioned from other Group members.

Arising as it does from the interest and work of a variety of individuals, it is not intended to be a comprehensive and definitive history of Victorian Ludlow, but the range of subjects which it covers has been chosen in order to reflect, in this local context, some of the major social and political issues which dominated Victorian England and, in so doing, to throw light upon the key elements of the life of the town during those years. Even with this limited intention, we hope that the reader will come to recognise, as we have done, that the story of Victorian Ludlow cannot and should not be dismissed as "a dowdy postscript to a glorious past".

The Editors wish to thank all who have helped in any way in the preparation and production of the book. They are too numerous to name individually here (particular acknowledgements are made appropriately in the text), but it would be improper of us not to pay tribute to the present chairman of the Research Group, Jean Brown, whose energetic advocacy of the project has sustained it from its inception. We would also wish to express our gratitude, as always in any endeavour which relates to Shropshire history, to the support given by Mary McKenzie, the County Archivist, and the staff at Shropshire Archives in Shrewsbury. Finally we record our thanks to our publisher, Andrew Jenkinson, and his team at Scenesetters for dealing so patiently and professionally with the demands which we have made upon them.

CHAPTER 1

EMPLOYMENT AND SOCIETY

DAVID LLOYD

Fig.1 Right: Princess Victoria as portrayed two years before her visit to Ludlow by the society painter, Sir George Hayter. The dog was her spaniel, Dash.
Left: This imposing house in Broad Street, built by Richard Salwey Esq. in the 1740s, became the Crown Inn in 1816. In 1832 it was renamed The Royal Kent, Victoria and Crown in honour of the royal visit. It was later replaced by the Wesleyan Methodist Chapel.

THE VISIT OF PRINCESS VICTORIA, 1832

On Sunday, 4 November, 1832, Princess Victoria and her mother, the widowed Duchess of Kent, visited Ludlow.[1] Recognised for some years as heiress presumptive to King William, the fourteen year old Victoria was being prepared for sovereignty by regional tours, which attracted enthusiastic crowds and official receptions. Coming from Oakly Park, where they were guests of R.H. Clive Esq. and Lady Harriet, the royal party was met by the "body corporate in their robes", and taken to the door of the church. The congregation, "more numerous than ever before witnessed", stood as the visitors were escorted to their seats by the

Rector, the elderly Revd Richard Baugh, and the officiating Minister, the Revd John Hinde. Later, in the castle, they were formally greeted by the Corporation, and presented by the bailiffs with "two pairs of gloves each: the principal manufacture of the town". This episode offers an appropriate introduction to a book on Victorian Ludlow.

The year of the visit was that of the great Reform Bill, which received royal assent five months before the Princess came to Ludlow, the first in a line of legislation which was to change many aspects of English society during her reign. Several of the topics covered in later chapters consider the impact of this legislation on Ludlow, taking their starting point before the Queen's accession in 1837. So 1832, for the purpose of this book, may be seen as the entrance into the Victorian era – a period in Ludlow's history down to 1901, the year of the Queen's death, which has its own unity and coherence.

One of the themes of these years is economic change, of which the presentation of gloves to the Princess and her mother affords a particular example. Glove making had indeed been the town's "principal manufacture" for nearly two centuries. In 1812 "the number of men, women and children" employed amounted "to several hundreds", but there was a sharp decline in production after 1815, in part due to renewed competition from French manufacturers.[2] There was a recovery in the 1820s, with eleven master glovers listed in Pigot's 1828 Directory, but

decline had resumed by the time of the royal visit, with only five producers in 1835, two in 1841 and just one in 1851: Mary Bottomly, at 1 Bull Ring.[3]

ECONOMIC CHANGE AND POPULATION

The purpose of this chapter is to explore the main elements of this economic change. They will be considered systematically, using the categories recognised by the Leicester University Small Towns Project. The classification, set out in Fig. 2, deals first with those who are employed, grouped by economic function, and then with those who are not remunerated for their work, but are either of independent means, or dependent on others,

Code	Class	1841 Ludlow	1841 parts of Stan.Lacy/ Ludford	1841 All	%	1901 All	%
	Fig. 2: Employment and Dependency, 1841 and 1901.						
	Percentages below refer to the total number of persons employed						
Employed							
1	Agriculture	106	33	139	6	141	5
3	Extraction	2	4	6	0.3	76	3
	Building	181	4	185	8	215	8
5	Manufacturing	596	21	617	28	454	17
6	Transport	18	2	20	1	164	6
7	Dealing	208	6	214	10	454	17
8	Financial	17	0	17	1	32	1
9	Labour	181	39	220	10	280	11
10	Public service & professional	112	2	114	5	228	9
11	Service: domestic	579	41	620	28	468	18
11	Service: other	54	4	58	3	144	5
	TOTAL EMPLOYED	2054	156	2210		2656	
	Water works construction (temporary)					124	
	Percentages below refer to the total population						
				2210	**40**	**2780**	**44**
Living on income							
12	Independent	277	5	282	5	141	2
Dependent							
13	Dependent: institutional	50		50	1	44	1
	Dependent: other	2683	226	2909	54	3332	53
	TOTAL	**5064**	**387**	**5451**		**6297**	

Fig. 3: Population of Ludlow and its suburbs, 1841 to 1901.		
	1841	**1901**
Ludlow St Laurence	5064	4552
Ludlow Castle	with above	5
Historic Borough	**5064**	**4557**
Stanton Lacy	283 [1]	1457 [3]
Ludford	104 [2]	253
Suburbs in 1901	**387**	**1710**
Enlarged borough in 1901	**5451**	**6267**
Outside Ludlow Borough in 1901		30 [4]
TOTAL	**5451**	**6297**

[1] That part of Stanton Lacy parish which was absorbed into Ludlow in 1901

[2] Holdgate Fee 44, Ludford Rock Lane 50, Paper Mill cottages 10.

[3] East Hamlet 1322, Rock Lane 135

[4] In Ludford parish

Research on these figures by Chris Train is gratefully acknowledged.

yet nevertheless are a significant part of the town's economy and social life.[4] Economic activities are the heartbeat of all communities, and the topics considered in later chapters rest on this foundation. To set the context for this discussion a brief survey of the town's population at the beginning and end of the period is required.

Published census figures from 1841 to 1901 give the population of Ludlow Borough as declining from 5,064 to 4,557.[5] If the suburbs are included, however, the population in fact rose, from 5,451 in 1841 to 6,297 in 1901 – an increase of 15.5%.[6] The figures are shown in Fig. 3 Disregard of the suburbs (whose growth is fully discussed in chapter 2) can lead to a serious misunderstanding of Victorian Ludlow, as occurred in such a highly regarded work as the *Cambridge Urban History of Britain*, Volume III, 1840-1950. Citing the census totals of 4,691 for 1851 and 4,552 for 1901, Stephen Royle drew the erroneous conclusion that "Ludlow lost population" during this period.[7] The reverse was in fact the case.

The figures show that Ludlow experienced modest though not spectacular growth in these years. Comparisons with other towns must be cautious, for all census figures can be distorted by boundary changes, but the evidence suggests that Ludlow's growth rate gave it an intermediate position amongst Shropshire towns. It was well behind Shrewsbury and other towns in the north, particularly Oswestry and Wellington, but ahead of other south Shropshire market towns, such as Bishop's Castle, Cleobury Mortimer, Clun, Church Stretton and Much Wenlock, some of which lost population.

This growth in population was accompanied by a growth in the numbers and proportion of people in employment – from 2210 in 1841 to 2780 in 1901, an increase from 40% to 44%. But that increase conceals variations between employment sectors. These are discussed in the following sections.

EMPLOYMENT

Agriculture: a stable employment sector

The number of people in agriculture in Ludlow remained almost constant, as shown in Fig. 2, though the nature of the work often changed. In 1841 there were 99 agricultural labourers, many of them working on farms outside Ludlow. By 1901 this number had fallen to 31, but there were many others, still essentially labourers, whose occupations were specified, for example as cowman, shepherd or wagoner. By 1901 there were also machinists, two of them threshing machinists. A number of small scale farmers lived in the town, such as William Pitt of Springfield Dairy in Lower Gaolford, farming eight acres in 1881.

One of the growth areas was gardening. There were 21 gardeners in 1841, but this number more than doubled by 1901. Some were market gardeners, such as Thomas Piller, whose nursery and garden ground south east of Friars' Walk occupied nearly two acres in 1847.[8] Another well known garden was that of John Collier, florist and nurseryman, shown in Fig. 4. There were also orchards in Linney, on the east side of Corve Street and elsewhere, covering nearly four acres. Most of the Borough's agricultural land was meadow for hay and grazing, innkeepers and butchers being the chief users. In 1841 there was only one veterinary surgeon – James Brookholding Jones – but by 1901 there were three, two of them with assistants. No statistic speaks more clearly of Ludlow's developing role as a service centre for a farming area.

This is illustrated further by the high profile of the annual show of the Ludlow Agricultural Society, formed in 1847. Held after harvest in late September, it attracted large crowds, ending with a dinner for the organisers, many of them Borough Councillors.[9] As well as promoting good farming practice, with prizes for best animals and ploughing, there were 14 prizes for servants in the hope of inculcating what were considered good habits, such as length of service and thrift. In 1853 the first prize in this category, for "the man who, by his daily labour, has reared the greatest number of children without parochial aid", went to John Davies, "in the employ of Mr Bishop of Rowton, for having reared ten children".[10] Participants came from a wide area, though the only prize winner from Ludlow was William Bytheway, maltster, servant to Mr Penny of Corve Street, for 30 years in one service in Ludlow.

Fig. 4: This detail of a panoramic view of Ludlow, photographed by Thomas Jones in the 1880s, shows an area of intense market gardening in Dinham, between the town wall and Camp Lane. The proprietor was John Collier, florist and nurseryman.

Brick-making and quarrying: a sector of rapid growth

The steep west facing slopes of Upper Gaolford and Gravel Hill have yielded brick-making clays since the Tudor period. There were only six brick-makers in 1841, but this rose to 20 by 1901, as new works were opened northwards. The leading manufacturer was Thomas Sheffield, described in 1856 as "brick and tile manufacturer, Station Yard"; his son John was still in business in 1895. The 1885 Ordnance Survey map shows seven kilns, five of them in Fishmore Road, where the proprietors by 1900 were Thomas Greenwood and Sons,

Fig. 5: Loaded rail wagons of the Clee Hill Granite Company, awaiting transit down the incline to the railway at Bitterley, and then to Ludlow.

brick and pipe makers, a branch of a Westbury firm. The growth in this sector must surely have been in response to the demand for bricks for the houses which began to spring up in the suburbs from the 1850s onwards.

Quarrying on Clee Hill generated more jobs, with about 50 workers living in Ludlow by 1901. The Dhustone quarries opened in 1863, sending stone for roads and other purposes to many parts of the country; and the closely linked granite quarries a few years later.[11] By 1891 the output of Dhustone was 90,000 tons a year, while the granite quarry reached 125,000 tons by 1911. Before 1900, nearly all the stone was moved by rail, using an inclined railway and a branch line from Bitterley to Ludlow, which opened in 1864, generating more employment. Loaded wagons waiting for downhill transport are shown in Fig. 5. From 1868 the General Manager of both quarries was Thomas Roberts who lived at 12 Corve Street, where the companies had their offices. Roberts became a leading Ludlow citizen, serving as Mayor in 1879-81 and again in 1893-1895.

Builders and their craftsmen: another stable sector

Numbers in the building trades rose, but only moderately. A few were master builders who employed others, though sometimes they called themselves by trade names, especially joiner and mason. As in previous periods some builders were from dynasties of two or three generations such as the Steads of Castle Street, the Russells of Old Street, the Grosvenors of Corve Street and, from the 1870s, the Weales of New Street. Samuel Stead (1788-1857), who employed eight men in 1851, enjoyed a particularly high reputation. After employing him at Oakly Park and at Killerton in Devon, the architect C.R. Cockerell, described him in 1838 as "the best artist mason I ever met with".[12] Some of these families came from local villages – the Steads from Eye, the Weales from Onibury – and saw opportunities in Ludlow. Several were developers and speculators, among them Benjamin Weale, as described in chapter 2. The master builders employed many operatives, with more decorators, plumbers and gas fitters late in the reign.

A study of Ludlow's Victorian buildings awaits another publication, but a short overview is appropriate here. With better communications enabling London architects to undertake more work in the provinces, it is understandable that some major building projects in Ludlow were designed elsewhere: the restoration of the parish church in 1859-61 by George Gilbert Scott, the new Town Hall in 1888-89 by Henry Cheers (Fig. 6), the re-casing of the church tower in 1889-91 by Arthur Blomfield. Yet the town's own architects are not without merit. Matthew Stead the younger, nephew of Samuel the builder, designed the Workhouse and the Assembly Rooms, though his miscalculation of the costs of the former – a little over £2,000 initially, £4,500 two months later[13] – hardly inspired confidence. Nevertheless, the magisterial Assembly Rooms, with bold Italianate features, are a fine memorial to him and his uncle. In contrast, another Ludlow architect, Herbert Evans (1842-91), son of Charles Evans surveyor, employed "the eclectic, latitudinarian style" of the mid-Victorians, as seen at 1 Dinham (Fig. 7) and Kennet House, Sheet Road (affectionately known as "the pepper pot"), both probably built in the early

Fig. 6, Top right: The new Market Hall, a few days before its unveiling on 17 October 1889 by Col. The Hon. G.H.Windsor Clive. The building gave late Victorian Ludlow fine facilities, including an elegant Council Chamber. Amidst great local controversy it was demolished in 1986 "for structural reasons".

Fig. 7, Right: No.1 Dinham, where Evans, perhaps influenced by the writings of Ruskin, followed a Ludlow tradition of tall, jettied buildings with steeply pitched roofs, but used different kinds of brick and stone to produce a striking polychrome effect. The house is a monument to both Victorian technology and aesthetic taste.

1870s.[14] Evans is remembered for collaboration with William Russell (1821-84) of Old Street, builder, but outside building contractors were sometimes used, such as R. Price of Shrewsbury for the Town Hall.[15]

Manufacturing: a sector in decline

The decline in manufacturing typified many market towns, as local manufactures were undermined by goods from more favoured production areas, brought in by improving transport. Some "entrepreneurial towns" were boosted by continuing production of a local speciality, e.g. Burton on Trent by brewing and Kettering by shoes.[16] At Ludlow, however, as shown above, the staple industry, glove-making, was in decline, contrary to what is said in the *Cambridge Urban History of Britain*, where Stephen Royle, commenting on Henry James' observation that Ludlow in the 1870s was a "town not disfigured by industry", remarks incorrectly "though by that time, Ludlow…did have an industrial centre, in malting, glove making and paper manufacturing."[17]

In fact, malting was another casualty. In the early 19th century this was a leading industry, with 24 Directory entries in 1842. By 1879, in the face of competition from national brewers such as Bass and Alsopps, the number had dropped to two, one of them the large Corve Street premises of Henry Lloyd, Mayor in 1888. An associated trade was the making of mineral waters by A.R. Cartwright at 116 Corve Street, established after 1895.

Two other industries which disappeared were cloth manufacture, the medieval and Tudor mainstay of the economy, and paper-making. In 1841 there was only one employer in cloth manufacture: William Evans. His Lower Broad Street premises (Fig. 8), rebuilt in 1856 as the town's first purpose built factory, were bought by a Bradford mill owner, who used water power to manufacture worsted blankets at the Teme Mill Company, an example of outside capital invested in Ludlow.[18] From 1835 or earlier to 1860 the Steventon paper-mill, which

had one "beating engine", was operated by John Wade, paper maker, who presumably employed the 13 paper makers in the 1841 census; but in 1861 there were only three employees, and by 1871 none.[19]

Other industries declined but were not obliterated. There were 29 nailers in 1841, many of them supplying ironmongers, but only two by 1901. Eleven men worked in non-ferrous metals in 1841, but there were only four – all tin plate workers – in 1901. The leather preparation trades, which had once supplied the glovers, employed only 16 men in 1841, and this had dropped to six by 1901. The numbers involved in making clothes were much larger: 263 in 1841, but dropping to 155 in 1901, as more ready made garments and shoes came into town. In contrast, female dressmakers, seamstresses and milliners increased. Many were women working at home, such as Emma Whitehouse, wife of the Gas Works manager, who made shirts.

A number of industries held their own, including watchmakers, printers, saddlers and wheelwrights, the last two reflecting the continuing importance of horse-drawn transport. To offset in part the many declining industries there were some growth areas. Ludlow was one

Fig. 8: The cloth factory in Lower Broad Street, photographed in the early 20th century, when it was used as a furniture store by Bodenham and Sons Limited (see chapter 3).

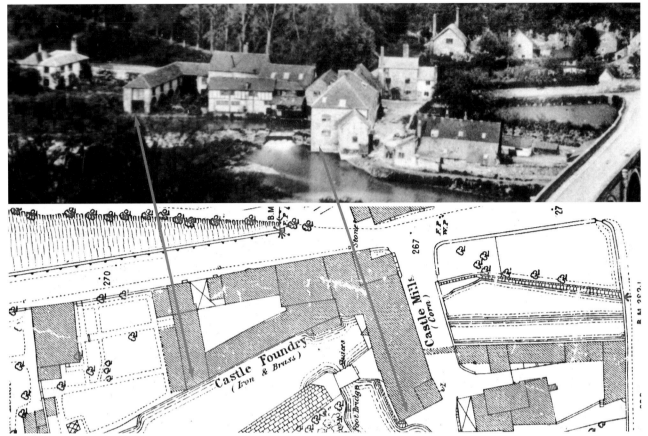

Fig. 9: A detail of a photograph taken from Whitcliffe in 1870, with part of the O.S 1:500 map of Ludlow. Chaplin Hodges' foundry was the eastern part (left) of the mill complex. In 1893, when advertised for sale, it was described as "for many years used as an iron and brass foundry". The buildings included a casting shop, capital workshops, a smith's shop and "an office with large pattern rooms over".

of several Shropshire towns to have a foundry, said by Trinder to be "a sign of virility".[20] It was owned by Chaplin Hodges, who had moved to Castle mills shortly before 1839, taking advantage of water power. A picture of the site, with an accompanying map, is shown as Fig. 9. The work was dangerous, Thomas Hamer in 1846 losing three fingers to the cutting blades of a circular saw.[21] Products included water-wheels, cast and wrought-iron shafting and cellar doors, of which about a dozen Ludlow examples survive. In 1890 the firm was taken over by its manager, W.J. Roberts, who moved to the Phoenix Foundry in Gravel Hill. Reflecting Ludlow's links with Clee Hill quarrying the Foundry specialised in casting jaws for stone breaking machinery. Comparable in size was the carriage building works in Lower Raven Lane,

employing 17 men by 1901. The last of a series of owners were Edward Clift and W.G. Kingston, partners by 1888. Baking and milling also expanded, reflecting rising population and decline in home baking. By the late 19th century most of the Teme mills were producing flour, including Steventon Mill, where the Day brothers installed roller milling in the early 1880s – an innovative technique which was to "transform the flour milling trade".[22]

Transport: a burgeoning employment sector

There were 17 transport workers in 1841, including three carriers, a carrier's clerk, two carters, seven hauliers – one of them a woman – and four coachmen. By 1901 the number had escalated to 164. Even if some who were described as labourers were involved in this sector in the earlier period, this is a remarkable increase, which highlights a principal reason for Ludlow's Victorian well-being: its role as a focal point in an economy of increasing mobility. In 1901 almost a third of transport employees were on the roads. There were 16 hauliers, the term perhaps being used more comprehensively than in 1841, though some of those who operated carrier services lived elsewhere along their routes. There were 19 road labourers and stone breakers, and three men who operated a traction engine: driver, stoker and flagman. The traditional carter's covered van was still in use, as shown on Fig. 10.

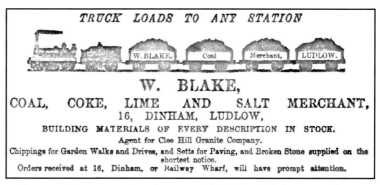

Fig. 11: An 1884 advertisement of William Blake, one of ten coal merchants then in Ludlow.
He lived in Dinham but had his depot at Station Drive.

The remainder – a total of 119 – worked on the railways. The opening of the line from Shrewsbury to Ludlow in 1852 and its extension to Hereford in 1853 are described in chapter 10. The opening of the Clee Hill railway in 1864 made Ludlow a junction, with considerable traffic in quarried Dhustone, and increased the demand for railway operators, maintenance men and support staff. Those living in Ludlow in 1901, many of them in the northern suburbs, included 24 platelayers, 18 porters and 13 engine drivers, as well as a range of specialists such as a station master, a yard foreman, a goods agent and a signal painter. Most of Ludlow's coal now came by rail, as suggested by Fig. 11.

Dealing: raw materials and foodstuffs

The number of dealers in Ludlow more than doubled between 1841 and 1901. Greater production and improved transport, especially the railway, caused more goods to circulate, and Ludlow was one of the market towns where exchange took place. Such towns, it has been written, like Thomas Hardy's Casterbridge, formed "the pole, focus or nerve-centre of the surrounding countryside".[23] Dealing in shops is covered in chapter 3, but other kinds of trade are considered here, as are the town's inns, hotels and lodging houses.

Porter's 1840 Directory lists two coal dealers, Richard Bird and David Dodd, both of Bridge End in lower Corve Street. They and other carriers used large wagons to fetch coal from Clee Hill, weighing the coal in Gaolford before its distribution.[24] After 1853 cheaper coal came by railway from South Wales, which was distributed in 1888 to ten coal

Fig. 10: A pencil drawing by Ellen Wilkinson, made about 1900. It shows a carrier's wagon in lower Corve Street, then the main road into Ludlow from the north. The large wheels took the weight of the wagon while the smaller front wheels facilitated steering.

merchants, four of them in Station Drive. A series of timber merchants occupied premises in Upper Gaolford, including John Thomas in 1840 and James Hine in 1875. In 1901 coal and timber distribution together had 26 employees.

Dealing in grain and foodstuffs was the core of the town's economy. Much of the business was handled by the Borough Council and its employees. In the 1840s the "principal grain market" was on Mondays, and "smaller markets for provisions" on Wednesdays, Fridays and Saturdays. George Griffiths, the Bewdley corn factor, was a regular buyer at Ludlow market, held "in the ancient building

Fig. 12: The Market House in Castle Square, with "the long room" above, where balls were held before the Assembly Rooms opened in 1841. The building was erected in 1702 and demolished in 1888 to make way for the new Corn Exchange and Town Hall. People have interrupted their business to pose for the photograph.

with open sides" (Fig. 12), where, he observed in 1837, "the class of farmers assembling here are of a better sort than most, particularly those from Corve Dale".[25] Many farmers belonged to well established dynasties, some of them familiar names in the twentieth century. Those listed in Slater's 1879 directory included five Bachs, two Froggatts (Richard's Castle and Ashford Bowdler), a Reynolds (at Snitton Farm, Bitterley), seven Smalls and four Whitemans. Other country folk also swarmed into town. Visiting Castle Square in 1860 the writer Walter White described "the noisy market place", with "rustics clad in fustian" and "smock-fronted boys", phrases such as "Be you a gween hoam a'ter market?" ringing in the air.[26] When the market hall was rebuilt in 1889 (Fig. 6), it was called The Corn Exchange, though after 1900 it was usually The Town Hall. The Monday market boosted the town's economy, one trader observing in 1900 that "a market day is worth the next three days".[27]

Initially, bakers and millers shared this trade, but in the late Victorian period it was dominated by one firm: "Marston Brothers, millers, bakers and corn dealers".[28] With roots in the Bishop's Castle area, William Marston had a baker's shop at No. 25 Bull Ring by 1863.

Fig. 13: This fine building, commonly known as Marstons' Mill, was built in the late 1890s. For nearly a century it was a focal point for much of the trade in agricultural products in and out of Ludlow. The mill was sensitively converted for modern use a few years ago.

When he died in 1874, his widow Margaret sustained and expanded the business, which was controlled by two of her sons William Hodgkinson Marston and Charles Bright Marston. In 1891 they acquired land off Portcullis Lane, close to the railway station, and erected one of the Ludlow's most characteristically Victorian buildings, an imposing five storey, nine bay milling warehouse (Fig. 13). Such buildings went up in many late Victorian towns, that of Rogers and Son, Flour and Corn Mills, Market Drayton, being another Shropshire example. The Marstons were enlightened employers, with echoes of such Victorian philanthropists as Lever and Cadbury. William Marston was Mayor in 1895, while Charles was a pillar of the Baptist Church in Rock Lane, evangelising the temperance movement among his employees. The firm encouraged fitness, with an early 20th century cricket team called the Corncrakes.

Dealing: livestock

Although some farm produce was sold on market days, the principal sales of animals were at fair days. There were eight annual fairs by 1849, some of them ancient, such as that on 21 August, a replacement for the medieval fair on St Laurence's day (10 August); but others were more recent, like that secured by lawyer Thomas Blainey in 1769.[29] Cattle, horses, sheep and pigs were sold, each at particular places round the town, with hops, butter and cheese at some fairs. By 1890 there were twelve fairs, held on the second Monday of each month. Rampaging bulls were a hazard, like the one that "broke away" on Ludford Bridge in 1847, finally being caught "near to Corve Turnpike Gate".[30] The May Fair, an ancient event revived in the 1820s, was the occasion for hiring servants, and developed as a pleasure fair, to which, on 1 May 1844, "thousands of persons from the surrounding districts resorted to this town".[31] The following year the fair was described as "a scene of considerable animation, the country people exhibiting every symptom of mirth and happiness".[32] The shows, on that occasion, were "extremely numerous", with "a large supply of cattle, sheep and pigs", and "considerable business done".

The removal of livestock markets to edge of town sites was a widespread aspiration. That of Shrewsbury moved to Raven Meadows in 1850, that of Kidderminster in 1857.[33] Proposals to move the Ludlow market near the station in the early 1850s collapsed, but in 1861 a move did

occur to "upwards of four acres" in Lower Gaolford.[34] Later, this site, close to the railway but without a siding, lost out to private enterprise in the vicinity of the station. William Urwick, auctioneer, bought land south of Station Drive that was already an auction yard in 1880.[35] This was sold to George Morris, auctioneer, who by 1900 was a partner in Morris, Marshall and Poole, auctioneers and stock salesmen. Press reports reveal fluctuations in trade, but there were many good sales, as in October, 1884, when "customers were numerous for store cattle, including the usual Birmingham and Wolverhampton dealers".[36] By 1895 rival auctioneers, Jackson and McCartney, had bought a neighbouring site, and in the twentieth century the firms merged as McCartneys.

The livestock market, like the trade in grain and foodstuffs, was responsive to the state of farming in the surrounding countryside. There is general agreement that agricultural depression replaced prosperity in the 1870s, though its extent and chronology varied regionally. A basic cause was competition from developing primary producing countries such as

Fig. 14: Though this photograph was taken in 1916, it shows the livestock market in Corve Street much as it was in the late Victorian period. In the foreground are cattle pens east of Portcullis Lane, in the area which is now part of Tesco's carpark. Beyond, on the left, an arched roof covers sheep pens. On the right is the other market area, owned in the 1890s, as in 1916, by Morris, Marshall and Poole.

Canada and Argentina, which depressed prices.[37] This was accompanied by "atrocious" harvests between 1878 and 1882. The malaise spread to market towns, Trinder finding at Banbury that "every indicator suggests a lowering of the rate of activity".[38] There are signs, however, that the Welsh border, with its mixed agriculture, was not so badly affected as areas where arable farming predominated. In an overview of recent research, Trinder has written:

"Shropshire, with its many dairy and sheep farms, was less affected by the Agricultural Depression of the late 19th century than regions where there was more arable cultivation, although the county suffered as much as any from the succession of wet seasons, foot and mouth epidemics and other disasters of the 1870s and early 1880s".[39]

Dealing: inns, hotels, and lodging houses

There were 54 inns in Ludlow in 1841, three of which – the Angel, the Crown and the Golden Lion – were also posting houses. This meant that there was one inn to every 100 Ludlow residents, though much of the trade came from travellers, visitors and market goers. Later in the century, though coaching had declined, the larger establishments were usually listed separately as "Inns and Hotels", of which Ludlow had six in 1879, and the rest as "Taverns and Public Houses", of which there were 42 in 1901.

In 1843 16 of the inns were owner occupied, including five of the ten with the highest rateable values, among them the Crown, the Golden Lion and the Bull.[40] By 1901 there were still 16 owner occupiers, though only one, the Queen's Arms in Corve Street, was held by the same family, the Birds. One prominent innkeeper was Robert Edwards (1826-90), who came from Denbighshire, to be first landlord of the Angel, then owner and later landlord of the Feathers, where he was succeeded by his son Charles (d.1898). Robert was Mayor in 1870-72. Another prominent family were the Sheldons, Edward Sheldon, landlord and owner of the Horse and Jockey, serving as Mayor 1902-04. By

1901 16 establishments were owned by breweries – four by the local Ludlow and Craven Arms Brewery, and ten by Ind Coope of Burton on Trent.

Much social and sporting life centred on the inns, especially for men. Several had their own Friendly Societies, such as the Bear and White Lion Society, whose members paraded the streets with a military band before the 1847 annual dinner.[41] Business was transacted, at least seven inns having market or commercial rooms, and auctions were often held.[42] Horse drawn conveyances such as chaises and flies could be hired from inns, as illustrated by Fig.15. Inns were also depots for carriers, where goods were left or collected. In 1879, two carriers terminated at the Compasses in Corve Street, two at the Dolphin in Upper Gaolford and six at the George in Castle Street. In 1901 the inns had stabling for 269 horses, with the greatest capacity at the Portcullis in Upper Gaolford, with 25 stables. At the larger inns, travellers were well received. The corn factor George Griffiths and the coachman were "waited upon like lords" when they arrived from Bewdley for breakfast at the Rose and Crown in 1837.[43] Cheaper accommodation was available at lodging houses, as at 73 Corve Street in 1871, where Michael Cassidy, hawker, and his wife Mary, had eight lodgers, including a shoemaker, a haulier, two Irish hawkers and two musicians from Naples.[44] In 1900 several establishments offered "furnished apartments" for lodgers, such as Mrs Harriett Lidstone, at 51 Mill Street.

Banking: a measure of confidence

Finance had seven employees in 1841, increasing to 32 in 1901. This kind of rise was experienced in many places, as local, regional and national economies became more complex. The core of the financial system was banking. In the 1820s two Ludlow banks had failed – Prodgers in 1824, Coleman and Wellings in 1826 – so the priority was to rebuild confidence.[45] This was done by making local banks part of a wider network, first regional and then national. The only bank operating in Ludlow in 1835 was Rocke, Eyton and Co., a Shrewsbury firm (Salop Old Bank) with members of two long established county families as partners. In the 1840s a successful local chemist, Henry Whittall, Mayor in 1844-45, ventured into banking, but was soon part of the Ludlow and Tenbury Bank, which drew on Worcester and later traded as Worcester City and County Bank.[46] Together with a locally run Savings Bank, these provided banking for Ludlow and district until the 1880s, when the Worcester Bank became part of Lloyds Bank Limited. In 1885 the Birmingham, Dudley and District Banking Company, with links to London and Manchester, purchased 3 King Street for £1,400, then commissioning a complete rebuilding. In 1889 Lloyds followed this lead by rebuilding their premises at 16 Broad Street.[47] This double investment, perhaps spurred by competition, testifies to the perceived economic potential of Ludlow and its countryside.

Labour: "in the sweat of thy face"[48]

In spite of the spreading use of steam – on the railways, for threshing engines, for road rollers – much hard and tedious work remained to be done by hand. The figures cited in Fig. 2 refer to those called "labourer", "general labourer" or "day labourer" in the census returns, but there were also specific kinds of labourer in other occupational groups, such as "agricultural", "foundry" or "road", which increases the numbers in this general class from 220 to 316 in 1841 and 280 to 351 in 1901, about an eighth of the work force. In 1841, unusually, one labourer, Amy Hoskins, was a woman.

The bland term "labourer" reveals little of the work done. Examples from elsewhere in England are a man who was at various times "builder's labourer, farm labourer, marl digger and fish hawker", and another who was "labourer, thatcher and quarry man".[49] Thirteen of those in the 1841 census for Ludlow were "day labourers", implying short term hiring for particular tasks. The social status of labourers generally was low, the average rateable value of their houses in 1843 being £3 17s, less than

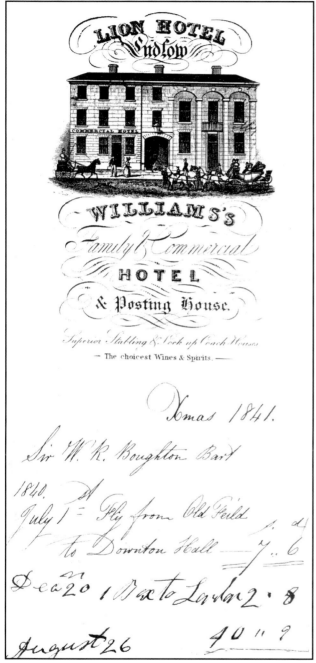

Fig. 15: This bill was sent out by John Williams, the proprietor of the Lion (later the Golden Lion) Hotel in Old Street, to Sir William Rouse Boughton of Downton Hall. It illustrates two of the services provided by inns: hiring horse drawn vehicles, and transporting parcels to London.

those in skilled manual trades, such as £4 16s 10d for bricklayers and masons. Only one of the 220 labourers listed in 1841 owned his own house – Samuel Hill of Camp Lane.

Of a sample of 100 labourers in the 1901 census, 38 had been born in Ludlow, twelve of whom were from families listed in 1841. Another 29 came from within ten miles of the town, but only three were Welsh, all of them from Montgomeryshire. One man, Thomas Wilson, had recently migrated from Chester, where his five year old child had been born, whereas three others had been born in Kent, Lancashire and Norfolk. A number of well known twentieth century Ludlow names appear in the 1901 list of labourers, among them Bradley, Bufton, Pound and Weaver. Slightly less than half of the 1901 sample were married men, many of the others being sons of labourers or of others doing menial work, such as housepainters, platelayers and carpenters. Fourteen of the sample were lodgers or lived in boarding houses, though in 1901 there were no such establishments as that of Thomas Jones in Upper Gaolford in 1881, where the 17 inmates included five labourers.

Fig. 16: A scene at Ludlow Station in the 1890s, with a policeman escorting a hand-cuffed man. The bystanders on the right, probably railway workers, appear to be taking little interest in the event.

The realities behind such statistics can be illustrated from the family of Joseph Maggs (1769-1836), a hatter from Winterbourne in Gloucestershire, who went "on the tramp" before his marriage to Margaret Smith of Ludlow in 1793.[50] Their ten children, most of them with biblical names, were baptised in Ludlow between 1794 and 1825, some staying in the town as adults. Among them were Israel (1805-75) and Lott (1810-), both of Frog Lane and usually described as labourers, though Israel was a chimney sweep in 1828 and a mason in 1834.[51] Others, however, moved on, among them Noah Maggs (1813-69), who became a nailer in Crickhowell.

Public services and the professions

As elsewhere, this was another growth area, with the numbers employed increasing by 100%. A large increase was in public services. The number of policemen rose from three in 1841 to seven in 1901, with five constables, a sergeant and an inspector – James Perry. One of these is shown in action in Fig. 16. They dealt with occasional serious crime, such as the attempted murder at The Angel in 1840, and a series of lesser offences.[52] These included thefts from shops, "obscene language in Raven Lane", assault, drunkenness on Mafeking night, and the behaviour "of all females of bad character on the streets at improper hours".[53]

The postal services increased, from four workers in 1841 to 24 in 1901. In 1841 the postmaster was Nicholas Sankey, also a maltster, who operated from his home at 51 Broad Street; while later the service was run by the grocers, Valentines. By 1895 there was a specialist Post Office in what became known as Post Office Square, at the eastern end of Castle Street. The service had nine postmen – and three deliveries a day! There was a fire engine station at Castle Walk by 1856, with Thomas Cook of Old Street as engineer, assisted by part-timers.

The professionalisation of the Borough Council also created a number of jobs, as did the Workhouse and the administration of Poor

Relief. More systematic management of public affairs is a Victorian trademark, but services were locally driven, with tentacles of county and state control not yet reflected in employment. Indeed, the number of excise and inland revenue employees in Ludlow dropped from six in 1841 to five in 1901.

In education there was rapid growth, in part due to the development of elementary education. Employment in the arts remained stable, with five people in photography in 1901 replacing the four artists who lived in Ludlow in 1841, while the numbers in music rose slightly: in 1901 there was a professor of music, two music teachers, two pianists, a dancing teacher and a piano tuner. The clergy, retired as well as those with cures, also showed stability, with eleven in 1841 – four of them non-conformists – and 13 in 1901.

Two more "learned professions" remain to be considered: law and medicine. The rise of the professions as an "urban elite" was an eighteenth century phenomenon, but their prestige and influence continued into the Victorian period, especially in market towns.[54] The lawyers, in particular, were a well-established and prosperous group, their rateable house values in 1843 averaging £33 17s 1d, the highest of any occupational group. They lived in some of Ludlow's finest properties while Humphrey Salwey, in practice by 1835, built The Cliff in Halton Lane.[55] The grandest life style was that of Robert Marston, in partnership with his father Richard. He lived at Castle House from 1888, adding a splendid ball room in 1904 (Fig. 17), before later purchasing an estate at Oaker in the Clun valley.[56]

There were 13 practising solicitors in Ludlow in 1841 and 12 in 1888, making up six or seven firms, such as that of Lloyd and Southern featured in chapter 10. Many clerks were also

Fig. 17: Robert Marston's luxurious Castle House, seen across the spacious garden. The house had been built after 1810, adapting a Tudor indoor tennis court as a service range on the right of the picture. The dining room and drawing room were on the ground floor of the gabled cross wings on the left.

employed. As in many towns, some firms lasted over two or more generations, sometimes absorbing new families. Thus Anderson, Downes and Anderson of 1835 had become George and Rodney Anderson by 1851, and in 1900 was Anderson, Son and Tyrell. Nearly all the solicitors had their roots in the surrounding countryside. Some came from long established land-owning families, such as George Dansey, third son of Richard Dansey, Esq., of Easton Court in Little Hereford, whose pedigree went back to the 15th century.[57] Others were from yeoman stock, such as Thomas Weyman, practising in Ludlow by 1844, whose family had held land at Hopton Castle for several generations.[58] Most of the lawyers were prominent in town affairs, six serving as Mayor, holding the office eleven times between them (see Appendix 1 for a full list of Ludlow Mayors during this period). One of the Mayors, Henry Weyman in 1886-87, was also an assiduous local historian, whose work is still authoritative (Fig. 19). Obituaries suggest that many solicitors were well regarded. Luttrell Lewin Clark, who practised from 1825 until 1875, was described as "a man of the strictest honour and of the most

Fig. 18: Rodney George Bridges Anderson (1809-1893), whose professional life as a solicitor embraced most of Victoria's reign. He was Mayor four times, more than any other Victorian. After living in a series of large town centre houses, he moved to Fishmore Hall, half a mile out of Ludlow.

Fig.19: Henry Weyman (1851-1942), elder brother of the historical novelist Stanley Weyman. He succeeded his father as senior partner in the family firm of solicitors. As well being Mayor and Alderman, he was active in many other spheres of public life, especially education.

sterling worth".[59] Others attracted controversy, especially in the post-Reform years, among them William Downes, a Reformer who was elected Coroner for the South Division of Shropshire in 1834 by 3,145 votes to 2,953, after a passionate campaign against the candidate of the Clives.[60]

The number of doctors fluctuated slightly over the period, with nine the norm. Distinction between the more highly qualified physicians and the humbler surgeons faded during the period, all eight doctors being listed together in 1888. They had times of great business, as in 1845, when "a dreadful scourge of smallpox" was raging, with funerals "a daily occurrence".[61] Some came to Ludlow from careers elsewhere, among them David Lewis (d.1837) and Richard Guise (1881 census), both of the Bengal medical service.[62] Others spent their whole career in Ludlow, including Richard Valentine (1802-67), who practised at 2 College Street; Henry Hodges (1807-93), at 40 Broad Street; and Henry Meymott (1807-95) at 49 Broad Street. Valentine, the son of James Valentine, grocer, and Hodges, the son of a long serving curate of Bromfield, were local men, but Meymott came from Southwark.[63] Two doctors – John Southern in 1862 and Job Edwin Brooks in 1884 and 1885 – served as Mayor, and others held office as Poor Law Guardians or Municipal Charity Trustees. Some doctors became involved in public controversy on health matters, but others retained the goodwill of the town: Henry Hodges was described at his death as "the poor man's friend".[64] Some doctors took a leading role in intellectual life, especially Thomas Lloyd (1802-49), founder member of Ludlow Natural History Society in 1833, and later honorary curator of the Museum.[65] The doctors tended to reside in the more prosperous parts of the town, with Broad Street sometimes known as "Ludlow's Harley Street".[56]

Medical facilities improved during the period. At first dental care was provided by itinerant dentists, such as Mr Grenville Jones, "Surgeon Dentist". In January 1840 he had been at Shrewsbury, but was "now at Ludlow" where he could be "consulted every day this week at Mr Maund's, Mill Street" (now no. 39).[57]From 1856 there was at least one resident dentist, usually in Broad Street, with two next door to each other in 1868, Appleby King at 32, Charles Gaine at 33. In 1835 there was a dispensary, "affording relief to the sick poor"; but only four nurses are recorded in Ludlow in 1841. The doctor giving longest service to the dispensary was John Southern, from 1856 or earlier until after 1885. By 1885 the dispensary had an average of 350 patients and the former College in College Street had become a Cottage Hospital.

Service: a declining sector but always the major employer

In 1841 there were 620 residential domestic servants in Ludlow, more than a quarter of all employees. Predictably, those with four or more were independent and professional families and the larger inns, but many humbler householders had one or two living-in servants, e.g. twelve of the seventeen tradesmen in High Street had one each. By 1901, the number was reduced to 468, less than a fifth of employees, but this remained the largest single economic group.

A number of people were employed in other service trades, including chimney sweeps and hairdressers. From 1888 the former included John Bursnell of 76 Lower Gaolford, whose family continued the business until the 1970s. There were also many women, most of them working at home, who were laundresses or washerwomen. The number of these rose from 30 in 1841 to 76 in 1901, probably a response to the reduced number of living-in servants. For the same reason, there were also 48 charwomen in 1901.

Temporary Works

In the energetic Victorian years, with massive feats of large scale engineering straddling the country, small towns sometimes had great but short-lasting influxes of working men. This must have occurred in the early 1850s, when the Shrewsbury to Hereford railway was constructed, and again in 1862 when the branch line was being built to Clee Hill. In both cases, the decennial census came too early to record the numbers involved. In 1901, however, the census was taken when work was in progress on the pipeline from central Wales to Birmingham, an ambitious project resulting from the Birmingham Corporation Water Act of 1892.[68] "The waterworks" brought 124 temporary residents to Ludlow, many of them taking lodgings in the town, ten of them in the house of Edward Prosser in Holdgate Fee. Others stayed with their families in hired houses. They ranged from two contractors, a manager and an engineer, through skilled workers such as a crane driver and five excavators, to 50 navvies and 30 labourers. Tunnelling was required, especially through the southern slopes of Titterstone Clee

Fig. 20: The construction of an aqueduct two miles west of Ludlow, to carry the pipeline from Elan Valley to Birmingham. Birmingham Corporation was renowned for its "Civic Gospel": the energetic promotion of projects to enhance the quality of life for its citizens.

Hill, so there were four tunnel miners and some "underground navvies". The work was often dangerous, a William Yates being injured in 1900 by a delayed blast of gelignite, "seriously injuring his eyes, face and hands".[69]

SOCIETY: THOSE NOT IN
EMPLOYMENT

Of independent means

Heads of household described in the census returns as "independent", "annuitant" or "living on own means" accounted for 5% of the town's population in 1841, dropping to 2% by 1901. Many of the persons described in this way, also occur among the names listed at the beginning of Ludlow entries in trade and postal directories. In 1842 these are grandly headed "Nobility, Gentry and Clergy", but from 1863 the more prosaic "Private Residents" was generally used.

Only a few of those permanently residing in Ludlow in 1841 were from the rural landowning gentry families who had been so prominent in late Stuart and Georgian Ludlow, causing the town to be celebrated for "its very good company".[70] John Syer, Esq. at 11 Dinham, from Norton in Culmington, and Emma Dansey, at 114 Corve Street, widow of Richard Dansey, of Easton Court, Little Hereford, were examples.[71] Others did retain town houses, notably Gustavus Hamilton, 6th Viscount Boyne of Burwarton, who owned and occasionally resided at 40 Broad Street – with its ball room next door at what is now 40A – and Edward Rogers Esq. of Stanage Park near Knighton. Edward's father, Charles Rogers (1753-1821), "an opulent East India merchant" with yeoman roots in Wentnor, had purchased Stanage Park in 1779, and in 1787 bought the house now called High Hall as a Ludlow residence.[72] This was sold about 1822 to the Clee Hill ironmaster, Thomas Botfield, but Edward Rogers, M.P. for Bishop's Castle from 1820 to 1832 and later Sheriff of Radnorshire, rented other Ludlow houses when required, such as Dinham Hall in 1840.[73]

By the 1860s most such families had severed their links with Ludlow, causing the American novelist Henry James to observe in 1877:

"The place seems to say that a hundred years and less ago it was the centre of a large provincial society, and that this society was "very good" of its kind. It must have transported itself to Ludlow for the season – in rumbling coaches and heavy curricles – and there entertained itself in decent emulation of that metropolis which a choice of railway lines had not as yet placed within its immediate reach….It is a place on which a provincial "gentry" had left a sensible stamp."[74]

Victorian Ludlow attracted a number of retired people. In spite of attempts to develop a medicinal spring on Titterstone Clee Hill in 1840, the town was never promoted as a spa, though Revd George Hunstley of Devonshire, who died aged 72 in 1846, had been "sojourning there a short time for the benefit of his health".[75] A study of Ludlow in the 1840s has revealed several retired people from elsewhere, including John Hutchins, a banker from Somerset, who lived at 31 Broad Street; Allen John Nightingale, a former Assistant Commissary General, at Mary Vale Cottage; and Sir Edward Thomason (Fig. 21), a successful Birmingham inventor and manufacturer, who rented High Hall from his relative, Thomas Botfield.[76] Such people and their families contributed much to local life. Thomason, for example, was elected a Municipal Charity Trustee in 1837; in 1838 he was a committee member of the Company for erecting the new Assembly Rooms; and in 1841 he spoke at the opening of the Mechanics Institute, in a way suggesting he had been a prime instigator.[77] Another immigrant, who lived at Castle Lodge from 1828 or earlier until her death, was Mary McGhie (1770-1844), spinster.[78] She was a noted amateur botanist, contributing to Flora of Shropshire, published in 1841; was famed for her "charitable disposition", being "a true friend and benefactress to the poor"; and had links

Fig. 21: Sir Edward Thomason (1769-1849), son of a Birmingham buckle maker, thrived in "the city of a thousand trades", specialising in metal goods of artistic quality. He presented elaborate medals of biblical subjects to all the sovereigns of Europe, receiving many honours in return, including a knighthood from William IV. In retirement at Ludlow, he was a lion of local society.

with the West Indies, the bequests in her will including £1,500 in trust for three children born in the 1790s to Grace Cameron, a slave on Greenside Estate, Jamaica.[79]

Of 282 householders described as "independent" in 1841, 71 can be linked with trade and 33 with the professions. Jemima Adams, for example, was the widow of Philip Birt Adams, surgeon, who had died in 1832, leaving her "all my freehold, leasehold and copyhold messuages, on trust, to receive the rents during her lifetime".[80] Data from later censuses show many annuitants supported by property, though Percival and Emily Sykes of 25 Broad Street enjoyed income in 1881 "from railway stock and government property". Some widows received pensions, as did Hester Baker of 110 Corve Street, whose husband, Captain Vashon Baker, RN, had died in 1878.[81] Some of those classed as independents were retired businessmen, such as Robert Atkins (1791-1869), described as "stone mason and maltster" in 1856, but as "independent" in 1861.

Non-residential nobility and greater gentry

Though these persons were rarely resident in Ludlow during the Victorian period, and are not included in the population totals shown on Fig. 3, they continued to have influence on Ludlow life in a variety of ways, especially during the early years. Their political activities are considered in chapter 5. Their custom was eagerly sought by Ludlow tradesmen. When Benjamin Griffiths opened his "hair cutting and shampooing rooms" at 69 Broad Street in 1884, he "respectfully informed" the "Nobility, Clergy and Gentry", ahead of "the inhabitants of Ludlow and neighbourhood".[82] Donations were regularly given to a range of local causes. To the ten charities reported on in 1869, the Earl of Powis, George Windsor Clive M.P. and Sir C.R. Boughton of Downton Hall were frequent and generous subscribers.[83] When the restoration of St Laurence's tower was announced in 1889, at a cost of over £8,000, £4,000 was immediately donated: £1,500 from Lord Windsor, £1,000 from Windsor Clive, and £500 each from Sir C. R. Boughton, Mrs and Miss Johnstone Foster – new owners of the Moor, Richard's Castle – and £500 from the Rector, whose wife was of the Clive family.

Birthdays and marriages of local landowners were celebrated enthusiastically in Ludlow; and their funerals marked with respect. In 1846 a public dinner was held at The Crown for "the majority" of Henry Rouse Boughton of Downton Hall.[84] In 1861 "church bells rang merrily" in honour of the birth of a son and heir to the Hon. G. Russell Hamilton Russell, son of Lord Boyne of Burwarton.[85] The greatest euphoria was reserved for the Clives of Oakly Park. At the coming of age of Lord Clive in 1846, the church bells pealed from 7 a.m., cannons fired volleys and a band processed from 9 a.m.[86] At noon there was a public feast for 1400 people in the castle, followed by "rural and manly sports", attracting "an immense concourse of persons". The occupants of the Almshouse and the Workhouse were given roast beef and plum pudding, the day concluding with fireworks on the castle tower. Two years later the mood changed, when there was "universal regret in the town" for the death of the Earl of Powis, many shops "not taking their shutters down all day".[87]

The great houses of the neighbourhood were the venues for sporting and social events, which were attended by the elite of Ludlow. In August 1838 the Herefordshire Company of Bowmen – archery was a fashionable recreation – had a meeting at Stanage Park, the seat of Edward Rogers, Esq. Upwards of "200 of the nobility and gentry attended", enjoying a "sumptuous dinner", with a military and quadrille band in attendance.[88] On 12 August 1846 the large crowd at the fourth anniversary of the Bromfield Horticultural Show included the Mayor of Ludlow as well as other town residents, with a long list of county worthies.[89]

Later in the Queen's reign such events were more restrained, reflecting a national trend of "less deference to birth", now that there were other sources to land and wealth.[90] However, Col. Windsor Clive retained the goodwill of the town, sitting as Ludlow's only Member of Parliament between 1867 and 1885.[91]

Dependent persons

The other principal non-employed category were the dependants. There was a small and over the period constant group in almshouses. The town had two anciently endowed almshouses, Hosier's in College Street, "for thirty three poor indigent persons", and Foxe's in Corve Street, where there were four sets of chambers. Both were eventually administered

Fig. 22: Oakly Park, the Bromfield house of the Clives and their successors, the Earls of Plymouth. Though not commensurate in size or grandeur with the status of the Clives and their relatives the Earls of Powis, the house reflected their informed classical taste, as illustrated by the one storey screen with symmetrical porches added by C.R.Cockerell in the 1820s.

Fig. 23: Three of the five almshouses at the lower end of Corve Street endowed by Louisa Powell in 1876. The other two were at the back and could be reached through the side passage. A tablet bearing the arms of the Powell family, with details matching those of the windows, can be seen towards the left.

by the Ludlow Municipal Trustees, set up in 1837 in line with the post-Reform insistence that municipal and charity money should be separate. From 1833 Lane's Asylum in Old Street, endowed in 1674 but previously used as a Workhouse and House of Correction", was also an almshouse.[92] In 1876 new almshouses (Fig. 23), with five accommodation units, were endowed by Louisa Powell, the philanthropic widow of Charles Powell, Esq. of Sutton Court, Diddlebury, the tenants to be "poor persons being agricultural labourers".

But by far the largest single group within the town's population, more than half, were those who depended upon the earnings or income of others – wives, children and the elderly. Their numbers increased between 1841 and 1901 broadly in line with the overall population growth, so, as a proportion of the total population, they remained virtually the same (54% and 53% respectively). So large a group played a vital part in the social, cultural and economic life of the town, but a discussion of that is beyond the scope of this study; chapters 7 and 8 on the Poor Law, chapter 9 on education and chapter 11 on the church deal with some aspects of their lives.

The chapter began with the proposition that the Victorian period was one of economic change for Ludlow. Its main elements have been identified as follows:

• There was a decline in manufacturing of traditional made goods, such as gloves and woollen items, and in malting. In all of these, outside competition, facilitated by improved transport systems, increasingly secured the market.

• There was a similarly significant decline in the numbers of household servants – a national trend.

• The town's marketing of agricultural produce continued and it played a developing role as an agricultural service centre for the local farming area. This role was sustained, though fluctuations in agricultural production in the surrounding countryside, especially "the great depression" of the late 1870s and beyond, had some impact on the town.

• There were substantial increases in all aspects of dealing, as greater production and improved transport caused more goods to circulate. Ludlow was the local market town where exchange took place and whose facilities were used by people visiting for that purpose.

• The town's role as a service centre for the local area developed, with growth in the numbers offering professional services of all kinds and in those involved in the provision of transport services.

The notion that these were years of economic stagnation and associated population decline in Ludlow has been shown to be erroneous. In fact the evidence points in the opposite direction. Ludlow had long since lost its national importance as the seat of the Council of the Marches. Its Georgian heyday as a fashionable place of retirement for the gentry would soon become a distant memory. Yet it still retained its importance as a market town, developing and adapting to changing economic circumstances. Also, as the next chapter will confirm, it kept its attractions as a place to live, attractions which still have potency today.

APPENDIX I

Mayors of Ludlow Borough, 1836 to 1901

Year(s)	name	occupation	residence
1836-37	William Edwards	draper	King Street
1837-38	Richard Wakefield	surgeon	Corve Street
1842-43	George Anderson	solicitor	Mill Street
1843-44	James Baxter	Esq.	Broad Street
1844-45	Henry Whittall	chemist	Bull Ring
1845-46	Benjamin Urwick	tanner	Corve Street
1846-47	Francis Massey	wine merchant	Bull Ring
1847-48	Horatio Russell	schoolmaster	Mill Street
1848-49	Ambrose Grounds	chemist	King Street
1849-50	Joshua Cooper	ironmonger	Castle Street
1850-51	Richard Marston	chemist	Broad Street
1851-52	Benjamin Urwick	tanner	Corve Street
1852-53	Ambrose Grounds	chemist	King Street
1853-54	Rodney Anderson	solicitor	Mill Street
1854-55	George Anderson	solicitor	Mill Street
1855-56	Samuel Valentine	grocer	Broad Street
1856-57	Francis R. Southern	solicitor	Mill Street
1857-58	Rodney Anderson	solicitor	Mill Street
1859-60	Rodney Anderson	solicitor	Mill Street
1860-61	George Cocking	chemist	Bull Ring
1861-62	Rodney Anderson	solicitor	Mill Street
1862-63	John Southern	surgeon	Broad Street
1863-64	Edward Foster	chemist	Castle Street
1864-65	John Harding	grocer	King Street
1865-66	Francis R. Southern	solicitor	Mill Street
1866-67	William Whitman	maltster	Old Street
1867-68	John Griffin	corn factor	Corve Street
1868-69	Edmund Bluck	ironmonger	Corve Street
1869-70	Edward Morris	publican	Lower Broad Street
1870-71	Robert Edwards	innkeeper	Bull Ring (Feathers)
1871-72	Robert Edwards	innkeeper	Bull Ring (Feathers)
1872-73	Samuel Watkins	builder	Lower Broad Street
1873-74	Thomas Sheppard	wine merchant	Bull Ring
1874-75	John Adney	currier	King Street
1875-76	William Bessell	draper	King Street
1876-77	Heber Rickards	ironmonger	Bull Ring

1877-78	Ernest Davies	solicitor	Lower Gaolford
1878-79	Heber Rickards	ironmonger	Bull Ring
1879-80	Thomas Roberts	quarry manager	Corve Street
1880-81	Thomas Roberts	quarry manager	Corve Street
1881-82	John Valentine	grocer	Broad Street
1882-83	John Cross	stationer	King Street
1883-84	Thomas Sheppard	wine merchant	Bull Ring
1884-85	Job Edwin Brooks	surgeon	Broad Street
1885-86	Job Edwin Brooks	surgeon	Broad Street
1886-87	Henry Weyman	solicitor	Mill Street
1887-88	Thomas Morris	grocer	King Street
1888-89	Henry Lloyd	maltster	Corve Street
1889-90	John Valentine	grocer	Broad Street
1890-91	John Valentine	grocer	Broad Street
1891-92	William Bessell	draper	King Street
1892-93	William C. Tyrell	solicitor	Mill Street
1893-94	Thomas Roberts	quarry manager	Corve Street
1894-95	Thomas Roberts	quarry manager	Corve Street
1895-96	Wm Hodgkinson Marston	corn dealer	Bull Ring
1896-97	Thomas H.Atherden	banker	Broad Street
1897-98	Thomas H.Atherden	banker	King Street
1898-99	Gaius Smith	grocer	King Street
1899-1900	Robert Marston	solicitor	Corve Street
1900-1901	William Chubb	draper	Castle Street

Although attributed to one author, this chapter owes much to the constructive comments and criticisms of members of the editorial team. Chris Train, in particular, has redrafted some sections of the text and corrected points of detail.

1   *Salopian Journal*, 7 Nov.1832.

2   Felton, W., *A Description of the Town of Ludlow, 1811*, p.116.

3   Unless otherwise stated, all dates cited in this and later chapters are those of the decennial censuses of 1841 to 1901, or the year of publication of commercial and postal directories: Pigot 1835, Robson 1840, Pigot 1842, Pigot 1844, Slater 1849, Slater 1850, Bagshaw 1851, Kelly 1856, Cassey 1858, Harrison and Harrod 1861, Kelly 1863, Slater 1868, Kelly 1870, Cassey 1871, Cassey 1875, Mercer and Crocker 1877, Slater 1879, Crocker 1884, Kelly 1885, Porter 1888, Kelly 1890,Kelly 1895, Kelly 1900.

4   Armstrong, A., "The use of information about occupation", in Wrigley, E.A.(ed.), *Nineteenth Century Society. Essays in the Use of Quantitative Methods for the Study of Social Date*, 1972, pp.191-310.

5   Census totals and other population information in this section from *Victoria County History of Shropshire*, Vol.II, pp. 219-229.

6   These figures exclude the occupants of the Workhouse in East Hamlet, since they came from the whole of the surrounding district as well as from Ludlow itself.

7   Royle, S.A., "The development of small towns in Britain", *The Cambridge Urban History of Britain, Vol.III, 1840-1950*, 2000, pp.155, 169..

8   Ludlow Tithe Map and Apportionment, 1847.

9   *Hereford Journal*, 3 March, 1847; *Ludlow Advertiser*, 30 Sept., 1876.

10 Poster showing results of the 1853 Agricultural Show (in author's possession).

11 Trinder, B., *The Industrial Archaeology of Shropshire*, 1996 p.96; Jenkins, A.E., *Titterstone Clee Hills: Everyday Life, Industrial History and Dialect*, 1982, p.31.

12 Watkin, D., *The Life and Work of C.R.Cockerell*, 1974, p.180.

13 Williams, D., "Building the Ludlow Union Workhouse", *Ludlow Heritage News*, no.27, 1987, p,1.

14 Inf.ex Colin Sheward, who has made a detailed study of the work of Herbert Evans, initially for an O.U. assignment.

15 Interview with the late Marjorie Russell, great-grand-daughter of William; caption of picture of new Town Hall (fig. 6).

16 Everitt, A., "Country, County and Town: Patterns of Regional Evolution in England", in Borsay. P (Ed.), *The Eighteenth Century Town*, 1990, pp.99-100; Lewis, S., *A Topographical Dictionary of England*, 5th.Ed., 1844. Vol.1, p.438; Vol.2, p.653; West, J., *Town Records*, 1983, pp.312-13, 320-21.

17 Royle, op. cit, p.163.

18 Deeds of Teme mills, Ludlow Museum.

19 Lloyd, L.C., "Paper-Making in Shropshire, 1656 to 1912", *T.S.A.S.*, XLIX (1938), pp.166-67.

20 Trinder, B., op. cit., p.47.

21 *Hereford Journal*, 22 July, 1846.

22 Trinder, op.cit., p.47.

23 Everitt, A., "Dynasty and Community since the Seventeenth Century", in Everitt (Ed.).*Landscape and the Community in England*, 1985, p.320.

24 Felton, W., *A Description of the Town of Ludlow*, 1811, p.116.

25 Griffiths, G. *Going to Markets and Grammar Schools, 1830-1870*, 1870, p.117.

26 White, W., *All Round the Wrekin*, 1860, pp.89-90.

27 *Ludlow Advertiser*, 12 May, 1900.

28 Kelly, 1895, p.127; much of this paragraph is based on research by the staff and Friends of Ludlow Museum Resource Centre..

29 Slater, 1849, p.26; Jones, E., *Party Feeling in Old Ludlow*, 1913; *Shrewsbury Chronicle*, 21 Feb.1789.

30 *Hereford Journal*, 31 March, 1847.

31 Ibid, 8 May, 1844.

32 Ibid, 7 May, 1845.

33 Marsh, P., "Shrewsbury Markets in the Nineteenth Century", Trinder, Ed., *Victorian Shrewsbury*, 1984. p.23; Lloyd, D., *A History of Worcestershire*, 1994, p.100.

34 *Ludlow Advertiser*, 14 August, 1861.

35 This paragraph is from private deeds, examined 1993, when in custody of South Shropshire District Council.

36 *Ludlow Advertiser*, 25 Oct., 1884.

37 Thompson, F.M.I., "Free Trade and the Land", in Mingay, G.E., *The Victorian Countryside*, 1981, pp.103-08.

38 Trinder, B., *Victorian Banbury*, 1982, pp.77-93.

39 Trinder, B., *A History of Shropshire*, Darwen County History series, 1983, p.105.

40 Shropshire Archives LB 1996/17/1, Ludlow Borough rate book, 1843.

41 *Hereford Journal*, 21 July, 1847.

42 County of Salop: *Return of Licensed Houses in the Borough of Ludlow*, 1901.

43 Griffiths, G., op. cit. p.110; *The Old Tower*, Bridgnorth magazine, Feb.1878, p.152.

44 Trinder, B., notes on Victorian Market Town Lodging Houses, given out at a lecture on 19 April 1999 to The Friends of Ludlow Museum.

45 Grant, G.L., *The Standard Catalogue of Provincial Banks and Banknotes*, 1977, p.52.

46 Robson, 1840, p.67; Pigot, 1844, p..23.

47 SA DA3/7/110/1.

48 Genesis, 3, v.19, cited by Howkins, A, in "The Labourer and Work", Mingay, G.E.(ed.), *The Victorian Countryside*, Vol. 2, 1981, p.506.

49 Howkins, op.cit. p.506.

50 Inf.ex. Roger Maggs of Sheffield.

51 From Ludlow Parish Registers after 1812, transcribed by Queenie Haydon, Gillian Sharpe & Dorothy

Arrowsmith.

52 *Ludlow Standard*, 22 Aug., 1840.

53 *Hereford Journal*, 19 March, 1851; *Ludlow Advertiser*, 20 March,,1861; *Ludlow Advertiser*, 15 July, 1876; ibid, 26 May,1900.

54 Sweet, R., *The English Town 1680-1840*, 1999, p.181.

55 Burke, *The Gentry*, 1934, p, 2238.

56 Martin, E., "The Family of Marston of Afcote", *T.S.A.S.*, ser.4, ix (1923); Fuller ref. DA3/710/12.

57 Robinson, C.J., *A History of Mansions and Manors of Herefordshire*, 1872, p.50.

58 Edwards, O., "Stanley Weyman", *Country Quest*, Nov. 1875, p.37.

59 Undated, Packer scrapbook.

60 *Shrewsbury Chronicle*, 17 Oct.1834.

61 *Hereford Journal*, 1 Jan.1845.

62 MI St Laurence's; 1881 census.

63 MI St Leonard's; LPR, p.1116; 1843 rate book; various directories.

64 Packer scrapbook, undated obituary.

65 Lloyd, D., *The History of Ludlow Museum, 1833-1983*, 1983, pp.4-5.

66 Inf.ex. the late Mary Lloyd, who spent her childhood at the Broadgate, Ludlow.

67 *Salopian Journal*, 22 Jan.1840.

68 Rowlands, *The West Midlands from AD 1000*, 1987, p.296.

69 *Ludlow Advertiser*, 6 Jan.1900.

70 Macky, J., *A Journey through England, in Familiar Letters from a Gentleman here to his Friend Abroad*, ii, 1724, p.130.

71 SA Hardwick, Addenda to Pedigrees of the Heralds Visitation of Shropshire, Vol.2, p.51; Robinson, C.J., *The Mansions of Herefordshire and their Owners*, 1872, p.50.

72 Williams, J., *A General History of the County of Radnorshire*, Brecon, 1905, pp.240/41; Oman, C., *Ayot Rectory: A Family Memoir*, p.29; Weyman, H., "MPs for Bishops Castle", *T.S.A.S.*, 2nd.ser., x, p.66.

73 Deeds of 20-22 Castle Street.

74 James, H., *Portraits of Places*, 1883, p.285.

75 *Hereford Journal*, 17 June 1846.

76 Deeds of 31 Broad Street, Ludlow Museum, conveyance 2 Aug, 1825; *Salopian Journal*, 28 Feb., 1844; ibid, 5 Sept., 1838.

77 *Salopian Journal*, 14 Feb., 1838; *Introductory Addresses and Speeches at the opening of the Literary Association and Mechanics Institute of Ludlow*, Ludlow 1841, pp.20-21.

78 SA DA3/100/2, p.5: Borough Council lease to Mary McGhie, 16 Nov.1838.

79 Sinker, G.A.and others; *Ecological Flora of the Shropshire Region*, Shrewsbury, 1985, pp.27-28; *Hereford Journal*, 3 July, 1844; will, P.R.O., 26 July 1844.

80 H.R.O. will,15 May 1832.

81 Inf.ex. Mary Blount, Ludlow, a descendant.

82 *Ludlow Advertiser*, 25 October, 1884.

83 Ludlow. Report for the year 1869 of ...(named charities), 1870, p.1-20.

84 *Hereford Journal*, 7 Jan.,1846.

85 *Ludlow Advertiser*, 4 Jan., 1861.

86 *Hereford Journal*, 28 May, 1845.

87 *Salopian Journal*, 2 Feb., 1848.

88 *Salopian Journal*, 22 Aug.,1838.

89 *Hereford Journal*, 19 Aug., 1846.

90 Young, G.M., *Portrait of an Age: Victorian England*, 1934, 1977 ed., p.148.

91 Mason, J.F.A., Parliamentary Representation, *Victoria County History: Shropshire*, Vol. III, 1979, pp. 338-339.

92 Weyman, H., *Ludlow in Bye-Gone Days*, 1913, pp.66-67.

Chapter 2

The Growth of Victorian Ludlow

Christopher Train

"Lonsdale" 33 Julian Road the home of the Misses Grieves from the 1880s.

In 1901 the Misses Grieves, Amelia, Mary and Jemima, were living at what is now 33 Julian Road, a house then called Lonsdale. They had been there for more than twenty years. All were born in Ludlow, daughters of John Grieves, a chemist, of Old Street. The eldest was Amelia, born in 1831, so her life had more than spanned Queen Victoria's reign.

Had she been asked in January 1901 what were the most striking changes she had seen in Ludlow during the late Queen's reign, she might have mentioned the coming of the railway fifty years past, or the building of the grand new Market Hall in the late 1880s, but she would surely have drawn attention to the growth of the town on its eastern side into the sandpits, fields, and nursery gardens of her childhood.[1] Her memory can be confirmed by comparing two maps which span almost exactly the same period: one of 1832 which shows the limits of the Borough of Ludlow for the purpose of electing Members of Parliament [Fig. I] and the 1902 Ordnance Survey Map [Fig. II].

In 1832 the physical extent of Ludlow was much as it had been since medieval times – the core of the town around the market place along the crest of its hill, ringed by what remained of its ancient walls, with extra-mural settlement down Corve Street, lower Corve Street and St Mary's Lane as far as the bridge over the river

Fig. I: Map showing later Stanton Lacy and Ludford suburbs of Ludlow in 1832.

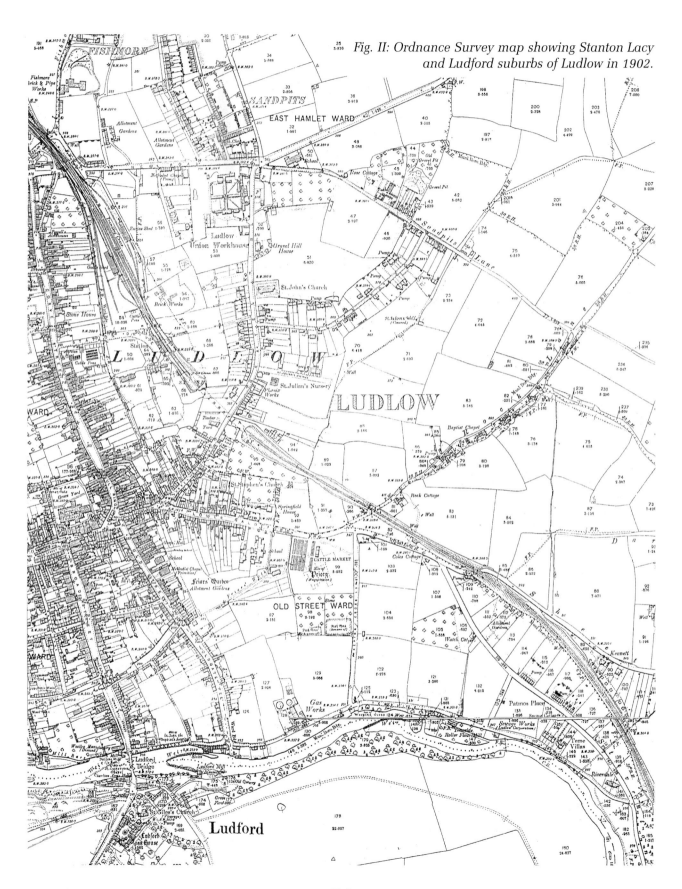

Fig. II: Ordnance Survey map showing Stanton Lacy and Ludford suburbs of Ludlow in 1902.

Corve by what is now The Bridge Inn, in Lower and Upper Gaolford, and down Mill Street, Broad Street and Old Street as far as the natural boundary provided by the river Teme. Ludlow at this time was essentially the ecclesiastical parish of St Laurence, with some small trespass two hundred yards or so up Upper Gaolford into the parish of Stanton Lacy and, at the bottom of Old Street on its eastern side, the area known as Oldgate or Holdgate Fee, which lay in the parish of Ludford. Beyond that, with one exception, there were only scattered settlements and houses; a cluster around the Mitre Inn and the Fishmore Tollgate by the Corve Bridge, some cottages in the brickyard on the northern side of what is now New Road, another cluster by the Tollgate at East Hamlet, with Gravel Hill House and a couple of houses below it on the road into town, and only the Paper Mill on the way to Steventon. The exception was the cottages lining Rock Lane, which lay either in Stanton Lacy or Ludford Parish. These were typical squatters' cottages, some of which had been there since the seventeenth century.

By 1902 there were terraces in Fishmore Road, on either side of New Road from the bottom to the top, a large estate at East Hamlet, the Ludlow Union Workhouse and substantial villas in Gravel Hill, the Julian Road estate and the beginnings of St Julian's Avenue, properties by the Teme towards Steventon, and three substantial terraces in Steventon New Road. All of these had been incorporated into Ludlow Borough by the Ludlow Extension Order 1901[2], East Hamlet having already in 1880 been brought into the ecclesiastical parish of St. Laurence.[3]

Over the sixty years from 1841 to 1901 the population of what was to become the extended Borough of Ludlow grew from 5,451 to 6,297.[4] But that concealed a decline in the population of the ancient town, from 5,064 to 4,557, while the suburban population increased from 387 to 1,740, that is more than fourfold. By far the largest contributor to this was the suburb which grew up in the southern part of the parish of Stanton Lacy, as may be seen from the graphs [Figs. III and IV]

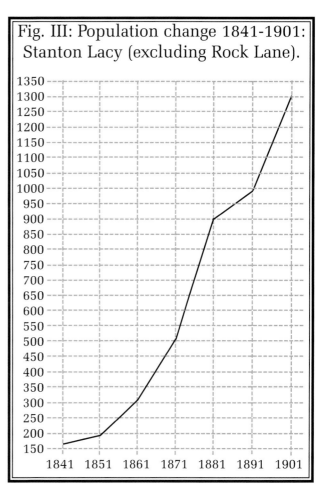

Fig. III: Population change 1841-1901: Stanton Lacy (excluding Rock Lane).

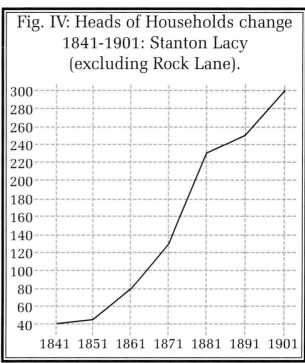

Fig. IV: Heads of Households change 1841-1901: Stanton Lacy (excluding Rock Lane).

Fig. V Right: Stanton Lacy Parish with later Stanton Lacy suburb, 1847.

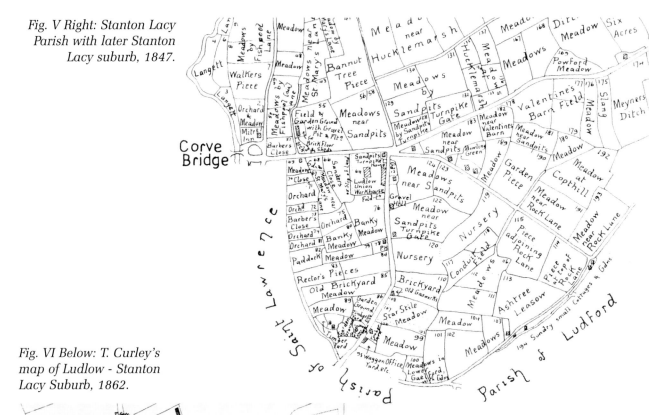

Fig. VI Below: T. Curley's map of Ludlow - Stanton Lacy Suburb, 1862.

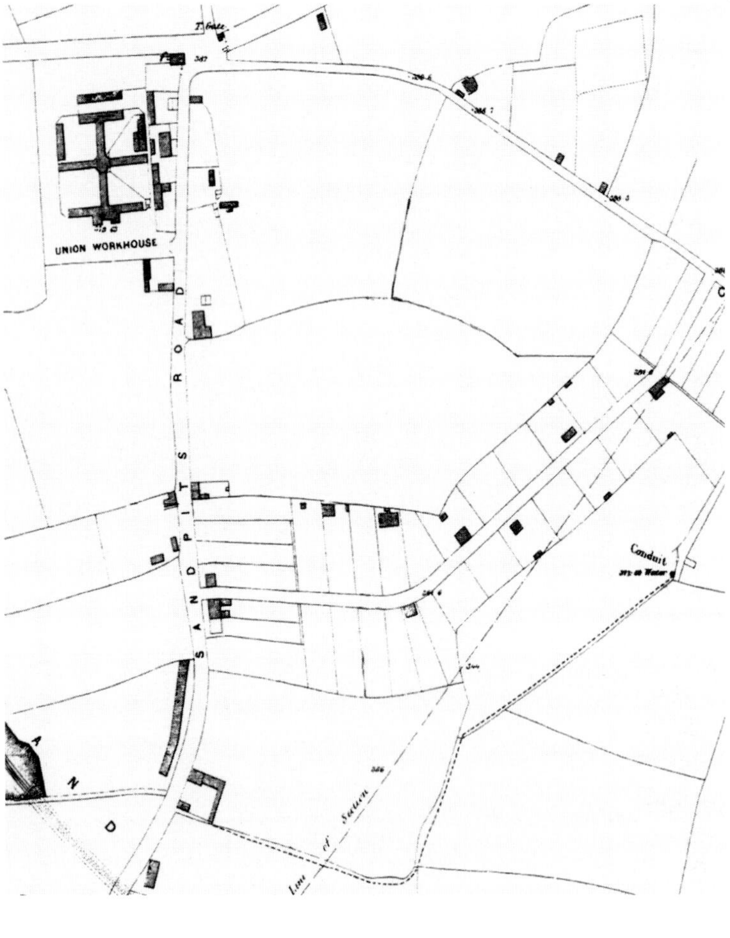

showing the increases in population and in the number of heads of households (that is, of dwellings) there during the period. These clearly show that the two decades from 1861 were the years of the most dramatic growth, Again available maps bear this out.

The Tithe Apportionment Map of 1847 [Fig. V][5] shows little change from 1832. The Union Workhouse has appeared with adjacent housing. One of these was "all that genteel and newly erected dwelling house, together with garden and appurtenances thereto belonging" advertised in the Shrewsbury Chronicle of 21 May 1847.[6] But, apart from Gravel Hill House, a house below it and what is called a public house in the hands of John Harding, on the western side opposite, there was still no development up the hill from Upper Gaolford, nor any in New Road nor along Sandpits Road. Fifteen years later T. Curley's Map of 1862 [Fig. VI][7] appears

Gravel Hill Terrace built in the early 1850s.

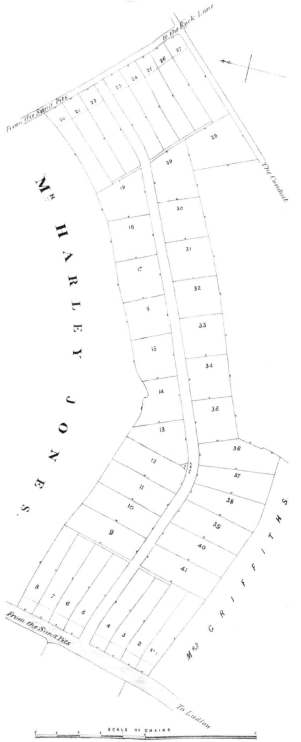

Fig. VII: Plan of Julian Road estate for sale by Rodney Anderson Esq. January 1859.

to show a short terrace on the eastern side of what the map designates as Sandpits Road (now Gravel Hill) below the old Gas Works. Further up on the western side Gravel Hill Terrace had been built and the Julian Road estate laid out with some houses already built.

The seven houses in Gravel Hill Terrace (now 17-29 Gravel Hill) were built on land acquired at auction on 4 March 1852 by Francis Bursnell, a whitesmith or cutler of Old Street, from the Ludlow Corporation for £256 7s 6d[8] (about £16,250 in modern terms), the sale being confirmed by the Council in February 1853.[9] Bursnell himself was to occupy Number 1 Gravel Hill Terrace until his death in December 1879. This was one of a series of sales of municipal land in the late 1840s and the 1850s which were forced upon the Borough Council to pay off the debts it had incurred as a result of what is known as 'the Great Law Suit' over the disposition of the Ludlow Charity estates.[10]

On 30 December 1853 the Council resolved that a further sale of lands should be arranged, the arrangements for and management of the sale being left to the Mayor, who was Rodney Anderson, a solicitor of Mill Street and clerk to the trustees of the Ludlow Charities.[11] On 23 June 1854 the Corporation sold to Rodney Anderson himself the two fields on the eastern side of Gravel Hill which stretched up to Sandpits Road and comprised what was known as the Tea Garden Nursery, in 1847 run by Miss Elizabeth Winwood, Anderson taking a mortgage of £600 on the following day against the property from Thomas Weyman, a fellow solicitor.[12] Four years later, this land, now divided into forty one lots with a road constructed through it and access to a well [Fig. VII], came on the market and sales of the plots began, surviving deeds giving 1 January 1859 as the date of conveyance.[13] Plots were sold to a variety of people, for example plot 4 to Elias Rollings, blacksmith of Upper Gaolford, plot 6 to William Coates, brewer and landlord of the Globe Inn, and plot 41 to Charles Davies, an auctioneer; prices recorded were £37 7s 1d for plot 13, £37 12s 6d for plot 32 and £40 13s 9d for plot 39 (all around £2,000 in modern terms).

Plaque on Prospect Place, Julian Road, in 1881 the home of Herbert Hammond, its probable original owner.

Because the plots were in different hands the building development was piecemeal. Curley's Map shows eight more or less substantial buildings in place by 1862, but some of these may have been no more than barns, since a number of the plots were used as gardens or allotments for many years, as later maps show. Indeed the original plot 31, immediately above the present numbers 36 and 38 Julian Road, remains a garden to this day.

The house on the corner of Sandpits Road and Julian Road carries the date 1863 with the initials H.H. and its name, Prospect Place. It seems almost certain that this was Herbert Hammond, a grocer at 132 Corve Street.[14] So building was proceeding apace. By 1871 there were 23 householders with a Julian Road address (this includes the houses which back onto Sandpits Road, known as Prospect Place and Julian Terrace, but not those fronting Gravel Hill), with one house empty, and in 1881 there were 37 householders with three houses empty. The Ordnance Survey Map, surveyed in 1883/4, shows what had happened [Fig. VIII].

Fig. VIII: Ordnance Survey map, 1883/4, showing Stanton Lacy and Ludford Suburbs.

Deeds of three houses give a glimpse of some part of this process. The plot of land upon which Number 8 Julian Road, The Manse, now stands was originally bought by John Pearce, a labourer, and then sold on in 1860 to Edward Thomas, a shoemaker. He in turn sold part of the plot to Miss Sarah Price of Broad Street in 1872, who then took out two substantial mortgages, almost certainly to build the house, known as Claremont House when it was let to the church as the Industrial Home in 1878.[15] On the other side of the road, the plot of Number 1, The Firs, and Number 3 similarly passed through several hands after its original purchase in 1859 before being acquired in 1877 by a local builder, James Hine of Corve Street. In March 1878 Hine took a mortgage against the "two houses then in course of construction", and sold The Firs in June 1880 to Thomas Sheppard, of 135 Corve Street.[16] James Hine was also the builder of Numbers 9, 11, and 13, whose plot had likewise passed through several hands

before he acquired it in May 1878, selling the newly erected houses to William Powell, a jeweller of 14 High Street, in September 1880.[17]

There had also been building on Gravel Hill since the early 1860s. Substantial villas now stood on all the plots facing Gravel Hill which Rodney Anderson had sold in 1859 – Gothic Villa, now Arran House (Numbers 42 and 44 Gravel Hill), occupied in 1881 by Henry Skarratt, a retired jeweller, Glenview (Number 54), the home of the High Street draper and outfitter, William Bodenham, and Holly Lodge (Number 56), occupied in 1881 by the Reverend Thomas Bennett, Lecturer of Ludlow. St. John's church, Gravel Hill had been open since 1880.[18] On the

Glenview, Gravel Hill, the home of William Bodenham.

The Firs, 1 Julian Road.

Victoria Terrace, Gravel Hill, built in the early 1880s.

other side of the road another terrace of four superior villas had appeared. The land was bought by William Bodenham in June 1881 for £915 (some £47,000 in modern terms) – it included a house and cottage, which were, presumably, knocked down – and the houses, to be known as Victoria Terrace and in later years to be the residences of various of William's sons, were erected over the next year or so. Down the hill closer to town Glebe Terrace had appeared between and abutting the short terrace of cottages shown on Curley's map and the Iron Foundry. These four houses were there by 1881, as were the two larger semi-detached villas opposite, known as The Laurels and The Yews.

However, much the most substantial development since 1862 had been in East Hamlet, an area which the Census enumerators and the maps designate as Sandpits. The 1861 Census gives seven properties in Sandpits (these include some few along what is now Sandpits Road). In 1871 there were 26.[19] In 1881 there were 100, with 9 under construction. There were three principal elements to this growth: an estate of essentially working men's terraced housing, which comprised New Street, Chapel Row and Dodmore Lane; an estate of middle class villas looking out across the Corve and Teme valleys to the town, the Castle, Whitcliffe and Bringewood – Castle View Terrace; and a variety of houses on New Road itself, including a group in a side road below the Zion Chapel which had been built in 1878 (now Bellevue Terrace, but then called Chapel Fields). The development differed from those in Gravel Hill and along Julian Road in that much of it derived from the initiative of one man – Benjamin Weale.

Benjamin Weale was born in 1845 at Vernolds Common, Onibury, the third son of a carpenter. Described as a general servant at the age of 15 in 1861, he married a girl from Stanton Lacy, Betsy Evans, and they had their first child, Mary, at Church Aston, Newport before moving to Sandpits in or around 1870.[20] The 1871 Census described him, at the age of 25, as a builder and timber merchant, and he already had one servant. In 1881 there were seven children and three servants, living in the largest house in the district, Sandpits Villa in New Street (his business in 1879 being described by Kelly's Directory as "Weale, Benjamin and William [a younger brother], builders and timber merchants, Sandpits and at Church Aston, Newport". By now the estate was nearly complete; New Street, Chapel Row and Dodmore Lane were built and only six houses remained in build in Castle View Terrace. With the certain exception of Numbers 3 and 4 Castle View Terrace, which were built by John Baxter in 1873/4 on land which Weale had sold to him in July 1872[21], all of the rest, including a small Primitive Methodist Chapel in New Street, which later was used as a schoolroom, were built by Weale's firm, work having begun almost as soon as he arrived in East Hamlet.[22]

On the other side of New Road from this development the Board of Guardians of the Ludlow Union in 1878 sold part of a block of

Benjamin Weale outside Sandpits Villa in 1903 at the wedding of his daughter Minnie May Weale to Oscar John Morgan of Marlbrook Hall, Burrington.

land, which they had recently purchased[23], below the Workhouse in New Road to various buyers, one of whom was Gaius Smith, grocer of 42 Bull Ring. Gaius Smith offered this land to the local Methodists for the erection of a larger chapel than the one in New Street, and the Trustees appointed in August 1878 for the purpose of supervising the building, among them Benjamin Weale and Gaius Smith himself, duly commissioned the erection of the Zion Chapel by Benjamin Weale, its foundations having been laid on 17 October 1878 (the names of members of the Weale family appear on several of the dedicatory stones). Shortly after this, work began on properties below the Chapel and in what was called Chapel Fields, now Bellevue Terrace, two being offered for sale in June 1880 and five more in April 1882, all described as newly built.[24]

Many of these properties remained in Weale's own possession for years, the land valuation records under the Finance Act 1909/10 showing him as the owner of the whole of New Street, seven cottages in Chapel Row, all of Dodmore Lane beyond Chapel Row, 16 – 25 Castle View Terrace, as well as properties at the top of New Road and in Chapel Fields. He had however substantially reduced his estate by the time of his death in 1920.[25]

Still on the northern outskirts of the town but somewhat away from the New Road and East Hamlet developments, Fishmore Terrace, beyond the brick and pipe works, was built in the 1860s and added to in the 1870s – there being 9

households in 1871 and 13 in 1881. On the hillside above it the cottages around the Old Brickyard continued to be fully occupied as they had been since before Victoria came to the throne.

The growth in the population to the north-east of the town over the two decades from 1860 to 1880 had, as has already been remarked, caused the church authorities, both Anglican and Non-Conformist, to provide local places of worship. And by 1870 it was clear that a school was going to be needed for the area (in 1871 there were forty six children of school age in the Sandpits district, a number which had risen to

Castle View Terrace.

New Street.

The dedication stone on the Zion Methodist Chapel on New Road Bank, showing the names of the trustees.

Left: Chapel Row.

Below: The original Methodist Chapel in New Street, later a school, which gave Chapel Row its name.

over a hundred ten years later). In December 1870 the Stanton Lacy Vestry resolved to provide a school at Sandpits, accepting the Rector of Ludlow's offer of part of the glebe land for a site.[26] It was to be six years before East Hamlet school was opened on the corner of Sandpits Road and Henley Road.[27]

After 1884 the pace of development slowed, but did not entirely cease, as a comparison between the Ordnance Survey Maps of 1883/4 and 1902 [Figs. VIII and II] shows. In October 1893 St Julian's Nursery, on the eastern side of Gravel Hill below Julian Road, was put on the market by Francis Calver, seedsman and florist of The Bull Ring. The land was divided into 16 plots and a new road was constructed, to be known as St Julian's Avenue. Norton's advertisement observed that "the plots were laid out to attract persons seeking to build desirable houses, and are on land sloping to the south on red sandstone formation with extensive views down the valley of the Teme, well sheltered from the north and east." Only nine of the plots (on the northern side of the Avenue) were sold in the first instance, among the purchasers being the grocer Gaius Smith and George Partington.[28] Partington's house became number 9, called, to begin with, Lorenzo. The contractor's specification of March 1895 provided that it should be built of good, sound

The top of New Road from an early photograph. East Hamlet School can be seen in the distance.

Fig. IX: Front Elevation of Lorenzo.

9 St Julian's Avenue, the house built for George Partington, originally called "Lorenzo".

Ludlow bricks; the stonework was to be of the best description of Grinshill stone, except for the steps which were to be of York stone. The roof was to be of medium quality Portmadoc slates and the ridge of red Ruabon cresting bed.[29] The proposed elevation for it is Fig. IX. By 1902 there were five houses in St Julian's Avenue, and one by the foundry on the corner of Gravel Hill built in 1897 for Francis Calver.[30]

At the same time gaps on the western side of Gravel Hill were filled. In April 1894 the glebe land between Gravel Hill Terrace and Victoria Terrace was sold at auction in four lots – "good frontage to Gravel Hill Road, would attract persons seeking to build desirable houses; it is outside the Borough and not liable to its rates. Close to St. John's Church and the Railway Station. Gas and Water can be laid on" ran Norton's advertisement.[31] The lower one was sold to Edmund Jones, grocer of 15 High Street, who had two houses built on the plot, living in the bottom one, Bringewood, himself.[32] The top three were sold to William Putman and in August that year tenders for the erection of six houses in Gravel Hill Road were sought, the plans and specifications being available at Fair View House (part of Victoria Terrace).[33] This was then the home of Mr Putman, described in the 1891 census as a lessee of granite quarries.

Finally and before 1900, since they were occupied by then, as the 1900 Kelly's Directory shows, the three houses next to Victoria Terrace directly opposite St John's Church and the two beyond them were built, the first group being owned by William Harris, a Great Western Railway Agent, and the second by Charles Marston, the miller and corn merchant, who lived at Hill Crest.

Elsewhere in this area Julian Road continued to grow and Benjamin Weale was still busy in East Hamlet, building two houses in New Road for Gaius Smith in 1895 (Numbers 21 and 23 just below the Chapel) and a terrace of four in Chapel Fields for Henry Hodges, a local doctor (Numbers 9-12 Bellevue Terrace). At the bottom of New Road before the Railway Bridge Numbers 70-74 carry a plaque "Railway View 1892", number 76 "Diamond Jubilee 1897", and on the other side there is "Jubilee Cottage 1887".

The shape and extent of the Victorian suburb in Stanton Lacy to the north-east of the town was now settled. That in Ludford to its south-east was less extensive, less coherent and less sustained. It may be more briefly described. At the beginning of the period, apart from the houses at the bottom of Old Street on its eastern side, in Holdgate Fee, which had for centuries been in Ludford Parish, and the cottages on the

Ludford side of Rock Lane, only a couple of cottages around the Mill lay in what, by the end of the century, was becoming recognised as Ludlow. And, just as with Stanton Lacy, so it remained for twenty or more years. Sometime in the 1860s a few cottages and more substantial properties began to appear by the river towards Steventon. At the western end, before Weeping Cross and close to the town gasworks, these were known as The Folly or Folley; further on around the Mill the properties were called Teme Terrace. In 1871 there were six properties in The Folly and four in Teme Terrace – Kelly's Directory of 1870 recorded two private addresses in Teme Terrace, which suggests that it was already regarded as a desirable place to live.

Shortly after that the largest single development in the growth of the Ludford suburb of Ludlow started. From 1872 onwards plots of land on what was variously known as Cole's Meadow or Folley Meadow, land which had earlier belonged to Sir Rowland Hill, were put on the market by Arthur Markham, a Northampton man, the area having been divided into 26 plots and a road constructed through it – Steventon New Road [Fig. X].[34] On the side facing the river the plots were larger and some substantial villas were erected over the succeeding years – Teme Villas and a pair of houses, called Riverdale on the 1902 Ordnance Survey map, on the corner where Steventon New Road comes down to the river. The 1881 Census recorded 8 houses in this area, four being unoccupied. On the northern side of the new road three sets of terraced houses were built in the 1870s, nine being occupied in 1881, and six unoccupied. By 1891 there were twenty properties here, the two eastern

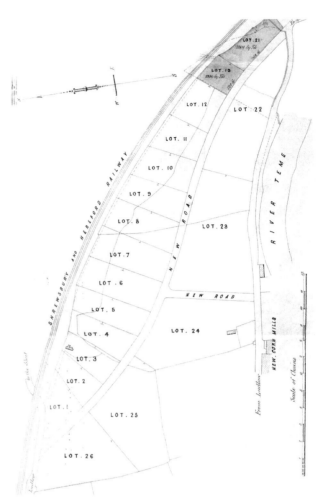

Fig. X: Plan of Steventon New Road estate to be sold by Arthur Markham in 1872.

Teme Villas, Temeside, Steventon.

Spring Cottages, Steventon New Road.

have been within the last fifty. A considerable number are now in course of construction close to the outlet of the sewer [near the Mill on Temeside], a large plot of ground called the Folley Meadows having been lately sold in building lots and new buildings are now being built thereon. Houses too, whether good, bad or indifferent are extremely difficult to be met with by people wishing to take them."[36]

It was the provision of a sewerage system for the Town which was the trigger for the incorporation of the new suburbs into the Borough. As early as November 1891 the Corporation of Ludlow had submitted a Memorial to the Local Government Board for a proposed extension of the Borough[37], but the proposal had fallen because there was "no effluent system of sewage disposal for the Borough. If that were provided,

terraces being known as Patmos Place and Spring Cottages, but further west and closer to town there was little building until well into the twentieth century.

To sum up this account of the physical growth of the Ludlow suburbs, in 1841 there were just over 100 properties outside Ludlow Borough in the area which was at the end of the century to be incorporated in it.[35] By 1901 this number had quadrupled to 415. John Williams, Town Clerk of Ludlow, in a letter to the Editor of the Hereford Times in 1874 about the provision of new sewers for the town (a saga which was to last for another twenty five years, until a system of sewerage and sewage disposal was constructed in 1900) gave a contemporary view. "Building too is going on to a great extent, more houses having been built within the last five years than

Installing services at the top of Gravel Hill, early twentieth century. The Workhouse is in the background.

then proposals for the extension might be entertained."[38] It has also to be said that at that time there seems to have been little support for the idea in East Hamlet. When the new Parish Council for East Hamlet under the provisions of the Parish Councils Act was elected in December 1894, Mr Passey, a retired farmer living in Gravel Hill Terrace, who chaired the start of the election meeting, observed that "He hoped the day was far distant when they should be put into the Borough of Ludlow, as they could do very well by themselves. When their Parish Council was elected and any grievances existed they had only to get three electors and they could call a parish meeting and have everything done as they wanted, but if they came into the Borough there would be sixteen gentlemen there dressed in their scarlet and fine linen to do it...." During the examination of the potential councillors several were asked if they would oppose annexation, and all did so explicitly, with the exception of Mr Gaius Smith who avoided giving a straight answer; he actually then lived in the Town and had been on the Town Council but had voting rights in East Hamlet as he owned property there.[39]

However, in April 1899 the East Hamlet Parish Council passed a resolution that "This Council is of the opinion that the time has arrived when in order to facilitate the efficient sewering of the district negotiations should be opened with Ludlow Town Council [for its inclusion in the Borough]." A month previously the Ludford Parish Council's resolution on the same subject was "That in the opinion of this meeting it would be of an advantage to a part of the Parish of Ludford to be incorporated with the Borough of Ludlow." The stage was now set.

Following a joint conference of representatives from the Ludlow Town Council, Ludlow Rural District, East Hamlet Parish Council and Ludford Parish Council in September 1900, a Memorial was produced in November setting out the case for extension. It was very similar to that submitted in 1891, its principal clauses being:

That the portion proposed to be included are the out-growths of the Borough, and contain an Urban district and a compact population which has grown up immediately round the Borough within the last 40 years.

That the said district has all the advantages of its proximity to the Borough without sharing its burdens.

That the present division is very arbitrary in many places: for instance in Holdgate Fee the one side of the street is in the Borough, while the other is outside the Borough. In Upper Gaolford the boundary runs across the street....

The out-district has no independent water supply and is dependent on the Borough for such supply. [This had been installed in 1890.[40]]

The present insanitary state of the out-district, there being no system of sewerage whatsoever, is a standing menace to the health of the Borough.

The Borough and East Hamlet portion of the district proposed to be added (by far the largest and most populous part of such district) now form one parish for ecclesiastical purposes.

The Burial Ground of the Parish of St. Laurence which is coterminous with the present Borough is now used both for the Borough and for the East Hamlet and Ludford districts. Such burial ground will shortly be full, and it is very desirable that the cost of a new ground should fall on the district using it.

The Ludlow Railway Station is in close proximity to the centre of the Town but is outside its present limit, and if brought within it would conduce to the advantage of the Borough.

A portion of the district proposed to be added is not lighted or paved, and some of the roads and streets are in a very bad state. If Urban Powers are obtained it would greatly benefit both the Borough and such district, and would encourage the building of villas and new houses.

That the proposed extension of the boundaries will on general grounds be advantageous to the Borough and to the district proposed to be added.

Although there were some make-weights in this – it is not immediately apparent why having the station within the boundaries of the Borough would conduce to its advantage – , the central argument was potent. The cost of running the Borough should be shared by all those who took advantage of its present or future facilities (advertisements for properties in the East Hamlet suburb had for some time been commending them on the somewhat provocative grounds that they had the benefit of being able to use the town and all its facilities without being subject to its rates). After a public enquiry in January 1901 and some to-ing and fro-ing with the Local Government Board the Ludlow (Extension) Order 1901 came into force in November of that year.

So it was that in the year that Victoria died the physical growth of Ludlow, which had been going on for the better part of her reign, was given statutory and administrative recognition by the incorporation of the suburbs into the town. But who were the people who had moved to live there? Why had they done so? And why had it happened at all?

The census of 1881 throws some light on the first two of these questions, since it was taken when most of the first wave of building was complete and families were becoming established in the new suburbs. The following table gives a social profile of the heads of households of the four principal areas of settlement in the Stanton Lacy suburb – Gravel Hill, Julian Road, the East Hamlet estate, including New Road and Fishmore Terrace, and Castle View Terrace (see Table 1).

Although the numbers are relatively small, a clear profile emerges, which is confirmed by the types of housing that were built. Gravel Hill and Castle View Terrace were predominantly middle class developments; there was rather more of a social mix in Julian Road; while the Sandpits/East Hamlet estate was predominantly working class. The contrast between Castle View Terrace and the other parts of the estate which Benjamin Weale had built is also detectable in another way. The average age of the head of household in the former in 1881 was 53, while, to take New Street which had the largest number of properties as the example, there it was 39. Of the 14 houses in Castle View Terrace then occupied only four had children of

Table 1: Occupations of Heads of Households in Stanton Lacy Suburb in 1881

	Retired/Independent Means/Widowed	Trades people	White Collar	Building and related trades	Railwaymen	Labourers and manual workers	Other
Gravel Hill	19	5					5
Julian Road	15	3	9	7	1	1	1
East Hamlet		10		20	23	20	13
Castle View - Terrace	8		4	2			1

Table 2: Places of Birth of Heads of Households in Stanton Lacy Suburb, 1881.

Location	Place of Birth (if recorded)			
	Ludlow/Stanton Lacy	**Within 10 miles**	**Beyond**	**Total**
Gravel Hill	5	11	13	29
Julian Road	11	11	15	37
East Hamlet, including Castle View Terrace	19	28	51	98
Total	**35**	**50**	**79**	**164**

school age, 9 children in all; of New Street's 32 houses 23 had children, 81 in all.

One other characteristic of the heads of household in the Stanton Lacy suburb in 1881 can be analysed – places of birth, which are set out in Table 2.

Two points need to be remembered in drawing conclusions from these figures. The fact that someone's place of birth is recorded as Ludlow or Stanton Lacy does not mean that they had lived there continually. Conversely, someone who is recorded as having been born out of Ludlow may have come to Ludlow as a child and have lived there all of his or her life. Put differently, the distinction between a "Ludlovian" and an "incomer" is not always clear cut. That having been said, it is clear that the creation of the suburb drew a substantial number of families into Ludlow, virtually half coming from a substantial distance, and a further 30% from out of town. So of the order of 80% were incomers. The smaller, but not insignificant, proportion came from the town itself.

The modern villas in Gravel Hill and Castle View Terrace, with their extensive views across the town to Bringewood Chase[41], and in Julian Road, with then similarly extensive views towards the town and to the south, proved from the beginning very attractive to retired people. Francis Bursnell, the original builder of Gravel Hill Terrace in 1852, had retired from his Old Street cutler's business, and he was joined from the early days by others in retirement. George Swift, a retired farmer, and Mrs Holden, a farmer's widow and her sister, Mary Swift, also a farmer's widow, were in Gravel Hill Terrace in the 1860s, Mary Swift moving on to Julian Road in the 1880s. Mrs Elizabeth Amies, widow of Thomas Amies, proprietor of the Rose and

Crown in Harp Lane, came to live at 3 Gravel Hill in the 1860s with her daughter, Caroline, who stayed there for some years after her mother died before moving to 16 Castle View Terrace in the 1880s. Mrs Annie Blakeway, described by the Census as a retired farmer, was at The Yews, Gravel Hill in 1881, and Henry Skarratt, a retired jeweller, was at Gothic Villas. Living in Julian Road in 1881 were Benjamin Griffiths, who had retired from his hairdressing business in Broad Street, Henry Jones from his printing, bookselling and stationery business at 10 Broad Street, and Thomas Pearce from keeping the Bear and White Lion at 99 Old Street, while the three Misses Grieves of

Gravel Hill from an early postcard.

independent means, daughters of the Old Street chemist, John Grieves, having first moved to Castle View Terrace, were now residing at Lonsdale, where they were to remain for the next twenty or more years.

Over the years from 1861 Gravel Hill and Julian Road also became the residential area of people who had businesses in town and who had lived or might have lived over their place of business. One of the first to come to Gravel Hill in the 1850s was Edward Harding, draper and outfitter of the High Street, who was to live at Gravel Hill Villa at the top of Gravel Hill by the

Union Workhouse for over forty years, and Jasper Cox, a general outfitter and boot and shoe maker of Broad Street, was an early resident in Gravel Hill Terrace. By 1881 Alfred Townsend, the manager of the Clee Hill Dhu Stone Company had come to live at The Laurels, below Gravel Hill Terrace; and at Glenview, next to Holly Lodge and St. John's church, William Bodenham, draper and outfitter in King Street, together with his wife, seven children, four apprentices and three servants, had taken up residence which was to last for the family here and over the road in Victoria Terrace into the 1920s. In Julian Road in that year were to be found the Relieving Officer for the District, William Harding, who had moved from Old Street, the Assistant Overseer and Registrar of Births and Marriages, William Broad, the Bailiff of Ludlow County Court, Thomas Williams, a solicitor and partner in the firm of Clark, Sudbury and Williams, John Bennett Williams, and three members of the Inland Revenue Excise Branch, Thomas O'Riordan, George Passmore and William Steenton.

The extent to which Gravel Hill, Julian Road, Castle View Terrace and, in the last decade of the century, St Julian's Avenue became fashionable places to live may be illustrated by a comparison of the number of private residents registering their address in Kelly's Directory in 1870 and in 1900. In 1870 19 out of 142 (13%) resided in these roads. In 1900 it was 62 out of 172 (36%).

Table 1 clearly shows the predominance of two groups of artisans in the Sandpits area in 1881 – workers in the building trade and railwaymen. In New Street ten out of eighteen heads of household were in the building trade, which strongly endorses the local memory that this was the principal street in which Benjamin Weale's work force lived. Benjamin himself, and his elder brother, Thomas, a carpenter, lived there from the early 1870s, and his younger brother, William, also a carpenter and with whom he later seems to have gone into partnership, had been lodging in Sandpits in 1871. William had moved to the Newport area in the late 1870s and ran the part of the business there, employing 35 men and 5 boys in 1881. He returned to Ludlow in 1885 and died there in 1890.[42] The building which went on in the suburbs almost continuously from the mid-1850s until the end of the century generated employment not only for skilled men (bricklayers, plasterers, carpenters) but also for general labourers, who are also to be found in significant numbers in this part of the suburbs.

The number of railway-men living in East Hamlet is not surprising, and all the streets had their share of them. For the first few years after the railway came through in 1852 only a small number of staff lived in the Stanton Lacy suburb. In 1861 there were two railway clerks, a porter and the

Benjamin Weale's workforce c.1890. Benjamin Weale is the bearded man in the centre. His elder brother Thomas is on the far left of the back row.

station master himself - the station lying outside the Borough – while in the Town there were twenty, many of them lodgers, mostly living close to the station, in Corve Street and Upper and Lower Gaolford. But after the opening of the branch line to the Clee Hill quarries in 1864, the number of heads of households living in the Stanton Lacy suburb who were railwaymen began to grow – 9 in 1871, 25 in 1881(of the sixty seven railway staff – either heads of households or lodgers – in this year half lived in East Hamlet), 29 in 1891 and 33 in 1901. The East Hamlet estate was attractive to them. It was close to their place of work, the properties were modern, of the right size for young men (as the majority of the railwaymen were) just starting families, and, no doubt, available for rent at a price which was within their means as railway servants. Most of them did not stay long, but there were exceptions. Samuel Cheese, a carriage examiner and repairer, was in New Street and then Sandpits Road from at least 1881 to after 1901; John Coates, a signalman, had a similar spell, first in New Road and then in New Street; John Pheasant, a platelayer, was in New Street for the whole period, as was Charles Worthen, a carriage examiner; while Frank Money, a railway cattle inspector, moved from 32 New Street, where he had been in 1881 and 1891, to 23 Castle View Terrace in 1901 as he came up to retirement.

This social mix is in some measure reflected in the outcome of the first election of East Hamlet Parish Councillors in December 1894. At least one hundred people were present at the meeting to elect eleven councillors from twenty one nominees. Benjamin Weale topped the poll with a hundred votes[43], followed by William Harris, Great Western Railway Agent of Castle View Terrace (90), Thomas Wyilde, locksmith of Sandpits Lane (82), George Berrington, bricklayer of Julian Road (81), Henry Wale, Inspector of Schools of Castle View Terrace (77), the Reverend Nicholl, chaplain to Ludlow Union and curate at St John's (69), Samuel Cheese, Railway Wagon Examiner of Sandpits Lane (64),

Thomas Williams, County Court Bailiff of Julian Road (62), William Roberts, Iron Foundry foreman of Julian Road (61), George Luscott, labourer of Dodmore Lane (59) and Charles Keysell, Wine Merchant of Gravel Hill (52). During the questioning before the election Mr Keysell had the following splendid exchange with the Reverend Chubb who asked him whether "if he were elected, he intended to represent the licensed victuallers or East Hamlet." Mr. Keysell replied, "The licensed victuallers have nothing to do with the meeting. So mind your own business." Among those failing to get elected were Mr Putman, quarry manager of Gravel Hill, who was about to develop more properties in the road, Francis Calver, the florist, who was launching the development of St Julian's Avenue, and Gaius Smith, one of the most influential men in Ludlow itself, but, as already mentioned, non-resident in East Hamlet at this time. The election having been on a show of hands, Gaius Smith moved for a poll to be held, but was persuaded to withdraw on grounds of the expense which would be incurred. "It was the first time he had withdrawn from a contest, but as there were a number of working men on the Council, he did not mind agreeing with their wishes."[44]

Although the numbers in the Ludford suburb were smaller than in East Hamlet, the census of 1891 (by which time the Coles Meadow estate was fully occupied) provides some picture of the social characteristics of those who had come to live there. It shows a broadly similar pattern of "incomers" and "Ludlovians" among the heads of household – some four to one, with just over 40% having been born further than ten miles from Ludlow. The Coles Meadow houses were occupied almost entirely by skilled and unskilled manual workers, as were those in The Folley, while the larger houses in Temeside, Teme Terrace and around the Paper Mill had attracted tradesmen, white collar workers, and retired people.

Some answers to the final question which was posed earlier – what caused the growth of the Ludlow suburbs in the second half of the nineteenth century? – have emerged from the foregoing account. So far as the Stanton Lacy suburb was concerned, the Corporation's need to generate capital to meet the debts it had incurred through the 'Great Law Suit' brought onto the market in the 1850s land which had hitherto been let for agricultural purposes but which might now be used for much more lucrative housing developments, both for sale and to let. Those developments, of commodious modern housing, were in a very pleasant area, with fine views, within easy distance of the town's amenities and close to the newly arrived railway. They were attractive, therefore, both to middle class people who worked in or wished to work in the town and to retired people with adequate means, not only from Ludlow but also from farther afield. The arrival and development of the railway also created the need for houses of a less expensive, but none the less up to date, sort to accommodate the growing numbers of railway staff. The provision of housing for these groups required a growing force of skilled craftsman and labourers and these too had to be similarly housed, in turn feeding the development of the suburbs.

The availability of land for new housing and a market for that housing were essential to the development of the suburbs but alone they were not sufficient. Also required were businessmen who recognised the opportunity offered by the availability of the land and the existence of a potential market for new housing, and were prepared to risk investing in it. Again, the story of the suburbs' growth has revealed who some of these men were: in the early days Francis Bursnell, the developer of Gravel Hill Terrace, and Rodney Anderson, who bought the land and laid out the site for the Julian Road Estate, and rather later when the way forward was clear, in Julian Road, the builder James Hine, in Gravel Hill, William Bodenham, William Putman and William Harris, in St Julian's Avenue, Francis Calver and Gaius Smith, who also had interests elsewhere in the district, and Arthur Markham, who laid out and sold the Steventon New Road Estate. But the most significant figure was Benjamin Weale, who, supported by his younger and elder brothers, William and Thomas, had the financial acumen, the resourcefulness, the foresight and the energy to create the Sandpits estate, and by whose business so many other East Hamlet houses were built. Looking on the ground today at what he achieved, one can understand why he was known as the "King of East Hamlet".[45]

Benjamin Weale, Mayor of Ludlow 1905-6.

1   Unless otherwise indicated the sources for this chapter are the censuses from 1841 – 1901, and trade and postal directories, all of which may be found either at the Ludlow Library or at Shropshire Archives in Shrewsbury. References to documents at Shropshire Archives are preceded by the initials SA.

2   See page 47 below.

3   See Chapter 11 The Anglican Church in Ludlow, 1867 – 1907, page 211.

4   These figures include the population of that part of Rock Lane which lay in the Parish of Ludford, although it was not brought into the Borough at that time, but exclude the occupants of the Ludlow Union Workhouse.

5   SA: P265/7/2, together with the actual apportionment: Stanton Lacy – Stanton [296] 29 – 296.2. Figure V is Foxall's Field name map based on the Tithe Apportionment. It is reproduced by permission of Shropshire Archives.

6   The advertisement continued "The house has been recently built in the most substantial manner, is replete with every convenience, and contains entrance hall, drawing room, parlour, 3 bedrooms and attic over, kitchen, larder, brewhouse and cellar". It was later to be known as Gravel Hill Villa and to be the house of the draper, Edward Harding, from at the latest 1861until his death in 1907.

7   Map with Geological Sections of the Borough of Ludlow shewing lines of the new sewers and the new cattle market.

8   I am grateful to Amy Ormond for this information.

9   (SA) Ludlow Corporation Minutes, DA3/100/2.

10   For an account of this see David Lloyd, *The Concise History of Ludlow*, Ludlow 1999, pp. 133-4.

11   (SA) DA 3/100/2.

12   (SA)2030/2/451.

13   See for example (SA) Salwey and Rickards Collection, 2030/2/455 Conveyance to Charles Brown of plot 32. Figure VII is reproduced from this document by permission of Phillips and Co., Corve Street, Ludlow.

14   Herbert Hammond and his wife Mary were living at Prospect Place by 1881 and their ages and places of birth correspond exactly with the Corve Street family of earlier years.

15   I am grateful to Adrian Williams for a sight of these deeds.

16   I am grateful to Joe Bishop, the present occupier of The Firs, for a sight of these deeds.

17   From an abstract of the deeds of Number 9 taken by David Lloyd with permission of the present owner, Brian Perry.

18   See Chapter 11, p.211.

19   In 1871 the census enumerator included some of the houses at the top of Gravel Hill in the Sandpits district, so these two sets of figures are not on exactly the same basis. However that does not invalidate the point being made about the substantial development here in the 1870s.

20   Mary was 2 in 1871 and their second child, John was 6 months, having been born in Stanton Lacy.

21   From the deeds of 3 Castle View Terrace kindly provided by Mrs Daphne Jones.

22   This is an inference drawn from a comparison of the 1871 Census and that of 1881. The former does not give street names in Sandpits, but Benjamin Weale himself, his elder brother, Thomas, a carpenter, Samuel Bytheway, a postman, Samuel Easthope, a railwayman, George Sheffield, a Brickmaker, and Thomas Venables, a carter, were recorded in both censuses and in 1881 are recorded respectively in New Street, 6 New Street, 5 New Street, 12 New Street,15 New Street, and 5 Chapel Row.

23   (SA) PL9/2/1/14 Minutes of the Ludlow Union Board of Guardians 28/6/1878. I am grateful to Derek Williams for this information.

24   (SA) Norton Collection 4924/2/7/33 and 4924/2/9/13.

25   (SA) WILL 1920/[296].

26   (SA) P265/C/1/1 – 2.

27   See Chapter 9, p.172 .

28   (SA) 4924/1/19/41.

29   (SA) PL/38/3/16 from which Figure IX is taken by permission of Shropshire Archives.

30   (SA) DA22/994/39/1-3.

31   *Ludlow Advertiser,* 7 April 1894.

32   (SA) Salwey and Rickards 4924/1/20/9.

33   *Ludlow Advertiser,* 11 August 1894.

34   Conveyance in the Morgan collection at Shropshire Archives (SA 5755/10/5), from which Figure X is reproduced by permission of Morgans, Solicitors, Mill Street, Ludlow.

35   This number includes properties in Upper Gaolford and Holdgate Fee, which had always been seen as belonging to the ancient town. It also includes the Ludford properties in Rock Lane, which were not brought in by the 1901 Extension, but which form a unit with the properties on the other side of the Lane which were.

36   (SA)DA3/990/1/1 Minutes of the Ludlow Urban Sanitary Authority 22 January 1874.

37   (SA)DA3/702/3 of 12 November 1891.

38   All of this section is drawn from the papers which deal with the Ludlow Borough Extension Order 1901 (SA) DA3/135/285 - 334.

39   *Ludlow Advertiser,* 8 December 1894.

40   Minutes of the Ludlow Rural Sanitary Authority 1889 and 1890 (SA) DA22/994/3.

41   The deeds of 8 Castle View Terrace have a covenant on them which precludes building in the garden on the western side of the road, so protecting the outlook (personal communication from Leslie Haynes, the present occupier).

42   I am grateful to Mrs Gwyn Tyrrell, Benjamin Weale's great-granddaughter for this information. She has also provided the pictures of Benjamin Weale, of the wedding party outside Sandpits Villa, and, from Mrs Watkins, another great-granddaughter of Benjamin, the picture of Benjamin with his work force.

43   Benjamin Weale was to become Mayor of Ludlow in 1905-06 and remained an Alderman of the Town, representing the East Hamlet Ward until his death in 1920.

44   *Ludlow Advertiser,* 8 December 1894.

45   Miss Marjorie Waite, who lives in Castle View Terrace, remembers that her father, who knew Benjamin Weale, told her that this was how he was known in his lifetime.

CHAPTER 3

SHOPS AND SHOP KEEPERS

DAVID LLOYD

Fig. 1: Picture of the 'hub of Ludlow', painted in the 1870s.

The ambience of a shopping day in mid-Victorian Ludlow is captured by the painting reproduced as Fig. 1. It shows the Butter Cross and the streets converging before it. Horse drawn carts and wagons are lumbering into town, while the rider in the middle of the picture is armed with a shopping basket. Goods are hanging outside some of the shops, while baskets of produce rest on the pavements, some of them with haggling customers. The picture reflects the leisurely pace of a country town, but on market and fair days it was much busier. This was the experience of the writer, J.J. Hissey, who visited Ludlow on a Monday in 1894 and found himself in streets so crowded that "progress towards the ancient Feathers Inn was somewhat slow".[1]

The artist, Edward Phipson, contrives to magnify the buildings by making people smaller

Fig. 2a: Ludlow Town centre in 1884 - East Area
based on Crocker's Directory of Shropshire published in that year.

Broad Street

1	Sarah Amies	Berlin & fancy
2	Mary Taylor	baker
3-5	John Valentine	grocer
6	Herbert Smith	boots & shoes
7	Edmund P. Thomas	draper
8	William Tillett	grocer
10	Samuel Bridges	general dealer
13	Mary Howells	milliner
55	William Boucher	music dealer
56	James Nixon	chemist
58	Charles Partridge	bookseller
59	George Collier	cabinet maker
60	Robinson Brothers	watchmakers
67	Christine Boulton	milliner
68	Thomas Lowe	fishmonger

Bull Ring

1	Thomas Blackmore	boots & shoes
2	George Woolley	bookseller
3	George Adney	draper
4	James Eldridge	boots and shoes
5	Elizabeth Cook	cooper
6-7	Heber Rickards	ironmonger
8	Samuel Davies	baker
9	George Crundell	stationer
10	Charles Doble	fishmonger
11	Henry Crane	grocer
12	John Daulby	saddler
13	Henry Blackmore	fancy goods
16	William Cooke	furniture dealer
20	Emma Hean	milliner
21		unoccupied
22	William Cooke	cabinet maker
25	Margaret Marston	baker
26	John Watkins	butcher
27	Charles Doble	greengrocer
33	John Stevens	tailer & hatter
34	Charles Williamson	gunmaker
41	Charles Davies	tobacconist
42	Gaius Smith	grocer
43-44	Dawes and Bowen	wine merchants
45	George Woodhouse	chemist
46	Charles Keysell	wine merchant
47	Turner & Co	boots & shoes
48	Mary Brown	glass & china
49	Alfred Marston	chemist
50	John Anthony	hairdresser
51	Francis Calver	seedsman

King Street

1	Willima Holyoake	glass & china
3	Challoner Bros.	ironmongers
4	James Evans	draper
5	William T. Bessell	draper
6	Gaius Smith	grocer
7	James Wainwright	boots & shoes
8	Richard Evans	poulterer
9	George Menhencott	grocer
10	Thos.Vickerstaff	grocer
11	Robert Gross	tailor
12	John Fennell	butcher
13	Thomas Micklewright	cabinet maker
14	Mary Ashwood	general dealer
15	John Adney	leather seller
16	John Cross	stationer
17	Maria Baker	milliner
18-20	William Bodenham	draper

Old Street

1	James Jones	butcher
2	George Williams	butcher
3	Edwin Nickols	baker
98	Charles Mansfield	boots & shoes

Tower Street

3	Martha Davies	tobacconist
4	Charles Brown	grocer
5	William Pugh	butcher
6	George Jones	baker
9	James Driver	saddler
10	Charles Gore	baker
12	Richard Grainger	draper
13	George Rix	grocer
14	Mary Cox	shopkeeper
15	William Barber	saddler

Fig. 2b: Ludlow Town centre in 1884 - West Area
based on Crocker's Directory of Shropshire published in that year.

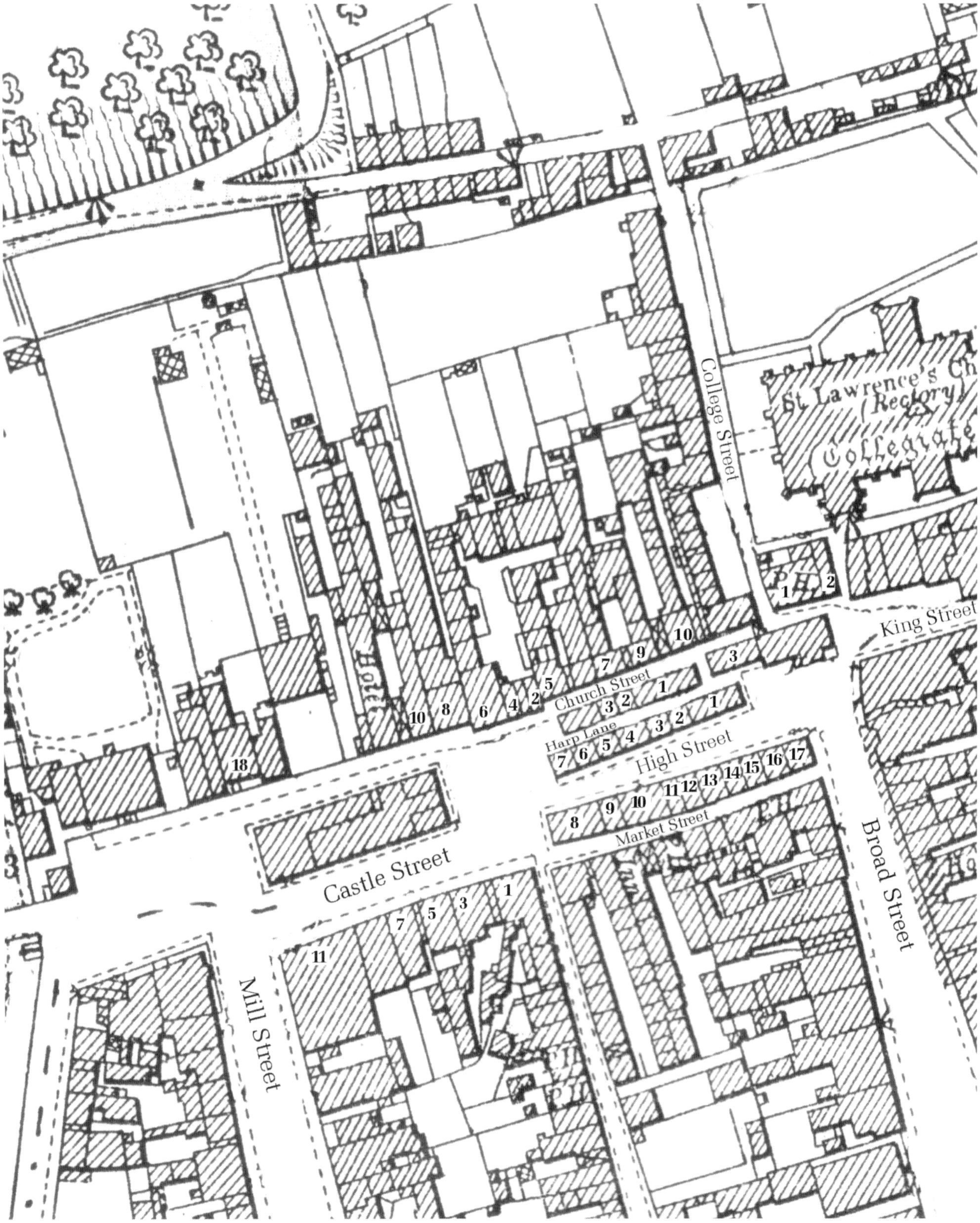

Castle Street

1	James Lang	draper
2	Gutta Dicks	boots & shoes
3	William Honeyfield	ironmonger
4	John Henner	butcher
5	Frederick Smith	chemist
6	William Chubb	draper
7	Thomas Collings	baker
8	Walter Hobday	draper
10	William Bright	butcher
11	Josiah Smith	bookseller
18	George Beeston	wine merchant

Church Street

1	John Watkins	glass & china
2	Thomas Palmer	watchmaker
3	Elizabeth Vale	dressmaker
4	Thos. Wainwright	saddler
5	James Brandford	butcher
7	William Davies	seedsman
9	Edwin Morgan	tailor
10	James Challoner	ironmonger

The Cross

1	John Wollaston	wine merchant

2	Robert Sweetman	chemist
3	Thomas Morris	grocer

High Street

1	John Langslow	draper
2	Wiliam Robinson	boots and shoes
3	Daniel Crundell	draper
4	William Webb	boots & shoes
5	Bessell and Raymond	tailor & hatter
6	John Chambers	draper
7	Rowland Edwards	watchmaker
8	Edward Harding	draper
9	George Prinn	hairdresser
10	Benjamin Williams	draper
11	Penny & Co,	tobacconist
12	Elizabeth Botfield	milliner
13	Singelton Tomlinson	cabinet maker
14	William Powell	silversmith
15	Jones Edmonds	grocer
16/17	Edward Leake	draper

Market Street

1	William Sharp	hairdresser
2	Henry Gatehouse	wine merchant
8	Richard Wellings	grocer

---

than life size, but his details are generally accurate.[2] No. 1 High Street, partly masking the Butter Cross, was the property of John Langslow, draper, whose cloths and carpets can be seen on display.[3] To the left, at No. 2, is the small workshop of William Robinson, boot and shoe maker. Facing his premises, on the right of the picture, are the wares of Joseph Price, basket maker. Ahead, at No. 2 Broad Street, is the shop of William Taylor, baker, with a timber framed facade. To the left, on the ground floor of a jettied building dating back to the early fifteenth century, were two smaller shops: first, that of Sarah Amies, "Berlin wool dealer", and then, on the corner, that of William Bodenham, draper and outfitter, whose business expanded later to become one of the success stories of late Victorian Ludlow. Beyond, in King Street were larger shops, including, on the right, the premises of William Thomas Bessell of Commercial House (now Mackays).

For many people, shopping in Ludlow was a mundane event. For others, it was a social and at times an exciting occasion. This was especially so for people from the countryside. "Dang my buttons, I never seed such sights or such a noise never before in my life", observed one country lad visiting Ludlow in 1861.[4] His utterances are a bucolic version of a remark made about Salisbury, admittedly a larger market town than Ludlow, that "the mere sight of it exhilarates like wine".[5] Meetings with friends, acquaintances and celebrities gave spice to expeditions to town, as when Anna Maria Fay went into a shoe shop in June 1852 to discover Lord William Powlett, a candidate at the forthcoming parliamentary election, "canvassing the vote" of the proprietor.[6] For others, shopping was a nostalgic experience. When Mary Brown, who as Mary Sneade had been "the belle of Ludlow" in the 1790s, came on holiday to Ludlow in 1854, she found that "the baker's shop under the corridor was still selling the same cakes and wigs as it had done thirty five years past".[7]

THE NUMBER OF SHOPS IN VICTORIAN LUDLOW AND THEIR LOCATION

In spite of the agricultural depression after 1870, which affected the prosperity of many market towns, the Victorian period was a time of retailing growth. This was part of an increase in consumption, the process which the writer Samuel Smiles (1812-1904), the son of a shopkeeper, described as "a harvest of wealth and prosperity".[8] The historian John Walton has described how most families now began to afford "new ready made clothes, substantial furniture and ornaments to gather dust in the front parlour".[9] There was, he continues, "a whole cornucopia of non-essential items, some of which were recent inventions, which reached out into hitherto distant realms of fashion, fantasy and frivolity".[10]

In 1840 there were 144 shops in Ludlow. For more than half of these – booksellers, butchers, drapers – selling was the primary activity. But two fifths of the shops were outlets for manufacturing craftsmen, who sold their products directly to consumers. Bakers, cabinet makers and shoemakers are examples of such trades. Later this distinction became blurred, as many products of traditional crafts were displaced by those of mass production, imported from elsewhere. There were also shops linked with the professions, particularly the chemists – the successors of earlier apothecaries – and some that offered personal services such as hairdressing. By 1870 the number of shops had risen to 154, and by 1900 there had been a further slight increase to 158.[11]

A high proportion of these shops – 82% in 1840, 67% in 1900 – were in the town centre, along and close to the medieval market place which ran from the castle to the Bull Ring. Here continuous shop frontages lined the principal streets, in places adjoining inns, banks and public buildings, while until 1862 the streets themselves were the venues for weekly markets and occasional fairs. This area, shown on Figs. 2a & b, was Ludlow's principal trading zone, the core of its being as a market town. The generic term High Street is often used for such zones of intense economic activity, though urban

Fig. 3: High Street about 1900, with small shops adjoining each other on both sides. These shops, with cellars below and living accommodation above, were at the heart of Ludlow's Central Business District. This had been a specialist shopping area since the Middle Ages.

historians prefer either Central Business District or Special Retail Nucleus.[12] Outside this town centre, shops occurred sporadically along most of the main streets and in some of the narrow lanes. The largest number was in Corve Street, which had four in 1840, seven in 1870 and ten in 1900. Such shops were usually part of larger buildings, and were in areas of mixed residential and industrial development. There were also a few small shops serving the expanding suburbs of Gravel Hill and East Hamlet.

TOWN CENTRE SHOPS IN 1884

Crocker's Directory of 1884, which lists properties by streets and postal numbers, provides a summary of Ludlow's Town Centre shops (Fig. 2). There were 117 shops, most of them small businesses operated by a few people. In 1884 only one shop, Turner and Co.'s Boot and Shoe Shop at No. 47 Bull Ring, had a manager for owners outside the town. There were a few family partnerships, such as Challoner Brothers, ironmongers, at No. 3 King Street. A number of other businesses, though headed by one person, were family concerns, such as that of James Lang, draper at No. 1 Castle Street who was assisted by two sons. In 1884 there was only one partnership not within a family: that of Dawes and Bowen, wine merchants, at Nos. 43/44 Bull Ring.

There were 16 drapers in the town centre in 1884, often under titles to show they provided ready-to-wear clothes. In High Street both Edward Harding and Benjamin Williams styled themselves "drapers and outfitters". There were still eight boot and shoe makers, six milliners and three tailors

in the town centre, one of the latter also calling himself hatter. The town centre had many food shops, including 12 grocers, eight butchers and seven bakers, with a few fishmongers, poulterers and greengrocers. Some of these retained links with the production of the goods they sold, such as Thomas Collings who was miller as well as baker. There were three saddlers and two ironmongers; and others in these trades outside the town centre, such as Bluck and Everall, ironmongers and agricultural implement agents, at No. 140 Corve Street, where a large property, reaching to Portcullis Lane, provided the space necessary for their wares. The presence of a gunsmith, three watchmakers, five wine merchants, a furniture store, three glass and china dealers and six booksellers reflect other aspects of Victorian consumption, while the town centre also had four chemists and three hairdressers.

Most businesses were confined to a single site, though Charles Doble had different shops for fish and greengroceries. In 1884 Gaius Smith,

Fig. 4: This photograph of part of the west side of Corve Street was taken in 1909 but it shows a street scene little different from that of the late Victorian period. A number of small shops can be seen, intermingling with other buildings. In 1884 the shop on the far left, No. 18, part of the Eagle Inn, was that of George Robinson, shoemaker. Right of the alley, at No. 19, was Richard Waite, tobacconist. The other shop, No. 22, partly obscured by the horse and cart, was a public house in 1884 but later became the premises of George Wagstaff, pork butcher.

grocer, had shops at Nos. 42 Bull Ring and 6 King Street, but he soon consolidated his business by acquiring Nos. 9 and 10 King Street, which had been the premises of two other grocers. John Valentine, grocer, had acquired three adjoining properties – Nos. 3, 4 and 5 Broad Street – where he operated a long established family business and ran the Post Office. In 1884 William Bodenham, draper and outfitter, had one shop, at No. 19 King Street, but within a few years his family firm had expanded into adjoining properties and had a furniture business at No. 59 Broad Street.[13] Twelve of the shopkeepers were women, some of them widows maintaining family businesses, such as Margaret Marston, widow. [14]

HIERARCHIES OF SHOPS AND SHOPKEEPERS

Using 1841 census returns and a Ludlow Borough Rate book of 1843, hierarchies of Ludlow shops can be compiled, as tabulated in Fig. 5. These enable the nature of the businesses and their role in the town to be better understood. The main categories of shops (column B) are ranked by the mean number of residential servants per household, the term including all those who were employed in the shop, as well as domestic servants. Drapers and mercers, chemists, ironmongers and grocers headed the hierarchy, with the craft trades occupying lower positions. The apprenticeship system, once a feature of nearly all Ludlow trades, was still operational in some cases, especially among the drapers, mercers, chemists and grocers. John Shepherd, mercer, at 55 Broad Street, had four boy apprentices, while three drapers had two each.[15] Some older assistants, including journeymen who had completed apprenticeships, were living-in employees, especially with the drapers, mercers, and bakers. An exceptional situation was that of John Wilding, silk mercer, who had six residential assistants at his premises at the Cross (now the Church Inn). Overall, however, more than half of all residential employees were

domestic servants, 67 of the 87 shopkeepers employing at least one, though none had more than two.

The second method of ranking is by mean value of properties occupied by each group of shopkeepers, calculated from Rate Book valuations. Ironmongers, chemists, drapers and mercers are again the leading trades. The ranks of the grocers and butchers have dropped, both trades having some shopkeepers in small properties, such as John Coates, grocer, at No. 8 Tower Street, whereas saddlers and cabinet makers occupy higher positions. Just under half the shops were owned by their occupiers, while the rest had tenants. This was so for ironmongers and chemists as well as for less prosperous trades such as milliners and shoemakers. Notable shopkeepers who rented their premises included Joshua Cooper, ironmonger, at No. 3 Castle Street, who was a tenant to Thomas Botfield, the Coalbrookdale ironmaster[16]; and Thomas Coleman, butcher, who rented No. 3 Broad Street from Elizabeth Cropper of Birmingham, the widow of a former Ludlow butcher.[17]

Later in the century, a number of shopkeepers were able to buy their own properties, among them Charles Evans, born of a poor family in Frog Lane in 1832.[18] In 1857 he bought No. 8 Broad Street for £400 (£19,924 in modern terms), running it as a grocer's shop until 1873, when he sold it as a business to William Tillett, which enabled him to retire to Gravel Hill. He is an example of a self-made Victorian. There were even more spectacular success stories, such as Gaius Smith, grocer, and William Bodenham, outfitter, who bought a number of town centre properties, as well as residences in the new suburbs at Gravel Hill and Sandpits.[19] Later information on property ownership for the whole town centre is not readily available, but data on residential assistants and servants in 1881 are presented in Fig. 5C. The grocers and drapers now have the highest ranks, with the bakers and butchers higher than they were, while some of the craft retailers retain a low position.

Fig. 5: Hierarchies of shopkeepers in Ludlow Town Centre 1841 & 1881.

A	B	C	D	E	F	G	H	I	J	K	L
	Type of shopkeeper	**Ownership**		**Residential assistants and servants**						**Property**	**Rank**
		No.of shops	self owned	assis-tants	journey men	appren-tices	serv-ants	total	mean per household	mean value £ s d	

A In rank order of residential assistants and servants per household, 1841

A	B	C	D	E	F	G	H	I	J	K	L
45	drapers & mercers	10	5	9	0	12	14	35	3.5	31 12 00	1
65	chemists	5	2	1	0	7	8	16	3.2	31 18 00	2
52	ironmongers	5	2	1		5	6	12	3	36 09 00	3
46	grocers	11	5	4	2	8	13	27	2.45	23 02 00	4
31	bakers	8	4	1	7	3	8	19	2.4	20 15 00	5
46	butchers	8	3	4		3	8	15	1.9	17 04 00	6
21	saddlers	4	3	0	0	0	6	6	1.5	27 01 00	7
52	china & glass dealers	3	1	0	0	0	3	3	1	17 05 00	8
19	cabinet makers	4	1	0	1		2	3	0.75	25 18 00	9=
51	booksellers & stationers	4	3	0	0	0	3	3	0.75	26 16 00	9=
29	milliners, hosiers & glovers	6	1	0	0	0	4	4	0.67	18 00 00	11
29	hatters & tailors	7	3		1		1	2	0.5	16 14 00	12
29	shoemakers	8	3	0	0	0	2	2	0.25	11 11 00	13=
34	watchmakers	4	3	1	0	0	0	1	0.25	18 10 00	13=
	total	87	39	21	11	38	78	148	1.9		

B In rank order of mean property value, 1841

A	B	C	D	E	F	G	H	I	J	K	L
52	ironmongers	5	2	1		5	6	12	3	36 09 00	1
65	chemists	5	2	1	0	7	8	16	3.2	31 18 00	2
45	drapers & mercers	10	5	9	0	12	14	35	3.5	31 12 00	3
21	saddlers	4	3	0	0	0	6	6	1.5	27 01 00	4
51	booksellers & stationers	4	3	0	0	0	3	3	0.75	26 16 00	5
19	cabinet makers	4	1	0	1		2	3	0.75	25 18 00	6
46	grocers	11	5	4	2	8	13	27	2.45	23 02 00	7
31	bakers	8	4	1	7	3	8	19	2.4	20 15 00	8
34	watchmakers	4	3	1	0	0	0	1	0.25	18 10 00	9
29	milliners, hosiers & glovers	6	1	0	0	0	4	4	0.67	18 00 00	10
52	china & glass dealers	3	1	0	0	0	3	3	1	17 05 00	11
46	butchers	8	3	4		3	8	15	1.9	17 04 00	12
29	hatters & tailors	7	3		1		1	2	0.5	16 14 00	13
29	shoemakers	8	3	0	0	0	2	2	0.25	11 11 00	14
	total	87	39	21	11	38	78	148	1.9		

C In rank order of the number of residential assistants and servants per household, 1881

A	B	C	D	E	F	G	H	I	J	K	L
46	grocers	11		8		9	10	27	2.45		1
45	drapers	13		12		4	10	26	2		2
31	bakers	6		5			6	11	1.8		3=
46	butchers and fishmongers	10		5		3	10	18	1.8		3=
65	chemists	5				1	7	8	1.6		5
48	wine merchants	5					7	7	1.4		6
51	booksellers	6		4			4	8	1.33		7
52	ironmongers & china dealers	3				1	2	3	1		8
29	milliners & tailors	9		6		2	4	12	0.75		9
20	cabinet makers	3					2	2	0.66		10
21	saddlers	3					1	1	0.33		11
34	watchmakers	3					1	1	0.33		12
29	shoemakers	6					1	1	0.17		13
	total	83		40	0	20	65	125	1.92		

from: A: code system of occupational classification; B: type of shop; C: 1841 census; D: 1843 Borough Rate Book SA (LB 15/2/245); E-H: 1841 census; I: calculated; J: calculated: K: as D; L: calculated

The total number of residential staff shows a 15% decline, from 148 in 1841 to 125 in 1881, but this does not necessarily mean a drop in the number of employees. Information given by enumerators for the 1881 census shows that these numbers had a wide range. Thomas Lowe, fishmonger, at No. 68 Broad Street, had just one man, while John Watkins, butcher, at No. 25 Bull Ring, had two men and one boy. The largest number of employees noted in the census is the eleven men and two boys employed by William Bessell. Other sources show that some of the town's most successful shopkeepers had even more employees, e.g. John Smith, ironmonger, at No. 3 King Street, had 19 men in 1851.

THE PLOTS OCCUPIED BY LUDLOW SHOPS

Central Ludlow was a mosaic of plots, usually but not always rectangular. They pertained to the twelfth century town plan and its later development. Because the perch was used as the basic measure, both linear and aereal, many properties still related to that unit (16 feet 6 inches) and to its multiples and fractions. Many of the largest properties were medieval burgages, abutting onto the original High Street market place.[20] The longest, 346 feet, were those on the north side of Castle Street, most of which had complex tenurial histories, with shops and their premises occupying only part of the property. Other original burgages, as on the east side of Old Street, had lengths over 160 feet. All had substantial back development, with slaughter houses and other buildings. Those on the west side of the Bull Ring, restricted by the churchyard, had shorter lengths, for example Nos. 12 and 13, which were 124 feet deep and 49 feet 6 inches wide.

Quite different in their progeny were the many small plots which began as medieval stalls or selda. These are seen most clearly in High Street, where the properties on the north side, with those on the south side of Church Street, were the medieval shambles, separated by what is now Harp Lane (Fig. 6). The original plots often survive, as at No. 2, which is a square perch exactly. Unable to expand in any direction, such properties are often very high. No. 2, occupied by William Robinson, boot and shoe maker in 1884, has a cellar, a ground floor and three upper stories. Other infill rows of selda were wider, especially that on the south side of the Bull Ring, where tall, imposing buildings have resulted, as at No. 45, occupied by chemists: first Whittall, then Cocking, finally Woodhouse.

Elsewhere, rows of small shops were built up against earlier properties, as at Nos. 2 and 3 at the west end of the north side of Tower Street, where there are very shallow properties with no back yard (Fig. 7). In 1871 these were occupied by John Vale, general dealer, and Albert Davies, tobacconist. On the north side of King Street the pattern is different again. The properties near

Fig. 6: Though there have been some amalgamations of the adjoining properties, the plan of the medieval shambles can be discerned. In the seventeenth century the shops adjoining High Street were known as Shoemakers' Row. Harp Lane was named after the Harp Inn which was at its eastern end in the eighteenth century.

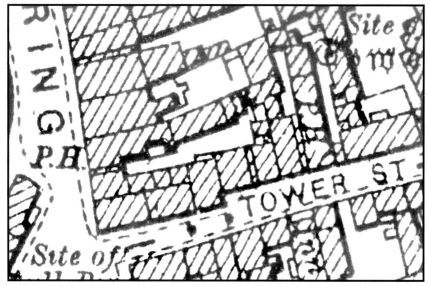

Fig. 7: An extract from the 1885 OS map showing a complex pattern of medium length burgages running east from the Bull Ring and north from Tower Street. There has been a considerable amount of back building, and a number of boundary changes.

the Butter Cross, built on what was once the edge of the churchyard, are 45 feet deep, with little or no back yards, but further east they are deeper, because their front premises have encroached into the street to form "The Narrows".

SHOP WINDOWS AND THE DISPLAY OF GOODS

In the nineteenth century "a new competitiveness appeared", as a result of which "high streets all over England were substantially changed".[21] One result was a transformation of shop windows, to allow greater opportunity for display. In the early years some shops had simply open spaces, which were closed at night by shutters, but others had windows which "were generally made up of small panels of glass".[22] Plate glass was introduced in the 1830s, becoming what Charles Dickens, in Sketches by Boz, called "the epidemic", with an "inordinate love of plate glass".[23] Initially, shops were fitted with three panes of glass, "before having, at the end of Victoria's reign, large single sheets which encased the whole frontage".[24]

Examples of all these kinds of windows occurred in Ludlow and can be seen on contemporary illustrations, though the pace of change was slower than in larger urban areas. They are usually part of what Mark Girouard has called "an architectural melange", with windows for display fitted into buildings of different periods.[25] Examples of such adaptation occur on the south side of the Bull Ring, where shop fronts were fitted into medieval and Tudor

timber framed buildings; and on the south side of Castle Street, where the host buildings were Georgian and Regency (Figs. 8 & 9).

The most basic window was an opening with no glass, though shutters were erected at the end of the working day. Such a shop was that of William Ward Evans, butcher, at No. 25 Bull Ring now part of The Feathers Hotel (Fig. 10). More common in Victorian Ludlow were glass windows of small panels, some of which had been inherited from earlier periods.[26] Such a window in 1856 was that at No. 17 High Street, illustrated on a bill head of Thomas Jones (Fig. 11). The window was "slightly damaged" in May 1861, when a frightened horse, pulling a gig, "ran against the shop of Mr Jones", but the panes or their replicas were still there when a photograph was taken in 1900.[27] Windows of this kind have survived at a few Ludlow shops, such as No. 9 Church Street and No. 11 King Street.

The earliest known windows with larger expanses of glass were those of James Harding and his son Edward, drapers, clothiers and hatters, whose new building at No. 5 High Street heads a bill dated 1864; and of Edward Partridge, bookseller, at No. 58 Broad Street, which was described by Anna Maria Fay as "a very fine new shop" in the same year[28] (Figs. 12 & 13). Glass was used even more spectacularly by Alfred Marston, chemist and druggist, at No. 49 Bull

Ring. The main shop windows have glass panels running horizontally, while the glass conservatory above – a useful facility for a druggist – has faint echoes of the Crystal Palace, and must have been a show-piece of Victorian Ludlow.[29]

The largest new shop in Victorian Ludlow was that of Gaius Smith, grocer, at Nos. 9 and 10 King Street, which was completely rebuilt in 1884 (Fig. 15). This was an imposing four storey, three bay emporium in rather brash yellow brick. The dominant feature was the arena of display on the ground floor, with sheets of plate glass supported by slim metal columns. The erection of this building, in place of a sixteenth century house and shops, induced the charge of "Vandals" in The Antiquary, an indication that Ludlow's conservation lobby was already at work.[30] A few years later Bodenham and Co., drapers and outfitters, rebuilt No. 18 King Street, with almost continuous glass frontages.[31] (Fig. 16). Though later condemned as a "Victorian abomination"[32], this building is Ludlow's ultimate in nineteenth century commercial display, a local example of the widespread practice of making shop fronts "larger and grander" for the purpose of selling goods at a profit.[33]

At the other end of the spectrum were small

Fig. 8: *A continuous line of shops occupies the ground floor of medieval, Tudor and 17th century buildings on the south side of the Bull Ring.*

Fig. 9: *Beginning at the shop of Thomas Collings baker (now Prices, bakers), shops stretch continuously along the south side of Castle Street.*

Fig. 10: *The open front of the shop of W.W. Evans, butcher, on the east side of the Bull Ring. This a detail of a picture of the adjoining Feathers Inn, drawn in 1846.*

Fig. 11: *The small panes of glass in the windows of No. 17 High Street can be detected in this faded bill head of Thomas Jones, tailor and woollen draper, dated 13 June, 1856.*

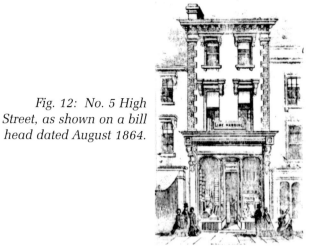

Fig. 12: No. 5 High Street, as shown on a bill head dated August 1864.

Fig. 13: No. 58 Broad Street, as it is in 2004. In 1864 it was described as a "new shop".

Fig. 14: This late 19th century trade card shows the Bull Ring premises of Alfred Marston, Chemist.

Fig. 15: Gaius Smith's premises taken from a paper bag, issued about 1914. It shows the front of the building as it was after 1884.

Fig. 16: By 1898 Bodenham and Sons Ltd. had aquired an imposing group of buildings on the corner of King Street and Broad Street. This advertisement shows them to maximum effect. No. 18 King Street, on the far left, formerly a Georgian house, was rebuilt with large expanses of glass on the ground and first floors.

shops such as that at No. 70 Corve Street, where the ground floor of a narrow house had been converted to a shop, with shelves behind the window (Fig. 17).[34] In a few cases, as at No. 104 Corve Street, more display space was created by a bow window, which in 1894 was being fully utilised by the tenant, Emma Morris, grocer and provision dealer (Fig. 18). Little shops are often held in great affection by those who use them, and occasionally catch the attention of writers or artists, as happened here.[35]

SHOP INTERIORS

Most Ludlow shops had small interiors, as shown by the photograph of Edward Robinson, watch maker and jeweller, in his shop at No. 60 Broad Street (Fig. 19). Display rooms and warehouses were often very crowded, sometimes causing hazards, as at No. 3 Castle Street, the premises of Cooper and Bluck, ironmongers, in January, 1847.[36] An upper room was "well stored with turpentine, oils, pitch, tar and other inflammable materials", but had an escape from fire, when a brick was left out of the flue of a chimney in an adjoining warehouse. Retailing businesses crowded into historic houses used several rooms for display. This was so at No. 18 Bull Ring, where a sale catalogue in

1890 described 760 items of furniture in five rooms.[37] Premises built later in the century, on two or more historic plots, sometimes offered more space, such as that available to Gaius Smith, where the illustration shows female assistants packing flour (Fig. 20).[38]

Specialist shops had their own fittings and furniture. When John Edwards, baker, of Upper Gaolford, "declined business" in 1840, the sale items included a shop counter with drawers, cake and peppermint moulds, and flour scales and weights.[39] A few Victorian fittings survive in Ludlow shops, as at Nos. 6 & 7 Bull Ring, where Heber Rickards took over an ironmongery business from the Eggington family in 1865. The firm is still in business, in 1995 inspiring journalist Julian Critchley, an enthusiast for Victoriana, to write an article headed "shopping in aspic".[40] He describes the "rows and rows of wooden boxes" and "upright desks a-la Bob Cratchit". Another period piece is the dispensing sign of Alfred Marston inside No. 49 Bull Ring, still a chemist's shop.

Fig. 17, left: This twentieth century photograph of No. 70 Corve Street shows the building as it probably was before 1901.

Fig. 18, right: This sketch of No. 104 Corve Street appeared in a travel book, The Marches of Wales, *which was published in 1894.*

Fig. 19: Edward Robinson, watchmaker and jeweller, in his shop at No. 60 Broad Street. The business was established by 1879 and lasted until the 1940s, with two generations of owners.

Fig. 20: This indistinct picture of the premises of Gaius Smith, taken from a mutilated copy of The Grocer, *is one of the few illustrations of Ludlow shop interiors in the late 19th and early 20th centuries.*

Fig. 21: These shop fittings are still in place at Rickards and Son Ltd., ironmongers, Nos. 6 & 7 Bull Ring.

Left: Boxes with their original labels in the shop itself.

Right: Shelves in a rear storeroom.

The Shopkeepers and their Employees

Some indication of the stability of Ludlow shops and of migration by shopkeepers can be obtained from trade and postal directories. In the 1870 edition of Kelly's Directory, 160 shopkeepers were listed, but only 35 of these – slightly more than a fifth – had matching entries in Robson's Directory of 1840, the entries in the earlier year either being for themselves or for a close relative, often their fathers. Of the 1870 entries there were just 29 (18%) who had matching entries in Kelly's 1900 Directory. Only seven families were in all three directories. In most cases shopkeepers were in the same trade throughout, sometimes in the same premises, as were Valentines, grocers, at and around No. 4 Broad Street and the Watkins family, glass and china dealers, at No. 1 Church Street. In other cases, there was movement within the town. Joseph Harper, cabinet maker, was at No. 59 Broad Street in 1840 ; his son John Harper was a furniture dealer at No. 133 Corve Street in 1870; but by 1900 he was an "antique and modern furniture dealer" at No. 28 Corve Street.

A turnover of some 80% over thirty years suggests substantial migration and mobility. Analysis of the 1881 census shows that only 23 of 94 heads of shopkeeping households in the town centre had been born in Ludlow, the rest coming from elsewhere. Another 27 of these had been born within twenty miles of Ludlow, but the remainder – 53% – came from further afield, covering a total of 17 counties. In some cases, the birthplaces of children enable the movements of families to be traced before their arrival at Ludlow. William Bessell, draper, a native of Marlborough, came to Ludlow from Bristol; James Lang, draper, from Cheltenham; and Josiah Smith, bookseller, from Surrey. The movement of such men to Ludlow shows their perception of opportunities in the town, sometimes for purchasing a business.

Analysis of the birth places of 69 town centre apprentices and assistants shows a similar pattern, with 15 (22%) born in Ludlow, 14 (20%) in the surrounding villages, and the remainder (58%) further away, including one person from each of Berkshire, Hampshire, Northamptonshire and Wiltshire. In total, just over half of all town centre shopkeepers, assistants and apprentices were born more than twenty miles away, a higher proportion than has been found in studies elsewhere.[41] For both heads and assistants combined, it is surprising that only eight (5%) had been born in Wales.

A special group of Ludlow shopkeepers were those who became Mayor. Between 1836 and 1901, 23 shopkeepers occupied the civic chair on 33 occasions, that is for 51% of the time, most other incumbents being from the professions. During these post-Reform years, more tradesmen, doctors and solicitors – sometimes called "the new squirearchy" – were taking public office.[42] The early Mayors, and the councillors who elected them, were political Radicals, three of the Borough's first Aldermen, appointed in 1836, being shopkeepers: William Edwards, draper, John Smith, ironmonger, and William Harding, grocer; but some of their successors as Mayor were Conservatives, such as the chemists Edward Foster and Richard Marston.[43] Of the shopkeeper Mayors who held office more than once, John Valentine, grocer, came from Bitterley, and Heber Rickards, ironmonger, from Wistanstow, but the others were born far from Ludlow: Edward Foster, chemist, in Maidenhead, Ambrose Grounds, chemist, in Wisbech, and Thomas Sheppard, wine merchant, in Berkshire.

In later years, as the heat went out of Ludlow politics, leadership on religious and moral issues became more relevant. George Cocking, chemist, was "a pillar" of Ludlow's Congregational Church[44], while Gaius Smith, grocer, said to be "as hard as granite" on matters of principle was a passionate Methodist, who caused controversy by "taking the maces to the Wesleyan Chapel" on his first Sunday in office in 1898.[45] Others were Anglicans, 58 of the 74 churchwarden-ships at St Laurence's between 1870 and 1907 being held by shopkeepers.[46]

Samuel Herbert Valentine, an assistant to his father and then his successor, as well as being Mayor on four occasions, was "for more than 50 years a member of the choir in the parish church of St Laurence, and Churchwarden from 1902 to 1909 and again in 1923".[47] Such public service brought high esteem, manifesting itself in impressive funerals. When John Valentine, three times Mayor, died in 1892, every place of business was closed for his funeral, and on the following Sunday he was described in a memorial sermon as "a public man", the text being: "Their works do follow them" (Revelation xiv, v.13).[48]

The early years as a shop-keeper brought hard work rather than public dignity. Apprentices also worked hard, as feelingly described by Henry Peach Robinson (1830-1901), who on his fourteenth birthday was apprenticed to Richard Jones, bookseller.

"Long years they are too, working from seven in the

From Top:
Fig. 22: William Harding (1784-1867) grocer and tea merchant. Mayor of Ludlow 1838-39.

Fig. 23: George Cocking (1809-1866), chemist. Mayor of Ludlow 1860-61.

Fig. 24: John Valentine (1831-1892), grocer. Mayor of Ludlow 1881-82, 1889-90, 1890-91.

Fig. 25: Gaius Smith (1848-1914), grocer. Mayor of Ludlow 1898-99.

morning till nine at night is nothing but slavery and I shall hail the morning on 9th July 1849 with the greatest joy."[49]

At the beginning of the period, shop hours were indeed extremely long for all assistants and apprentices – and for many employers. In 1849 a letter signed by 43 young men was sent to the Mayor, asking him to:

"Take into consideration the best means of effecting the early closing system now so generally carried on throughout the towns of England. We still have to work from seven in the morning till nine at night and in some shops much later than that, so that we hardly have a moment for exercise, improvement or study."[50]

The reply was disappointing, the Mayor, Joshua Cooper, ironmonger, insisting that "it would not do for me to interfere". Mayors did intervene sometimes, however, as on 2 February 1848, when "the Mayor, Ambrose Grounds, requested that shops should shut between 12 and 4 o'clock" on the day of the funeral of the Earl of Powis.[51] By 1862 shops were closing at 7 p.m., as can be inferred from the correspondent to The Ludlow Advertiser who complained of hazards from shutters and iron bars when the "drapers are closing their shops at 7 p.m."[52] Later in the century, Thursday half day closing was introduced, with a Grand Promenade Concert on Castle Green on a Thursday afternoon in July, 1889, and a football team known as "the Half Holiday Club".[53]

SHOPKEEPING DYNASTIES

The Valentines were one of a number of families who traded in Ludlow over two or more generations. In such families, one or more sons often succeeded fathers in the business and daughters sometimes married into other shop keeping families. An unmarried shopkeeper was sometimes succeeded by a nephew, as happened in 1863 when John Valentine took over from his bachelor uncle Samuel Valentine. The longevity of such families made them eligible for leadership roles, and as shown above a number had representatives on the Borough Council. The process occurred in many towns and persisted into the twentieth century, as noted by Reeder and Rodger:

"…..the adaptation of small businesses, with their dynastic ability to survive and grow, frequently provided a degree of continuity and leadership within towns and cities all over Britain".[54]

But such families often had wider horizons than Ludlow, and many younger sons, in particular, sought their fortunes elsewhere, especially in London, in the burgeoning towns of the Midlands or in the expanding Empire.

Such a family were the Hardings, whose pedigree is shown in Fig. 26. Their status in Ludlow was established by John Harding (1748-1831), wine merchant, who owned Nos. 68/69 Broad Street (now Silver Pear).[55] His probate estate was valued at "under £9,000", an enormous sum for that date.[56] His eldest son, William, became a grocer, who in 1806 married Mary, daughter of George Whittall, the King Street grocer with whom he had probably served his apprenticeship.[57] Whittall and then Harding were tenants of shops in King Street, later Nos. 9 and 9A, which were part of a large Corporation property, once called Kingston Place. William Harding was able to acquire the leaseholds, one in 1822, the other in 1831, for the latter no doubt using some of the £2,000 left to him by his

Fig. 27: A picture of Nos. 7 to 10 King Street, taken before 9 & 10 were replaced by Gaius Smith's new shop in 1884. The third and fourth shops along, which together became No. 9 when postal numbers were introduced before 1863, were the premises of the Hardings.

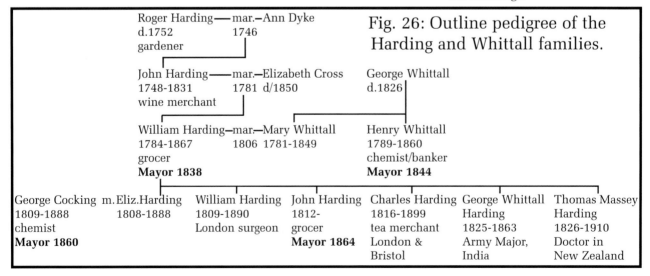

Fig. 26: Outline pedigree of the Harding and Whittall families.

Roger Harding — mar. — Ann Dyke
d.1752   1746
gardener

John Harding — mar. — Elizabeth Cross   George Whittall
1748-1831   1781 d/1850   d.1826
wine merchant

William Harding — mar. — Mary Whittall   Henry Whittall
1784-1867   1806 1781-1849   1789-1860
grocer   chemist/banker
Mayor 1838   **Mayor 1844**

George Cocking m. Eliz.Harding   William Harding   John Harding   Charles Harding   George Whittall   Thomas Massey
1809-1888   1808-1888   1809-1890   1812-   1816-1899   Harding   Harding
chemist   London surgeon   grocer   tea merchant   1825-1863   1826-1910
Mayor 1860   **Mayor 1864** London &   Army Major,   Doctor in
                                                                   Bristol   India   New Zealand

father; and in 1848 he bought the freehold from the Borough Council.[58] By the 1860s Hardings were one of the town's leading businesses, describing themselves as : "William Harding & Son, wholesale & retail grocers, tea, coffee and spice dealers, cheese factors, hop merchants, tallow chandlers and melters, King Street."

As leaders of "the large and important Harding family", William Harding and his brother in law Henry Whittall were at the heart of the Ludlow commercial establishment, but yet felt able to absorb a new-comer from Kent. This was George Cocking, a young chemist from Sandwich, who came to Ludlow in 1831 or earlier, probably in response to an advertisement by Whittall for an assistant.[59] In 1833 he married Elizabeth, William Harding's eldest daughter. They had thirteen children between 1807 and 1826, ten of whom lived beyond childhood.[60] The eldest son, John, followed his father in the

Fig. 28, Left: Edward Davies (1793-1862), a Bull Ring tailor in the early Victorian period. His smart clothes are a good advertisement for his trade.

Fig. 29, Right: Thomas Davies (1825-1899) and his wife Martha (1824-1899), confectioner and general dealer at No. 16 Corve Street. The photograph was taken in their garden.

Fig. 30, Below left: The shop at No. 16 Corve Street, taken, like many Victorian photographs, at a time when there were few people about.

Fig. 31, Below right: This fragmented photograph shows No. 16 Corve Street some years after 1900, with a trade sign painted on the first floor.

King Street grocery business, but the younger sons made their way in London, Bristol, India and New Zealand, one of them, an Army Major, dying in battle in November 1863 near Peshawar on the North West Frontier.

Other pedigrees show different kinds of networks. A family with rural gentry roots were the Marstons of Afcote in Wistanstow parish.[61] Richard Marston (1792-1866), son of John Marston Esq. (1778-1831) became a chemist at No. 56 Broad Street, and was Mayor in 1850, while Alfred Marston (1834-96), Richard's nephew, was also a chemist, at No. 49 Bull Ring. Richard's elder son, John (1836-1918), migrated to Wolverhampton, where he pioneered Sunbeam cars and became Mayor.[62] Another Marston network, emanating from Bishop's Castle, was that of William Marston (1826-74), who was a baker and corn factor at No. 25 Bull Ring by 1868.[63] His widow Margaret continued the business, which later expanded under William Hodgkinson Marston (1858-1918) and his younger brothers. Networks occurred too at humbler social levels, for example that of Edward Davies (1793-1862), a tailor at No. 42 Bull Ring[64] (Fig. 28). This was a small property, valued at £11 a year, where Davies was a tenant. He and his wife Ann had eight children, one of whom, Thomas, was later a wholesale and retail confectioner at No. 16 Corve Street, which he eventually owned, together with two other Corve Street properties (Figs. 29-31).[65]

CUSTOMERS, CASH AND CREDIT

Most Ludlow shopkeepers were retailers, selling direct to customers, though a few also advertised themselves as wholesalers, perhaps supplying suburban and village shops.[66] Such a trader was Joseph Allen, grocer, who in 1876 "supplied the trade", but also "waited upon families for orders".[67] Some shopkeepers dealt directly with distant suppliers. In 1838 Francis Massey, wine merchant, was receiving Guinness and porter "direct from Dublin", while in 1891 Bessells were offering Nottingham Lace Curtains "direct from the looms".[68] Links with the world of fashion were vaunted, especially by Bodenham and Sons, who were "sole agents in this district for Liberty and Co., Regent Street."[69] In May 1891 they had "the latest London and Parisian styles in millinery, mantles, jackets, laces, flowers, feathers and ribbons".[70] Several Ludlow shopkeepers were agents for brand products, e.g. George Cocking, chemist, in 1869, for "Dr Clee's Herbaceous Pills for indigestion and stomach complaints" ; or Edward Larcombe in 1893 "for Singer's Sewing Machines".[71]

The larger Ludlow shops drew customers from the surrounding countryside. In 1861 Bessel and Son, Drapers and Carpet Factors, claimed "the largest stock in the District", while in 1876 Joseph Allen, grocer, was delivering goods "carriage free, within 20 miles of Ludlow", either by rail or "our own vans".[72] Analysis of the day book of Heber Rickards, ironmonger, for November 1864, shows that he

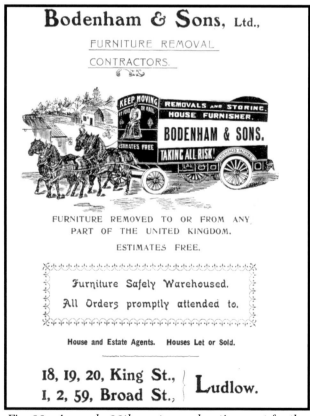

Fig. 32: An early 20th century advertisement for the furniture removal side of Bodenham and Sons.

Fig. 33: An attractive advertisement for the mail order business which Bodenham and Sons operated briefly soon after 1900.

Fig. 34: This small advert, dated 22 August 1840, is an example of fixed prices.

Fig. 35: This advert is dated 4 September, 1869. Hobdays at No. 8 Castle Street, sold ready-made clothes. aiming at the cheaper end of the market.

gave credit to 92 customers, spread over 18 parishes around Ludlow. In 1893, from 82 consecutive entries in a ledger, there were customers from 26 parishes, with four from further afield, including Cheltenham and London. Many country customers were farmers, but there were also gentry households, such as the Knights of Downton Castle and the Salweys of Richard's Castle.[73] A business with an even wider orbit was the furniture branch of Bodenham and Sons, who in the late 1890s removed furniture "to or from any part of the United Kingdom".[74] The outfitting side of this enterprising firm also made a short excursion into "Shopping by Post", inspired, perhaps, by the success of Pryce Jones's Royal Welsh Warehouse at Newtown, which had a mail order business encompassing the globe.[75]

The use of fixed prices, in place of the former practice of haggling, became general practice in England from the 1830s, a Frenchman noting in 1856 that a London shop assistant "stiffened visibly like a man of honour" when he tried to bargain.[76] Prices are listed in early advertisements, such as that placed in the short-lived Ludlow Standard in 1840 by Walter Bluck[77] (Fig. 34). Later advertisements claimed cheapness as well as quality, like that of Walter Hobday in 1869.[78] When Thomas Blakemore moved his Boot and Shoe Warehouse from No. 13 Tower Street to No. 1 Bull Ring in 1876, he claimed that his new stock "will be found to equal any house in the county, either for excellence of Manufacture or Cheapness, combined with Durability in their wear".[79] Sometimes competition degenerated into trade warfare, as can be inferred from Gaius Smith's Christmas advertising in 1884, their punch line being "the lowest price is not always the cheapest"[80] (Fig. 36).

Many counter sales were for cash, handled, in later years, by such tills as that now in Ludlow museum (Fig. 37). For some Ludlow and country customers, however, facilities for credit

SMITH AND COMPANY,

In the NARROWS,

ARE wishful to remind everybody that all kinds of

Xmas FRUITS and Specialite's

can be bought at their Stores, of the best quality at the Lowest possible price.

SMITH & CO., say that it has been a wet season in the fruit districts causing some to be damaged.

SMITH & CO., have been told that some of this kind has found its way to Ludlow, and is being offered at extraordinary low prices, very likely, but if anybody can sell at a low price, then Smith & Co., are the people, but S & Co like to sell good quality, such as will give satisfaction, and cause their customers to say 'Its worth the money,' the lowest price, is not always the cheapest, anyhow Smith & Co will not dirty their hands with common stuff. Best quality at the lowest price, at which best quality can be sold, shall be Smith & Co's HARBOUR of refuge.

SMITH & CO., print the names of a few articles with the CASH price opposite, which buyers will find good value for money.

Fig. 36, Left: This advertisement by Gaius Smith & Co. is dated 20 December 1884, and reflects keen competition with other grocers for the pre-Christmas trade.

Fig. 37, Right: A late Victorian till, displayed in Ludlow Museum.

Fig. 38, Bottom: An account of John J. Smith, ironmonger, dated Christmas 1855. It was probably written by his clerk.

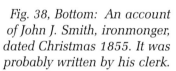

were expected, and often given, albeit reluctantly. The annual account shown in Fig. 38, from John Smith, ironmonger, of No. 3 King Street to the church wardens of St Laurence's, lists items purchased between February and December 1855. Payment was not made until November 1856, but as this was within a year of when the account was submitted, no 5% charge was incurred.[81] In 1875 Davis and Menhencott promised "due consideration to those who prefer making cash payments", while in 1888, John Vale, "dealer in all kinds of Sewing, Washing, Wringing and Mangling Machines", offered "liberal discount for cash".[82] The best slogan was that of Bodenhams, who proclaimed in 1876 that "the nimble ninepence is worth the slow shilling".[83] Rickards' ledger shows that most accounts sent out in November 1893 were settled in 1894 or 1895. One however, for repairing the bicycle of Miss Stevens of Oxfordshire, was not settled until 1902, while two others were never paid: one for 4s 3d to a Hopesay rabbit catcher, who died; and £1 10s 2d to a farmer at Farlow, who went bankrupt.

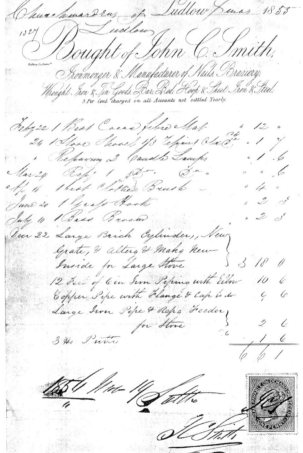

Fear of bankruptcy was a sword of Damocles to shopkeepers, with the credit system causing them many anxieties. A conspicuous failure was that of William Edwards, mercer and draper, in 1847, whose premises were at No. 5 King Street.[84] An active Reformer for many years, he had been the first Mayor of the elected Borough Council in 1836.[85] Francis Southern comments on the case in the first entry of his diary, 29 April 1851, reporting that Mr William Edwards…"died at the Isle of Man some days since". Southern recalled seeing him "only once…in his shop, very soon after he had made an assignment for the benefit of his creditors…but he has been absent from Ludlow nearly ever since."[86] There were at least two more bankruptcies in the 1840s, when trade in Ludlow was notoriously difficult, allegedly due to the "vexatious Corporation bill".[86]

Shopkeepers and advertising

Ludlow shopkeepers had been inserting advertisements in newspapers since the eighteenth century, but this increased as newspapers proliferated and became cheaper. The weekly publication of The Ludlow Advertiser from 1856 encouraged this process and front page advertisements across two or more columns became a regular feature. There are some earlier examples, many of them produced by the Ludlow printer Thomas Griffiths.[88]

Cartoon-like drawings were a feature of Thomas Griffiths's advertising in the 1840s. The example shown was for William Harding, the successful King Street grocer, whose public career has been outlined above. Later in the century, the style became more verbose, the advertisement of Edmund Philip Thomas, draper, for example. It is packed with information and uses bold fonts for headings.

The quality of local products was often stressed, one speciality being sausages. When Mr Griffiths of Corve Street succeeded Mr. E.H. Hopkins in Castle Square, he pointed out that sausages would "still be made from Mrs Hopkins's recipes".[89] In 1893 F. Clayton called himself "the celebrated sausage maker", while James Branford of Church Street – later described as "purveyor to the Queen" – announced that he "has commenced making the celebrated Shropshire sausages".[90] Ludlow bakers also enjoyed a high reputation, a Presteigne correspondent asserting in The Hereford Journal in 1846 that "better bread is not made in any town than in Ludlow".[91] High quality items came too from local jewellers, such as the two keys made by Edward Robinson

Fig. 39: This attractive advertisement, making use of cartoon-like caricatures and doggerel, plays on the popularity of ladies tea parties in early Victorian Ludlow.

Fig. 40: The advertisement of E.P. Thomas, draper, whose shop at No. 7 Broad Street was later absorbed by Poyners.

for presentation to Col. Windsor Clive, M.P. for Ludlow since 1860. Made of 15 carat gold, the keys had the Borough arms on one side and those of the Clives on the other, and were presented in light blue velvet cases.[92] Ludlow chemists had home produced remedies, for example Alfred Marston who claimed to be "Proprietor of the Celebrated Corn Eradicator".[93]

Products advertised by chemists reflect the local importance of agriculture. In 1879 George Woodhouse's stock included "improved fly powder for sheep, footrot ointment and Pix Campo for preventing the ravages of birds and vermin." Ironmongers also had rural links, as shown on Thomas Everall's advertisement (Fig. 41). He had a number of agencies, including Ransomes of Ipswich, who had emerged as "the dominant but not unchallenged, leader among mid-Victorian agricultural engineers".

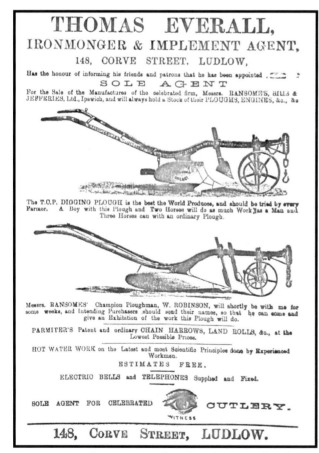

Fig. 41: An advertisement by Thomas Everall, who was an agent for several suppliers of farm machinery.

The bill head of John Hawkins, grocer, (Fig. 42) is a reminder that this was an age of Empire and world trade. In 1839 Richard Marston, chemist, was importing cigars "direct from an eminent West India Merchant".[94] In December 1875 Josiah Smith, stationer, widened his range of goods to include cabinets "in elegant wood, lacquer and beautiful straw work, china vases and boxes of ivory and sandal wood", as well as "curious tortoises" and "pekin ink bottles".[95] These items were "direct from Canton, Shanghae, Pekin and Yokohama", and had been received "by the short route through the Suez Canal". In 1898 G.H. Smith, butcher, was selling "Finest Quality Canterbury Mutton", while in Castle Square, William Chubb, general draper, displayed "home and colonial outfits".[96] But the Imperial drum beat loudest for T. and E. Bradley of No. 16 King Street, tobacconists, who, they proclaimed in 1910: "have faithfully represented your wants in the Ludlow portion of His Majesty's Empire for over 20 years."[97]

Some types of shopkeepers rarely advertised in the press, especially the saddlers and butchers, but photographs of both kinds of shops show fulsome displays.[98] In the 1840s the butchers were famous for Christmas shows of meat, Mr Evans (25 Bull Ring), Mr Pitt (High Street), Mr Dayus (26 Bull Ring) and Mr Towers

Fig. 42: The bill head of John Hawkins, No. 22 Broad Street, whose premises were outside the town centre. Though his entry in Kelly's 1856 Directory was as "grocer and tea dealer", the title used here, and the images above it, give a more exotic feel to his products, and suggest what some people saw as the romance of the Empire.

Fig. 43: People living in the Victorian and Edwardian countryside had great need for horse-drawn transport and implements. James Price, of No. 15 Tower Street, was one of the local saddlers who provided harness and a range of other goods.

Fig. 44: In an age still free of strict hygiene regulations, butchers were able to mount lavish displays of fresh meat outside their premises. This is the display at No. 14 High Street by Robert Carpenter, who moved here between 1900 and 1905, having previously traded in Castle Square.

(King Street) being praised in The Hereford Journal "for their display last Monday".[99] Several Ludlow traders were opportunists, among them Bessell and Co, who advertised "flags, banners and decorations" in September 1889, just before the opening of the new Town Hall.[100] Christmas, made much of by the Victorians, brought an annual glut of spending, with W.E. Sharp, hairdresser, holding a "Christmas Bazaar of Fancy Goods and Toys" in 1884.[101] Another hairdresser, Joseph Price, perhaps copied this initiative, for early in the twentieth century he urged customers to visit "Toy Land: the Home of Father Christmas".[102] "Every Child", he said, "must come and bring his or her mother; Every Mother must come and bring her children".

MEASURES OF SUCCESS

As argued in chapter 1, Ludlow's 15.5% growth in population between 1841 and 1901 owed much to its role as a centre of exchange. Alongside the livestock and street markets, shops played a major part in the exchange mechanism by recycling wealth created in town and countryside. The farmer who sold cattle at the Smithfield in Lower Gaolford and then bought a new plough at Bluck and Everalls was part of that process. Some of the "conglomeration of bonnets and shawls" noted by Anna Maria Fay in the streets of Ludlow in 1852 and the mens' "coats of every shade of gray and brown and black" may have been made by village dressmakers and tailors, but many of them must have been the work of Ludlow traders.[103]

A proportion of the takings of the town's businesses was consumed by the various rates – the Borough rate, the Poor rate and the rate levied by the Council acting as a Local Board of Health – and helped the town to sustain and expand its public services.[104] But private enterprise by the more successful shopkeepers was of equal if not greater benefit to the town. As shown above, only a few – Edward Partridge, Edward Harding, Gaius Smith – completely rebuilt their town centre properties, though many carried out alterations and enhancements. What many shopkeepers did do was to build new houses in the town's expanding suburbs.

In 1841 almost every town centre property had people living "over the shop", but by 1901 numbers were greatly reduced. For example, in 1909 the nine properties on the east side of Broad Street, between King Street and The Angel, had 14 residents in only three properties, compared to 59 in 1841; and one of the these families, the Valentines, moved to Julian Road before 1909.[105] Migration started slowly, with Edward Harding and William Bodenham the only leading tradesmen in Gravel Hill before 1884.[106] By 1900, however, there were 20 practising or retired shopkeepers in the Gravel Hill area, and 21 by 1913. A few found new homes closer to the town centre, such as William Chubb, ex-Mayor and retired draper, who was living at No. 4 Brand Lane in 1900, while in 1913 Edward Rickards, ironmonger, was at No. 36 Broad Street, once the town house of gentry.[107]

A broader picture of the material success attained by shopkeepers comes from their wills, a selection of which is shown in Fig. 45. The valuations include moveable goods, investments and money owed to the testator, but not property. Net values are only available after 1910, so have been estimated for earlier wills. At the top of the scale was Gaius Smith, grocer, whose fine house at Overmead, built after 1901, stood in a spacious estate, which originally had a small farm attached. He was followed by Charles Keysell, wine merchant, whose shop was at No. 46 Bull Ring, almost directly opposite Gaius Smith's premises. As shown on Fig. 45 both Smith and Keysell had estates valued at over a million pounds each, regardless of property. No other shopkeeper rivalled such opulence, though five were worth over £200,000 in modern terms, and six more over £100,000. Ten shopkeepers in the sample, however, were valued at under £20,000, the lowest being John Adney, though he owned five small properties. The properties owned by many shopkeepers were substantial, six having estates out of Ludlow, with one of these, Edmund Bluck, ironmonger, choosing to retire to Aston-on-Clun, some twelve miles north west of Ludlow.

There is evidence, too, that the more successful shopkeepers enjoyed higher social status during these years. In the early years of Victoria's reign there was a clear social distinction between the charity balls in the Assembly Rooms, patronised by aristocracy and local gentry, and the commercial balls, held at one of the local inns.[108] But by the 1860s, as Ludlow's role as a fashionable social centre diminished, the two events came together as "The annual agricultural and commercial ball", with gentry and leading tradesmen attending.[109] Not everyone approved of this newly won status, however. Henry Peach Robinson observing in his diary of the 1849 Shrove Tuesday rope pulling: "The tradesmen used to pull but they have left off of late years thinking it beneath them to mix with men who have not had the fortune to be as rich as themselves."[110]

CHANGE AND CONTINUITY

The Victorian years were the apogee of the family business. Ludlow's single shop managed for an owner outside the town in 1884 had become six by 1900. One of these was Freeman, Hardy and Willis, boot and shoe dealers, the first well known chain store to be established in the town; while W.H. Smith, newsagents, had a kiosk at the railway station.[111] By 1917 Smiths had taken over George Woolley's stationery and

Fig. 45: Selected wills of Ludlow shopkeepers, 1830-1925.

year	[1]	surname	first name	occupation	valuation gross £	[2] £	(3) £	known Ludlow property	known rural property
1831	HRO	Harding	John	wine merchant	9,000	6,000	295,120	several messuages	
1840	HRO	Eggington	John	ironmonger	6,000	4,000	192,730	messuages	
1840	HRO	Hodson	Richard	ironmonger	800	533	25,680	messuage Castle Street	
1840	HRO	Payne	William	watchmaker	200	133	6,408	messuage King Street	
1841	HRO	Wilkes	George	shoemaker	200	133	6,577	house in LG	
1841	HRO	Williams	Charles	butcher	800	533	26,359	messuage Bull Ring	Farlow, Stottesdon
1853	PRO	Massey	Francis	wine merchant	4,000	2,660	145,222	house in Corve Street	
1857	SA	Smith	Humphrey	ironmonger				3 in Ludlow centre	Overton
1857	SA	Robinson	John	shoemaker	900	600	28,909	2 High Street	
1860	SA	Jones	Harley	draper	8,000	5.667	267,313	High Street, Gravel Hill	
1862	SA	Egginton	William	ironmonger	450	300	14,410		
1866	SA	Marston	Richard	chemist	3,000	2,000	95,680	messuage in Mill Street	
1866	SA	Nash	John	butcher	600	400	19,136	Sandpits,Stanton Lacy	
1868	SA	Harding	William	grocer	8,000	5,333	256,169	King Street shop/others	
1871	SA	Foster	Edward	chemist	3,000	2,000	93,871	Castle Street shop	
1872	SA	Collings	George	baker	450	300	13,489	house in Bell Lane	
1872	SA	Dayus	Samuel	butcher	1,000	667	29,993	fields	Cockshll Lydiatt
1872	SA	Grieves	John	chemist	3,000	2,000	89,933	freehold in Ludlow	& elsewhere
1879	SA	Partridge	Edward	bookseller	3,000	2,000	102,432	freehold house/shop	
1885	SA	Griffiths	Benjamin	hairdresser	300	200	12,079	all estate	
1886	SA	Adney	John	leather seller	100	67	4,457	5 premises Corve/ King St.	
1888	SA	Cocking	George	chemist	1,236	824	53,159	The Hollies	
1894	SA	Bluck	Edmund	ironmonger	16,504	9,070	572,733	Corve Street	Aston-on-Clun
1907	SA	Harding	Edward	draper	10,024	6,682	401,515	messuage Gravel Hill	farm at Wigmore
1908	SA	Bessell	William T	draper	2,608	1,738	101,469	house & shop	
1912	SA	Fennell	John	butcher	5,764	2,068	128,352	freehold King Street	freehold Julian Rd
1914	SA	Smith	Gaius	grocer	38,339	24,853	1,342,859	house Overmead/ meadow	Stoke Prior
1914	SA	Keysell	Charles F.	wine merchant	29,895	22,000	1,188,706	Bull Ring, Gravel Hill	various
1918	SH	Evans	Charles	grocer	1,087	1,041	25,844	house	
1920	SA	Woodhouse	George	chemist	8,433	7,205	172,343	Pengwern, St Julian's Av.	
1925	SA	Chipp	Edward	cattle dealer	1,403	977	35,450	of 22 Gravel Hill	all estate

1) Where probate is held: HRO: Herefordshire Record Office; PRO: Public Record Office; SA: Shropshire Archives; SH: Somerset House

2) Estimated before 1910 on average difference from gross after 1910.

3) The formula used for converting to modern values is that devised by John J. McCosker, "Comparing the Purchasing Power of Money in Great Britain from 1284 to any other year including the present", Economic History Services 2001; copyright © 2004 by EH.NET

bookselling business, and by 1934 the Woodhouses had sold out to Boots, and Lang's, drapers, had become Woolworths.[112] The number of corner shops, too, declined, though new ones developed to serve new suburbs.[113]

The two leading grocers, however, Valentines' and Gaius Smith's, and Marstons, corn merchants, continued as limited companies until after 1967, while Bodenhams and Rickards, founded respectively in 1863 and 1864, survive into the twenty first century, the former now owned and managed by the great-grand daughter and great-great-grandson of the founder. The names of other Victorian shopkeepers live on in tangible ways. There is a Valentine's Walk, running from Broad Street along the side of a historic burgage plot, while the name of Gaius Smith is still to be seen, high on the gable of his now much altered shop, but visible to the observant pedestrian in Tower Street and the Bull Ring.

Fig. 46: Freeman, Hardy and Willis, boot and shoe dealers, opened a branch in Ludlow between 1895 and 1900, at first occupying Nos. 5 and 6 Broad Street, premises which later became DeGreys Cafe.

1 Hissey, J.J., *Through Ten English Counties*, 1894, p.263.
2 Edward Phipson was a Birmingham artist specialising in townscapes.
3 This, and other identifications in this paragraph, are derived from Casey, 1871, pp.212-216, Casey, 1875, pp.211-216, Mercer and Crocker, 1877, pp.56-59, Slater, 1879, pp.52-57, and Kelly, 1879.
4 SJ, 8 May 1861.
5 Hudson, W.H., *A Shepherd's Life*, Everyman, 1910, p19. Although published in 1910, much of the book relates to the late nineteenth century. The passage is cited by Everitt, A., in "Town and Country in Victorian Leicestershire: The Role of the Village Carrier", in Everitt, A., *Perspectives in English Urban History*, 1973.
6 Fay, *Victorian Days in England*, 1851-52, p.233; Weyman, H., *Ludlow in Bye-Gone Days*, 1913, p.51.
7 Oman,C, *Ayot Rectory: A Family Memoir*, 1780-1858, 1965, p.206.
8 Cited by Asa Briggs in *A Social History of England*, 1983, p.190.
9 Walton, J.K., "Towns and consumerism", in Daunton, M., *The Cambridge Urban History of Britain:* Volume III 1840-1950, 2000, p.527.
10 Ibid.
11 These numbers are based on Robson 1840, Kelly 1870 and Kelly 1900, supplemented in some cases by census returns. Though the main shops are easily identifiable, a number of judgements have been made as to whether a particular craft has enough retailing for it to be counted as a shop. These sources are used for all references to these years, unless stated otherwise.
12 Girouard,M., *The English Town*, 1990, p.223; Whitehead, J.W.R., *The Urban Landscape*, 1981, pp.59-74; Walton, op.cit., p.720.
13 Lloyd and Moran, *The Corner Shop*, pp.43-44.
14 William Marston, baker, died in 1874 (SA 1874/82).
15 The method used for locating Ludlow properties is described in Speight and Lloyd, *Ludlow Houses and their Residents*, 1977.
16 Burke, *Landed Gentry*, 1846, p.122.
17 Deeds of 7-10 King Street (private), from which details of the Croppers can be deduced.
18 I am grateful to Jean Brown for this information of Charles Evans.
19 See chapter 2.
20 A burgage was a unit of land held by a burgess, in return for services or a small rent.
21 Girouard, op.cit., p.224.
22 Baren,M., *Victorian Shopping: How It All Began*, 1998, p.7.
23 Cited in Evans, E. and Lawson, A., *A Nation of Shopkeepers*, 1981, p.9.
24 Baren, op.cit.
25 Girouard, op. cit., p.229.
26 e.g. that at No. 10 Broad Street, Lloyd and Klein, p.74.
27 SJ, 22 May 1861, p.6, col.3.
28 Fay, op. cit., pp.244-245.
29 I am most grateful to Mr and Mrs James, former proprietors of Brown and Francis, for drawing my attention to this illustration, which they have reproduced as a trade card.
30 *The Antiqary*, Vol.X., July-Dec.1884, p.83.
31 LA, 8 January 1898. Advertisement by Bodenham and Sons stating that "Business will be carried on as usual in every department during the rebuilding of the premises".
32 Clifton-Taylor, *Six English Towns*, 1978, p.166.
33 Mercer, E., *English Architecture to 1900: The Shropshire Experience*, 2003, pp.268-69. Mercer cites comparable examples at Bridgnorth (1884), Church Stretton (1901) and Whitchurch (1904).
34 Private deeds; 1841 census, when the tenant was Hanna Weaver, shopkeeper.
35 Harper, C.G., *The Marches of Wales: Notes and Impressions on the Welsh Borders*, 1894.
36 HJ, 10 Feb., 1847, p.4, col.5.
37 SA, Norton 4924/3/2/1.
38 An early edition of *The Grocer*, donated by the late Mr Campbell, manager of Gaius Smiths.
39 Griffiths scrapbook, Ludlow Museum, p.2d.
40 The Sunday Telegraph Magazine, 19 November, 1995.
41 e.g. Trinder, *Victorian Banbury*, 1982, p.77. Dr Trinder's figures, however, refer to the total population, not only to shopkeepers. I am most grateful to Dr Trinder for helpful discussion on this topic.
42 Gerrard, J., "Urban elites, 1850-1914; the rule and decline of a new squirearchy?", *Albion*, 27 (1995).
43 1840 Poll Book.
44 Davies, A.W., *The Cockings of Ludlow*, 1959, p.10.
45 Unidentified press obituary, written after Smith's death on 13 Jan.1914, given to the writer by the late Mary Andrews, a relative of the Smith family.
46 I am grateful to Chris Train for this information.
47 MI St Laurence's, St John's Chapel.
48 LA 1 Oct.1892.
49 Peach Robinson, diary p.12.
50 Ibid.
51 HJ, 2 Feb.1848.
52 LA, 25 Oct.1862.
53 LA, 27 July, 1889.
54 Reeder,D.and Rodger,R., "Industrialisation and the City Economy", in Daunton, *The Cambridge Urban History of Britain*, Vol.III, 1840-1950, 2000, p.584.
55 PRO: IR 23/71.
56 HRO 14 November 1831.
57 Easter Book entries, 1806, 1807.
58 SA LB 2/1/7,p.366; LB 2/1/8,p.48; conveyance 4 May 1848 (private deeds).
59 Davies, op.cit., p.8.
60 This paragraph is based almost entirely on the genealogical research of Robin Newman of Sutton Coldfield, who is a descendant of Charles Harding.

61 Martin, E.H., "The Family of Marston of Afcote", T.S.A.S., 4th ser., vol.8, 1921-22.

62 Ibid.

63 Slater, 1868; Kelly, 1870

64 Information about the Davies family kindly supplied by Ann Jones, 24 Bell Lane, Ludlow, who is a descendant.

65 Kelly, 1895; will of Thomas Davies, SA, 1900/36.

66 e.g., in Bagshaw's Directory of Shropshire, 1851, pp.531-51: Clee St Margaret: Samuel Hall, weaver & shopkeeper; Peaton: William Dyer, shopkeeper; Holdgate: Ann Harper,shopkeeper; Munslow: John Stubbs, shopkeeper; Stanton Lacy: Edward Farmer, farmer & shopkeeper; Stoke St Milborough: John Humphries, shopkeeper.

67 LLH, 19 May, 1876.

68 SJ,4 April, 1838.

69 LA 28 May 1892.

70 LA 2 May 1891.

71 LA 4 Sept. 1869; LA, 14 Oct. 1893.

72 Kelly, 1861, advertisement; LLH, 19 May, 1876.

73 I am grateful to Sybil Marsh, manageress of Rickards and Co., for allowing access to the Day Book and Ledger.

74 Kelly 1895 lists Bodenhams only as "drapers and oufitters", but in Kelly,1900 they are "drapers, outfitters and furniture dealers".

75 Richards, R., A History of Newtown, 1993, pp.82-83.

76 Cited in Adburgham,A., Shops and Shopping, 1800-1914, 2nd.ed., 1981 p.142. Adburgham shows that haggling was more common in France than in England.

77 LS, 22 Aug. 1840. The Ludlow Standard was published for a few months only in 1840. There are some copies at the British Library (Colindale).

78 LA 4 Sept. 1869 Kelly,1870.

79 LA 15 July, 1876.

80 LA 20 Dec., 1884.

81 LA, 15 Mar., 1856.

82 Porter's Directory, 1888.

83 LLH, 19 May, 1876.

84 Private deeds of No. 5 King Street.

85 Easter Books, Voting books and other records.

86 Southern p.1; Edwards was buried at in Ludlow on 20 April 1851, in the churchyard now known as St Leonards.

87 HJ 13 Mar. 1844.

88 Griffiths scrapbook, op. cit.

89 LA 29 Mar. 1890.

90 LA 13 Aug. 1893; LA 2 May 1891; LA 10 Dec.1893; Kelly, 1890.

91 HJ 15 April 1846.

92 LA 19 Oct. 1880 Weyman, 1895, pp.52-53.

93 LA 26 Mar. 1892; ibid, 28 May 1892.

94 SJ 6 Nov. 1839.

95 LLH, 17 Dec. 1875.

96 LA Almanack, 1898.

97 LA 10 Dec. 1910.

98 I am grateful for the photograph reproduced as Fig.43 and information about the Price family to Karen Price of Riverdale, Western Australia.

99 HJ 24 Dec. 1845.

100 LA 20 Sept. 1889.

101 LA 13 Dec. 1884.

102 LA 17 Dec. 1910.

103 Fay, op. cit., p.179.

104 I am grateful to Martin Speight for this information,

105 Census returns; Kelly, 1909.

106 Crocker, 1884; there were already 41 houses in Gravel Hill, 13 in Castle View Terrace and 37 in Julian Road, but there were no other "substantial shop keepers" among them.

107 Kelly, 1900; Private deeds of 4 Brand Lane; Lloyd, Broad Street, p.27 (the Dunnes of Gatley Park, Leinthall Earls).

108 SJ 26 Dec. 1838: commercial ball at the Angel; HJ 31 Jan. 1844: public ball at the New Buildings in aid of Ludlow Winter Charities.

109 LA 25 Jan. 1861.

110 Robinson Diary p.19.

111 The other four were: Scales and Sons, Boot Makers, The Cross; E.W.and W. Phillips, tailors, 17 High Street; Imperial Vaults, wine merchants, 2 Old Street; Exchange Wine and Spirit Vaults, The Cross.

112 Kelly, 1917; ibid, 1935.

113 e.g. Biggs's stores in Sandpits Road.

CHAPTER 4

BEHIND THE FACADE - DOMESTIC SERVANTS IN LUDLOW

JEAN BROWN

Fig. 1: The presence of at least one residential servant in nearly all its substantial houses was a feature of Victorian Ludlow. For the stretch of Broad Street on this 1880 photograph, the 1881 census recorded 12 such servants.

Victoria's reign encompassed massive industrial development, and with it came social change that was reflected in the lives of many women. The growing economic power of the middle classes enabled more women to remain within the home. If the wife was to indicate to the world her leisured status, and her husband's success, this was primarily achieved by the employment of servants. The servants had to perform their functions efficiently while remaining discreetly in the background, preserving the facade of respectability and status. Charles Booth, in his extensive study of London poverty, chose to use the employment of servants as a category that divided the social classes. In his work based on the 1891 Census he showed that in London over ten per cent of households had servants, which he used as an indication of middle or upper class status.[1]

Pamela Horn describes this social phenomenon: "....there developed the view that the employment of domestic staff was in itself a sign of respectability and an indicator of social status, rather than a mere aid to the smooth running of the household. And as small shopkeepers, tradesmen and clerks moved in growing numbers into the servant-keeping classes, so the distinctions between employer and maid were more firmly drawn."[2] It is difficult to see how far this would be true in Ludlow but social distinctions were clear in speech, dress and place of residence. In most houses with limited physical space the servant (often the only one employed) could not be the invisible retainer that was possible in large establishments.

To examine the nature of domestic employment there are a number of sources available. The national census, newspapers, trade directories, and workhouse records have been examined for Ludlow and have provided information which is both statistical and personal. The ages and birthplaces recorded in the census give the general trends and some analysis can also be made of the types of occupation recorded under the general heading of 'servant'. Also, the census describes the composition of each household, so it can be seen what possible burden of work was placed upon the servants.

It is also important to compare the local with the national scene. Much has been written on the social impact of the increase in women employed in domestic service. The main source of information is the national census carried out every ten years by the Registrar General from 1841 onwards. Each census redefined certain questions and so it is not always possible to make satisfactory comparisons. The 1841 census did not state relationships within each household, and birthplace was only noted as being within the same county or outside it. Gradually, however, there is more specific information. It needs to be remembered that the census is a 'snapshot' of one day. In 1851 of the women in employment 25% were in domestic service, rising to 44% in 1881. The rate of growth slowed down but the figure was still 40% in 1901. In Shropshire in 1851 there were over twelve thousand female domestic servants, and by 1881 this had risen to over fifteen thousand, an increase of 25%, although the county population had only increased by 8%.[3] The rapid increase in the demand for female servants was met usually by country girls seeking employment in larger towns and cities. Although domestic service remained a major source of employment until the first World War, other opportunities became possible for girls. This was reinforced by the introduction of compulsory education and the decrease in the rural population as the agricultural economy changed.

For the women who employed servants there was a plethora of advice in books and magazines. The works of Mrs Beeton are the most famous of these, with their guidance on how to regulate the ideal household.[4] These manuals were addressed to women as wives, mothers and as servants, and contain a mixture of recipes, household hints and moral encouragement. Even if the wife was to remain at home she needed to be manager of the establishment, giving orders and trying to maintain harmonious relationships with her staff. This often proved to be a fraught exercise as many young wives soon learned. Mrs Abell, writing in 1852, goes in quick succession from the preparation of meat, how to serve afternoon tea, how cooks should carry out their work, comments to the housewife on the "treatment of domestics", and then on to gardening.[5]

Very few personal reminiscences were recorded from the mid-nineteenth century, but later writers began to collect the stories of men and women in domestic service and many of these were developed into full autobiographies.[6] The diaries of Hannah Cullwick (1833-1910), born in Shifnal, are an exceptional record, kept at the request of her husband, Arthur Munby, to whom she was secretly married.[7] The frequent changes of jobs, the loneliness of the single servant, the lack of privacy and free time are chronicled and give a different perspective to the advice laid down by authors such as Mrs Beeton. Hannah's diaries are the most accessible insight into the world of the servant, particularly where only one was employed, as a 'maid of all work'.

Although the experiences of Victorian servants in Ludlow have not been recorded, two accounts exist which give the employer's perspective in the years 1851-2. These reflect both modest and wealthy households.

Anna Maria Fay (1828-1922) was a wealthy American girl who came to stay in Ludlow from November 1851 to August 1852. Her uncle and aunt, Richard and Catherine Fay, had rented Moor Park from the Salwey family and moved within the local aristocracy and gentry. Anna Maria's letters to her mother in Boston are illuminating for they show a world where servants were critical to the life of the wealthy family. The Fays had four children and their household is described as comprising a German maid (Fischer) for Catherine, Miss Dodd the governess, and Shaw the butler with a boy under him. Completing the indoor staff were a porter, chambermaid, laundry maid, cook and scullion. Outside servants consisted of a gardener, a keeper and coachman.[8] While the Salweys were still in residence on 30 March 1851, the date of the census, the household was two adults, two children, aged 12 and 10, and ten servants. Two of these were governesses, one of whom was only 19 and came from Paris. The other indoor servants included the cook (a widow aged 60 from Ludlow), a kitchen maid, a butler, a nurse (for the children), two maids, a housemaid and a laundry maid. This represents a fairly typical pattern of employment for a family of this social status. Although servants moved frequently, it is interesting to note that William Vale, the butler, aged 44 and described as married in 1851, had been present on the staff ten years previously but named just as a servant.[9]

Anna Maria Fay visited many of the local gentry houses and was much impressed by the liveries of the staff, including the coachman of Moor Park with his green coat, gilt buttons, buff breeches and top boots. She was invited to dinner at Oakly Park by Lady Harriet Clive and recorded: "Two footmen in red plush breeches and blue coats and silver buttons, and the groom of the chambers in black, received us in the vestibule, where we took off our cloaks."[10] In a later visit they were received again by the butler, "and the footmen, this time in undress livery, blue coats and silver buttons, gray tights and unpowdered heads".[11] Oakly Park was one of the most aristocratic houses in the Ludlow area, and Shaw, the butler at Moor Park, was obviously gratified to receive a visit from the Clive family. "It would be impossible to describe to you Shaw's gratification when the yellow coach and four, with postillions and footman, drew up before the door."[12] The Fay family also had regular social contact with the Rouse Boughton family from Downton Hall. Sir William Rouse Boughton was a widower with five daughters ranging in age from 12 to 21. He employed a companion and a governess for his daughters, a housekeeper, lady's maid, three housemaids, butler, coachman and footman. It is surprising that there is no designated cook.[13] By contrast, when Anna Maria visited Ludford House, the home of Mr Charlton, she found that "he keeps but one servant in the house to wait on him, but the stud of horses which he retains are well provided with grooms".[14]

While the Fay family were moving within the upper echelons of society, Francis Southern was a Ludlow solicitor whose extant diary covers the period from April 1851 to December 1852. Southern makes little mention of his servants. His own household in Ludlow is not immediately obvious as on the night of the 1851 Census he was staying with his mother in Condover. In September of that year he mentions that one of his mother's servants had died supposedly from 'brain symptoms'.[15] He frequented the Angel Hotel a great deal and commented in March 1852 – "Afterwards to The Angel. A new barmaid, a Miss Williams arrived. Didn't like her appearance. Miss Wainwright left about a fortnight ago."[16] Miss Wainwright does not seem to have been resident at The Angel in the 1851 Census. He was much put out when his servant was ill for three days in October 1852.[17] One of his occasional social contacts was with Elizabeth Jones, a governess, and he mentions meeting her after she had left employment with Mr Shield in Clun and was staying with Francis Southern's mother. Elizabeth Jones then went to work for a family in Wigmore.[18] The status of the governess was an awkward one in Victorian society, as can be seen in novels such as *Jane Eyre*. They were often young middle class women forced to take employment, but their status within the household could be a difficult one, somewhere between the family and the rest of the servants and truly accepted by neither.

The Fay and Southern documents raise questions concerning the employment of servants. One of these is recruitment. Mrs Beeton describes the ways in which servants can be found, recognising that advertising locally was the most common method. But she also mentions that contacts may be made through trades people. Professional agencies were another source.[19] In larger cities these agencies

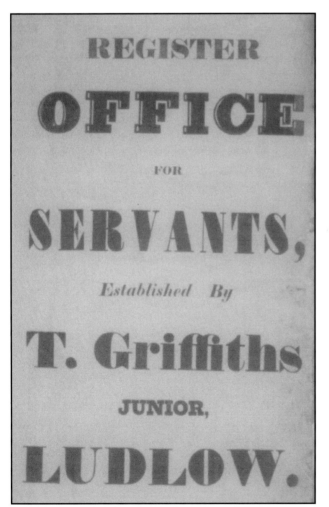

Fig. 2: Printer's bill from the Thomas Griffiths Specimen Day Books 1840-44. Shropshire County Museum Service.

were often regarded with some suspicion by both employers and employees, but in Ludlow there would have been more personal contact. Thomas Griffiths, a local printer, produced a bill to advertise an employment agency on behalf of his son, also Thomas, in the 1840s (Fig. 2). This service was still available when he advertised in the Ludlow Advertiser in 1863 – "Wanted – a number of first class servants. Fancy Repository Broad Street". A month later in the same newspaper Mrs Leaver was advertising a "Registry of respectable servants. No. 8 Harp Lane".[20] In 1888 an advertisement appeared stating "Registry for Families and Servants conducted by Mrs Langslow, 1 High Street".[21] This may be the wife of John Langslow who ran a draper's shop at the same address in 1881. Not many copies of the Ludlow Advertiser survive, but in the twenty one issues available for 1885 there were five requests for servants. These included a footman, a cook who was also capable of managing a dairy, a good general servant who could do plain cooking, a nurse for four children and two servants for the Charlton Arms. In 1881 there was just one request for employment from a servant, "a young person wanting a situation in a private family as Plain Cook or Housemaid, in or near Ludlow. Apply RS 27 Old Gate Fee".[22] However, the census of only three months earlier reveals no one of that name at that address, so this may have been a relative of the family. In the trade directories for Ludlow only three advertisements were found. Miss Elizabeth Ashworth advertised a Registry for Servants at 18 Brand Lane in 1879[23] and Mrs Elizabeth Vale of 8 Church Street advertised in 1879 and 1885.[24]

Servants came from a wide area to work in Ludlow, but it would appear from Mrs Beeton's suggestions about recruitment that personal local recommendations were important. The local gentry or clergy might also be consulted. Anna Maria Fay mentions another source, that of finding places for girls straight from school. On the Oakly Park estate at Bromfield a school had been established and Lady Harriet Clive was much involved in its governance and the care of the girls. "When the girls are fourteen or fifteen, they go out to service in Ludlow or the neighborhood, and if they do well Lady Harriet recommends them whenever she can".[25]

Some girls were employed direct from the workhouse and the Admissions and Discharges book of the Ludlow Union gives many examples. On 20 September 1851 Margaret Morgan had been brought to the workhouse by the Revd and Mrs Hodges from her situation at Onibury "having no other home". On 24 September she "Went upon trial to Mr Thompson the blacksmith of Ashford". In December she is mentioned as having gone to service to Mr Hammond of Hopton Cangeford.[26] It appears from even a limited study of the records of Ludlow Union Workhouse that Margaret Morgan was not untypical of the servant girls who found themselves destitute, often with children to care for.

From the biographical accounts of wealthy families it is evident that retainers were often kept on or maintained long after they had ceased to work for the family in any formal way. Nannies could often be found helping with a second or third generation of children. But for the more general servant, retirement was not an option in the days before pensions. Losing their employment could lead to severe poverty. The giving of references was a questionable business, since employers might provide a good one just to get rid of an unsuitable servant, or provide a negative one if they were vindictive in their attitudes. Horn cites Joseph Chamberlain when he gave evidence to the 1893 Commission on the Aged Poor. Chamberlain reported that no one would employ a servant past 50 years of age and almost by necessity they had to go into the workhouse. In the Birmingham workhouse in that period there were 438 inmates over 65 and more than a third had been directly connected with domestic service. In 1871 one third of the female inmates in St George's workhouse, in Hanover Square London, had been domestic servants, and nearly one half of those were over

60 years of age.[27] Servants must have been aware of this possibility and in a book addressed to footmen and butlers in 1823 it is recognised that servants "have found, to their unspeakable disappointment and distress both of body and mind, the master or mistress whom they have served all the prime of their days, has either died without mentioning them, or lived beyond

TABLE 1: WOMEN CLASSIFIED AS SERVANTS RESIDENT IN LUDLOW WORKHOUSE 1851 & 1881

Age Range	1851	1881
15-24	6	6
25-34	10	4
35-44	2	5
45-54	0	2
55-64	0	1
65 and over		11*
Total No. of servants	18	29
Total of female residents	50	59
% of females who were servants by occupation	36	49

*This does not include the only man classified as a servant of 104 male residents, who was an unmarried coachman.

Marital Status

In 1851 all 18 women were classified as unmarried. By 1881 this had changed considerably

Unmarried	11
Unmarried with children with them	7
Total	**18**
Married	1
Married, children with them	2
Total	**3**
Widows	3
Widows with children with them	1
Total	**4**
Married with spouse in workhouse	2
No status given	2
Total	**4**
Total no of female servants	**29**

Source: National Census for England and Wales 1851 and 1881 for Ludlow, Stanton Lacy Parish

their income, so that they could not refund the money which was their servants' due".[28]

Table 1 shows the number and ages of servants in Ludlow Union Workhouse in 1851 and 1881. In 1851 36% were classified as servants, higher even than the proportion quoted for London and Birmingham. In 1881 this percentage was 49%. There was also 1 man classified as a servant. The economic uncertainties and the greater number of servants available for employment may have contributed to this larger percentage of destitute servants. Although relationships between the inmates are not specified it appears that several of the women had children of school age with them, and of these the largest proportion were unmarried.[29]

The problem of illegitimate children was a source of concern to the Victorians, as many such offspring were the result of seduction by members of the family or fellow servants. Whatever the paternity of the child the disgrace usually led to the firing and subsequent destitution of the servant girl involved. Some managed to have their children without their families ever knowing, and then faced the problem of caring for, fostering or even abandoning their child. Francis Southern reports the tragic outcome of such a situation when he attended a case at the Shrewsbury Assizes in August 1851. A servant girl, named Elizabeth Rogers, was convicted of murdering her illegitimate child by drowning it in a pool near Church Stretton.[30] Horn discusses the problem of illegitimacy in relation to workhouse inmates, quoting from the Kensington Workhouse where in April 1871 there were thirteen unmarried servants with their young babies, nearly one in ten of all the servant inmates. She goes on to describe how these girls had to make arrangements for their babies. "Occasionally the infants were allowed to stay in the workhouse infirmary and were then left to the tender mercies of the Poor Law".[31]

The Admissions and Discharges book for Ludlow Union Workhouse in 1851 provides a local example. Catherine Reece of Stanton Lacy was admitted as pregnant on 21 February and the census of that year shows her as still resident in the Workhouse in March, being unmarried and 27 years old. Her daughter Mary was born on 6 July, but on the 21 July Catherine left of her own accord taking her baby with her. However, she must have entered the Workhouse again, for she left to go into service at Bitterley in August. She returned unwell in October, followed shortly by her baby. Sadly in December the baby died and after some further two months in the Workhouse Catherine Reece left, perhaps to find new employment on her own.[32] In 1881 six servants were admitted as pregnant and of these three births are recorded within the Workhouse.[33]

In assessing the nature of domestic service in Ludlow during the Victorian period a study was made of certain streets from the 1881 Census held on Sunday 3 April.[34] From the census returns for that year, available in computerised form, it became possible to carry out an in-depth analysis, particularly in examining the characteristics of households in which servants were employed. The streets chosen represented different social and occupational strata of Ludlow. Broad Street has been a major thoroughfare since Norman times, with a considerable proportion of large houses and some commercial properties. Lower Broad Street, divided from its more prosperous neighbour by the medieval Broad Gate, was an area of artisan dwellings, having been associated traditionally with the weaving industry. Since these two streets had a similar number of residents and households the comparisons are of interest. Corve Street had many more inhabitants, with smaller properties and a high concentration of skilled and specialist craftsmen. Gravel Hill (in Stanton Lacy parish) was the product of the Victorian expansion into the suburbs, with many large individually designed terraced and detached houses.

The data for the four streets are shown in Table 2. The high proportion of servants in

TABLE 2: SERVANTS AND HOUSEHOLDS 1881				
Individuals (male and female) classified by occupation as servant				
	Broad St	**L.Broad St**	**Corve St**	**Gravel Hill**
Population of street	319	300	778	158
No. of households	60	66	164	34
Total No. of servants	75	9	56	27
No. of households employing servants	40	2	31	18
% of total households	73.3	13.6	23.8	52.9
No. of individuals related to the head of household, described occupationally as servants	4	7	11	0
Age range of all servants	13-57	15-54	13-56	12-51
Average age	22.4	27.4	24.3	24.0

Source: National Census for England and Wales 1881 Ludlow St Lawrence and Stanton Lacy parishes.

Broad Street is an indication of social class and occupation. Gravel Hill, which was developing as a suburb shows a higher proportion of servants than Corve Street. Lower Broad Street presented quite a different picture, as will be described below.

National studies indicate that most servants were under 24 years of age. The average age shown in Table 2 supports this finding, (Lower Broad Street being different in that most of the servants were not resident in their place of employment).

"Going into service offered a girl food and shelter, as well as, if she was fortunate, the possibility of saving some money, which might later be used to set her sweetheart in a trade...... The 1851 Census shows that the majority of general domestic servants were girls between fifteen and twenty five, whereas the majority of charwomen, washerwomen, manglers and laundry keepers were middle aged and older."[35] It would be rare, and perhaps only in very large houses, that married women could remain working. In the Ludlow sample around 70% of all the servants were aged twenty four or younger. Of the total number of servants 13% were aged 40 or over and only 3% were in their

TABLE 3: SERVANTS IN LUDLOW SAMPLE		
Place of birth in distance from Ludlow 1881		
Distance	**Number**	**Percentage**
Ludlow	38	23%
Within five miles	32	19%
From 5 to 10 miles	48	29%
From 10-20 miles	12	7%
From 20-30 miles	10	6%
Over 30 miles	19	11%
Not given	8	5%
Total	**167**	**100%**

fifties. With an abundant supply of labour, younger girls could be employed in quick succession, and only a few remained in domestic employment as a long term career. It is relevant therefore that twelve of these older women had higher status jobs within the hierarchy of domestic service. Eight were housekeepers, three were cooks and one a professional nurse. Six of them were unmarried, with one widow. The one married woman was in the position of being head of a household and working for another family.

In analysing the birthplace of servants, as is shown in Table 3, information is revealed on the patterns of job-seeking in the nineteenth century. The majority of servants found their first residential job within their own neighbourhood, and then, to gain experience, often sought jobs further afield.

Over the four streets a high proportion of the servants had been born within ten miles of Ludlow, the percentage being 71%. 23% of the Broad Street servants had been born more than ten miles away, compared with 29% in Gravel Hill and 30% in Corve Street, but there is no apparent explanation for this.[36] Local employment would be easier to procure and more reassuring for young girls leaving home for the first time. As with other general patterns of migration it is possible to suggest that those who had been born in more distant places had moved in search of work. Many servants did not stay in one position for more than eighteen months or two years. Within the sample, only one example was found where a servant had stayed in the same employment for more than a decade. Jane Thomas, in Corve Street, had remained servant to Henry Whittall for over twenty years. There is no consistent pattern in the more distant places of birth which included Worcester, Walsall, Salford, Manchester, Newbury, Wareham and Bath.

The status of the really young servant was very low, and there is plenty of evidence to suggest that they were the most exploited by their employers and other servants. In the sample there were thirteen young servants between the ages of ten and fourteen. Ten, including one boy, aged 14, are described as General Domestic Servants, and three as Nurses. All but two of the group were born in Ludlow and the others came from about five miles away.

It has been possible to locate the family of one of these young servants by reference to the 1871 Census. Jessy Meale was the fifth of six children of Edward and Annie Meale living in the Linney. Edward was a nailmaker. His eldest daughter, Clara, had left home to become a servant in Ludlow where she is recorded as such in 1881. In that same year two children

aged 24 and 11 remained at home, while Jessie was the only resident servant to two sisters in Corve Street. Another sister, then aged 18, had also left home. Mary Bluck was another young girl who was recorded as a General Servant in 1881, but was still living at home in Lower Gaolford with her parents and siblings. Of these the four oldest, including Mary at 14, were all employed and the remaining six children ranged in age from eleven down to one year. Martha Oakley, aged fourteen, was the only resident servant to the Revd Josiah and Mrs Tallady, the Wesleyan Methodist Minister living in Broad Street. Harriet Pugh, aged 12, was the youngest of the group, and was also the only resident servant to Edward Russell, in Gravel Hill. The household consisted of a family of four plus two lodgers. One can only hope that there was other non-resident domestic help or young Harriet must have worked long hours indeed.

One of the constant challenges faced by the Registrar General in the formulation of the census questionnaires was classifying occupations. There were attempts over the decades to provide a better analysis into which all occupations could be slotted, but it never proved entirely satisfactory.[37] An example of this can be found in the gradations of domestic service. These ranged in status from the housekeeper at the top, down through nanny, lady's maid, cook, housemaids, kitchen maids and, at the bottom, the scullery maids. For this study governesses were not included. In a larger establishment it might be easier to assign particular duties to each member of staff, but most houses in Ludlow had only one or two servants. The occupational title of General Domestic Servant covers over 50% of all the servants in this sample. In Broad Street 40% are classified as General Domestic, but this is the one street where there is a greater number of servants per household and so more distinctions between staff. There were fourteen cooks, five housekeepers, fifteen housemaids, and one lady's maid in Broad Street to support this view.

It has been noted that there were thirteen servants between the ages of ten and fourteen in the sample and that three of these were described as 'nurses'. The first job given to a young girl on leaving home was often to look after the children of her employer. In Broad Street, Mary Davies aged 14, was in a household with two children aged 1 and 2 years, with one general domestic servant as well. Susan Price, aged 13, lived in a household with 5 children, two of whom were under school age. The family also employed one general servant. In the household of William Bodenham in Gravel Hill, Mary Longford, also 13, must have been responsible for the care of the two youngest children, aged 3 and 1 years, in a family where there were also five older children.

The number of men servants in the sample is small, being only five of the total of 167. The employment of men within the house declined rapidly during the nineteenth century. A tax was placed on male servants in 1853, revised in 1869 to 15s per annum for all male servants, and this was not abolished until 1937.[38] It became more common for men to be employed outside the house, in gardens and stables, and only larger houses would have a valet, butler or footmen.

The discrepancy between the national figures and that for all servants in Shropshire in 1851 and 1881 set out in Table 4 may reflect the large estates in the county which would have employed more men. If only domestic indoor servants are compared the ratio is nearer the national figure. In St Laurence Parish in 1881 there was a much greater proportion of men employed as servants than in the national figure. In the sample of four Ludlow streets the proportion is much lower. The five men in the sample were described as a baker's boy, valet, billiard marker, and two ostlers. An indication of the change in the percentage of male servants employed can be found by comparing Broad Street in 1861 where there were nineteen resident male servants, with 1881 when the total had decreased to three.[39]

An area which proved difficult to classify in the census was the employment of servants in inns and hotels. With a resident family running the establishment there would be a need for domestic help both for the family and for the guests and customers. In 1881 the Raven Inn in Gravel Hill and the Barley Mow in Lower Broad Street had no resident staff, while the Wheatsheaf in Lower Broad Street had one girl, aged 18, doing general domestic work. Since there were two adults and seven children in the Rodgers family at the Wheatsheaf it might be assumed that her work was confined to looking after them, but this may not have been so. The Angel Inn in Broad Street run by the Chirm family had only two adults in the family, but there were three boarders and seven servants. Defined as being part of the Inn were the barmaid, the billiard marker (a man aged 20), the waitress, the chambermaid, a general servant and a housemaid. The cook is not designated specifically to either the inn or as a domestic servant but it may be assumed that she cooked for all the residents.

In the census of 1881 the landlord of the Feathers Hotel and his wife had two children and a visitor staying with them. The resident staff consisted of a barmaid, a waitress, a chambermaid, cook and two men working as ostler and 'boots'. Another ostler was living

TABLE 4: RATIO OF MALE TO FEMALE SERVANTS		
		Male to female
National figures	1800	1:8
National figures	1851	1:10
Shropshire – all servants	1851	1:6
National figures	1881	1:22
Shropshire – all servants	1881	1:5
Shropshire – indoor domestic servants	1881	1:18
Ludlow St Laurence parish	1881	1:10
Ludlow sample	1881	1:32

adjacent to The Feathers in the Bull Ring.

The occupational classification of married women proved a constant challenge to the Registrar General. By 1881 married women were given the status of their husband, unless they stated a specific occupation outside the home. Part-time or temporary employment was necessary for many women at this period to augment the family income but this remains a hidden statistic. Widowed mothers, unmarried sisters and relatives were often described as 'housekeepers', looking after the households of their close families. Charles Evans, a Ludlow grocer in Broad Street from 1857 to 1873 had his widowed mother as housekeeper. By 1881 when his mother had died and he was living in Gravel Hill this role had been assumed by his unmarried niece Ellen. This remained so until her death in 1909. She had been living with the family since the age of five after her own mother's death. The housekeeper in a larger establishment was a person of importance, controlling all the domestic staff outside the kitchen, and being of a similar status to the butler. However, the job of housekeeping raises the question relating to all servants as to whether they were employees or relatives. Of the eleven housekeepers in the sample, two in Corve Street and two in Broad Street were sisters to the head of the household. Five women were classified occupationally as 'servants' but were in fact heads of their households. Ann Hughes was one of these, with a family of eight people, and one young servant girl of 15, who was described as 'a maid of all work'. Twenty individuals were 'servants' by occupation but were related in some way to the head of the household in which they lived. Three other 'servants' in the sample were living as lodgers. Historians have examined this question of 'kin servants' as opposed to 'true servants' and the way in which the earlier censuses did not always distinguish between the two. A recent study of servants in Tenbury Wells supports the view that the employment situation was sometimes unclear. So the status of a servant could range from a paid employee resident in the household to a reluctant relative assuming the role for the family.[40]

From 1851 the census data show the relationship with the head of the household, age, marital status, occupation and place of birth. This has enabled historians to study the patterns of family life in the nineteenth century and to reveal the complexities of who actually resided with whom. A 'household' could comprise two or three generations, siblings and other relatives, lodgers, boarders, apprentices, servants, assistants and visitors. From the 1881 sample it is possible to look at the situation in Ludlow to assess the number of servants in relation to the overall household. This can be seen in Tables 2 and 5.

During the nineteenth century many employers and their families still lived over or near their working premises and Ludlow was no exception. The Rickards family owned a large ironmongers business in the centre of Ludlow, in the Bull Ring. The premises, now used completely for shop storage, still bear the elegant wallpapers and interior decor for what comprised the upstairs accommodation for the family. In 1881 Heber Rickards was Deputy Mayor of Ludlow and a Justice of the Peace, aged 43. He had five children from 13 down to

TABLE 5: NUMBER OF RESIDENT SERVANTS PER HOUSEHOLD IN LUDLOW SAMPLE 1881				
	Broad St.	Lower Broad St.	Corve St.	Gravel Hill	Total
1 servant	21	2	20	12	55
2 servants	15	0	7	4	26
3 servants	4	0	3	1	8
4 servants	0	0	1	1	2
Total	40	2	31	18	91

2 years, and his mother-in-law lived with them. An apprentice was also part of the household. Mary Taylor, aged 24, was the cook and there was a nurse, Mary Powell, aged 16. She was one of the nine girls described as 'nurse'. This was a household of eleven people, living in a large apartment, as part of their business premises. In Broad Street, John Valentine, the grocer still lived over the shop with his family, including eight children, three shop assistants, and four apprentices. Two of his wife's sisters were also resident with them assisting in the house and in the post office section of the shop. This large household was looked after by a cook and a general servant.

By contrast, some employers were beginning to move out to the new suburbs, but the pattern remained of a large mixed household. William Bodenham lived in Gravel Hill, and his shop, a drapers and outfitters, was in the centre of town in King Street. His household in 1881 comprised eighteen people, including seven children, two male apprentices and two male assistants. To care for this large number there was a cook, a housemaid, aged 19, and the previously mentioned young nurse Mary Longford, aged 13. Edward Harding was another draper who had moved to Gravel Hill, again with an extended household. With his wife and seven children there were also two male apprentices, both born in Gloucestershire. There were two female general servants, aged 40 and 19. By contrast with the apprentices, both women had been born locally.

These suburban houses afforded very suitable accommodation for a large family with resident servants. Since the houses are still there, although modernised, the space allocated to servants can be estimated. Fig. 3 shows three of these large late Victorian houses in Gravel Hill. Holly Lodge, the centre house in the photograph, was the home of Thomas Bennett, described in 1881, as the Lecturer of Ludlow, an Anglican clergyman, from County Derry in Ireland. His wife, also aged 26, had been born in Bath. They had two children, aged 1 and 2 years old, and four servants: Jane Lucas, aged 22, a cook from Wareham, Mary Summers, aged 19, a housemaid from Ledbury, Eliza Hall, aged 17, a nursemaid from Ludlow. The fourth servant was Emily Sadd, aged 24, a nurse who came from Bath. It might be assumed that there had been a local connection between her and Mrs Bennett. The house is on four floors, including a cellar. The ground floor has three reception rooms and a kitchen with outbuildings which may have been stabling. There are now three bedrooms and a bathroom on the first floor and the same on the second floor. These are well proportioned rooms, but while the two top front rooms have dormer windows, on the rear elevation there are only roof lights. It is possible from the plans of this house to see how the four servants probably shared two of these bedrooms

Fig. 3: Houses in Gravel Hill.

at the back of the house, each room being approximately four by three metres and with a fireplace.[41]

Table 5 shows how the sample streets varied in the number of resident servants employed per household. Corve Street and Gravel Hill have over a third of households employing more than one servant, while in Broad Street the number is nearly half of the households. But Thomas Bennett was unusual in having four servants, as 60% of the households had only one resident servant. This is higher than the figure of one third of households employing one servant, quoted for London by Charles Booth in 1891. A greater disparity in social class and income might be expected in the capital in comparison with a rural market town such as Ludlow.

Perhaps the most intriguing household in the sample is that of the Tickill family in Corve Street, where six children and three servants are recorded, but no parents. One can only presume, that if alive, the adults were staying elsewhere on the night of the census. Booth also noted that over half the total number of female domestic staff were employed in households with only one or two servants.[42] In the Ludlow sample 81 women out of 162, precisely 50%, were in such households. The workload of the single servant was hard indeed, and by the mid Victorian period three fifths of servants were classified as general domestics. They were expected to fulfil a large range of tasks, even though some outside help might be brought in as occasion demanded. Hannah Cullwick's diaries show what the daily schedule could mean.

"Saturday 28th July 1860. Lighted the fire. brush'd the grates. Clean'd the hall & steps & flags on my knees. Swept & dusted the rooms. Got breakfast up. Made the beds & emptied the slops. Cleaned & wash'd up & clean'd the plate. Clean'd the stairs & the pantry on my knees. Clean'd the knives & got dinner. Clean'd 3 pairs of boots. Clean'd away after dinner & began the preserving about ½ past 3 & kept on till 11, leaving off only to get the supper & have my tea. Left the kitchen dirty & went to bed very tired & dirty."[43]

Even Mrs Beeton was aware of the plight of the single domestic servant: "deserving of commiseration; her life is a solitary one, and in some places, her work is never done. She is also subject to rougher treatment than either the house or kitchen maid, especially in her earlier career; she starts in life, probably a girl of thirteen, with some small tradesman's wife as her mistress, just a step above her in the social order."[44] The physical presence of the 'baize door' which separated family and domestic staff was restricted to larger houses, but in practice the servant was often confined to the kitchen for her working and sometimes sleeping hours. At Laugharne, in South Wales, is preserved the one chair that Dylan Thomas' parents allowed their servant to use in the first two decades of the twentieth century.

With a large proportion of Ludlow servants working not more than ten miles from their birthplace there would be opportunities to visit family. However, time away from the job was minimal and a Christmas visit might have to be made in the new year. Hannah Cullwick tried to maintain contact with her family, although visits to Shifnal were infrequent, but she did keep in touch with servants with whom she had worked. In Ludlow there must have been socialising, even with limited free time. Compulsory attendance at church by servants was often demanded by employers. Commentaries from elsewhere would suggest that Ludlow families would have been unusual if they had not practised such religious observance. Some households would also have maintained a regular daily time for prayers.

Within the sample of Ludlow inhabitants studied in 1881 there were marked differences between two particular streets, Broad Street and Lower Broad Street.

Here, in essence, is the great divide between the servant and non-servant employing households. As can be seen from Table 2 the number of households and individuals is similar, but there all resemblance ends. An analysis of the inhabitants reveals more discrepancies. In Broad Street sixteen residents lived off independent incomes, and the recorded occupations include bank managers, shop owners, booksellers, chemist, clergy, doctors, solicitors and some skilled craftsmen. In Lower Broad Street occupations included several skilled craftsmen such as master baker, blacksmith, cabinet makers, stone mason, painter, a dozen dressmakers, gardeners, and several apprentices and journeyman attached to various trades. Whereas in Broad Street less than 25% of the residents were aged fourteen or under, in Lower Broad Street it was 40% . Considerable research has been done on the properties in these two streets and the architectural distinctions are clearly related to the social class structure.[45] The census data for 1861 show that there were sixty eight servants in Broad Street with eight in Lower Broad Street. The comparable figures for 1881 are seventy five and nine.

Ludlow, as a town, was a relatively contained unit in the nineteenth century and it presents a community which fulfilled most of the needs of its people. There were extreme differences between the rich and the poor, in types of housing and in the size and composition of households. The statistics relating to servants bear comparison with other local and national studies in age, birthplace and kinship relationships, and demonstrate the importance of the servant in the Victorian period. In a town the size of Ludlow properties can be identified and the relationship of family size to the number and type of servants employed can be analysed. It is also possible to build up a picture of individual households. However, the census presents a static picture for one date and does not show what was happening to individuals and families in the ten years in between. Other sources such as newspapers, trade directories and the Poor Law records have provided more personal detail to add to the statistics.

The personal accounts of Anna Maria Fay and Francis Southern are a glimpse into the world of the employers, but in Ludlow the servants do not speak for themselves. It is appropriate, therefore, to leave the last word to Hannah Cullwick, to highlight the fundamental distinctions between employer and servant. Her writings emphasise the role of the servant, not only as domestic help, but as the means of maintaining a social facade. Hannah, the Shifnal girl, began her working life at the age of eight in her home town, before moving to other employment in a wide variety of places. She chose to remain a servant even though she could later have enjoyed the privilege of being a middle class wife. As Hannah wrote in her diary in July 1860, "I've been busy cleaning windows and glasses this month, for the flies and the dust make so much dirt. My hands are very coarse and hardish, but not more so than usual. Mrs J [Mrs Jackson for whom she had worked for over four years] has very white hands and she often comes and lays her hand lightly on mine for me to feel how cold they are – we say it's to show the difference more than anything else."[46]

ENDNOTES

1   Booth, Charles, *Life and Labour of the People in London*, Vol 17 London Macmillan 1903 p. 8.
2   Horn, Pamela, *The Rise and Fall of the Victorian Servant*, Dublin, Gill and MacMillan 1975 (1990 edition) p. 13.
3   1851 Census of England and Wales Report. Enumeration Abstract Vol 1 p. 456 1881 Census of England and Wales Report Vol 111 p. 240.
4   Flanders, Judith, *Domestic Life from Childbirth to Deathbed in the Victorian House*, Harper Collins, 2003. The introduction on 'House and Home' gives a good resumé of the many manuals available, and the book has an excellent bibliography.
5   Abell, L.G., *A mother's book of traditional household skills*, The Lyons Press 2001. Original edition 1852 by R.T. Young p. 160ff.
6   Dawes, F.V., *Not in front of the Servants*, Century 1989 Published in association with the National Trust. An excellent account of 'life below stairs', based on servants' accounts. Thompson, Flora, *Lark Rise to Candleford*, OUP 1945 as a trilogy, reprinted Penguin Classics 2000. Although Flora Thompson was not a servant she sees the effects of being a servant within her own village community.
7   Stanley, L. (ed), *The Diaries of Hannah Cullwick Victorian Maidservant*, Virago 1984 pp. 35-52 (Hannah's Places) and p. 96.
8   Fay, Anna Maria, *Victorian Days in England*, Letters home by an American Girl 1851-1852 Ludlow The Dog Rose Press 2002 p. 13.
9   1881 Census of England and Wales.
10 Fay op. cit. p. 78.
11 Ibid p. 116.
12 Ibid p. 154.
13 1851 Census of England and Wales Census Enumerators Books HO107/1982 352 Ludlow 2 Fiche 1+ p. 34.
14 Fay, op. cit. p. 47.
15 Francis Southern Diary 26 September 1851 Further analysis of this diary will be found in a separate chapter.
16 Ibid 9 March 1852.
17 Ibid 31 October 1852.
18 1851 Census.
19 Beeton, Isabel, *Mrs Beeton's Everyday Cookery and Housekeeping Book*, Ward Lock Second edition 1880 p. 541.
20 *Ludlow Advertiser*, 17 January and 7 February 1863.
21 *Ludlow Advertiser*, 14 July 1888.
22 *Ludlow Advertiser*, Copies for 1885, and 30 July 1881.
23 Post Office Directory of Shropshire 1879.
24 Kelly's Directory of Shropshire 1885.
25 Fay, op. cit. p. 121.
26 Ludlow Union Workhouse Admissions and Discharges 1851.
27 Horn, P., op. cit. p. 186.
28 The Footman's Directory and Butler's Remembrancer printed by J. Hatchard & Son 1823. Facsimile Reproduction Pryor Publications 1998 p. 243 Although slightly earlier in period this gives a complete advice manual to male servants, both practical and moral.
29 Census of England and Wales 1851.
30 Southern, op. cit. 2 August 1851.
31 Horn, P., op. cit. p. 156.
32 Admissions and Discharges for Ludlow Union Workhouse, Shropshire Archives PL9/19/1/2 1851.
33 Admissions and Discharges for Ludlow Union Workshouse, Shropshire Archives PL9/19/1/9 1881 Census of England and Wales 1881.
34 All data hereafter given from the Census for England and Wales have been transcribed from the Census Enumerators Books by the Ludlow Historical Research Group. This was part of a larger study of Ludlow in the Victorian period, with a sample of five streets using data in the 1841, 1861 and 1881 censuses.
35 Mitchell, J & Oakley A., *The Rights and Wrongs of Women*, Penguin 1976 p. 98.
36 The calculation of distance from Ludlow was taken from 1881 Census data by locating the birthplaces on an Ordnance Survey map.
37 For an analysis of the problems facing the Registrar General in defining occupations in the nineteenth century refer to: Woollard, M., *The Classification of Occupations in the 1881 Census of England and Wales*. Department of History, University of Essex, Colchester 1999. Historical Censuses and Social Surveys Research Group. Occasional Paper No 1.
38 Horn. P., op.cit. Chapter 5.
39 The sources for the proportions of male to female servants were taken from Horn P, Shropshire figures: Official Report of the Census 1831 Vol 1 Ludlow figures: General Census of England and Wales 1881.
40 Adair, W.D., *Can we trust the Census Reports*: Lessons from a study of domestic servants in Tenbury, Worcestershre 1851 and 1861 Family and Community History Vol 5 No 2 November 2002 p. 99.
41 Details of property by permission of current owners 2003.
42 Booth, C. Cited in Horn, P, op. cit. p. 26.
43 Stanley, L., op. cit. p. 109.
44 Mrs. Beeton Cited in Horn, P, op. cit. p. 19.
45 Lloyd, D., *Broad Street*, Studio Press, Birmingham 1979. New edition Ludlow Historical Research Group, St Leonard's Press Ludlow 2001.
46 Stanley, L., op. cit. p. 11.

CHAPTER 5

PARLIAMENTARY ELECTIONS IN LUDLOW BETWEEN THE REFORM ACTS, 1832 -1867

MARTIN SPEIGHT

WE HAVE NO TORIES OR RADICALS: WE ARE CALLED CLIVITES AND REFORMERS[1]

Edward Herbert, 2nd Earl of Powis (1785-1848) by Sir Francis Grant. As Lord Clive, he represented the borough from 1806 to 1839, when his elevation to the peerage was the cause of the notorious corrupt by-election.
(Photograph: Powis Castle, The Powis Collection (The National Trust) / NTPL / John Hammond.)

The Parliamentary Reform Act which became law in 1832 was the successful culmination of a campaign lasting over several decades. Its main aims, as summarised in the preamble to the act, were threefold: to remove the right of representation from the worst of the rotten and pocket boroughs, where the choice of a Member of Parliament was the prerogative of one family, and to distribute the seats among large and unrepresented towns; to extend the right to vote to a proportion of the male population who had hitherto been deprived of the franchise; and to reduce the expense of elections.[2]

These aims were achieved to a varying degree, though many of the more radical supporters of the measure were disappointed when the act failed to bring in anything approaching adult male suffrage. The success of the act in achieving its other aims was sometimes dependent upon local factors, and in the case of Ludlow the short-term results of the reform of Parliament were at odds with the intentions of the government.

The outline of Ludlow's parliamentary history has been fairly well-known since the publication of Sir Lewis Namier's ground-breaking study of *The Structure of Politics at the Accession of George III* (1928). Namier, pioneering the methodology for which he was to become famous, made a detailed examination of Shropshire politics as part of an investigation of the sources of political influence in the country. He found an extensive web of influence woven by the family of Lord Powis, and was particularly struck by the tenacity of the hold of the Herbert and later Clive families over the borough of Ludlow, which survived, to a somewhat diminished extent, after the Reform Act. Between 1832 and the abolition of the Ludlow borough constituency in 1885, there were only eight years when a member of the Herbert-Clive family did not hold one of the Ludlow seats.[3]

Following the pioneering work of Namier, Ludlow's parliamentary history, including events after 1832, has received the attention of a number of historians. Norman Gash, in his study of *Politics in the Age of Peel* (1953), drew attention to the 1839 Ludlow election not only as an example of corruption increasing after Reform, but also as an early example of national party organisations intervening in a local contest in the depths of the provinces. More recently, Ludlow's parliamentary history has come under the scrutiny of Namier's monumental offspring, the *History of Parliament*, and the equally authoritative *Victoria County History* (1979). In view of the fact that this subject has been examined by such an array of august scholarship, it may seem strange that a further foray into Ludlow electoral politics should be undertaken here. Justification for doing so must rest upon the fact that in all the cases quoted above, the perspective has been that of the outside observer putting Ludlow under the lens – in the case of Namier and Gash to provide illustrations and support from the localities to be extrapolated on a wider national scale, and in the case of the History of Parliament and the Victoria County History to provide authoritative works of factual reference. The present chapter seeks, at least in part to reverse the procedure and to consider the question from a Ludlow perspective, in doing so examining peculiarly local circumstances, which it is contended often eclipsed the wider issues of the time. The main point at issue is contained in the quotation below the title of this chapter, namely whether local personalities and conditions, rather than national political trends, were the determining factors in Ludlow's electoral behaviour during this period.

DEVELOPMENTS PRIOR TO 1832: THE MAKING OF A POCKET BOROUGH

In order to address this question it is necessary first to examine briefly the transformation of Ludlow into a virtual pocket borough controlled by the Clive family in the century prior to Reform, and secondly to outline the history of the borough representation between the first two Reform Acts. It should then be possible to analyse some of the factors which influenced the processes. Like the majority of borough constituencies in England, and in common with the other Shropshire boroughs, the franchise in Ludlow prior to 1832 was vested in the free burgesses. Between 1661 and 1698, the right to vote had been restricted to resident burgesses, but in the latter year the by-law governing this was repealed, and the franchise opened to non-resident burgesses. This rapidly increased the electorate from 90 in 1679 to over 700 by 1727, the last seriously contested election before 1832. Throughout the 18th century the out-voters (non-resident burgesses) outnumbered the residents, a common situation in borough constituencies at the time, and one which greatly increased the expense of elections. The transporting of electors from distant places to the poll, provision for their entertainment, accommodation, and often corruption meant that the cost of an individual vote could be disproportionately large. In Ludlow the situation changed rapidly in 1727 when both seats were captured by members of the Herbert family of Oakly Park, who built up a power base by swearing in many of their supporters as out-voters. This marked the beginning of the domination of Ludlow by the Herberts and their relatives the Clives, which was to survive the Reform Act, albeit in a weakened form. By 1750 the appointment of Ludlow's members had passed in practice from the electorate into the hands of the head of the Herbert clan, the Earl of Powis, who generally nominated his relations or trusted friends to the seats. This situation was not accepted unreservedly, and there were abortive attempts to mount a challenge to the Powis candidates, in 1774, 1780 and 1784, but these failed in the face of the overwhelming financial power and political influence of the Earl of Powis. From 1806 until 1832 the Ludlow seats were shared by Edward Herbert, Lord Clive and a succession of his relations.

EARLY ATTEMPTS AT OPPOSITION

The one serious attempt to challenge the Clives at the polls came in 1826. Opposition to the Clive dominance of the borough, both through its Members of Parliament and the increasing number of the family's associates appointed to the Corporation, had for some time been coordinated among the largely disfranchised tradesmen and artisans by the Ludlow printer, William Felton. By publishing a number of tracts concerning the largely diminished rights of the burgesses, and by promoting a costly and ultimately successful lawsuit against the Corporation for demolishing St Leonard's Chapel, Felton and his associates had developed some nuisance value when dealing with the political establishment of the borough. They lacked an influential leader until this role was assumed by the unlikely personage of Edmund Lechmere Charlton, the eccentric squire of Ludford. In 1823 Charlton, a member of the Corporation since 1810, had begun to challenge the right of non-resident burgesses to serve on that body. This campaign had taken the form of a series of unsuccessful Quo Warranto actions in the Court of King's Bench which challenged the non-residents to prove their entitlement to hold office. Though the actions failed, they established Charlton, who in most

respects was a hard-line Tory, as the unlikely leader of the town's Reformers. In the General Election of 1826 Charlton stood on a programme of opposition to the Clives and their influence, and claimed, with no foundation, that resident householders were allowed to vote. A poll was held in which fourteen burgesses voted for the Clives, while Charlton received a mere two votes. This somewhat farcical episode was the only time between 1727 and 1832 that a challenge to the Herbert/Clive hegemony was ever carried to a poll, and Charlton was rewarded with a large piece of silver plate to which the Reformers of the town had subscribed.[4] In 1830, however, following the mediation of two influential Tory politicians, Charles Greville and C.W. Wynn, Charlton became temporarily reconciled to the Clives, who had paid him £1,125 towards his outstanding legal costs, and mutual compromises were made regarding the question of the non-resident burgesses. This was not to be the last occasion when Charlton was bought off, and not surprisingly it was regarded as an act of gross betrayal by his former allies, the Reformers.[5]

This ornate piece of silver was presented to Charlton by the Reformers of the town in gratitude for his campaign against the Clives in the 1820s.
It was purchased for Ludlow Museum in 1980, but stolen within a few months of being displayed.

The Influence of the 1832 Reform Act

The Reform Act of 1832 brought significant changes to the borough. The franchise was extended to all adult male householders occupying property to an annual value of £10, subject to various minor qualifications. This added over 300 electors to the roll. Prior to 1832 a rigid check on the admittance of new burgesses to exclude, as far as possible, those opposed to the Clives had reduced the electorate to under a hundred. The Reform Act further reduced the number of 'old-right' voters to 57 by finally disfranchising the non-resident burgesses.[6] As 'old-right' voters who failed to re-register at every election automatically lost their vote for ever, it was hoped that in a few years this class of voter would have disappeared. By 1840, the date of the last surviving poll book during this period, the number had fallen to 45.[7] The abolition of the non-residents or out-voters had been intended to reduce substantially the cost of elections, one of the main aims of the Reform Act. It was also hoped that enlarging the electorate would make bribery and corruption less practicable. On both counts the act failed dramatically in most boroughs, as candidates were able to concentrate their financial resources on corrupting a relatively compact community of electors, rather than wasting large sums on unreliable out-voters. In Ludlow, the absence of elections for most of the previous century had meant that, apart from the regular sweetening of supporters at the time of the uncontested elections, opportunities for overt corruption were almost non-existent. This situation was changed dramatically by the Reform Act.

In 1832 the first election under the Reform Act witnessed a major upset in Ludlow, for although Lord Clive headed the poll, the other sitting member, the Hon. R.H. Clive, was beaten into second place by Edward Romilly, a moderate Reformer from Glamorgan. R.H. Clive regarded the result as "an act of unexampled deceit and treachery", and turned his back on Ludlow, being elected one of the new members for the Southern Division of Shropshire a few days later. The lesson of this contest was not lost on the Clives, for although they retained one Ludlow member for all but eight years between 1832 and 1867, they never again attempted to contest both seats. In 1835 the Conservatives, as they were now officially known, captured both seats, with Charlton narrowly unseating Romilly in the last hour of the poll. Charlton's brief parliamentary career was fiery and unorthodox, and culminated in a spell in the Fleet prison for contempt of a Master in Chancery.[8] In June 1837 the death of William IV necessitated a General Election, in which Clive and Charlton faced a pair of Reformers, Colonel Salwey, the scion of the leading local family of Reformist gentry, and a stranger from Surrey, Thomas Alcock, who had represented a Lancashire constituency before Reform. At the nomination Charlton unexpectedly withdrew from the contest, thereby ensuring that at least one of his opponents, in the event Salwey, was elected. Charlton had been bought by Alcock, who had agreed to purchase his mortgages.[9] Having betrayed both sides, Charlton now lost all political credibility.

Post-Reform developments

In 1839 the elevation of Lord Clive to the earldom of Powis led to a ferocious by-election contest between Henry Clive and Alcock at which both sides practised extensive acts of bribery and intimidation. Alcock won the seat by a slender margin on appeal, but was unseated on petition on the grounds of bribery. As Clive was found to be equally guilty of malpractice, the election was declared void. At this time the government was attempting to clamp down on electoral corruption, and had deprived St Albans and Sudbury of representation for this reason. Ludlow and Cambridge, which had both held very corrupt contests in 1839, narrowly avoided disfranchisement when Tory members secured the passage of the writ for a new election by parliamentary legerdemain. The

Clives prudently abstained from the new contest, and the by-election of 1840 saw a new Conservative candidate, Beriah Botfield, easily defeat another imported Liberal, George G. de H. Larpent, whose many names excited great ridicule among Tory wits. In the General Election of 1841 Botfield was joined by a second Conservative, James Ackers of Heath House, Clungunford, while the Liberals fielded Salwey and Alcock. Following an unsuccessful attempt by the Liberals to secure a compromise election of Botfield and Salwey,[10] Alcock withdrew, and Botfield and Ackers swept home. It is significant that at this contest the Conservatives captured all twelve Shropshire seats, as they had done in 1835, and Sir Robert Peel was able to form the first majority Conservative government since the Reform Act.

In 1846 Peel split his party over the repeal of the Corn Laws, and Botfield, who had supported Peel, lost his seat, as did Tomline of Shrewsbury. The significance of the Corn Laws and other issues in determining the election will be discussed in more detail below. There ensued a period of five years when the Ludlow seats were shared by the protectionist Tory, Henry Bailey Clive, and the Liberal, Colonel Salwey. This initiated a period of unbroken Clive and Herbert representation which survived the reduction of Ludlow to a single member constituency in 1867, and lasted until the Third Reform Act deprived the borough of its own member in 1885. The Clive and Herbert members after 1852 were Robert Clive, son of the former member R.H. Clive, (1852-54); General Percy Egerton Herbert (1854-1860), a Crimean War hero who subsequently represented South Shropshire until 1876; and Colonel G.H. Windsor Clive (1860-1880). Significantly there were no contested elections in Ludlow between 1852 and 1865. In 1852 the second seat had been easily won by Lord William Powlett, a Peelite Conservative and son of the Duke of Cleveland, whose family owned 25,000 acres in Shropshire. In 1857 he was replaced by Beriah Botfield, who held the second seat until his death in 1863, after

Beriah Botfield MP shown grieving on the monument of his mother (died 1825) at Norton by Daventry, Northamptonshire. Photo: P.M. Bolton

which it passed briefly to a stranger, Sir William Fraser (1863-65), who retired when faced with a contest in 1865. The second seat was easily captured by J.E. Severne of Wallop, who beat the Liberal candidate into third place by 209 votes to 137. After the 1867 Reform Act, the electorate was significantly enlarged, and the constituency lost its second member. Colonel Clive easily retained his seat in the three contests prior to the demise of the constituency in 1885.

THE RESILIENCE OF THE CLIVE INTEREST

Perhaps the most obvious feature of this summary of the parliamentary history of the borough after 1832 is the resilience of the Clive interest. This appears even more remarkable when it is remembered that members of the Herbert and Clive families represented the Southern Division of Shropshire between 1832-1859 and 1865-1876, and that the son of Colonel Clive, the last Ludlow borough member, sat for the Ludlow Division of Shropshire between 1923 and 1945.[11] This does not quite compare at first glance with the record of the Whitmores of Apley Park, who held at least one of the Bridgnorth seats without a break from 1734 to 1870, and the Foresters of Willey who held a seat at Wenlock from 1734 to 1885 with the exception of a few months in 1780 and 1784.[12] Even so, the Herberts and Clives held at least one seat at Ludlow from 1737 to 1839 and from 1847 to 1885. Behind this apparent survival of the territorial interest, several interesting divergences may be observed. While Bridgnorth and Wenlock both boasted continuous Tory representation of both seats after 1832, the split in the Conservative party after 1846 saw the gradual defection of the Peelite member in each constituency to the Liberals. Although on three occasions in the period under examination Ludlow had one Liberal member (1832-1835; 1837-1841; and 1847-1852), and briefly two in 1839-1840, after 1852 the seat became solidly Conservative. It is therefore necessary to examine in some detail a range of factors which may have determined the course of elections during the period. These include the importance of the personalities of individual candidates; the relationship between parliamentary and municipal politics; the influence of national parties and political issues; and the role of electoral corruption.

Names.	Residence.	Profession.	Vis Clive	Romilly	Charlton
Hodges, Richard	Broad street, and Steventon, in the parish of Ludford, Shrops	Gent	1		1
Hodges, George	Felton, in the parish of Bromfield, Shrop	Gent	1		1
Hodges, Richard Christie	Steventon, Shropshire	Gent	1		1
Hodges, John Julius	Corve street	Clerk	1		1
Hodson, Richard	Broad street	Gent	1		1
Hodson, Edward	Broad street	Printer	1		1
Hodson, Edward (the younger)	Broad street	Printer	1		1
Hodson, George	Old street	Chandler	1	1	
Hodson, William	Castle street	Ironmonger	1		1
Harding, Richard Hodson	Whitcliff, in parish of Bromfield, Shrops	Maltster	1		1
Lewis, William Thomas	Corve street	Gent	1		1
Lewis, James George	Knowlbury, in parish of Cainham, Shrop	Gent	1		1
Lewis, Samuel	Ledwich, in parish of Ludford, Shrops	Gent	1		1
Lloyd, John	Broad street	Gent	1		1
Lloyd, William	Mill street	Gent	1		1
Lloyd, Thomas	Broad street	Doctor of Medicine	1		1
Russell, William	Corve street	Gent	1		1
Rocke, Thomas	Corfton, in parish of Diddlebury, Shrop	Clerk	1		1
Salwey, John	Moor, in parish of Richard's Castle, Shr	Esquire	1		1
Salwey, Theophilus Richard	Lodge, in parish of Richard's Castle, Shr	Esquire	1		1
Salwey, Edward	Ditto	Esquire	1		1
Salwey, Theophilus	Ashley Moor, parish of Orleton, Herefordshire	Esquire	1	1	
Salwey, Gilbert	Ditto	Gent	1	1	
Salwey, Erasmus	Ditto	Gent	1	1	
Sandiers, George Urwick	Corve street	Maltster	1		1
Thomas, John	Corve street	Currier	1		1
Urwick, William	Mill street	Gent	1		1
Walcott, Charles	Bitterley, Shropshire	Clerk	1		1
Wellings, Thomas	Bromfield, Shropshire	Clerk	1		1
Wood, John	Castle street	Toyman	1	1	
White, James	Mixen lane	Tailor	1		1
Wellings, George	Broad street	Gent	1		1

Left: Extract from 1835 Poll Book: Freeman votes. Note the unanimous support for Clive.

Opposite Page: Extract from 1835 Poll Book: Note that support is more divided in these householders than among the freemen.

FACTORS IN ELECTORAL BEHAVIOUR
CANDIDATES' PERSONALITIES

The role of the individual candidate in an election is a factor upon which there is disagreement even today, for while it is usually discounted, most general elections will produce a few examples of an apparent 'personality' vote. In the years between the first and second Reform Acts, when party divisions were less pronounced, and party organisations, particularly in relatively backward constituencies like Ludlow, were fairly undeveloped, it is particularly hard to estimate the strength of personality relative to other factors. As a general rule, it would seem that a link to the locality, by family or estate, was normally a prerequisite for electoral success. In the case of the Clives, they had inherited a political interest in the borough which dated back to 1737, although this had not been sufficient to secure the return of R.H. Clive in 1832. Whether this reflects dislike of one Clive is dubious. The result was caused by those voters who split their votes across party lines: no less than 43 voted for Lord Clive and Romilly, while 13 split their support between R.H. Clive and Romilly. One split between R.H. Clive and the second Reformer, Davies. In a sense this may have been "an act of unexampled deceit and treachery" as alleged by Clive, in that the voters concerned had no doubt accepted money from both sides, and had neutralised their vote accordingly. Most voters on both sides had voted on strict party lines, and there were few 'plumpers' or single votes to offset the damaging effect of the split votes.[13] R.H. Clive's failure to be re-elected in 1832 may be interpreted as a personal rejection by a section of the electorate, but there is insufficient evidence to confirm or deny this.

The success of Romilly, whose interests lay in South Wales, shows that it was possible for candidates opposed to the Clives to win a Ludlow seat, even without local connections.

Names.	Residence.	Profession.	Vis Clive	Romilly	Charlton

HOUSEHOLDERS, &c.

Names.	Residence.	Profession.	Vis Clive	Romilly	Charlton
AMIES, THOMAS	Harp lane	Victualler	1	1	
Ashworth, John	Broad street	Hatter		1	
Anderson, George	Broad street	Gent		1	
Ashcroft, Edward	King street	Shoemaker	1	1	
Amies, Samuel	Bull ring	Saddler		1	
Atkins, Robert	Corve street	Stone-mason	1		1
Booty, Rev. William	Dinham	Clerk	1		1
Berrington, Benjamin	Tower street	Mason	1		1
Baxter, James	Mill street	Esquire	1		1
Baines, James	Mill street	Surgeon	1	1	
Barker, Thomas	Broad street	Shoemaker		1	
Boulton, Francis	Broad street	Draper	1		1
Bowen, Thomas	Broad street	Gardener	1		1
Bishop, Benjamin	King street	Grocer		1	
Bradford, Joseph Powell	Bull ring	Brazier	1		1
Bright, Francis	Tower street	Victualler	1	1	
Blayney, James	Lower goalford	Ditto		1	
Bidlake, James	Old gate's fee	Dissenting Minister		1	
Bosworth, Charles	Lower goalford	Dyer		1	
Bennett, Richard	Lower goalford	Turner		1	
Bowen, John	Old street	Painter	1		1
Barnes, Henry	Old street	Shoemaker		1	
Bawcombe, John	Old street	Victualler	1		1
Bishop, John	Bull ring	Hair dresser		1	
Bowen, George	Corve street	Joiner	1		1
Burrows, William	Corve street	Gent	1		
Clark, Luttrell, Lewin	Mill street	Gent	1		
Copner, Henry	Old street & King str	Draper		1	
Cranage, Thomas	Castle street	Shoemaker	1	1	
Clay, John Granby	Dinham	General in Army	1		1
Cox, Richard	Bell lane	Gardener	1		1
Cooper, Joshua	Castle street	Ironmonger	1		1
Coates, William	High street	Grocer		1	
Cooke, John	Lower broad street	Mason	1	1	
Cooke, William	Lower broad street	Shoemaker		1	
Cooke, Edward	Broad street	Victualler	1		
Coleman, Thomas	Broad street	Butcher	1		1
Cooke, James	Bull ring	Cooper		1	
Crundell, John	Tower street	Baker		1	

The victory of Alcock in 1839 might also be cited as an example of this, although it was almost certainly secured by corruption. It is significant that the only other Liberal to represent Ludlow during the period, Colonel Salwey (1837-41; 1846-52), was a member of one of the oldest Whig families in the district, whose credentials dated back to the Civil War. However even he claimed to have been defeated in 1852 by "a combination of family influences such as few men would have the stamina to oppose."[i.e. that of the Clives][14] For the most part the non-Clive Conservatives who represented Ludlow were relatively local men like Beriah Botfield, the Clee Hill coal magnate (1840-46; 1857-63), and James Ackers of Heath House (1841-46), or Shropshire landowners such as Lord William Powlett (1852-57) and J.E. Severne (1865-67), who was related to Sir Charles Rouse Boughton. The only non-Salopian to sit for the Conservatives, Sir William Fraser (1863-65), withdrew after two years as Member rather than fight an election.

The one figure who might well be expected to have possessed a personal following was E.L. Charlton. A skilled self-publicist, Charlton took the credit for unseating Romilly in 1835, though the margin of victory was narrow (five votes) and achieved in the last hour of the poll.[15] An examination of the poll reveals, however, that all but two of Charlton's 159 votes were shared with Lord Clive, and he failed to achieve a single plumper. While no less than 55 voters split their votes between Clive and Romilly, only two voted for Romilly and Charlton. This would suggest that the Reformers had, not surprisingly, failed to forgive Charlton for his desertion from their cause in 1830. It is also clear that the support of the Clives was a most significant factor in Charlton's victory. In 1837, after withdrawing from the contest, Charlton claimed to have given his support to Salwey and Alcock. What this meant in electoral terms may be discovered by a comparison of the poll books for 1835 and 1837. The vast majority of those who had voted for Clive and Charlton in 1835 plumped for Clive in 1837. Similarly all but one of those who had plumped for Romilly in 1835 voted for Salwey and Alcock two years later. A further 29 voters who had split between the parties in 1835 did so again in 1837. There were however seven Ludlow householders who switched completely from Clive and Charlton in 1835 to Salwey and Alcock in 1837, suggesting that they may have been the core of Charlton supporters who had followed their leader's defection. It is less surprising to note that in 1835 five out of six Ludford voters had supported Clive and Charlton, compared with nine out of ten for Salwey and Alcock in 1837. They were nearly all

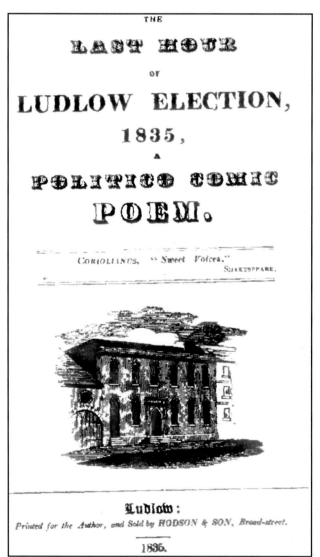

THE

LAST HOUR

OF

LUDLOW ELECTION,

1835,

A

POLITICO COMIC

POEM.

CORIOLANUS, "Sweet Voices."
SHAKESPEARE.

Ludlow:
Printed for the Author, and Sold by HODSON & SON, Broad-street.

1836.

Title page of 1835 election squib published by Charlton.

tenants of Charlton. It may therefore be assumed that if Charlton commanded any personal following after betraying both political groups in the town, it consisted of little more than a handful of voters, half of whom as his tenants possessed little choice in the matter. It is therefore possible to conclude that the personal following of individual candidates had only limited importance in the heyday of party activity before 1850, and considerably less in the years which followed.

THE RELATIONSHIP BETWEEN PARLIAMENTARY AND MUNICIPAL POLITICS

It is hardly surprising that, given the exclusion of the ratepayers from local government before the Municipal Reform Act of 1835, the election of councils under the terms of that Act should have resulted in the overwhelming victory of the supporters of that reform in virtually every borough in the country. Ludlow was no exception to this, and on 1 January 1836 a council of 12 members, all Reformers, took office, and promptly appointed a further four of their colleagues as Aldermen. It is significant to note that this took place at a time when all 12 parliamentary seats in the county had been won by the Conservatives, as the party led by Peel was now officially called. The Reformers maintained their monopoly on Ludlow Borough Council until November 1841, when the Conservatives at last began to make inroads at the polls, capturing all four seats which were up for election.

While it might appear that national and municipal politics were operating in separate spheres, there was one area of considerable overlap. This centred upon the matter of the municipal charities, a cause dear to the heart of E.L. Charlton. Charlton's conversion from an advocate of the reform of municipal corporations to a bitter opponent had become complete by 1835. His implacable opposition to the Reformist council which took office in 1836 may, as frequently alleged, have been due to the Council's failure to honour its predecessor's agreement to pay Charlton £500 compensation for road-widening work at the Charlton Arms.[16] Charlton crossed swords violently with the council on the issue of municipal charities, which, in common with those of most unreformed boroughs, had been used to augment borough revenue rather than to carry out their original charitable role. In 1841 a compromise was tentatively agreed between the Charity Trustees and the council which would have increased the money received by the charities, but this was challenged in court by Charlton and his co-petitioner Revd Arthur Willis, headmaster of the Grammar School. This began the so-called 'Great Lawsuit' which ultimately led to the council selling all the corporation lands in order to defray the costs of the action. This deprived the town of a major financial asset, and may well have contributed to the fall of the Reformist council in 1843, and the ensuing ten years of Conservative rule.[17]

Thus the major change in municipal politics in Ludlow in the 1840s would appear to have been caused by a combination of purely local factors and a national swing to the right following the 1841 General Election, when the Conservatives captured all 12 Shropshire seats and formed a majority government under Sir Robert Peel. When the Reformers or Liberals regained control in 1853, the result was a low-key affair which did not merit a report in either of the county's two Shrewsbury-based newspapers. In marked contrast to the fierce spirit of party which had existed until the mid-1840s, it became the custom for the candidate for mayor to be proposed by a leading member of the opposition group.[18] It has already been noted that the year 1852 marked the start of a period of uncontested parliamentary elections which lasted until 1865, and it would appear that during this period Ludlow had developed a system of Conservative domination of the parliamentary sphere, combined with an element of power-sharing at local level.

The Impact of National Issues

It is difficult to estimate the effect of the great national political issues upon the behaviour of voters in a constituency as remote from the centre of government as Ludlow. Once a measure of Reform had been achieved in 1832, many of its middle-class advocates lost their enthusiasm for a further extension of the electoral franchise, and the issue appears to have largely disappeared from the political menu in Ludlow. Certainly Ludlow's largely agriculturally-based economy, initially dominated by malting, did not contain an industrial proletariat like the textile workers who made the market towns of Montgomeryshire a hotbed of Chartism. Similarly anti-Catholicism, which was virulent in many towns in the early Victorian period, was relatively restrained in Ludlow.[19] There was no Irish immigrant population, and for centuries Protestant and Catholic landowners had lived together in harmony. From the mid-1840s Conservative candidates made routine commitments to support the Irish Church against the threat of disestablishment, and to oppose government funding for the Roman Catholic seminary at Maynooth.[20] Disquiet about Catholicism or crypto-Catholicism was not the prerogative of any one party, and at the same meeting Colonel Salwey, many of whose supporters were protestant nonconformists, expressed disquiet at the state of the Church at Oxford, then experiencing the first flush of Tractarianism.[21]

The issue which could have been expected to raise most interest in the Ludlow area was the repeal or retention of the Corn Laws. These had originally been passed by the government after the Napoleonic Wars, as a means of protecting British farmers by banning the importation of foreign grain. Although the adverse effects on the poor in times of dearth had been considerably mitigated by Huskisson's modifications to the Acts in the 1820s, political opinion polarised over the issue of repealing the Corn Laws completely. The Conservatives, whose power-base was largely rural, were committed to the Corn Laws, while their opponents embraced repeal and free trade as basic articles of faith. The Irish Potato Famine of 1845 strained Peel's commitment to the Corn Laws, which he eventually repealed in 1846, a second act of 'treachery' for which his party never forgave him.[22] This action split the Conservatives, who failed to gain a parliamentary majority again until 1874.

As an area of mixed rather than arable farming, the Ludlow district was less directly affected by the Corn question. Agricultural Protection Societies were established in Shrewsbury, Bridgnorth and elsewhere, but not apparently in Ludlow. In February 1846 the two Clives, who represented the Southern Division of the county, were given a somewhat rough ride by the Shrewsbury Association, which suspected that they intended to support repeal. In the event, they split, as did the borough members. Botfield supported repeal, while Ackers opposed it. Significantly, in the ensuing election in 1847 Botfield was rejected by the voters, while a new protectionist Tory candidate, Henry Bailey Clive was elected. Ackers did not stand, and for five years the seat was shared with the Liberal, Colonel Salwey. Free trade continued to be a basic article of Liberal faith for many years, but the issue lost most of its fire during the 1850s. Indeed in 1852 Lord William Powlett claimed to be as much a free trader as Salwey and was still returned as a Conservative member. The period of unopposed Conservative representation after 1852 brought an end to much of the public debate over these issues. In 1865 the three candidates stressed their moderation, differing only on details. Thus Severne (Conservative) expressed support for reforms which were "essential to the progressive spirit of the age", while Yardley (Liberal) credited his party's rule with preserving the Indian Empire, and rebuked his supporters when they hissed Severne, remarking that they were there "to argue rather than to clamour".[23] Clearly Ludlow elections in 1865 were very different from those of the 1830s.

ELECTORAL CORRUPTION

It is ironic that one of the main aims of the Parliamentary Reform Act of 1832 was a reduction in the expense of elections. In practice, as has already been noted, the reverse was achieved and it is significant that Dickens' famous portrayal of the corrupt election at Eatanswill dates from 1836, and depicts a post-Reform contest.[24] The 1839 by-election brought the world of Eatanswill to Ludlow, although in many ways it represented a more flagrant instance of what had rapidly become normal practice. Electoral corruption was the direct consequence of the system whereby votes were cast in public, and afterwards published for all

Bribery Row, Bell Lane. The extension of the vote to householders in 1832 gave the owners of tenanted properties, such as these early Victorian houses, control over a number of votes.
The commercial value of such influence was soon exploited by property auctioneers.

to see. The secret ballot was regarded as 'un-English', and not introduced until 1872, at a stroke almost ending electoral corruption.[25] Corruption took a number of forms, the simplest of which was straightforward bribery – the making of a cash payment for a vote. The erection of houses to be let to political supporters was a more expensive long-term investment. Local tradition asserts that the row of early-Victorian houses in Bell Lane known as 'Bribery Row' were built specifically to be let to Whig voters in the immediate post-Reform years. A similar tradition alleges that Cliff Villas in Ludford were built by E.L. Charlton to create householder votes favourable to his interest. Very prevalent, but less effective was the treating of electors (and often non-electors), who expected to be plied generously with free food and drink during a contest. A third form taken by corruption was the intimidation of voters. This could be achieved by the use or threat of violence from bands of hired thugs, or in more subtle ways, such as the eviction of tenants from their houses, employees from their work, or the removal of contracts from tradesmen. These elements were commonplace, although the pre-1832 situation had given Ludlow voters relatively few opportunities to experience them. The 1839 by-election is of interest by virtue of its detailed documentation in the Report of the Select Committee of the Commons appointed to investigate the question, and because of the involvement of the national party agents in the process.

Simple bribery was no doubt widespread, but the enquiry concentrated on a few test examples. The main instance was that of Samuel Cook, who had been paid £30 by the landlord of the Compasses on behalf of the Liberal agent, James Coppock. The evidence that Cook received three £10 notes was sufficient ultimately to convince Alcock and his legal team to abandon his seat in Parliament, but not before launching a counter petition against Clive. While £30 was quite a high price to pay for a vote, some electors seem to have been offered considerably more. John Wade, the proprietor of the Paper Mills in Ludford, allegedly refused an offer of £250 to vote for Clive, though the witness who made the allegation was unreliable.[26] The same witness also reported a conversation at the Feathers with John Williams, the former Town Clerk, where it had been agreed that £75 would be a reasonable price for a vote, although another witness claimed that he had been unable to obtain an offer of more than £50 to vote for Clive. It was clear that both sides had paid bribes, and for that reason Clive was also found guilty, and therefore unable to take the seat to which he would otherwise have been entitled after the withdrawal of Alcock.

Treating was also widely established, and a time-honoured practice. By 1839, however, pretexts had been adopted to avoid possible prosecutions for corruption by the forming of 'committees' at various public houses in the interests of the respective candidates. The 'members' of these committees were entitled to free drink and refreshment. Alcock's general committee met at the Rose and Crown every day except Sundays for a fortnight before the election under the secretaryship of Rodney Anderson, a leading solicitor and Reformer. Here supporters were treated, and on the morning of the election regaled with a breakfast for a hundred. This exercise in voter entertainment brought the landlord, Thomas Amies, the doubtless welcome sum of £140. Similar treating in Alcock's interest took place at the Compasses, where the landlord received £124: 10 shillings for his services. Under examination by the Parliamentary Select Committee, Anderson produced a sheaf of bills from a further 14 public houses who claimed to have entertained voters in Alcock's interest The adjacent Castle Street houses, the George and the Sun, were the chief meeting places for Clive's supporters, who no doubt had as wide a range of other places of refreshment as their opponents.

Intimidation was a feature of electioneering which became, if anything, more widespread after Reform, with gangs of thugs being used to threaten or even abduct voters.[27] In 1839 the Clives employed a pugilist by the name of Tom Brown, together with some 60 'bludgeon men' to overawe opponents. Whether Brown had orders to kidnap Alcock's supporters is not known, but the threat was used to persuade a group of 60 doubtful voters to stay overnight at the Compasses before the poll to avoid being kidnapped or thrashed by Brown and his men.[28]

IN THE BOROUGH OF LUDLOW.

Particulars and Conditions of Sale
OF
VALUABLE FREEHOLD HOUSES
AND LANDS,
ALL OF THEM WITHIN THE
BOROUGH TOWN OF LUDLOW
With the capability of
SECURING SIXTEEN VOTES;
ALSO,
KNOWBURY FARM,
CONSISTING OF
138 ACRES,
ABOUT FOUR MILES FROM LUDLOW.

The First Portion of this Property claims especial attention from its manifest and highly
Important Political Influence,
As it cannot be doubted that it will
SECURE BOTH SEATS IN PERPETUITY;
As it regards the Freehold Farm,
COAL HAS ALREADY BEEN DISCOVERED;
AND, LASTLY,
THE VERY ADVANTAGEOUS MORTGAGE OF
TWENTY THOUSAND POUNDS;
Which will be Sold by Auction
BY
Mr. GEO. ROBINS
AT THE GOLDEN LION INN, LUDLOW,
On MONDAY, the 26th day of APRIL, 1841,
AT ONE FOR TWO O'CLOCK EXACTLY, IN TWO LOTS.

Particulars may be had, Three Weeks before the Sale, of W. Downes, Esq., Town Clerk, Ludlow; at the Golden Lion Inn, Ludlow; also the Hop Pole, Worcester; of Messrs. Parke and Freeth, Solicitors, Lincoln's Inn Fields; the Auction Mart; and at Mr. GEO. ROBINS' Offices, Covent Garden.
(WHITING, LONDON.)

Property sale notice (1841). The value of the political interest was clearly rated more important than the discovery of coal on the Knowbury property.

Ironically, as the landlord was instructed that on no account were any of these men to be let out, it was as much an instance of 'cooping' as that from which they had been supposedly delivered.

PARTY ORGANISATION AND INVOLVEMENT

A feature of the 1839 contest which marked it out from previous elections was the extent of the involvement of party organisations. Possibly as a result of its tradition of uncontested elections prior to 1832, Ludlow did not have a developed system of political clubs such as were to be found in towns like Colchester, or political quasi-benevolent societies such as those in Lewes or Bristol.[29] Revis claimed to have established a Conservative Institution in Ludlow in 1836, but little is known of it.[30] Certainly, in 1839 the Conservative campaign received assistance from the party in Shrewsbury, in the form of the architect Edward Haycock together with John Frail, the barber who virtually ran Shrewsbury Conservatism for several decades, and was in charge of the 'dirty work' in Ludlow.[31] In addition, the Clive campaign received the semi-professional assistance of William Holmes, a former member of one of the Shropshire county seats who had risen in the national party hierarchy. Alcock employed an experienced professional election agent, James Coppock, who had managed a number of campaigns for rising Liberal candidates, including William Cobden. Alcock had been dissatisfied with the efforts of a local attorney, William Downes, as his agent, preferring to put his trust in a professional, although he later claimed that Coppock had been sent from the Reform Association in London against his own wishes.[32]

The election of 1839 could have had disastrous consequences both for the borough and for Coppock, had not a considerable amount of legerdemain been employed. Although electoral corruption had in many ways increased rather than lessened after the Reform Act, there was nevertheless a mood among many members of Parliament that boroughs where malpractice had been proved should lose their right to representation. This was to be the fate of St Albans and Sudbury, and was nearly that of Ludlow. As Clive had not been awarded the seat vacated by Alcock by reason of his own use of bribery, it was necessary for a writ to be moved for a new election. The Liberals wished to consider the Ludlow case in tandem with that of Cambridge, where the sitting member had also been disqualified for gross corruption. Lord John Russell, a leading member of the government, particularly wished to speak on the matter, but was absent from Parliament following the murder of his uncle. The Tories took advantage of his absence, and his supporters' uncertainty about how to proceed successfully to move a writ for a new election at Ludlow. Thus the borough was able to retain its members. The narrow escape was, however, fully appreciated.

For Coppock, the election could have ended his career, as an action was brought against him under the Bribery Act for having authorised the payment of £30 to Samuel Cook. Coppock rapidly brought his own successful, and probably collusive, action against Cook in order to claim immunity from action against himself

An engraving of The Feathers in the mid 1850s, taken from a photograph by Henry Peach Robinson. The gallery had been added a few years previously for electioneering purposes.

on the grounds that he had within twelve months of the alleged offence successfully prosecuted another for bribery.[33] Although this defence was rejected, Coppock was acquitted by a Shrewsbury jury in August 1840. Two other cases arising out of the same contest (Hall v. Coleman; Sharpe v. Tilley) also produced verdicts in favour of the defendants, illustrating the reluctance of juries to convict in bribery cases.[34] In future Coppock conducted his electoral business with much more discretion.

The lesson of 1839 was not lost on the politicians of Ludlow, and the borough rapidly moved from the world of Eatanswill to that of comparative electoral rectitude. It is significant that the 1840 by-election which followed the events discussed above which "had excited interest and anxiety throughout the country, seemed of very secondary importance to the inhabitants of the borough" until the actual morning of the nomination.[35] The Conservative Salopian Journal commented that there was no treating, no bribery, and no drunkenness, and that there had been no need to call upon Brown and his 12 colleagues, who had been kept in readiness at Bromfield. The Shrewsbury Chronicle noted that the nomination was attended by a number of elegant ladies, whose presence was to become a feature of future nomination meetings. In the General Election of 1841 the Conservatives engaged most of the musicians in the town to form bands, while groups of supporters paraded through the town under the respective banners of the Conservatives (crimson, green and white) and Reformers or Liberals (yellow and blue). While there was a skirmish outside the Golden Lion, the proceedings passed off peacefully.[36] The general carnival atmosphere tended to be repeated at most subsequent contests.

Soliciting votes without the aid of bribes and beer meant that candidates had to interview electors individually, and endeavour to win their support by persuasion and argument. One of the best descriptions of electioneering under the new conditions comes from the pen of an American visitor to Ludlow in 1852. Anna Maria Fay, perhaps oddly for one brought up in the democratic citadel of Boston, commented that it was "not so pleasant" for Robert Clive to have to solicit the votes of a neighbour's servants, and expressed her mortification at the "elegant gentleman" Lord William Powlett "asking the vote and hearing the reproaches of a vulgar Radical."[37]

The events of 1839 were never to be repeated, and candidates frequently repudiated corruption in their speeches.[38] The extent to which party organisation developed in the succeeding years is hard to determine, as the conduct of elections became increasingly decorous, and the two county newspapers contain little information relevant to party activities in a borough which was on the fringes of their readership. It may with confidence be suggested that outside interest on the scale shown in 1839 was not exercised again during the period under consideration.

CONCLUSION

The intention of this chapter was to examine the factors which influenced Ludlow parliamentary politics in the period between the first two Reform Acts, and in effect to test the truth of the assertion quoted at the start of the chapter. It is clear that different factors operated at different times, and that some which have received the greatest attention, namely electoral corruption, may be regarded as the exception rather than the rule. Yet despite the inter-action of a variety of influences, one continuing thread which cannot be ignored is the persistence of the influence of the Clive family which lasted virtually unabated until the borough lost its separate representation in 1885. The "long-cherished family associations"[39] with the borough were undoubtedly a significant factor in determining the nature of parliamentary representation in Ludlow, but it is likely that they coincided to a considerable extent with the naturally conservative inclinations of a majority of the electorate.

ENDNOTES

1 Comment by John Williams, landlord of the Golden Lion, Minutes of Evidence taken before the Select Committee on the Ludlow Election Petitions, 1840.

2 2 Will. IV, c. 45, quoted in Costin, W.C. and Watson, J.S., *The Law and Working of the Constitution*, Vol. II, 1784-1914, (1964), p.55.

3 Namier, op.cit., pp.242-245.

4 This tureen was offered for sale at Sotheby's in 1983, and was purchased for Ludlow Museum by the Friends of Ludlow Museum and the Ludlow Civic Society. After some months on display, it was stolen and never recovered.

5 Weyman, H.T., The Members of Parliament for Ludlow, Transactions of the Shropshire Archaeological Society, 2nd Series, Vol. VII, (1895) pp.48-9.

6 List of the Poll for the Borough of Ludlow…1832.

7 List of the Poll for the Borough of Ludlow…1840.

8 A full account of Charlton's exploits in Parliament may be found in Speight, M.E., "The chequered political career of E.L. Charlton, M.P"., Ludlow Heritage News, No. 31, (1999).

9 The truth of this allegation is confirmed by a recital in a deed of the Charlton Arms, Ludford of 1851, which quotes a mortgage of £14,500 from Lord Abinger and J.W. Farrer transferred to Thomas Alcock on 23 May 1838. (SA 5411/19/1).

10 *Salopian Journal*, 17 November 1841.

11 Namier, op.cit., p.245.

12 Ibid., p.243.

13 Two for Lord Clive, three for Romilly and one for Davies. List of the Poll for the Borough of Ludlow, 1832.

14 *Salopian Journal*, 9 July 1852.

15 Hence the title of his celebratory squib, The Last Hour of Ludlow Election 1835: a Politico Comic Poem, (1835).

16 There may have been some truth in this allegation, as the money was not paid.

17 See Lloyd, D.J., *Country Grammar School*, (1977) Chapter VI for a detailed account of the lawsuit. The same author's *Concise History of Ludlow*, (1999), pp.133-4, gives a lucid summary.

18 SA/DA3/100/2, Ludlow Borough Council Minutes.

19 Colchester, with a long tradition of Protestantism, was particularly receptive to Anti-Catholic sentiments at this time. Speight, M.E., *Politics in the Borough of Colchester, 1812-1847*, unpublished London Ph.D. thesis, 1969.

20 First made by Peel in 1845, to encourage the training of Catholic ordinands in Ireland rather than in Europe, where they might pick up revolutionary ideas. Many of his party were unconvinced, but Lord Clive supported the grant for the foregoing reasons. *Salopian Journal*, 9 July 1852.

21 Ibid.

22 The first was the granting of Catholic Emancipation in 1829, also against his own beliefs.

23 *Salopian Journal*, 7 July 1865.

24 Dickens, C., *Pickwick Papers*, (1836), Chapter XIII.

25 It should be remembered that it took over another century for Trades Unions reluctantly to accept the secret ballot. Their objections were similar to those of early nineteenth century Tories.

26 John Brook Revis, a polemical journalist, had worked for the Conservatives, but subsequently deserted them. *Shrewsbury Chronicle*, 8 April 1840.

27 Gash, N., *Politics in the Age of Peel*, (1953), p.144.

28 Minutes of Evidence taken before the Select Committee on the Ludlow Election Petition, (1840), pp.41-43.

29 Speight, op. cit., Chapter VII; Gash, op.cit., p.128.

30 Minutes of Evidence taken before the Select Committee on the Ludlow Election Petition, (1840), p.112.

31 Ibid., p.128.

32 *Salopian Journal*, 27 May 1840.

33 Gash, op. cit., p.425.

34 *Salopian Journal*, 12 August 1840.

35 *Shrewsbury Chronicle*, 22 May 1840.

36 *Salopian Journal*, 7 July 1841.

37 Fay, A. M., *Victorian Days in England*, (2002), pp.230-234.

38 "I challenge any man here to say that any tradesman has been threatened with loss of custom, or that any labourer has been threatened with loss of work on my behalf." Sir William Yardley, (Liberal), *Salopian Journal*, 14 July 1865.

39 Speech of Col. Clive, ibid.

CHAPTER 6

THE PROVISION OF LOCAL GOVERNMENT SERVICES IN LUDLOW, 1830 ~ 1880

MARTIN SPEIGHT

Lower Mill Street c.1880. River water was pumped from here to supply houses with non-drinking water until the inauguration of the new supply.

MUNICIPAL REFORM

On 1 January 1836 a Borough Council of twelve elected members took office in Ludlow, and proceeded to choose four further individuals to serve as Aldermen. This brought to an end a system of town government by the self-perpetuating groups of the Twelve and Twenty five, which dated back to the mid-13th century, and which had been ended by the Municipal Corporations Act of 1835. The 1835 Act was a logical conclusion to the process which had begun with the Parliamentary Reform Act of 1832. With the worst of the rotten and pocket boroughs removed, and the franchise extended to urban rate paying householders of properties worth £10 per year, the anomaly which excluded those same ratepayers from electing the corporations which governed the boroughs and cities was in urgent need of correction. The Poor Law Amendment Act passed in 1834 had already made the Guardians of the new Poor Law Unions subject to election by the ratepayers, and a Commission was duly set up to investigate the state of urban government as a prelude to legislation. While it is clear that many of the old Corporations had been at best inefficient, and at worst downright venal, many of the commissioners conducted their inquiries with a lack of objectivity reminiscent of Thomas Cromwell's commission of inquiry into the state of the monasteries some three centuries previously.

The results of the Municipal Corporations Act in Ludlow followed a pattern which was common to many towns. As the old Corporation had been identified with the Tory cause, the first council elections in December produced a council composed entirely of Radicals, who held power until 1847. In that year, when the novelty of Radical rule had worn off, the Conservatives gained power and held it for six years. After 1853 there was less violent change and a decline in extreme partisanship. The initial period of Radical control had been dominated by the vexed question of the Ludlow charities. The alleged misuse of charities was a wrong which 19th century reformers across the country were determined to right, though the effects of their actions were not always beneficial. In Ludlow the story had an unusual twist, for the Radical council became the defenders of a compromise settlement of the borough charities which was to the benefit of the Council, while the challenge was mounted by an unlikely partnership between Edmund Lechmere Charlton, the town's maverick Tory M.P. between 1835 and 1837, and the idealistic schoolmaster, Arthur Willis. The story of the Great Law Suit, which ultimately led to the sale of the properties which the town had inherited from the Palmers' Guild in order to pay the Council's legal expenses, has been well chronicled by David Lloyd, and needs no further elaboration here.[1]

The present chapter is not, however, concerned with the political aspects of Ludlow's municipal history in this period, but with the provision of public services. The main purpose is to attempt to discover whether the various changes in local government machinery which were enacted by successive governments actually brought about any significant changes in the services provided by the local authorities, and in the manner in which they were delivered.

Except in one particular area, namely policing, the 1835 Municipal Corporations Act had been concerned with the organisation of borough councils rather than with the services which they provided. Apart from the exclusiveness of their membership, the main accusations most frequently directed against the unreformed corporations concerned their alleged financial incompetence (or corruption), and their inefficiency. Ludlow was largely innocent on the first of these counts, having in 1828 commissioned a professional investigation into the chaotic state of the borough finances, the recommendations of which they had subsequently put into practice.[2] By the time the 1835 Act came into force, Ludlow would have been found to be solvent and reasonably well served by its financial procedures.

With regard to the performance of services, the position was more complicated. In theory the activities of the Corporations had been laid down by their charters, and this was often used as a convenient excuse for doing no more than what was strictly required. Ludlow Corporation's responsibilities had been fairly extensive and included the standard duties of maintaining law and order; the administration of justice in the borough courts; the provision of a gaol; the management of markets, fairs and tolls; the overseeing of the municipal charities, which included the Grammar School and the Almshouse; and the task of administering the large corporation estates, particularly those which had been inherited from the Palmers' Guild. In addition to these obligations, Ludlow Corporation had acquired a variety of other duties and responsibilities over the centuries. These included the provision of water from the engine and waterworks at the bottom of Mill Street; maintaining the streets and bridges; and appointing the assistant clergy in the parish church.

BACKGROUND TO IMPROVEMENT

In order to set the activities of the post-1835 Corporation into context, it is necessary to look back to the final years of the 18th century. The fact that the Corporation had for some time exercised responsibilities with regard to the maintenance of streets and bridges, and the provision of a public water supply, is interesting in view of developments at the end of the 18th century. At this period a standard response to the inactivity of borough corporations in such matters had been the establishment by Private Acts of Parliament of bodies of commissioners to carry out specific tasks which were not being provided by the borough authorities. These sprang up in towns all over England, and in 1793 Ludlow procured its own Act for 'paving the footpaths within the Borough of Ludlow ...and for lighting, watching and otherwise improving the same'. The purpose of this action would seem to have been to confer upon the Corporation additional powers to enable it to extend its activities in this area. Certainly all members of the Corporation were appointed Commissioners, together with an additional 20 members drawn from prominent residents and Anglican clergy.[3] In December 1794 the first paving stones were laid in Castle Street, in the presence of the High Bailiff and other civic dignitaries.

The precise nature of the operations and responsibilities of the Improvement Commissioners is not always clear, due to the absence of their minute books,[4] though surviving records throw some light upon their activities. These documents are largely concerned with leases of Commissioners' property, and also cases for the opinion of counsel in instances upon which the Commissioners were contemplating legal action.[5] In addition to paving the streets, the Commissioners sought to remove obstruction to the free flow of pedestrian and vehicular traffic. Fortunately for the character of the town, this was not prosecuted with the zeal employed by many of their fellows elsewhere, as in Hereford where most of the ancient lanes formed by medieval colonisation of the market place were swept away, or Shrewsbury where projecting front steps were removed from whole streets of houses. By comparison, the Ludlow Commissioners' actions were very modest. Projecting corners were modified in King Street, where the medieval corner post of 'the Corner Shop' was replaced by cast iron columns set back within the shop, and the ancient oak posts which supported the butterwalk at the top of Broad Street were similarly renewed in cast iron in 1795. The Commissioners were also concerned to control the erection of bow windows which projected into or over the footway, though it proved easier to regulate the practice by requiring the granting of prior permission than it did to enforce removal of structures which had already been erected. Counsel's opinion, sought in 1823 in a test case involving premises at the head of Broad Street, advised the Commissioners had no power to enforce the removal of projections above ground level, other than water spouts which discharged onto the highway. The authorities seemingly heeded this advice.

There would seem to have been a considerable overlap in the functions of the Commissioners and the Corporation, which was no doubt aided by fact that 37 of the 57 Commissioners were also members of the latter body. This blurring of distinctions between the responsibilities of public bodies in the town is observable throughout the period under examination. It is particularly evident in the whole question of the maintenance and improvement of the streets. Although the flagging of the pavements in Castle Street in 1794 was greeted with enthusiasm, the Corporation had involved itself with paving since at least the 16th century.[6] The main difference would appear to be that the project begun in 1794 was systematic rather than piecemeal. It is, however, significant that the major street improvement of the early 19th century, to Broad Street, was inaugurated and financed by the Corporation, who in 1829 engaged the elderly Thomas Telford to draw up a scheme for regrading the approach to the town above and below the Broad Gate.[7] Similarly it was the Corporation who in 1794 had engaged

Telford to improve the approaches to Dinham Bridge, and who in 1823 employed John Straphen of Shrewsbury to rebuild the old bridge, with the exception of Telford's work. It was also the Corporation who drew up plans, mercifully unexecuted, for replacing Ludford Bridge and totally reconstructing the southerly approach to the town.[8]

While the unreformed Corporation of Ludlow undoubtedly had shortcomings, its actions in the years prior to its reform show that it pursued an active policy of urban improvement, the origins of which may be traced back to the replacement of most of its public buildings in the previous century to the designs of eminent local architects. Reform made little significant difference to the responsibilities of the Council, except in one major respect. Under the terms of the 1835 Act, the Council was required to appoint a police force on the London model, which was to be administered by a Watch Committee. Unfortunately little is known of the operation of this body, as the minutes of the Watch Committee, in common with those of all other committees of the reformed Council, have not survived. As meetings of the full Council increasingly confirmed business done in committee without giving details, it is impossible to discover whether Ludlow suffered the teething problems encountered by other authorities when establishing their borough forces.

IMPROVEMENT AFTER 1835

As mentioned above, the early years of the new Council were dominated by the case of The Attorney General v. the Corporation of Ludlow, and for some years after 1846 it was considerably occupied by disposing of its properties under the terms of the Local Act of that year[9] in order to recoup the costs of this so-called Great Law Suit. It is ironic that the origins of this action can be blamed indirectly upon street improvements, for it is believed that the annoyance felt by the litigious E.L. Charlton at the reformed Council's failure to honour its predecessor's award of £500 in recompense to him for demolition of part of the Charlton Arms in widening Ludford Bridge led Charlton to take up the cudgels on behalf of Willis, the Grammar School headmaster. This preoccupation with the charity suit, and the enormous costs incurred, meant that the Council had little time for taking the initiative in public improvements in the town during the first two decades of its life. The Improvement Commissioners also seem to have taken a much less active role during this period, concentrating their efforts on their primary business of maintaining the paving of the streets.

However, one major development during this early period, which would now be termed a joint public/private initiative, was the lighting of the town by gas. A gas works had been established on Corporation land in Gravel Hill some time after 1823 by three partners from Wellington, William Edwards, Ann Buffery and John Lockitt. The Gas Company then appeared to have reached an agreement with the Commissioners to supply the town with gas lighting, with the Commissioners paying for the gas which was consumed. The initial experience of gas lighting was favourable, and by 1832 the Commissioners were canvassing for public subscriptions towards extending the scheme. This involved almost doubling the number of lamps from 37 to 70, which would be lit for eight months of the year, with the exception of five days around each full moon.[10] The estimated cost of the additional lamps was £100. To add to the confusion, the Corporation had also begun to provide gas lamps in parts of the town not yet covered by the scheme.[11] The early fortunes of the Gas Company were clearly mixed. As early as 1830, Edwards and his partners had requested an exchange of lands with the Corporation, having evidently found that erecting their premises in Gravel Hill was a mistake. By 1840 they had pulled out of Ludlow, for in that year the Commissioners entered into an agreement with William Richardson of Dudley for supplying the town with gas lighting.[12] This 'new' gas company had established its works on the banks of the river Teme, and had also contracted with the Council to light the Butter Cross clock.[13] In 1847 Edwards and his partners were given formal notice to quit their premises in Gravel Hill, although it was nearly two years before the affair was finally settled. The old gas works subsequently became an iron foundry.[14] The supply of gas for street lighting was to be a running cause of contention between the municipal authorities and the gas company, but with the latter possessing a monopoly it generally emerged victorious from these disagreements.

During the 1850s the Council began once more to adopt a more proactive approach towards the improvement of the town. The central government, partly as a reaction to the scourge of cholera, had begun to pass a series of measures to enable communities to carry out

Above: The forlorn remains of Ludlow's first gas works in Gravel Hill, photographed shortly before demolition in 2004. The building would originally have contained apparatus similar to that shown in the early 19th century engraving (below).

SUBSCRIPTIONS
In Aid of the Funds for Paving and Lighting the TOWN OF LUDLOW.

	£	s.	d.		£	s.	d.		£	s.	d.
The Corporation	50	0	0	T. A. Knight Esq.	5	0	0	J. H. Holder, Esq.	3	0	0
Earl of Powis	10	0	0	Sir W. R. Boughton Bart.	5	0	0	Mr J. G. Lewis	5	0	0
Viscount Clive	10	0	0	Thomas Botfield Esq.	5	0	0	The Gas Company	5	0	0
The Hon. R. H. Clive	10	0	0	Rev. S. Johnes Knight	5	0	0	Rev. Thomas Wellings	1	0	0

CASTLE-STREET WARD.

	£	s.	d.		£	s.	d.		£	s.	d.
Amies, Mr.	0	10	0	Hammond, Mr.	0	5	0	Nichols, Mr. William	0	5	0
Anderson, Mr. C.	0	5	0	Hinde, Rev. J.	1	0	0	Pritchett, G. Esq.	1	0	0
Baines, Mr.	1	0	0	Hodson, Mr. R.	3	0	0	Pugh, Mr. George	1	0	0
Baugh, Mrs. Lucy	1	0	0	Jones, Mr. Isaac	1	0	0	Russell, Mr. William	1	0	0
Baugh, Edward, Esq.	1	0	0	Leake, Mr. John	1	0	0	Salwey, Mr. H.	0	10	0
Baugh, The Rev. R.	1	0	0	Lewis, Dr	2	0	0	Sawyer, Mr.	0	10	0
Baxter, James, Esq	1	0	0	Lloyd, Mr. William	1	0	0	Stephens, Mr. J.	0	5	0
Booty, The Rev. William	0	10	0	M'Ghie, Miss	1	0	0	Syer, Lady	0	10	0
Burlton, Miss.	0	10	0	Matthews, Mrs.	0	5	0	White, Mr. Thomas	1	0	0
Clay, General	1	0	0	Meyricke, The Rev. Robert	2	0	0	Williams, Mr. John	1	0	0
Graham, Mrs.	0	10	0	Moythan, Mr.	0	10	0	Williams, Mr. Thomas	0	1	0

BROAD-STREET WARD.

	£	s.	d.		£	s.	d.		£	s.	d.
Anderson, Mr.	1	0	0	Green, Mrs.	0	10	0	Needham, Mr.	0	5	0
Baker, Mrs.	0	10	0	Harpers, Messrs.	1	0	0	Procter and Jones, Messrs.	1	0	0
Biddulph, —— Esq.	1	0	0	Hodges, R. Esq.	1	0	0	Rea, Mr.	1	0	0
Boulton, Mr	0	10	0	Hodson, Mr. E.	1	0	0	Rocke, Eyton, & Co. Messrs.	5	5	0
Britton, Mr. George	0	10	0	Hutchings, J. Esq.	5	0	0	Russell —— Esq.	1	0	0
Browne, Mrs. William	0	10	0	Jennings, Mr.	0	10	0	Russel, Mr. R.	1	0	0
Clarke, Mr.	1	0	0	Lloyd, Mr. H	2	0	0	Sankey, Mr.	1	0	0
Coleman, Mr. Thomas	0	10	0	Lloyd, Dr.	2	0	0	Smith, Miss	1	0	0
Cranage, Mr.	0	10	0	Lloyd, Mr. John	1	0	0	Thorpe, Mrs.	0	10	0
Ellis, Mr.	0	10	0	Marston, Mr. R.	1	0	0	Valentine, Mr.	1	0	0
Evans, Mr. William	0	10	0	Meymott, Mr.	1	0	0	Vashon, Mrs.	2	0	0
Garrett, Mr	1	0	0	Morris, Mr.	1	0	0	Whatmore, Mr.	0	10	0
				Mosely, Mrs.	0	10	0				

OLD-STREET WARD.

	£	s.	d.		£	s.	d.		£	s.	d.
Amies, Mr. S.	0	2	6	Gardner, Mr.	1	0	0	Oliver, Mr.	0	2	6
Ashcroft, Mr.	0	2	6	Griffiths, Mr. Thomas	0	10	0	Pearse, Mr.	0	2	6
Bishops, Messrs.	0	5	0	Griffiths, Mr. B.	0	5	0	Penny, Mr.	0	5	0
Blayney, Mr.	0	2	6	Griffiths, Mr.	0	2	6	Pillinger, Mr.	0	2	6
Bottomley, Mrs.	0	1	0	Grosvenor, Mr.	0	2	6	Potts, Mrs.	0	5	0
Bradford, Mr.	0	5	0	Hammond, Mr. P.	0	2	6	Rogers, Mr. William	0	3	6
Cantrell, Mr.	0	5	0	Hand, Mrs.	0	2	6	Sheppard, Mr.	0	5	0
Clarke, Mr.	0	2	6	Harding, Mr. William	1	0	0	Smith, Mr. H.	1	0	0
Crosse, Mr.	0	4	0	Hitchcock, Mr.	0	2	6	Smith, Mr. John, King's-street.	0	10	0
Davenport, Mr	0	10	0	Hockey, Mr.	0	2	6	Smith, Mr. Sen.	0	2	6
Davies, Mr.	0	2	0	Hodson, Mr. Thomas	0	10	0	Stedman, Mr.	0	2	6
Dyer, Mrs.	1	0	0	Hooper, Mr	0	5	0	Tinson, Mr.	0	5	0
Edwards, Mr. William	0	10	0	Hotchkiss, Mr.	0	10	0	Watkins, Mr. Alexander	0	2	6
Egginton, Mr.	0	5	0	Jennings, Mr John	0	5	0	Wayne, Mr.	0	5	0
Esp, Mr.	0	2	0	Jones, Mr. James	1	0	0	Whittal, Mr.	0	10	0
Evans, Mr. R.	1	0	0	Morris, Mr.	0	1	0	Williams, Mr.	0	5	0
				Nash, Mr.	0	2	6				

CORVE-STREET WARD.

	£	s.	d.		£	s.	d.		£	s.	d.
Acton, S. Esq.	1	0	0	Griffith, D. Esq.	2	2	0	Prichard, Mr.	0	5	0
Acton, Mr. William	1	0	0	Hand, Mr. Wm.	1	0	0	Roose, Mr	0	5	0
Armstrong Mr.	1	0	0	Harding Mrs.	0	10	0	Roberts, Thomas Esq.	1	0	0
Atkins, Mr.	0	5	0	Harding, Mr. H.	1	0	0	Spencer, Mr.	0	7	0
Baugh, Mrs.	0	10	0	Hodge, Mrs.	0	2	0	Slack, Mr.	0	5	0
Burrough, Mr.	0	2	6	Hodges, Rev. J.	1	1	0	Taylor, Mr.	0	2	6
Childe, Mr.	0	10	0	Hosie, Mr.	0	5	0	Taylor, Mr. R.	1	0	0
Coates, Mr.	0	10	0	Jolley, Mr.	0	10	0	Thomas, Mr. John	1	0	0
Cropper, Mrs.	0	5	0	Jones, William, Esq.	2	0	0	Tilley, Mr.	0	5	0
Davies, Mr. Jun.	1	0	0	Jordan, Mrs.	0	5	0	Urwick, Mr. B.	1	0	0
Davies, Mr. R.	0	5	0	Owens, Mr.	0	10	0	Urwick, Mr. William	1	0	0
Evans, Mr.	0	2	6	Palmer, Mr.	0	2	6	Wakefield, Mr.	1	0	0
George, Mrs.	0	2	6	Penny, Mr.	0	10	0	Weems, Mr.	0	5	0

The Commissioners for Paving and Lighting the Town in publishing the above List and returning their thanks to the Subscribers, beg leave to state that they have entered into a new contract with Messrs. EDWARDS and Co., the Gas Proprietors, who have agreed to extend the main Pipes to all the extremities and Lanes of the Town---to increase the Gas Lamps from 37 to 70---to light up eight months in the year with an interval of five nights only instead of nine, at the full of the moon, for rather less per Annum than was paid on the old plan, the balance in hand of the above Subscription is £86. 10s. 0d. but a further expense of upwards of £100 will be incurred for the new Lamp Posts, Lamp Glasses, Fittings, &c. and the estimated charge for repairing the Pavement is about £140. The Commissioners are therefore under the necessity of soliciting further Subscriptions to enable them to meet the above expense without infringing on their Annual Income.

Ludlow. February 21, 1832.

Printed by Charles Anderson, Castle-street, Ludlow.

Voluntary contributions made towards gas lighting in 1832.

public health measures more easily. In 1853 the Council voted to adopt the Health of Towns Act which had been passed five years previously, and the Common Lodging Houses Acts of 1851 and 1853.[15] It was, however, one thing to grant authorities the power to undertake functions which aimed to improve public sanitation. It was quite another to persuade them to take action. If no financial assistance was available, these powers were unlikely to be exercised by cost-conscious councils, and this proved to be so in Ludlow where health problems associated with the sewers were not addressed until the 1860s.

THE NEW CATTLE MARKET

The point about the effect of parsimony was illustrated clearly in the attempts of the Council to erect a cattle market in Corve Street. This would have removed the nuisance caused by beasts in the town thoroughfares on market days, and would have been adjacent to the newly opened railway station. The proposal was, however, costed at £6,000, so that the Council, still struggling to discharge its debts, made an unsuccessful appeal to raise the amount by public subscription.[16] A more economical proposal was then adopted, and an application was made to the Public Works Loan Commissioner for £4,000 under the Cattle Market Act.[17] This presumably failed. The scheme was, however, rescued by the passing of a further piece of legislation.

In 1858 the Government passed a Local Government Act which enabled borough councils to constitute themselves as Local Boards of Health, with additional responsibilities and the power to raise a further rate for carrying these out. The Council duly resolved on 9 March 1859 to adopt the act, and on the following 1 June the new Board met for the first time. One of its first actions was to petition Parliament for the repeal of the 1793 Ludlow Paving Act, as the new Board possessed the powers formerly exercised by the Commissioners.[18] This was granted by September 1860, although it took several demands before the Commissioners were prepared to surrender their papers.

The membership of the Board exactly replicated that of the Council, and in practice it acted very much like a mirror-image of that body. Even the officials, the Clerk, Treasurer, Surveyor and Inspector of Nuisances were already employed in those capacities by the Council, with the exception of the Inspector, whose duties were a rather unwelcome addition to those of the Superintendent of Police. Initially these duties were performed for no extra remuneration, but by September 1861 the Board was forced to recognise that the extra work incurred by its officials required additional salaries.

Armed with its new statutory powers, the Board began work on two major projects, one of which, the new cattle market, the Council had already attempted to initiate. The other was a comprehensive renewal and extension of the town's sewerage and for both schemes the Board engaged the services of Timothy Curley, an engineer who had already carried out major works for the newly-constituted Improvement Commissioners who had been established in Hereford in 1854 after an outbreak of cholera in the city.[19] On 11 October 1860 the Board resolved that it was "necessary and expedient" for a new cattle market to be provided, and the following June the tender of Messrs. Brassey and Field was accepted. As it happened, the choice of site was not good. Lands adjacent to the Gaolford toll gate had been purchased from W. B. Vaughan for £800, but unlike the site which had originally been proposed in Corve Street, there was no access to the railway, and a proposal to erect sidings came to nothing. The new municipal Smithfield was ultimately eclipsed by a rival private market established in Corve Street in 1885, and had fallen out of use by 1900.[20] In the course of site clearance, the remains of the Augustinian Friary were exposed, and it is an interesting reflection of the changed attitudes of the time that this led to considerable public interest. Excavation of the site was carried out with the active co-operation and interest of Curley, and the patronage of the borough Member of Parliament, Beriah Botfield, who was an antiquary of some reputation. The results of the excavation were presented to the Society of Antiquaries by Botfield, together with a reconstruction drawing made by the Ludlow architect Herbert Evans.[21] For all its short-comings, this must rank as the first scientific archaeological excavation in Ludlow, and the fact that it was carried out with the active support of the Mayor, George Cocking, shows that a new spirit of civic pride was stirring in the town.

MODERNISING THE SEWERS

The market was duly opened on 20 August 1862, and despite its relatively short life, it removed one of the major nuisances from the town centre. The sewerage question was tackled simultaneously with the building of the new cattle market. Curley prepared a detailed survey of the town which showed the sewers which he proposed to install, and for which he was paid the sum of £250.[22] The Board's task was to carry out the recommended works, and then to persuade property owners to connect their premises to the sewers. The Board's minutes record the steady progress of the sewer construction from 1862 to 1866, with contractors beginning in the town centre and moving out into the inner suburbs. The scheme was, no doubt, in accordance with the normal practices of the day, but was to lead to trouble in the next decade. The basic problem was that sewage was discharged into the River Teme at two points, one in the Linney, and one near the paper mills on Temeside. Although deodorising tanks were provided with the intention of removing one of the potential nuisances, the more significant hazards involved in pumping a far greater quantity of sewage than formerly into a river from which a large number of inhabitants drew their washing water was not appreciated.[23]

In fairness to the Board, it appears to have initiated Ludlow's first attempt to tackle industrial pollution when it began in December 1865 to investigate the problem of waste emissions from the gas works in Temeside into the river. The proposed solution was the construction of an intercepting wall, but when in May of the following year professional advice was that the scheme would be useless, the proposal was dropped.

SLUM CLEARANCE

Little more success attended the Board's first efforts at slum clearance. In February 1872, the Board resolved to ask the advice of the Local Government Board on how to proceed in the case of a number of ruinous buildings in lower Corve Street and St. Mary's Lane. The state of these cottages had been mentioned as "calculated to engender fever and other diseases" in a petition from Corve Street residents in September 1871. The owner of the cottages had been illegitimate and had died intestate, with the property reverting to the Crown on his death. The properties were in a ruinous condition; the tenants paid no rent and recognised no authority. The buildings constituted an eyesore at a main entrance to the town, and were unfit for human habitation. The problem for the Board was whether it possessed the legal authority to evict the tenants and demolish the houses. This was to enmesh it in the fine web of mid-Victorian bureaucracy. The Local Government Board wanted to know whether the problem was due to dilapidation. The Town Clerk replied that the only dangerous structure was the chimney, in reference to which the Local Government Board referred him to a relevant clause in the Towns Improvement Clauses Act of 1847. Again the Clerk replied that this only applied to the chimney - the three properties were not strictly dangerous to pedestrians, and the town wished to carry out an improvement by removing them. The officials in London then advised proceedings under the Nuisances Removal Acts, whereby the magistrates could order the shutting up of the properties until repairs were carried out - which in the circumstances would amount to a permanent closure. This did not, of course, mean demolition, which was what the Council desired, but in April 1872 they resolved to take what action they could, and the following month the tenants received 40 days notice to quit.

In the meantime the Public Health Act of 1872 had replaced the Local Board of Health with an Urban Sanitary Authority, which had greater powers, was subject to even greater central government interference, but which, like its predecessor, was composed entirely of the Borough Council. The responsibility for the Corve Street nuisance was taken up by the new authority, which in February 1873 had secured the closure of the houses under the Acts suggested by the Local Government Board. The Clerk now sought the advice of counsel as to whether any further action could be taken. The opinion suggested that the Authority risked an action for trespass if it moved in to demolish the buildings, and there the matter was left. Later in the decade legislation passed by the Disraeli government might have given the necessary backing for action in the matter, but the will to proceed seems to have been lost.

Waning enthusiasm for Improvement

With the exception of the unsuccessful instances noted above, the Local Board does not seem to have been at all proactive after its initial burst of activity in 1860. Much of its business was similar to that which the Improvement Commissioners had been carrying out three quarters of a century earlier, namely the control of nuisances from slaughterhouses, projecting spouting, noxious privies and the like; the attempted regulation of bow windows and similar encroachments upon the highway; and repairing the paving of the streets. The lack of enthusiasm for positive action on the part of the

Board of Health in its later years is dramatically illustrated by a total absence of references to cholera in 1866. It was in fact the Board of Guardians who took the initiative when an outbreak threatened, by establishing a Sanitary Committee under the Disease Prevention Acts. This committee required medical practitioners in the area of the Union to report any cases of cholera or unusually severe diarrhoea to the Board's Medical Officer, Henry Meymott. Happily, there were no cases of cholera in the area, with the exception of a Ludlow railwayman who exhibited symptoms after coming into contact with the corpse of a cholera victim on a train from Birkenhead. As he recovered and returned to work in a week, it may be assumed that fright rather than the infection had affected the man's bowels. The committee began to consider the question of sewerage in the district, but was firmly reproved by the Poor Law Board for exceeding its powers. Following this, the committee frequently had no business to attend to at its meetings, and in early 1867 appears to have lapsed.[24]

The Feud with the Gas Company

The inaction of the Local Board of Health in the face of the perceived threat of a cholera outbreak contrasts markedly with the single-mindedness with which it pursued a long-running feud with the Gas Company. The relationship was always potentially fraught, as the Board wished to light the streets as cheaply as possible, while the company naturally wished to make a profit for its shareholders. As a monopolist, it had an advantage, although it could not afford to alienate a major customer too greatly. In 1865 the Board had agreed new rates with the company for supplying gas to 83 street lights and the Butter Cross clock. All went well until in May 1870 the Board was faced with a quarterly bill for £18 for lighting the clock, which had been 17 shillings for the previous quarter. The company insisted that the meter was correct, and refused to reduce the

The site of the gas works on Temeside which replaced the original premises on Gravel Hill. Gas continued to be manufactured here until the advent of North Sea gas in the 1970s made the process redundant. The manager's house is in the foreground.

Mr Seaton, the manager of the gas works, and proposed a meeting with the directors of the company. This was refused by Ambrose Grounds, the company secretary, himself a former mayor. For a fortnight there was a stalemate before the directors backed down, and on 17 October 1871 agreed to meet representatives of the Board. The result of the meeting is not clear, the Board minutes merely recording that the minutes of the meeting with the Gas Company were read and adopted. No doubt minor concessions were made on both sides, but the company always had the advantage.

demand. Eventually in July the Board agreed to pay the sum of £16: 12: 1d, with the proviso that they were "of the opinion that the charge was a very exorbitant one." The Surveyor was then instructed to follow up a report that the Leominster Board had a very economical method of lighting their clock. In September it was reported that the Leominster clock was in fact poorly illuminated, and that further investigation had revealed that in Bridgnorth a well-lit clock was turned off by a time switch. While the technical implications of this device may have been too advanced for the Board, they did nevertheless resolve that the clock light should be turned off in the morning with the town lights rather than being allowed to burn through the day.

Disagreement flared again in August 1871 when the Gas Company proposed new charges of 13s 4d per month per lamp rather than the ten shillings which had been previously agreed. The Board refused to agree to the demands of

The Board almost immediately employed new tactics in their efforts to reduce the gas bill. A letter was sent to Seaton requesting that 60 of the lamps should be turned off at midnight, and the remaining 40 an hour before sunrise. Seaton replied that this was impossible, as it would entail the expense of an inspector to see that the arrangement was adhered to, but suggested that pressure could be turned down at the works at midnight, thus reducing consumption. The Surveyor was then instructed to check that pressure had been sufficiently reduced, and when this did not appear to be the case further correspondence ensued. Seaton replied on 8 February 1872 that pressure had been reduced as much as he dared, for further reductions would have threatened the supply to private customers, put out all ground floor lights, "and endangered Bedroom Lights, of which there are many in the town". This appears to have been the final word on the matter, and the dispute, which at times bordered on the farcical, petered out.

Typhoid and the Water Supply

Towards the end of the life of the Local Board, two problems began to surface which were to cause major difficulties for its successor, the Urban Sanitary Authority, which commenced its existence on 5 September 1872. These were the closely related areas of sewerage and water supply. Although Curley's system of sewers had been a major advance for the borough, the scheme had a number of drawbacks, particularly in the nature of the outfalls into the Teme. In October 1870 the Surveyor had been ordered to investigate a complaint that land near the Paper Mills in Temeside was "impregnated with sewage". The matter appears to have been dealt with, but re-surfaced in February 1874 with a heated correspondence in the Hereford Times. This arose from comments made at a meeting of Herefordshire sanitary authorities at Bromyard, where a speaker had alleged that people were moving out of the eastern parts of Ludlow due to the odours from the outfall, and that "the place was full of zymotic diseases in consequence of the direction of the mouth of the sewer". The allegations were robustly refuted by Curley, the author of the scheme; by Henry Meymott, who had been appointed Medical Officer to the Sanitary Authority; and by the Town Clerk. Meymott's letter contained some eccentricities, such as an attack upon water closets, and a number of hostages to fortune when he stated that the health of the borough was good, with no zymotic diseases. The Town Clerk went further, asserting that "Ludlow was never so free from disease as at the present time".[25] In his report delivered to the Authority at the same meeting, Meymott painted a glowing picture of the health of the borough. The public water supply was "remarkably free from deleterious sediment"; the public drainage was in good condition and free from "offensive emanations" from the sewers; the only noxious trade was the candle factory in Gaolford; and the death rate was below average. Less than eighteen months later Ludlow experienced a typhoid outbreak.

Between September 1875 and June 1876 over 30 cases of typhoid fever were reported in Corve Street. Meymott had written a letter in the Ludlow Advertiser to try to minimise the threat, but the residents of the street were not mollified, and one of them, E.S. Lowndes, wrote to the Authority on 6 July 1876 demanding that an independent engineer should be employed to assess the cause of the outbreak. The implications of the epidemic were beginning to be more widely felt. Meymott's re-election as Medical Officer in August was challenged by Dr Thursfield, the Officer to the Rural Sanitary Authority, and although he subsequently withdrew from the contest, it was clear that Meymott's days were numbered. Word of the outbreak had reached London, and on 22 August, notice was received that the Local Government Board had instructed their inspector, Dr Airy, to enquire into the 'Sanitary State of the Ludlow Urban Sanitary Authority'.

By late September 1876 the number of cases had risen to 85, all in Corve Street, and the wealthier residents of the street led by Richard Marston formed a deputation which demanded and received a meeting with the Council on 28 September. Marston, who had visited the sewage treatment plant in Linney with the Mayor, was convinced that the cause of the problem lay there, with a deodorising tank which regularly overflowed into the river, and inadequate filter beds. Another suggested cause was the state of the sewers, particularly with regard to lack of ventilation. The deputation had no confidence in the Borough Surveyor, whose dismissal they demanded. The Surveyor on his part refuted most of Marston's allegations, and reserved his explanations for the Authority. Alderman Southern quoted "eminent medical opinion" that sewer gas did not cause typhoid, and the Mayor closed the meeting with thanks to the deputation for their interest.

Meymott was the first casualty of the

meeting. Using the confusion over the advertising of the post in August as a pretext, they re-advertised it and on 5 October 1876 unanimously appointed Dr Jones of Castle Street as Medical Officer. Meymott wrote complaining letters to the Local Government Board alleging irregularities in the appointment of his successor, but to no avail. At the same meeting the Mayor announced, perhaps smugly, that the Corve Street sewer had been opened, and the sewage had been found flowing freely with no sediment. Significantly, in view of their denials of the harmful effects of sewer gas, the construction of vent pipes was ordered, and shortly extended to other parts of the town.

The report of Dr Airy arrived in the New Year, and was discussed at a special meeting on 14 February 1877. There were two main recommendations. The first was the provision of an entirely new water supply, to replace completely the river supply from Mill Street, which should be disconnected from all houses. In the interim, public notices were to be circulated warning that river water was unfit to drink. The second recommendation was the extension of sewer ventilation to the whole town. In fairness to the Council it had been aware for some time of the inadequacies of the borough's water supply. As the Board of Health it had commissioned a committee to examine the problem as early as July 1864, although concerns had been for the shortcomings in the supply itself, a cause of frequent complaints from residents, rather than the purity of the water. Improvements which were carried out were of a piecemeal nature, and always governed by the dictates of economy. Thus when in 1870 the Board had approached several hydraulic engineers for ideas on improving the pumping system, their recommendations were set aside in favour of employing a full-time official to turn the supply on and off. A new reservoir was constructed on Whitcliffe in the summer of 1871 to increase the supply of drinking water from the springs there, but this did little more than improve slightly a system

which was still totally inadequate. It took the involvement of the central authority to nudge the Sanitary Authority into action, and it was almost panicked into adopting a scheme to bring water from Stoke St Milborough on the day that Dr Airy's report was considered. This scheme had been drawn up by a firm of engineers, Messrs. Gotto and Beasley, who envisaged a supply sufficient to meet existing needs as well as those of the rapidly developing suburbs of Gravel Hill and Sandpits. The vicar of Stoke St Milborough, whose own water supply was partly threatened, objected strongly, and this provided members who had been pushed into a decision with an opportunity to force a rethink of the proposals.

In April the mayor reported that an analysis of the Stoke water pronounced it to be too hard for any purposes other than drinking, and suggested a new scheme which would involve improving the supply of river water for domestic uses and extracting a greater amount of spring water for drinking. Gotto and Beasley rejected this proposal in December 1877 for a number of reasons both practical and sanitary, and strongly recommended reverting to the Stoke scheme. Failing this, they could extend the Whitcliffe supply, and exploit the Boiling Well in Burway for just over £8,000. In the following weeks the Authority, which was disastrously split on the issue, rejected both proposed schemes, and prompted the central board, through its local inspector, Mr Dansey, to enquire what progress had been made towards implementing a better supply. Four months later the Local Government Board itself wrote with the same question. At the beginning of December 1878 a proposal from Gotto and Beasley to create a new supply from Whitcliffe and Bringewood sufficient to supply a population of 6,000 with 20 gallons a day each was held over when a counter-resolution to approach Timothy Curley was carried.

This inaugurated a veritable battle of the engineers. In a pamphlet printed by the Hereford Times and considered by the

Authority on 16 January 1879, Curley dismissed the Bringewood and Stoke schemes, with a neat swipe at his rivals. Curley was not surprised that Gotto and Beasley were in favour of the prohibitively expensive Stoke scheme "judging from their recommendation of spending a large and unnecessary sum on the Corve Street drainage".[26] Curley calculated that the Burway springs had a capacity 75% greater than Ludlow's needs, and that if the water was pumped by steam to a reservoir on high ground, there would be sufficient pressure to supply the workhouse or Castle View Terrace, both of which were outside the borough boundary. This was music to the ears of the more parsimonious members, and it was unanimously resolved to ask Curley to submit an estimate - though the supporters of Gotto and Beasley secured the same right for their preferred firm. The results were an estimate of £5,000 from Curley and one of £7,865 from Gotto and Beasley. Shortly after, in February 1879, Gotto and Beasley set out to demolish Curley's estimate, which they said omitted essential items totalling £2,736 bringing the two estimates within £150 of each other. Curley's supporters managed, however, to secure the acceptance of his scheme by eight votes to six.

Before work could begin, many preliminaries needed to be completed. It was necessary to obtain permission from Lord Windsor and Mr Parkinson of Ludford, the two landowners involved, to the siting of the reservoir and the associated pipework. Further delays arose as the Whitcliffe Commoners sought compensation for the diminution of their rights, to the extent that in August 1879 Curley wrote to the Authority assuming that the project had been cancelled, and enclosing his bill for work done. Even more time-consuming was the need to obtain sanction from the Local Government Board for a loan of £6,000, to be repaid in 30 equal instalments, to cover the cost of the work and a sewerage scheme for Friars' Walk. When approval finally came in October 1879, it was for £5,100, as the sewerage scheme had been

rejected for lack of purification before the effluent was discharged into the Teme. The proposals were then advertised for tender, and these were duly received from 14 contractors. Prices ranged from £3,508 from James Hine of Ludlow, to £5,819 from Messrs. Carter and Morris of Gracechurch Street, London. When it was pointed out that the two lowest tenders did not fully comply with the particulars of the work, that of Richard Davies of Rock Cottage for £3,555: 15: 3d was formally accepted. Work then proceeded apace, and by the summer of 1880 was nearing completion. In June 1880 all householders were instructed to connect to the new supply, and advised to employ Davies to carry out the work. On 6 August they were warned that on 1 September the old supply would be disconnected, and on the day after the official switch over the final accounts were rendered. In the end neither of the rival engineers had been fully accurate in their estimates. The total cost was £6,239: 12: 8d, an excess of almost £1,140 over the amount of the loan. Much of this entailed unforeseen work on the rebuilding of the turbine house in Mill Street and the hiring of a steam engine until the new turbine was operational. It was, however, considerably less than the estimate of Gotto and Beasley, and the Authority appears to have got value for money by employing Curley. There were, of course, complaints, particularly from the Whitcliffe Commoners and their ally, the architect Richard Kyrke Penson of Dinham House, all of whom objected to the way in which the works had been landscaped. Ludlow had, however, been given a supply of pure water for all purposes, and the anachronistic dual supply had been finally ended.

THE SEWERS RE-EXAMINED

The modernising of the water supply was undoubtedly the most ambitious project carried out in Ludlow during the period under consideration. The problem of the sewers was handled in a much more characteristically *laissez faire* manner. It was the contention of the Authority that the town's sewers were in a perfectly sound condition, and that the outbreaks of typhoid in Corve Street had nothing to do with the drains. In June 1876 the Sanitary Committee had examined the sewer in the High Street, and had found nine or ten inches of sediment. The response was to renew the sewer, and to provide a flushing well near the Market Hall, and also to provide a new sewer in Gaolford. This did not address the Corve Street problem, where the sewers had been deemed satisfactory, and in November 1878 a petition from the residents pointed out that a further 17 cases of typhoid had occurred the previous summer in houses which had been affected by the previous outbreak. The petition quoted that Gotto and Beasley had pronounced the Corve Street sewers badly laid and jointed, and alleged that the Authority "demur to carry out the advice [of professional engineers], whilst others ask for a manifestation of public opinion." Curley, who had devised the scheme, agreed to meet the petitioners, but insisted that there was no link between sewers and fever, and refused to take responsibility for work done 18 years before. The Authority's response was to open the street to construct manholes. On 5 December 1878 the Mayor reported, no doubt with delight, that when opened the sewer was found to be in perfect condition, with no sediment. The fact that the question appears to have lapsed after this may well have been due to the replacement of the town water supply which has already been discussed above.

CONCLUSION

It could hardly be argued that the Borough Council in Ludlow in the guise of the Local Board of Health, and later the Urban Sanitary Authority, embraced the 'Gospel of Public Health', which emanated in particular from Birmingham, with anything more than muted enthusiasm. Its approach was generally reactive rather than proactive, and the twin pressures of the central government, via the Local Government Board, and public opinion, were required to goad it into action. Economic considerations, which often appear as thinly disguised parsimony, were generally paramount, and many councillors preferred to 'make do and mend' rather than undertake costly projects of improvement. This may be clearly seen by the convoluted processes by which Ludlow finally received an improved and hygienic water supply in 1880. It is even more significant that the debate about the state of the town's sewers rumbled on until the end of the century, when it was revealed that only 11 of the 33 largest industrial towns in England had a death rate higher than that of Ludlow.[27] Even then there were still councillors who denied any link between drainage and disease. The long-awaited replacement of the borough's sewers was finally commenced in the autumn of 1900.

This lack of commitment to improvement towards the end of the period under consideration contrasts with the short-lived but significant burst of enthusiasm which accompanied the establishment of the Local Board of Health in 1859, and even more so with the situation in the earlier part of the 19th century. The establishment of the Improvement Commissioners in 1793 in part foreshadowed the duplication of authorities which characterised the later approach to the questions of health and improvement. The unreformed Corporation had in many ways been rather better than many of its contemporaries in its attitude to the provision of public services, and the Improvement Commissioners pursued their aims in a limited but fairly conscientious manner. The 19th century does not appear to have witnessed a growing commitment to improved public health on the part of the relevant authorities in the town, and the changes required by central government were generally only grudgingly accepted. The pattern of activity established by forward-looking elements at the beginning of the century had become ossified by the 1870s.

ENDNOTES

1   Lloyd, D. J., *Country Grammar School*, Ludlow, 1977, pp.115 -126.
2   SA, LB2/2/2/153-158, Corporation Minutes, 28 October 1828.
3   SA, LB7/1102, Ludlow Improvement Act, 1793.
4   A volume of Commissioners' minutes seen by Thomas Midgeley, the unofficial borough archivist, in the 1940s has since been lost.
5   These comprise a large collection of individual papers in the Ludlow Borough collection in SA, DA3/ 152/2/1 - 16.
6   Lloyd, D.J., *Broad Street*, 1979, p.15.
7   Ibid, pp.15-16. The scheme also involved the construction of a common sewer down the centre of the road, into which surface water would drain.
8   SA, LB2/2/2 Corporation Minutes, 25 January 1831; similar proposals had previously been advanced by the Herefordshire justices, SRRC, DP100. In the event a much less drastic scheme was implemented in 1835 in the last months of the Corporation.
9   9 & 10 Victoria, cap.18.
10 SA, DA3/152/2/4/12. Printed list of subscribers.
11 SA, LB2/2/ Corporation Minutes, 24 October 1833. Lamp on southern side of Ludford Bridge provided by the Corporation.
12 SA, DA3/152/2/12/2.
13 SA, LB Corporation Minutes, 7 May 1840. Both gas works were situated outside the boundary of the borough at the time.
14 Ibid., 4 September 1847; 23 May 1849.
15 Ibid., 4 August 1853; 12 October 1853.
16 Ibid., 4 October 1853; 4 May 1854.
17 Ibid., 2 May 1856.
18 SA, DA3/990/1/1, Ludlow Board of Health Minute Book, 24 June 1859. Unless otherwise stated all subsequent references are from this source, or from the minutes of its successor, the Urban Sanitary Authority, from 1872 - 1878. These are included in the same volume.
19 Mitchell, D.J., "Hereford in the Age of Reform, 1832-56", *Transactions of the Woolhope Naturalists* Field Club, 1982, pp.105-109.
20 Lloyd, D.J., *The Concise History of Ludlow*, 1999, p.141.
21 Dawson, M. and Sheward, C., "Herbert Evans and the 'restored' Friary", *Ludlow Heritage News*, No. 33, 2000.
22 The original plan is now in SA, ref. 522/8/926. Smaller versions were printed and published at the time.
23 Many Ludlow properties possessed a dual water supply. Drinking water came from springs around the periphery of the town, and was stored in cisterns prior to being piped to consumers. Water for other domestic purposes was generally drawn from the river by the water works at the bottom of Mill Street.
24 SA, PL9/2/1/11, Ludlow Board of Guardians, Minutes, August 1866-February 1867. I am grateful to Dr. Derek Williams for drawing my attention to this episode.
25 Quoted verbatim in the Authority's Minutes.
26 Curley, T., *Report on the Waterworks of Ludlow*, (1879), p.7. References to the proceedings of the Urban Sanitary Authority after 1 January 1879 are from SA, DA3/990/1/1.
27 Williams, D., "Ludlow - January to June 1900", *Ludlow Heritage News*, No. 32, (2000), p.6.

CHAPTER 7

THE LUDLOW UNION WORKHOUSE 1839-1900

DEREK WILLLIAMS

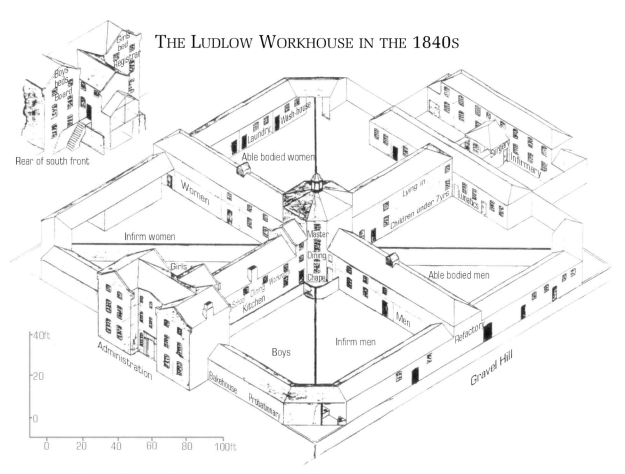

THE LUDLOW WORKHOUSE IN THE 1840s

Drawing of the workhouse based on plans approved by the Poor Law Commissioners in 1836 and later amended by the Ludlow Guardians.
(Ivan Hall, Ludlow Historical Research Group 2004).

Visitors to Ludlow between 1839 and 1870 would often include in their itineraries an inspection of the workhouse at Gravel Hill, and many would record their impressions in the Visitors Book. One of the first to call, within weeks of the opening of the workhouse in 1839, was the celebrated reformer and philanthropist Louisa Twining, who thought that it would be "a pleasure and a comfort" to inmates if they were given a few books to read. Such practical suggestions were infrequent. Most of the entries were confined to congratulating the Ludlow Guardians on the excellence of their arrangements. In 1843 W.M. Jones wrote that "it is a source of great gratification to live in a country where the poor are so well provided for; wisdom and economy are united, and I hope that the spirit of thankfulness will be engendered in the hearts of the poor". In 1851, the Reverend John Puckle of St Mary's Dover wrote "...how very compatible are the essential comforts, good order, cleanliness and discipline of (the) poor inmates, with the kindly and liberal system evidently maintained here."[1] If we were to rely on the Visitors Book, we might conclude that the inmates of the Ludlow workhouse were always contented and their conditions enviable.

The aim of this chapter is to describe what life was really like for the inmates. Many of the Ludlow workhouse records have been preserved. They include most of the minutes of the meetings of the Board of Guardians, and many records and reports prepared by the officers of the workhouse: the Master, Matron, Medical Officer, Schoolmistress and Porter.[2] For the local historian, the limitation of these records is that they provide a view of workhouse affairs from the perspective of those who administered the system. We have virtually no evidence of how the inmates felt about their lot. This presents few problems when we are studying financial or personnel statistics that more or less speak for themselves. When inmates' behaviour is being reported, however, the lack of explanation is sometimes disappointing. In October 1844 the Master recommended that John Pugh, a reliable elderly inmate who worked in the workhouse garden, "and is in consequence much exposed to the wet and cold", be allowed a little warm tea with his supper. This was refused without explanation. Two months later, Pugh was found sitting with other elderly inmates in the old men's kitchen. When ordered to return to work he refused, and was warned about his behaviour. In April 1845 he was found in the kitchen at 4.30am using a picklock to open the coalbunker. "His tales upon the subject (being) various and contradictory" it was ordered that he be taken before the County Magistrates,[3] and he disappears from the records. We can only guess at what punishment he received, and why John Pugh changed in 5 months from model inmate to malcontent.

The chapter begins by reviewing the main features of the reform of the poor law in 1834 that led to the building of the Ludlow workhouse. It explains why pursuit of the aims of 'less eligibility' and 'classification' made life undeservedly harsh for most Ludlow inmates. There were rarely more than a few able-bodied men in the Ludlow workhouse, but they were the targets of the entire regime. Some of the features of that regime are then examined: timetable, diet, work and accommodation. Complete conformity with the rules of the workhouse was expected, but 'refractory' behaviour was frequent and was punished severely. The special problems and circumstances of five particular groups are then reviewed: children, women, the elderly, lunatics and vagrants. By 1900, most of the Ludlow inmates were old and infirm.

THE 1834 REFORMS

At the beginning of the 19th century, poor relief was administered by Justices of the Peace and parish overseers through arrangements first introduced in 1601. There was widespread pressure to change this system, which was thought to be wasteful of the ratepayers' money and to tolerate unacceptably wide variations in the levels of relief provided in different parts of the country. The government was frustrated by its inability to influence either the pattern or the volume of relief, with the spending decisions being taken by some 15,000 unpaid, untrained and virtually autonomous parish overseers.

A Royal Commission was set up in 1832 to study the problem. Such was the pressure for reform, however, that before the recommendations of the Royal Commission could be digested the Poor Law Amendment Act of 1834 was on the statute book. The Act deprived parishes of their freedom to administer poor relief. Poor law 'Unions' were to be established, each comprising about 30 parishes. A Board of Guardians, elected by and from the ratepayers, would govern each Union and be answerable to a Poor Law Commission (PLC) in London. These Boards would set the poor rate for each parish in their Union and decide how the money would be spent, within certain national guidelines.

By establishing Unions, the government created a national structure of poor law administration. The 1834 Act also gave the Unions firm guidelines on how they should work within that structure. All relief for able-bodied persons and their families was to be provided in 'well-regulated' workhouses[4] wherein the conditions were to be made as comfortless as possible. This was because those who drafted the new legislation believed that the causes of idleness were personal and moral rather than social and economic. (The Royal Commission had begun to study the causes of unemployment, but the 1834 Act was passed before the research was finished.) There was, they believed, work for all who wanted it. Under the old system, many able-bodied applicants had been granted 'outdoor relief' i.e. whilst living at home. Now they and their families would face a stark choice: either enter the workhouse or find a job. It was thought that, faced with this choice, most applicants would prosper outside the workhouse. To encourage the able-bodied to make the right decision, there would need to be a suitable workhouse in every Union, complying with the principles of 'less eligibility' and 'classification.'

'Less eligibility' meant that the food, accommodation and other conditions in the workhouse should never be better than those that ordinary able-bodied labourers in the locality were able to provide for themselves and their families. 'Classification' meant that those entering a workhouse should be placed in one of seven discrete classes:

aged and infirm men
able-bodied men and youths aged 13 and over
youths and boys between 7 and 13 years
aged and infirm women
able-bodied women and girls aged 16 and over
girls between 7 and 16 years
children under 7 years.

Each class was to be accommodated in a separate part of the workhouse "in which they shall respectively remain without communication with any other class."[5] This rule was intended to punish the able-bodied but indolent married pauper, for whom life in the workhouse was to be as joyless as possible. Unfortunately, in the pursuit of this objective, life became unpleasant for everyone else: children were separated from their parents, elderly couples forced to live apart.

The Royal Commission had originally favoured another approach, in which there would be separate buildings for each class of pauper. Edwin Chadwick, the secretary of the Commission, said that they had hoped for arrangements in which "the old may enjoy their comforts, the children be properly educated" and the most rigorous discipline reserved for the able-bodied.[6] It was, however, soon realised that this approach was unworkable: it would have been too expensive to build and staff separate buildings for each class of pauper, and too complex to organise and administer several distinct regimes within one large institution. Moreover, as the overriding aim of the 1834 reform was to intimidate the idle, it was thought that one large building would have more effect than several smaller ones. The proposal to establish different regimes of varying severity within each Union was therefore abandoned.

THE LUDLOW WORKHOUSE

This was the background to the formation of the Ludlow Union in 1836. The Union brought together 32 parishes in South Shropshire and North Herefordshire.[7] Each parish was represented on the Board by one elected Guardian, apart from two of the larger villages with two each and the town of Ludlow with five. There was always a large majority of farmers on the Board, and several active and influential Anglican clergymen.[8] The Union inherited from its parochial predecessors 3 small workhouses in Corfton, Leintwardine and

Ludlow. None of these was suitable for development as the 'well regulated workhouse' expected by the Poor Law Commissioners, and one of the first decisions of the Board was to build at Gravel Hill, on the outskirts of Ludlow, a new workhouse capable of accommodating 250-300 paupers. A Ludlow architect, Matthew Stead, was engaged to design the building and supervise its construction. The drawing at the beginning of this chapter shows that Stead was influenced by the ideas of Samuel Kempthorne, who had proposed a 'panopticon' approach to the design of workhouses that had been commended by the PLC.[9] Neither Stead nor the Guardians had much experience of a project of this magnitude, and despite using an off-the-peg design the building eventually cost £7,000 against an original estimate of about £3,000, and opened nearly a year late, in April 1839.[10]

Lane's Asylum, in Old Street, Ludlow, was one of three small workhouses inherited by the Board of Guardians from its parochial predecessors in 1836. It was given up by the Union after the workhouse at Gravel Hill opened in 1839.
From Shropshire Archives:
copyright London Borough of Barnet Local Studies

Although, as the drawing shows, the primary requirement in the design of the workhouse was to keep apart the different classes of inmate, experience soon showed that this was difficult to achieve. One problem was that female inmates working as cleaners or washerwomen had to visit all parts of the workhouse. Another was that, whilst the need to accommodate able-bodied inmates had been overestimated, other needs had been underestimated or completely overlooked. There was, for example, inadequate provision for the chronically ill elderly, for lunatics, and for children and other inmates with infectious diseases. No arrangements had been made for the growing numbers of vagrants passing through Ludlow. As these deficiencies became apparent, the Guardians and their officers were forced into a series of *ad hoc* changes in accommodation that put great strain on the original intention to segregate the classes. In 1866, an internal report on the management of the Union described the lack of classification in the Ludlow workhouse as "disgraceful".

Within weeks of opening, there were more than 100 inmates in the workhouse. Over the next few years the numbers rose to nearly 200, although there were always more inmates in the winter than in the summer and autumn, the busiest times of the agricultural year. After reaching a peak of 196 in January 1842,[11] numbers gradually fell until in the late 1840s there were times when there were less than 100 in 'the house'. Thereafter the numbers varied between 100 and 150, and in 1872 the Local Government Board (LGB)[12] instructed the Ludlow Guardians to limit the number of inmates in the workhouse, apart from vagrants, to 132. For the rest of the century, the numbers in the workhouse remained near this level.

Even in the 1840s, when the workhouse was at its fullest, there were rarely more than a dozen able-bodied men in the house, and then only for short periods. Most inmates fell into three broad groups: children; the elderly and infirm; and unsupported women – widows with children, single mothers, and deserted wives. In the 1840s, more than half of the inmates were children, many of whom were illegitimate. Thus, in February 1841, 105 out of 179 inmates were children, and 46 of these were illegitimate.[13] In the second half of the century there were fewer children, and the number of elderly and infirm inmates rose. In 1874, the Medical Officer told the Guardians that since 1863 the number of 'invalids' in the workhouse had risen from 34 to 84 in a total workhouse population of 130. Ten years later, 79 of the 132 inmates were elderly and infirm, and 23 were children. There were broadly similar figures for the 1890s, although at the end of the century the total numbers began to fall below 130. In February 1900, at a time of the year when the workhouse was normally at its busiest, the Guardians' Visiting Committee reported that "we never saw the house so empty".

In summary, between 1840 and 1870 the workhouse was primarily a home for children and distressed women. Between 1870 and 1900 its main function became the care of the elderly and infirm. Throughout the century there were usually a few able-bodied men in the workhouse, who normally only stayed for a few weeks. There might be about a dozen at any one time in the winter, and fewer – perhaps none – in the summer. Nevertheless the entire workhouse regime was aimed at 'deterring' the able-bodied from what was presumed to be their natural inclination to be idle. The regime was applied with equal force to all classes of pauper, and was perhaps felt most keenly by those who least deserved it.

ENTERING AND LEAVING THE WORKHOUSE

Paupers ineligible for outdoor relief were normally 'offered the house'. In most cases, this decision depended on the judgement of the Guardians and their officers, especially the Relieving Officers whose functions are discussed in the accompanying chapter on outdoor relief. Despite the instructions of the PLC, many able-bodied paupers in the Ludlow Union continued to receive outdoor relief, partly because it was usually cheaper to sustain able-bodied men and their families at home than in the workhouse. There were, however, some categories of pauper for whom the workhouse was the only option. The Commissioners refused to allow outdoor relief for deserted wives, widows with children, and 'fallen women' – a category that included prostitutes and unmarried mothers. In 1839, the Ludlow Board resolved that "any illegitimate children who may hereafter be born shall not be relieved out of the workhouse and the mothers shall be obliged to go in with them".

On admission, all inmates were bathed – men by the porter, women by the matron – and examined by the Medical Officer to determine to which part of the workhouse they should be sent. Occasionally, in the early days, paupers would be refused admission on medical grounds. In 1837 Esther Matthews, aged 60, was considered by the Medical Officer to be "an improper person to be admitted in consequence of her being insensible to the calls of nature", which probably meant that she was incontinent. After 1850, such rejections were infrequent.

To be released from the workhouse, an inmate had only to give 3 hours notice, although the able-bodied were not allowed to leave without their children. In 1845, the Clerk to the Guardians wrote to the PLC to ask if anything could be done to prevent inmates from discharging themselves from the workhouse "before some wake, fair, race, market or other amusement and returning to it again when the tempting cause is over." Of particular concern were "the female paupers (who) not infrequently re-enter the house in a filthy diseased state." The Clerk wrote again in 1862 to ask if Guardians "had any power to prevent the indoor female paupers leaving the house immediately before the Ludlow May Fair, and whether the Guardians could refuse re-admission immediately after the Fair." The answer on both occasions was that neither departure nor return could be refused.

THE DAILY ROUND

Life in the workhouse was governed by rules and restrictions, and every day followed the same routine:

<table>
<tr><td colspan="3" align="center">The Workhouse Timetable</td></tr>
<tr><td></td><td align="center">SUMMER</td><td align="center">WINTER</td></tr>
<tr><td></td><td align="center">25 March-29 September</td><td align="center">30 September-24 March</td></tr>
<tr><td>Get Up</td><td align="center">6am</td><td align="center">7am</td></tr>
<tr><td>Breakfast</td><td align="center">6.30 – 7am</td><td align="center">7.30 – 8am</td></tr>
<tr><td>Start Work</td><td align="center">7am</td><td align="center">8am</td></tr>
<tr><td>Dinner</td><td align="center">12noon – 1pm</td><td align="center">12noon – 1pm</td></tr>
<tr><td>Stop Work</td><td align="center">6pm</td><td align="center">6pm</td></tr>
<tr><td>Supper</td><td align="center">6 – 7pm</td><td align="center">6 – 7pm</td></tr>
<tr><td>Go to Bed</td><td align="center">8pm</td><td align="center">8pm</td></tr>
</table>

Bells rang to mark the time to change from one activity to the next. One of Ludlow's early rules was that during meals "silence, order and decorum shall be maintained,"[14] but this was rescinded in 1842. Even so, workhouse food did little to relieve the monotony. The doctrine of 'less eligibility' required that the workhouse diet should be as dreary as possible. Unions were encouraged to choose one of six 'model dietaries' recommended by the PLC. In the model first chosen by the Ludlow Guardians, breakfast was always bread and gruel. (Gruel was a thin oatmeal porridge made with water: most inmates particularly disliked it.) Supper was always bread and cheese, as was dinner on four days of the week. On Tuesdays, dinner was cooked meat with potatoes or vegetables; on Thursdays, soup; on Saturdays, bacon with vegetables or potatoes. The three staple items in the workhouse diet were therefore bread, cheese, and gruel.

During outbreaks of cholera and other diseases the Guardians, on the advice of the Medical Officer, would approve temporary arrangements to make the diet more nutritious, but when the threat abated the basic dietary would be restored. In 1857, in a revealing report on Thomas Bishop, aged 30, the Medical Officer wrote "unfit for the workhouse: needs a nourishing diet." It was widely believed that the food in prisons and lunatic asylums, where 'less eligibility' was not a factor, was better than in workhouses. In Ludlow, there were instances of inmates being suspected of feigning insanity in order to be transferred to somewhere with better food.

In 1839, the Committee of Management for Regaling the Poor of Ludlow asked if the Board would allow the inmates of the new workhouse to be regaled "with about 80lbs of mutton, buns and plum pudding, with a pint of beer for each adult pauper in the House – free of all expense to the Union", to celebrate the coming of age of Viscount Clive. The Guardians agreed, but two weeks later Sir Edmund Head, the visiting Poor Law Inspector, 'disapproved' the arrangement and ordered that no such regaling be considered again. This uncompromising commitment to the 'principles of 1834' was soon abandoned. In 1840, the inmates were allowed to celebrate the birth of the Princess Royal with a "substantial roast beef and plum pudding dinner" on Christmas Day, paid for by the Mayor and several ratepayers and 'respectable inhabitants' of Ludlow. From 1847, the Guardians always gave the inmates a special meal at Christmas.

Despite these occasional feasts, there were no major improvements in the workhouse food before 1900. From time to time the Guardians would tinker with the dietary, for example by varying the days when meat was served or replacing potatoes with rice when the former were in short supply. Even the smallest change needed approval from London. In 1867 the Poor Law Board (PLB) rejected as "insufficiently nutritious" the Guardians' proposal to give the children rice only for their dinner on Wednesdays: "a small quantity of bread ought to be given with it". In 1883, in a bold innovation proposed by Henry Meymott, the Medical Officer, fish replaced meat as the Friday dinner. Cod or haddock was bought direct from Grimsby at 2d a lb, cleaned and ready for cooking. The experiment was viewed with suspicion by many inmates and some Guardians, and after 8 months, despite Meymott's recommendation that fish was "decidedly wholesome", was abandoned.

Towards the end of the century, the workhouse Medical Officers did what they could to make life easier for elderly inmates. In 1884, the Inspector startled the Ludlow Board with some figures on the amount of beer consumed in various Shropshire workhouses:

Weekly Consumption of Beer, Shropshire Workhouses. 1884

Workhouse	Inmates	Pints of beer
Atcham	393	25
Ludlow	**132**	**306**
Newport	89	7
Oswestry	162	21
Wellington	133	Nil
Whitchurch	188	15

Meymott admitted that he was regularly prescribing beer to 79 elderly inmates, and agreed to "gradually" reduce the amount. In 1887 the Inspector, Mr Dansey, reported to the Board that the cost per head of wines, spirits and beer in the workhouse had fallen from 10/4d in 1884 to 2d in 1886. Later that year, however, the Guardians discovered that expenditure on drink was rising again. Henry Meymott had retired, and been replaced as Medical Officer by his life-long friend John Southern. In the 6 months to September 1887, nearly £12 had been spent on stimulants prescribed by Southern, including 473 tots of whisky. He explained that "the life of many old people is prolonged by a glass of whisky or brandy" and, rather surprisingly, the Board accepted this. At the end of the century, most Guardians were also prepared to resist the pressure of the powerful Temperance Movement to ban intoxicants from the workhouse. In 1897, when the Ludlow and Craven Arms Brewery offered a kilderkin of ale to enliven the workhouse Christmas, a motion to decline the offer and serve only tea and coffee at the Christmas dinner was narrowly defeated.

The Guardians were willing to see the elderly 'consoled' with drink, but did little to raise the overall dietary standard. There was always a big difference between the amount and quality of inmates' food and that of the workhouse staff. In 1846, the then Medical Officer, Valentine, was asked to comment on the adequacy of the prevailing meat allowances, which were 9 ounces per week for adult inmates, 6 ounces a week for children, and 4 ounces per day for inmates on the sick list. The staff allowance was 10 ounces per day. Valentine wrote that the allowance to adult paupers "affords sufficient nourishment to sustain the wants required for the purpose of ordinary nutrition, considering that little exhaustion is occasioned by the inmates, which in many cases amounts to only the necessary degree of exercise required to ensure healthy assimilation." This was, perhaps, an ungenerous view of the work done by most inmates. The usual task for able-bodied men was stone breaking: in Ludlow that meant working for up to 10 hours a day using iron bars to break the notoriously hard 'Jewstone' or 'Dhustone', chippings from which would fly in all directions and often break windows around the work yard. Other tasks included gardening and drawing water from the well. When the well was dry, inmates had to haul water by cart from the Teme. Infirm men were sometimes employed picking oakum for stuffing mattresses; elderly men often worked in the garden. Women of all ages picked oakum and were employed on divers domestic tasks: washing, cleaning, sewing, cooking and nursing the sick.

Inmates who refused to work were punished severely. In 1841, John Mullard, a weaver from Stokesay, refused to weave in the workhouse unless 'encouraged' by some payment. He was taken before the Magistrates and sentenced to 14 days in Salop County Gaol. The Guardians never tried to help or encourage able-bodied inmates, even those with valuable skills, to find employment outside the house.

Accommodation for inmates was as cheerless as their diet. After supper they retired – in summer well before dark – to dormitories furnished with beds and little else. There were no bedside lockers, and nowhere for inmates to keep their personal effects, although in 1867 the Guardians agreed, on the recommendation of the Inspector, to provide small bedside tables in the sick wards. In the early days, some wards were overcrowded and others malodorous. In 1842 Valentine was brave enough to complain directly to the PLC about the offensive odour in the sick wards and the inadequate space – 15 inches – between beds in the children's wards.

The toilet facilities in the workhouse remained primitive until late in the century. In 1841 the Guardians described as "unnecessary and heavy expense" the Master's purchase of 4 dozen chamber pots, and forced him to return them to the supplier. Thirty years later, the Medical Officer of Health, in a report on the Ludlow workhouse, described the lavatory facilities as "combining all the worst features of the privy and the water closet." He also recommended that the house be fitted with gas, an idea that the Guardians had been resisting since it was first suggested in 1867, arguing that the inmates might interfere with the taps.

The Ludlow Guardians fought a long battle with the poor law authorities over the question of single beds. In 1858 the PLB, following an adverse report on the workhouse from one of its inspectors, asked that adult 'idiots' should not be allowed to share a bed. The Guardians agreed. Ten years later, the PLB made several attempts to persuade the Ludlow Board to provide single beds for all adult inmates. (In

1868, only 14 out of 64 women and 21 out of 49 men had single beds.) The Guardians always rejected these requests.

Towards the end of the century, conditions in the Ludlow workhouse may have fallen behind those in other places. In 1886 an inspector reported on Ludlow's cold wards, thin blankets and grim stone floors: he concluded that "it is impossible to report favourably of this workhouse."

DISCIPLINE AND PUNISHMENT

When the Ludlow workhouse opened, the Guardians published guidelines on the punishments that would follow any infringement of "the rules of the house". Only the Master was authorised to inflict punishment, which might entail the isolation of the offending pauper, a diet of bread and water for up to 24 hours, the enforced wearing of distinctive 'refractory' clothing, or various forms of corporal punishment. For what were considered more serious offences, the Guardians could also take inmates before the magistrates for possible committal to prison. The right of inmates to discharge themselves was suspended for those facing such charges.

In Ludlow, the most common offence was absconding "with the workhouse clothes" – a phrase always used by the authorities to justify the pursuit and arrest of offenders. Young women and children, for whom workhouse life must have seemed unbearably tedious, were the main absconders. Some boys showed extraordinary skill and ingenuity in escaping. Edward Lewis, a frequent absconder described by the Master as "a most daring fellow", was once put to stone breaking in the men's yard with his legs tied together: he escaped at the next meal break.[15] When Lewis was eventually recovered and taken before the magistrates, he was merely reprimanded and discharged. The magistrates were often reluctant to punish children for such adventures, but took a harder line with adult absconders. In 1842 Edward

Wall, an able-bodied inmate, was arrested in the Black Country and returned to Ludlow after a reward had been offered for his apprehension. The magistrates sent him to prison for three months.

This unflattering description of young Lucy Haycock shows how determined the Ludlow Guardians could be in their pursuit of absconders from the workhouse. Lucy was arrested in May 1873: the reward was paid to Superintendent Brookes himself.

For young inmates who wanted more than a short break from the tedium of the workhouse, the Black Country was a magnet of opportunity and excitement. In 1846 the Superintendent of Police in Bilston informed the Guardians that he

had detained a deaf and dumb lad wearing clothes marked 'LUWH'. The boy was Richard Bristow of Munslow. The Master was instructed to bring him back to Ludlow not, as one might suppose, to celebrate his courage and determination but "with a view to his being punished by the magistrates for his offence". Absconding became less frequent in the second half of the century, but when it happened it was punished severely. Six months after Charles White left the workhouse in 1877, without notice and wearing the workhouse clothes, he was arrested in Shifnal and given 14 days hard labour in Salop County Gaol.

Absconding children were not normally given corporal punishment, although when in 1845 three boys absconded and were brought back to the workhouse hours later they were "birched in bed" by the Master.[16] Flogging was the usual punishment for theft and violent behaviour. The boy Williams, "having used threatening conduct to the Matron," was flogged and kept away from school for a month. William Beaumont, aged 9, stole £2/0/6d from the desk of the Schoolmistress, Lavinia Moon, and hid the money under the floorboards in his dormitory. He was ordered a flogging, but Miss Moon persuaded the Guardians to suspend the punishment. For less serious thefts by children, other punishments were sometimes used. After Thomas Minton stole a book worth 1/- from a Ludlow bookshop, he was made to wear "a badge of disgrace on his breast and back with the word 'thief' upon it".[17]

The Guardians permitted premeditated corporal punishment but disapproved of its casual use. When it emerged that a newly appointed Master was in the habit of punishing naughty children by "cuffing them with his hand and other rough treatment" he was reprimanded and admonished to be "more temperate and cautious", to avoid summary corporal punishments and to follow the rules of the house, which provided for minor offences to be punished by putting children to bed early or 'mulcting' them of their dinner.

THE CHILDREN

Some children were orphaned or abandoned, and therefore alone in the workhouse; others had one or both parents in the adult wings. (Mothers were allowed to 'interview' their children daily, by arrangement with the Master or Matron.) It is hard to explain why so many of the Ludlow inmates were children – around 50%, against a national average of about 25%.[18] It may have been a consequence of the high illegitimacy rate in Victorian Shropshire, which in 1887 was 9.1 per 1000 births, against a national average of 4.8. Many children were born inside the workhouse, where there was no special food for expectant mothers and little expert care in childbirth. (There were no women on the PLC staff, and no female Guardians anywhere in England until late in the century.)

The workhouse was an unhealthy place in which to raise children. Some ailments were endemic, including diarrhoea and 'the itch'. The Medical Officer attributed the latter to too many children sharing the same bed. In 1840 it was therefore agreed that no more than 2 inmates, adults or children, should sleep in one bed. From time to time diseases like smallpox raged through the house. After the 1841 epidemic, the Guardians held an Inquiry into "The cause of illness of some of the younger children." They were satisfied that conditions in the workhouse were "perfectly healthy, the diet good and wholesome" and that the deaths that had occurred were due to "constitutional ailments and predisposed consumption". They did, however, decide that the children should get more exercise outside the workhouse, and more nutritious food. The Clerk was told to read formally before the (presumably reluctant) Schoolmistress and Master an order of the Board that the children should be taken for walks 3 times a week. In Ludlow, such resolutions were often short-lived. After a similar crisis in 1861, the Guardians allowed the Medical Officer to set a special diet for children for the next six months, and resolved that the children "should be taken outside the house occasionally when practicable in fine weather." When it was wet or cold, the children stayed in. The Master once suggested that the children, who usually went to church on Sundays, should have cloaks and asked for permission to buy 30 yards of material. The Chairman refused, writing "the children not to go to church in the winter" in the Master's Report Book.

Until late in the century, workhouse children were educated within 'the house'. Most workhouse schoolteachers were badly paid and untrained; some were illiterate.[19] The Ludlow school opened in 1839, with Mr and Mrs David Jones as Schoolmaster and Schoolmistress, on a joint salary of £26 *per annum*. (The porter earned £25). Within a few months, Mr Jones was dismissed for insolence and intemperance, and his wife continued alone, on a salary of £20, until she was sacked a year later. Thereafter the Guardians employed a series of resident schoolmistresses, seventeen altogether between 1840 and 1889, when the school closed. Under two of these teachers, Miss Moon (1848-1862) and Miss Clarke (1878-1883), the school flourished and received favourable reports from the poor law school inspectors. Most of the others stayed for only a few months, or for various reasons were asked to leave. In 1842, Miss Graham quarrelled with the Master. In 1862, another Master made Miss Beddoes pregnant. In 1870, it was discovered that Miss Sambrook knew no arithmetic, and in 1877 Miss Wright proved to be a poor disciplinarian. The last in the line, Miss Moran, had been appointed *in absentia* on a salary of £20 a year and on the strength of a photograph of herself that she had sent from Cambridge: she became redundant when the school closed in 1889. Thereafter the workhouse children went to the two National Schools in Ludlow.

The workhouse school curriculum, as originally defined by the PLC, had called for at least 3 hours daily instruction in reading, writing and the principles of the Christian religion, and "such other instructions …as are calculated to train (the children) to habits of usefulness, industry and virtue".[20] There was, however, a perpetual tension between these educational aims and the Guardians' view that the schoolmistress should also act as a general assistant to the Master and Matron. This often led to disputes over priorities. When, in 1848, the Poor Law Inspector advised the Ludlow Board that reference to this administrative role should be omitted from future advertisements for schoolteachers, the Guardians were unconvinced, and asked the PLB if schoolmistresses should really be expected to devote all their time to the children. They were assured that the Inspector was right.

The most serious disagreements between the Ludlow Board and the workhouse school inspectors occurred over what was called 'industrial training'. The inspectors repeatedly urged the Guardians to help the children to acquire practical skills. In 1851, the resourceful and determined Jehingir Symons, who had been inspecting the Ludlow school for several years, argued that even under a competent schoolmistress "what occasional work they do cannot fit these children for earning an independent livelihood and will therefore not prevent them from becoming paupers of the future." Symons felt that 'spade husbandry' was the key skill for boys, and urged the Board to recruit a gardener to teach it, whose salary could be recovered from Treasury funds. The Guardians always refused such offers, arguing that there was no time for industrial training when the boys' services were "greatly necessary at the pump and other household tasks". Eventually, however, they gave in and appointed a gardener, Symons having offered the Union £1 from the Parliamentary Grant for every boy efficiently taught.

There were similar problems with industrial training for girls. In the 1860s, the Guardians recruited someone to teach domestic skills, but the Inspector complained that although she was paid from the Parliamentary Grant she was "much employed as a servant in the workhouse". So the Board discharged her and gave the responsibility for girls' industrial training to an adult inmate. This experiment failed, the Master reporting that the inmate concerned used 'bad language', the girls were becoming insubordinate and that those prepared in this way "would not be likely to turn out so well as servants."

Two kinds of apprenticeship were available to boys from the workhouse. A few were bound to local tradesmen, often tailors. Many more became mining apprentices in the Staffordshire coalfield. In the 1840s and 1850s, dozens of Ludlow workhouse boys, some as young as 10, went to mines in the Black Country and several were killed or badly injured.[21] The Guardians continued to send boys into mining, even when the risks were known, and to employers who had mistreated previous Ludlow apprentices. There were few comparable opportunities for girls, although in 1846 nine Ludlow workhouse girls, aged between 12 and 20, were taken to work in a Stockport mill.

In 1869, the Ludlow Board decided that, ideally, boys should go into service with local farmers, and asked the PLB if they could be bound indefinitely into such service. The PLB replied that training in "ploughing, sowing, reaping, planting and the like" was acceptable, but that they could not condone boys being bound for several years "simply to act as agricultural labourers". In fact, most Ludlow workhouse boys ended up as unskilled labourers and most girls in domestic service.

At about this time, the Board made a commendable attempt to improve the quality of life of some workhouse children by boarding out orphans and deserted children with respectable cottagers in the Ludlow area. Each family received a weekly allowance of 2/6 to 3/- for board and lodging, and the children were given clothes "not of a workhouse character". The Board paid their school fees. At first, the experiment went well, but by 1872 the Guardians concluded that "it is very doubtful whether the children are not better taught and cared for in the workhouse than by Foster Parents", and a few years later, after alleged ill-treatment of some of the children, the scheme was abandoned.

SOME ADULT INMATES

The noisiest and worst behaved parts of most workhouses were usually the able-bodied women's wards.[22] Ludlow was no exception. As we have seen, some young women would discharge themselves before the Ludlow Races or the May Fair and return immediately afterwards. Although the Guardians could not prevent this practice, they tried to separate those they called "women of bad character" from other able-bodied women. Young women were in the workhouse for various reasons: some were widows or had been abandoned by their husbands. Many were unmarried mothers. There were also, in Ludlow as elsewhere, a number of prostitutes who used the workhouse as a safe haven. The Guardians tried to isolate them from male inmates and from the other women, but their efforts were often unsuccessful. At times, the Ludlow workhouse had a reputation for moral turpitude. In 1843 the Mayor of Ludlow was reported to have said in the Guildhall, in his "magisterial capacity", that certain inmates had been delivered of children "which must have been begotten in the workhouse." The Guardians disputed this, but the records show that the Mayor was right. Mary Sergeant's baby was born after an encounter with a stonemason working on the building, and Mary Banks conceived after intercourse in the hearse-house with a tramp.[23] Charlotte Green, aged 14,was sent to the Magdalen Hospital in London for 'reclamation', "she being a thief as well as a prostitute and in other respects exceeding depraved", but she was returned to Ludlow because she was suffering from venereal disease.

The Ludlow Guardians interpreted the term 'bad character' more widely than many would today. The Master was empowered to separate from other women those in the habit of using strong or obscene language, and unmarried mothers were sometimes treated harshly. In 1842 the Guardians ordered that the Master or the Porter should attend church on Sundays, taking any adult inmate who cared to attend except women with illegitimate children. (This order was later dropped on the advice of the PLC.)

In the second half of the century the workhouse became primarily a home for the old and frail. This change of function was partly due to changes in the attitude of the poor law authorities to the care of the indigent elderly. Until 1870, the PLC and its successors had condoned the payment of small amounts of outdoor relief to old people who were reluctant to go into the workhouse. After 1870, the poor law inspectors put pressure on the Unions to 'offer the house' to elderly applicants for relief, partly to encourage their relatives to take responsibility for them.

For the elderly, conditions in the workhouse were little better than those for able-bodied inmates. They were expected to work hard, and to wear 'parochial' clothes. There were few dietary concessions, even for those with poor teeth and digestions, although, as we have seen, sympathetic medical officers readily prescribed beer and whisky for the elderly infirm. Even in the 1830s, Boards of Guardians had had the power to provide, for elderly married couples, "sleeping apartments by themselves detached from the other paupers,"[24] but few Unions made such arrangements. The first time the Ludlow Board allowed an elderly couple to live together was in 1876, and ten years later the LGB was still reminding the Ludlow Guardians that elderly couples entering the workhouse should not be separated.

Life became more uncomfortable for elderly men in the Ludlow workhouse when, as sometimes happened, they were made to share their accommodation with mentally ill paupers, some of whom were violent. In 1850, the Master was trying to restrain Thomas Watkins, a violent 'lunatic'. He reported that "there has been the greatest difficulty in keeping him within the walls of the premises, and I have only been able to do so by locking him up with the old men in their dayroom".[25]

The workhouse always had about a dozen mentally ill and mentally handicapped inmates: 'lunatics' and 'idiots' were the terms then used. Unions were encouraged to transfer these inmates to the county lunatic asylums. There were usually about 20 paupers from Ludlow in these institutions, but for financial reasons the Guardians kept that number as low as possible. It cost about 12/- to 14/- a week to maintain a pauper in an asylum, which was much higher than the comparable cost of a place in the

Mrs Harriet James, who reached her 100th birthday in the Ludlow workhouse in 1916. By then conditions for the elderly had improved, but the Guardians refused a request to commemorate the event by giving the elderly women in the workhouse a special tea. Mrs James died in 1917.
Ludlow Museum photograph

workhouse, and in their search for economies the Ludlow Guardians obtained quotations from asylums as far away as Carmarthen.

From time to time, the Guardians ordered their medical officers to visit asylums where there were Ludlow paupers, to see if any could be returned to the workhouse. Paupers were brought back if the doctor believed that they were feigning insanity in order to enjoy the better conditions that prevailed in asylums. In 1850, Francis Havard was withdrawn from Kingsland Asylum after a Ludlow doctor reported that he was a "downright impostor". He soon showed what the Master described as his "unconquerable propensity... for striking other inmates." Within weeks of his return he was sentenced to 28 days in gaol for violent behaviour. Despite the magistrates' recommendation that he be sent back to an asylum, he remained in the workhouse until 1852 when he attacked two old men. He was then, by order of the magistrates, sent to the Salop Lunatic Asylum where he died in 1856.

From the 1870s onwards, the 'Commissioners in Lunacy' regularly inspected the Ludlow workhouse. They demanded better food and accommodation for their charges than did other poor law inspectors because they ignored the need to achieve 'less eligibility',[26] and their reports on Ludlow were often scathing. In 1879 they found the accommodation "dull and cheerless", with inadequate washing facilities and clothing that was too thin for winter wear. They made similar criticisms in 1888. In 1896 they insisted that inmates should be bathed weekly, and not once every two or three weeks as was the case in Ludlow.

The mentally handicapped were probably better off in asylums than in workhouses, where they were made to work for long hours at unpleasant tasks. Four 'idiots' in Ludlow operated the capstan pump, described by the Lunacy Commissioners as "not a cheerful occupation." (The Master reassured the Guardians that the 'idiots' only did this job for 3 or 4 hours a day.) There were also instances of monstrous neglect. When the young 'idiot' Jane Hughes was discharged into the care of her mother in 1861, she was found to be suffering from venereal disease. In the Inquiry that followed the mother's complaint to the magistrates both the Matron and the Nurse were formally censured.

VAGRANTS

No one knows how many vagrants were tramping the roads of Victorian England, some in search of work and others for whom vagrancy was a way of life. No national statistics were kept, but the Webbs estimated that when trade was bad there were about 80,000 on the roads, and half that number in good times.[27] Ludlow had more than its fair share: in the 1840s about 500 a year passed through the workhouse, and the numbers gradually rose until they reached 2,547 in 1880. In 1894 the workhouse took in about 4,500 vagrants, including nearly 400 in one fortnight in December, and the numbers remained at about 4,000 a year until the end of the century.

Ludlow, like other Unions, had made no preparations to accommodate vagrants. When the first arrived in 1839 the women were put into the coalhouse and the men into a clothing store. A special ward for male vagrants was built in 1843, with its own yard separated from the rest of the workhouse by a high stone wall. In the 1860s, when vagrancy was increasing, a detached room was provided for vagrants thought to be suffering from cholera.

The Guardians seemed indifferent to the comfort and dignity of vagrants. Like all those entering the workhouse, vagrants were bathed on arrival. But whereas the Matron bathed long stay female inmates, the porter bathed *all* vagrants. In 1881, Albert Worthington was reprimanded for unseemly behaviour when bathing vagrant women. The food offered to vagrants was meagre: only 2/3rds of the ordinary diet of the able-bodied inmate. They were also expected to work for their night's lodgings. Every male vagrant had to 'break small' 2½ cwt of Jewstone before breakfast, and every woman to pick at least one pound of oakum or cocoanut fibre. In 1843, the PLC approved an arrangement whereby male vagrants would be expected to break stone for two hours before breakfast and another two hours after.

As the numbers of vagrants grew, so did the determination of the Board to make their stay in Ludlow as uncomfortable as possible. In 1861

By the end of the 19th century, ivy had overgrown the administrative wing of the Ludlow workhouse, then known as Ivy House. Accommodation for vagrants, built in the second half of the century, can be seen to the right of the main building.
Shropshire Archives
PHL/31/13

the Guardians resolved that "a board only be provided for vagrants to sleep on, with one rug each for covering, and for supper and breakfast bread and water only be given to the able-bodied". The Assistant Commissioner immediately declared this resolution void. Two years later, vagrants visiting Ludlow were offered a choice: perform 'the usual task' and have breakfast, or leave without working but also without breakfast.

Whether it was a cause or a consequence of the treatment they received, many vagrants behaved badly: breaking windows, seducing the workhouse women, and refusing to work. The punishment for these offences was often severe. Two women were given 21 days in Shrewsbury gaol for breaking windows after the Master had withheld their breakfasts because they had used "bad and abusive language". Four men who refused to work after breakfast were given two months with hard labour, as were two others who broke 16 panes of glass in 1857. Some Ludlow magistrates, however, evidently felt that not even vagrants should be asked to work on empty stomachs. In 1859 they declined to punish a tramp for refusing to work before breakfast. The Guardians immediately changed the rules, and when, two weeks later, a vagrant refused to work *after* breakfast he was given three months in the County gaol.

In 1890, the board accepted an offer from the Tramp Mission to furnish the vagrants' accommodation with a small library of books "being of a strictly religious and non-controversial character" and various scriptural wall cards. This was the only recorded improvement before 1900 in conditions for vagrants using the Ludlow workhouse.

CORRECTION AND CARE

In 1868 John Southern, the Medical Officer for the Clee Hill district of the Ludlow Union, told the Board that surgical operations "in small and badly lighted cottages are attended with discomfort and danger", and it was agreed that,

where safe removal was possible, such operations would in future be conducted in the workhouse. This was a landmark decision. All the major additions to the workhouse after 1870, including fever wards and extensions to the infirmary, strengthened its medical functions. In 1839 the workhouse had been primarily a concentration camp for the supposedly indolent: by 1900 it had become a hospital and a home for the old and vulnerable.

This change of emphasis, from correction to care, might have been accompanied by improvements in the conditions of workhouse inmates, but those who managed the workhouse did not always understand the need for such changes. The Guardians were keen to safeguard the interests of ratepayers, and it was usually cheaper to preserve existing practices than to make improvements. The dietary, disciplinary and other systems that were first introduced to make the workhouse unattractive to able-bodied idlers had, in the second half of the century, settled into familiar routines that the Guardians and their officers were reluctant to abandon.

The two most influential groups on the Ludlow Board were farmers and Anglican clergymen from the villages around Ludlow. Both groups were innately conservative on social issues. As the Guardians were never given any training in how to administer the poor law, apart from the directives of the poor law authorities and occasional visits from inspectors, this conservatism tended to permeate the decisions of the Board. Nor were the workhouse officers active proponents of change. The first Masters were appointed when the prime need was thought to be to achieve an orderly and disciplined regime within the workhouse. (The PLC believed that the best Masters were former non-commissioned officers from the army or retired policemen.)[28] Such men set the pattern for those who followed. Moreover workhouse staff had little contact with the outside world. They worked long hours, had infrequent and unpaid holidays, and their only associates, apart from the inmates and the Guardians, were the other officers. In Ludlow, relations between officers were often stormy, particularly those between the Master and the Matron on the one hand and the Schoolmistress on the other. In such tense and claustrophobic conditions, and under the scrutiny of a conservative Board, Ludlow Masters usually felt more secure following their familiar custodial practices, and they maintained those practices long after their relevance for most inmates had passed.

Apart from a few courageous Medical Officers, there were no champions of reform in the Ludlow Union. Even if there had been, it is doubtful if they could have coped with two essentially contradictory functions: within one building, and under one management, to deter the idle and to care for the sick and helpless. Deterrence was usually the priority in the Ludlow workhouse, but it would be wrong to conclude that the inmates were treated with deliberate malevolence. The Guardians, and most of the officers, were honest and industrious. They were sometimes harsh, and often parsimonious, but their harshness and parsimony were consonant with their values and experience. If the Ludlow workhouse was a cruel place, it was the cruelty of prejudice, neglect and indifference. We know that many people in Victorian England would have preferred to starve than enter the workhouse. It was, perhaps, the loss of dignity and identity that they dreaded more than the bleak conditions and the awful food.

We cannot say how Ludlow compared with other workhouses, because this study has only been concerned with Ludlow. As we have seen, some inspectors were critical of conditions in Ludlow, but the differences between most workhouses were probably marginal. They all had to cope with what Crowther called the "unresolvable tension" between deterrence and care. Perhaps Ludlow was a little less generous than some of its neighbours. A vagrant once wrote this message on a wall where other vagrants could see it. "A stunning workhouse for a good supper and breakfast. Much Wenlock, lads, that's the place."[29] If only the Ludlow workhouse had such an epitaph.

Many 19th century workhouses have survived in the 21st century as parts of NHS hospitals. In this photograph, substantial elements of the original Ludlow workhouse, including the administrative wing and the Master's quarters, can be seen alongside the more modern parts of what is now Ludlow Community Hospital.

ENDNOTES

1. The main source of information on the Ludlow Union is the PL9 Collection in the Shropshire Archives, Shrewsbury. Occasional visitors to the Ludlow workhouse were able to write their comments in the 'Unofficial' Visitors Book, so called to distinguish it from the Visitors Books used by the Guardians in their weekly inspections.

2. Unless otherwise indicated, this chapter takes its evidence about life in the workhouse from the Minute Books of the Ludlow Board of Guardians, from PL9/2/1/1 (July 1836 to August 1838) to PL9/2/1/20 (February 1899 to January 1902).

3. Master's Report Book and Journal, October 1844 – February 1845 PL9/20/4/1.

4. Crowther M.A., *The Workhouse System 1834-1929* p.13.

5. Ludlow Workhouse Rules 1836 PL9/1/1/2.

6. Webb S. and B., *English Poor Law History* Part 2, Vol. 1 1963 p.129.

7. A map of the Union and its parishes accompanies the chapter on outdoor relief: see chapter 8.

8. For a review of the work of the Board, see Williams D. "The Ludlow Guardians 1836-1900" *Transactions of the Shropshire Archaeological and Historical Society* (forthcoming).

9. Englander D., *Poverty and Poor Law Reform in 19th Century Britain* 1998 p.31.

10. Hall I. and Williams D., Building the Ludlow Workhouse *Ludlow Heritage News* No. 27 1997.

11. Statistical Return for the quarter ending March 1842 PL9/4/2/1.

12. In 1847 the Poor Law Board (PLB) replaced the Poor Law Commission (PLC). This lasted until 1871 when, in another reorganisation, the PLB became a department of the Local Government Board (LGB).

13. Statistical Return for the quarter ending March 1841 PL9/4/1/2.

14. Rule XIII, 1836, PL9/1/1/2.

15. Master's Report Book April and July 1845 PL9/20/4/1.

16. Ibid., October 1845.

17. Ibid., June 1845.

18. Longmate N., *The Workhouse* 1974 p.14.

19. Ibid., p.14.

20. Establishment Order PL9/1/1/2.

21. For a fuller account of the experiences of boys from the Ludlow workhouse in Staffordshire mines, see D. Williams "Did he fall or was he pushed?" Ludlow Heritage News No. 28 1997.

22. Longmate, op. cit., p.13.

23. Master's Report Book January 1843 PL9/20/4/1.

24. Ludlow workhouse rules PL9/1/1/2.

25. Master's Report Book September 1850 PL9/20/4/2.

26. Webb., op. cit., p.339.

27. Ibid., p.403.

28. Crowther, op. cit., p.118.

29. Longmate. op, cit., p.238.

CHAPTER 8

OUT RELIEF IN THE 19TH CENTURY LUDLOW UNION

IVAN HALL

The Parishes of the Ludlow Union

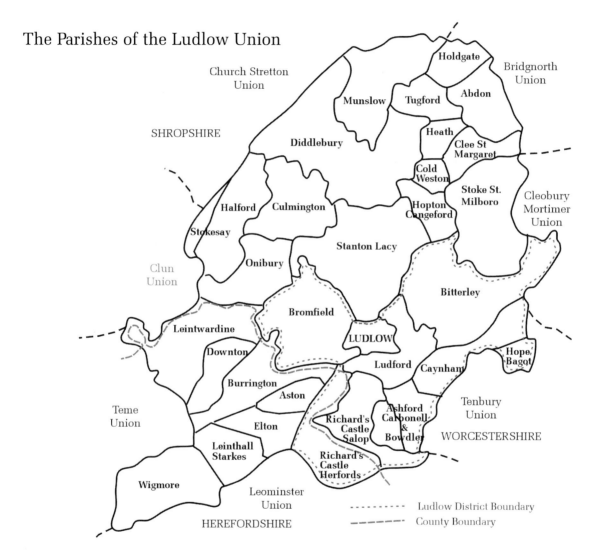

The Poor Law Amendment Act of 1834 was intended to reduce, or at least contain, the increasing cost of poor relief that was seen as a great burden on the ratepayers. The system whereby each parish, acting through its unpaid Overseer, relieved its own poor was abolished, and Poor Law 'Unions' of, on average, about 30 parishes were established throughout England & Wales to administer what became known as 'the new poor law'. Each Union was to be governed by a Board of Guardians, appointed by and from the local ratepayers, and accountable to the Poor Law Commission in London.[1] The Act required that relief to certain categories of paupers, including able-bodied workers and their families, and unmarried mothers and their children, should be provided only within strictly managed workhouses. Whereas the Commissioners insisted that the workhouse was the only form of relief to be offered to the idle and the morally degenerate, the Boards of Guardians were given some discretion in how they provided relief to other classes of pauper, including the indigent elderly, and the sick and handicapped. Relief for these groups might be provided in the workhouse or through 'out relief' that maintained paupers in their own homes.

The response of the Boards of Guardians to these provisions was extremely varied. Some Unions implemented the new system with enthusiasm; at the other extreme were Unions that would not even build a workhouse. But the majority, into which the Ludlow Union fell, chose to compromise, co-operating much of the time, but choosing to exercise local discretion, ignoring the regulations and exploiting the many allowed 'exceptions' to the full as it suited them. In fact, as Rose has written, "The grim workhouse is often seen as the symbol of the Poor Law, but only 10%-20% of paupers ever saw its inside."[2]

The Poor Law Commissioners attempted to influence the practice of the Unions with periodic Orders, but to little effect. Writing of the Shropshire Boards, Crowther says that they "persistently opposed the Commissioners, and local rather than central issues determined the treatment of the poor. Contrary to the whole intention of the Poor Law, how an applicant was relieved depended very much on where he or she lived."[3] Thus it was that throughout seventy years the Ludlow Union continued to issue to paupers money, food, clothing, footwear, port wine, and artificial limbs, and to provide medical attention, nursing and, finally, funeral expenses for a Christian burial. All such assistance was meagre; scarcely sufficient to keep body and soul together, but just enough to keep the recipient out of the workhouse. It is a consideration of this provision, known variously as out maintenance, out door relief, or out relief, that forms the substance of this chapter.[4]

In common with most other Unions in the country, Ludlow was at first unable to implement the provisions of the 1834 Act since it did not have the appropriate workhouse accommodation. There was a small rented workhouse in Old Street (now known as Lane's Asylum) and another at Leintwardine. Although they continued in use for a time, they were quite unsuitable and inadequate within the meaning of the Act. So, until a new house was built, the Union had no choice but to provide out relief, the Guardians receiving instructions and guidance from the Commissioners as to how this was to be done.

The Ludlow Union included 32 parishes in South Shropshire and North Herefordshire (see the accompanying map of the Ludlow Union and its constituent parishes) with a population of about 17,000 in the 1830s. To facilitate the payment of relief the area was divided into three (occasionally four) Districts. For each District it was necessary to appoint a salaried Relieving Officer. The system being new, there was no pool of trained or experienced men from which the Guardians could choose; they just had to advertise, and to appoint whom they thought fit. Together with a residential qualification, the essentials were literacy, numeracy, and integrity; references and a bond were required, for those appointed would be handling an average of £1,500 p.a. on a salary of £60. The appointment of a Relieving Officer always assured a good attendance at the Board of Guardians meeting, and no doubt a fair amount of lobbying went on. On the whole the Guardians' appointments were satisfactory, although on one occasion they did manage to appoint an illiterate, and one or two other Relieving Officers absconded with some of the funds.

It was the Relieving Officer's responsibility to enter in his Application and Report Book those paupers who had applied for relief, and to report to the Guardians' fortnightly meeting his assessment of the validity and necessity of the application. Age, sex, status, calling, income, health, disability, family size and composition

NAMES of APPLICANTS, their Wives, and Children under 16, dependent on them.	Age	RESIDENCE. Where, or with whom.	CALLING.	If Adult, whether Single, Married, Widower, or Widow; If Child, whether Orphan, Deserted, or Illegitimate.	Ordinary Able-bodied.	If partially or wholly Disabled, and the Description of Disability.	Medical Relief.	Regular or Temporary Relief, and say whether, and what Relief from Clubs, Charitable Institutions, Government Pensions, or otherwise; such Relief, Pension, Allowance, or Contribution to be described, and the Amount stated.	Present Cause of seeking Relief, or Nature of Application.
6th Week Cont.d Wednesday August 8th 1849									
Lloyd Philip	60	In the Square	Groom	Married	Yes	Neither	No	Neither	For the medical orders to and for 16/10 The expenses of
Late Elizabeth his Wife	56						Yes		
- Harriet	11								
- George	5								
Late Baynham Martha	27	Frog Lane	Servant	Single	No	Dead	Yes	none	For 16/10 the expenses of
Edwards William	69	Ludlow, but belong to Lindfield	—	—	No	Partially from a bad leg.	Yes	has 4/6 weekly	For 4 in addition to the
Jones Thomas	28	Absconded from his family	Labourer	Married	Yes	Neither	no	None	For 6 given & for 2/6 weekly
" Sarah Wife	27	Stone Yard Ludlow							till she hears from her hus
" Jemima	3½								band
" John	1½								
Surrall James	50	Frog Lane	Blacksmith	Married	Yes	Wholly from a broken leg.	Yes	has 5/ weekly	For the 5/ to be continued 2 weeks longer
" Elizabeth Wife	49								
" Eliza	8								
" Jane	4								
Prince James	63	Upper Goalford	Labourer	Married	no	Partially from Asthma	Yes	has had relief during illness	For 1/6 weekly given for weeks
" Eliza Wife	46								
Santram Derah	53	In Workhouse	Labourer	Widow	Yes	Neither	no	None	For Workhouse order
" John	10								
Maggs Hannah	50	Frog Lane	—	Single	Yes	Partially from a diseased leg	Yes	has 2/6 Weekly	For an additional
Powell Martha	82	Lower Goalford belongs to Hope under Dinmore	Labourer	Widow	no	Partially from age and infirmity	has 2/6 weekly	For 3/ Temporary

This page and next: A page from one of the Application and Report books kept by the relieving officers for all paupers receiving out relief.

(especially as to earners and dependants), family members outside the household who might be expected to give support – indeed anything that could have a bearing on the application – needed to be recorded. It should be noted that although children up to the age of sixteen were recorded, from the age of seven they were expected to be contributors to the family income.

On this information the Board would decide if relief was appropriate, and if so, whether it should be 'the house' or out relief; and if the latter whether it should be regular or temporary, in cash or in kind. 'In kind' sometimes involved a 'ticket' for specific foods. There was a period when bread was issued, baked in the work-house or in country parishes, and distributed from rented Bread Stations.

Paupers who, because of a permanent disability, chronic bad health, or old age, were never going to be able to support themselves alone, but with a little help could get by, were likely to be put on the regular list. By far the greatest amount of out relief was distributed to those on this list, averaging about six times as much as for those who received temporary relief although the numbers in each category were about equal (See Chart 1). In the early years of the Union the regular list was reviewed at six monthly intervals. Receiving a bare minimum, the 'regulars' might well have to apply on occasion for some extra temporary relief.

For the Quarter ending _Michaelmas_ **1849.**

OBSERVATIONS, and Names of Relations liable by Law to relieve the Applicant, distinguishing those apparently capable of assisting the Applicant.	Present Weekly Earnings, or other Income of Applicants, and Family dependent on them.	QUANTITY and DESCRIPTION of RELIEF IN KIND.				RELIEF ORDERED BY GUARDIANS.					Other Orders of the Board, (if any.)	Week when Order made.	Initials of Chairman or Clerk.	OBSERVATIONS.
		Reported as given by Overseer.	Given by Relieving Officer.	Value. s. d.	Date when given.	MONEY. s. d.	KIND.			For what Time allowed, or Nature of the Order made.				
							Quantity and Description.	Value. s. d.						
be confirmed at the Funeral	None	10/-				16 10	Funeral Expenses a/d						6 7CB	
the Funeral.						16 10	Funeral Expenses a/d						6 7CB	
allowed last Board day	uncertain			4	5th week	4	Temp'y						6 7CB	
				6	6th week	2 6	Weekly for Two Weeks						6 1CB	.
	none			allowed		5	Weekly for Two Weeks						6 7CB	
						3 6	Weekly for Two Weeks						6 7CB	
							to Workhouse order sent						6 7CB	
be confirmed ing						2 6 Refused	Weekly for Two Weeks						6 7CB	
						5	Temp'y						6 7CB	

Those receiving only temporary relief were usually (but not always) bread-winners who were experiencing a short period of difficulty as a result of accidents, ill health, bereavement or unemployment. Temporary relief was as a rule given for and reviewed at two-weekly intervals. There was no fixed tariff and the relief awarded could vary from as little as 4d for a pound of mutton to five shillings or more in rare cases.

Temporary relief of a different sort was given for what was, undoubtedly, the highest expenditure some poor families would ever face, the cost of a funeral. Many families might be existing precariously without relief, but the expense of a funeral would be beyond them and they would need to apply to "the Parish" as they would probably erroneously have called it. For this the Union had negotiated a contract with Prince, a local undertaker, with the cost of the funeral ranging from eight shillings to one pound four shillings depending on the size of the coffin.

More or less coterminous with but not completely coinciding with the Out Relief Districts were Medical Districts, each with its own Medical Officer appointed by the Guardians. If a pauper wished to consult the doctor he or she had first to apply to the Relieving Officer. "If in his superior judgement medical treatment was required he would report so to the Board which, if it approved, would make out the Medical Order for the District Medical Officer".[5]

At times of crisis the Relieving Officer was empowered to act on his own initiative but he had to justify retrospectively his activities to the

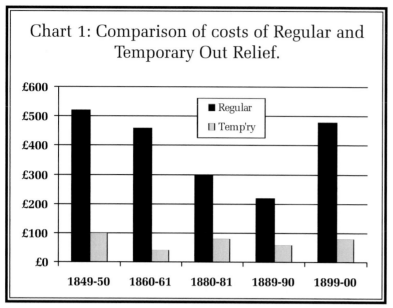

Chart 1: Comparison of costs of Regular and Temporary Out Relief.

£7,000, the parochial range being wide, from St Laurence, Ludlow at nearly £2,000 to Aston (£7) and Cold Weston (£2). When the list had been agreed it became known as the "Averages" and was intended to last for three years. Revision of the figures took place periodically in the light of the amounts actually spent by the Union on the poor of each parish. The Board issued to the parishes warrants, enforceable at law, for a proportion of the Averages, usually 10% in the first instance. From this the Relieving Officers were given a working balance of £18 to £20 from which to pay the paupers. The Clerk to the Board kept a running account of the monies paid in by each parish and that paid to the paupers of that parish, and if the latter exceeded the former further calls for a percentage of the Averages would be made. In essence, therefore, an important difference between the old arrangements and the new was that, whilst after 1836 each parish Overseer retained the responsibility to raise funds for the relief of paupers within his parish, he lost the right to determine how those funds should be spent. Many Overseers resented this, and many of the Ludlow Guardians – particularly those from the villages around Ludlow – sympathised with the Overseers to the point of publicly calling for a return to the old system, when unpaid Overseers with profound local knowledge decided who would get relief and how much.[7] But these protests fell on deaf ears.

Board. For example, he had the authority to offer relief in the house to single women who had a bastard or who were pregnant, for whom, as mentioned above, out relief was prohibited.

The Relieving Officers had to tread a narrow line between what the Guardians might see as excessive generosity and what might later be criticised as unduly harsh treatment. There were occasions in the Ludlow Union when Relieving Officers were fiercely criticised when neglect leading to starvation was suspected.

Although the parishes had, under the new arrangements, lost their freedom to administer relief to the poor, they were still expected to raise the funds that would now be spent by the Guardians and their officers. Each parish Overseer was required to collect from his ratepayers, enough money to cover the costs incurred by the Union in caring for the poor of that parish. In the beginning, the Union determined how much each parish should pay by averaging out the amount that that parish had spent on poor relief in the three years before 1836. The final decision on how much to collect from each parish was taken by the Board of Guardians, advised by the Assistant Poor Law Commissioner responsible for Ludlow and a number of neighbouring Unions.[6]

Initially, the total amounted to almost

Throughout England & Wales the administration of out relief was made extremely complicated by the laws governing the 'settlement' of paupers and their compulsory 'removal' from one parish to another. Under statutes that predated the 1834 reforms, parish Overseers had the right to return to the parish whence they came, or 'parish of settlement', any persons who had become a burden on the poor rates in a parish to which they subsequently moved, unless they had acquired a legal 'settlement' in that parish. The law required that the costs of such compulsory repatriation be borne by the parish of settlement. This led to a great deal of inter-parochial correspondence and litigation, described by one commentator as "15,000 republics engaged from time to time in bloodless war with one another."[8] In 1840, across England & Wales, some 40,000 paupers were removed from their places of residence to their parishes of settlement. Rather than bear the full costs of removal, parishes would often grant out relief to persons belonging to them but resident elsewhere, and arrange for the Union within which the pauper resided to administer such payments on their behalf. In England & Wales, there were 82,000 paupers in receipt of non-resident relief in 1846.[9]

In Ludlow, the Clerk dealt with questions of settlement and removal after noting from the Relieving Officers' records any discrepancy between an applicant's parish of residence and parish of settlement. In 1841/2, apart from interpreting various settlement issues within the Union, the Clerk dealt with 16 cases of individuals and families who had moved into the area from as far afield as Aberystwyth, Birmingham, and Bridgwater. Sarah Millman posed a particular problem. A single, 22 year old servant, she became pregnant and in June 1841 applied for relief. But Sarah was herself illegitimate and had been born in an 'extra parochial place' (i.e. a place which, for various historical reasons, was not attached to any particular parish; there were a number of such anomalies within the Ludlow Union). She therefore had no parish of settlement which meant that she could only be relieved in the Casual Ward – not an appropriate place to give birth. After consideration it was decided that she could enter the house. In December the Application and Report Book notes that a Workhouse Order was confirmed on her three month old daughter, Miriam, with a complaining note "Why chargeable to Ludlow?" By then Sarah had left the workhouse for employment in domestic service.

During the 19th century, the government made several attempts to mitigate the suffering amongst the poor caused by compulsory removal. The Poor Removal Act of 1846 rendered all those resident in a parish for more than 5 years "irremovable", and banned the removal of widows for a year after the death of their husbands, making the parish of residence responsible for their relief. In 1847, 'Bodkin's Act' placed the whole cost of relieving the irremovable poor on the 'Common Fund' of the Union, a fund which had hitherto been used mainly to finance certain general and administrative services. This meant that the Union as a whole and not the particular parish of settlement bore the costs of relief. By 1861 the cost of out relief for the irremovables had risen to be slightly higher than that for St Laurence Parish and formed almost 1/3 of the figure for the whole Ludlow District (See Table 1). In the same year the period of residence that conferred irremovability was reduced to 3 years, and the 1865 Union Chargeability Act reduced this period further, to one year. It also put the whole cost of all relief on the Union, making the Union the area of settlement, so that wealthy parishes from then on were obliged to help pay for relief in their poorer neighbours. By these means, settlement disputes in England & Wales fell from 16,000 *per annum* to 600.[10] These measures went some way towards reducing the misery caused by compulsory removal, but settlement disputes between Unions remained (there were 12,000 removals in 1907).

Changing definitions of irremovability and changes in accounting practices make it hard to compare the numbers and costs of out relief at different times between 1840 and 1900. With this proviso, the following account examines in more detail the working of the out relief system at approximately ten year intervals between 1839 and the end of the century. Most of the material used has been obtained from the Relieving Officers' Application and Report Books. Because of occasional ambiguities the

Table 1: Details of Out relief. Ludlow District. 1860-61 (PL9/24/19/3)						
	Regular.		**Temporary**			
Parish	**Number**	**Cost**	**Number**	**Dependants**	**Cost**	**Total**
Ashford Bow.	1	£5	None			£5
Ashford Carb.	5	£39	None			£39
Bitterley	29	£168	10	21	£14	£182
Cainham	30	£195	11	36	£25	£220
Ludford	3	£14	4	6	£1	£15
St Laurence	81	£456	44	65	£46	£502
Rich.Cas.Hfds.	11	£71	2		£5	£76
Rich.Cas.Slp.	10	£74	1			£74
Common Fund	58	£406	131	330	£117	£523
Non Settled	14	£100	None			£100
Totals	**242**	**£1528**	**203**	**458**	**£208**	**£1736**

accountancy is not 100% accurate, but the errors are not enough to distort the results, and they do give an idea of the personal circumstances of the applicants. Additional information has been gleaned from the Minute Books of Board meetings, and the Financial Statements presented to them.

The financial year of the Union began on 25 March (Lady Day). In the first full year of operation, 1837/38, total expenditure on poor relief was approximately £6,000, of which about £4,150 was for out relief, £231 on in-maintenance, with £72 for the rent of the two workhouses. The government was fortunate that the late 1830s were years of good harvests, so easing the burden of poverty during the period of change from the Old Poor Law to the New. (The pre-Union average was about £7,000.)

In the early days of the Union the accounting of the Relieving Officers was rather primitive – some of it on small pieces of unlined paper of various sizes, now held at the Shropshire Archive Centre. Fortunately the Ludlow Guardians – unlike most Shropshire Unions - had appointed a full time Clerk (Robert Thomas, a Ludlow solicitor). Working at first from temporary hired accommodation in the town, he it was who got things organised, but it took time to obtain the appropriate books. Even when they were in use the Relieving Officers needed to be

disciplined. A minute of 5 June, 1837 records a report from a special committee of Guardians that "the Relieving Officers' books are badly kept and many duties inefficiently performed, some totally neglected to the extent that it was difficult for the auditors and Clerk to make their returns to the Poor Law Commissioners. The weekly Outdoor and Receipt Books were neglected altogether." Again, the Committee discovered "many persons receiving relief who, though residing in the Union, had never been seen by a Relieving Officer, some parishes are seldom visited by them". The Officers were told that they had to visit parishes on given days at a certain hour every week and to make themselves thoroughly acquainted with each person. Another minute instructed that "the parish Officers be required to attend with the Relieving Officer to pay the poor."

By the year 1841/42 the new regime, with a purpose built Workhouse incorporating a boardroom and Clerk's office, had had two years in which to settle down. The cost of out relief in this year totalled a little under £3,600, a reduction on 1837/38, but it would not be so low again for many years (See Chart 2). In-maintenance costs had risen to about £1,200, so that the amount disbursed as out relief was almost three times as great. This ratio would at times increase over the next thirty years, and not

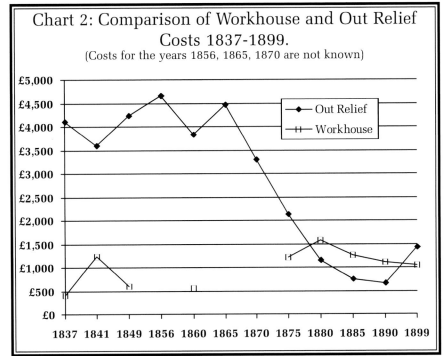

Chart 2: Comparison of Workhouse and Out Relief Costs 1837-1899.
(Costs for the years 1856, 1865, 1870 are not known)

children be removed to the Workhouse, a decision confirmed by the Poor Law Commissioners in spite of the fact that this contradicted that Order.

The Application and Report Book of the Relieving Officer for St Laurence Parish for 1841/42 was reasonably well kept, and gives a good insight into the living conditions of those Ludlovians who do not normally generate interest in an historic town. In most cases it gives the ages, status, and addresses of applicants, with the occasional explanatory note. However, it omits the paupers receiving regular relief, save those who were obliged to apply for additional temporary relief. There were fifteen such cases, mainly elderly – four of them were octogenarians – and widows with children. This may give a pointer to those who were receiving regular relief, but they might have been exceptions.

In all 91 paupers, with 125 dependants, made 221 applications for temporary relief for a total period of 257 weeks relief at a cost of £60. Nineteen funerals accounted for £16 of this total. Of the 91:

20 were 60 years old and over.

33 were married couples with a total of 80 children.

5 were widows and 2 were widowers under 60.

16 were single women; 7 of them pregnant, and 4 being servants.

13 were single men, mostly ill or disabled by accident. Typhus, fatigue through want of nourishment, crushed by cart, injured leg with stone hammer, fractured arm, are among the entries: funeral expenses of 4 of them were met.

4 were deserted wives with a total of 16 children.

until 1877 would the cost of out relief be brought down to the same level as that of in-maintenance. The question arises as to why the cost of out relief was so high.

In essence, the Guardians had an interest in keeping down the rates because they were all ratepayers, and all those who elected them were ratepayers. So they tended to adopt the cheapest option whenever possible, and in many cases this was out relief. Again, once inside the Workhouse the opportunity of a family finding employment – and much of it was of a very casual nature – would be more difficult, so that the social good was sometimes served by decisions aimed primarily at curtailing cost. In 1847 John Calstree of Leintwardine applied for relief. He had a wife and eight children to support on a labourer's weekly wage of 8s 0d. Due to the high cost of food he was unable to feed his family. Magistrates from the Leintwardine area, sitting on the Board as *ex-officio* Guardians, suggested that it would be cheaper to award 3s 0d weekly in out relief than to admit the whole family to the Workhouse, as required by the Outdoor Relief Prohibition Order. However, the full Board ordered that only two of the

Arising from these applications, the Guardians made 19 Workhouse Orders, 13 involving single women, and 6 single men.

Chart 3 shows the number of applications made during each quarter of 1841/42, beginning at 25 March. The number of applications gives a better indication of the need for relief than simply the number of applicants. It is noticeable that the number of applications increased quarter by quarter through the year, and that there was a dramatic increase in the final quarter (Jan. – March) of couples, most of whom had children. There was a similar increase in the number of Medical Orders authorised, with four times as many in the final quarter as the total of the three previous quarters. Many applications were solely for Medical Orders, indicating that there were families who coped until faced with the prospect of paying for a doctor. From the large number of Medical orders allowed it seems that ill health as much as unemployment was the cause of destitution.

These were the occupations of those who had recourse to poor relief in Ludlow at this time:

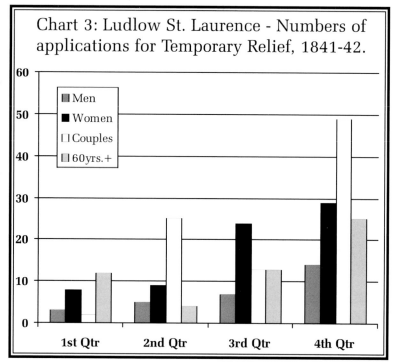

Chart 3: Ludlow St. Laurence - Numbers of applications for Temporary Relief, 1841-42.

Ballmaker	Besom maker	Blacksmith
Brickmaker	Cabinet maker	Carpenter
"Carries wood"	Charwoman	Cooper
Dressmaker	Fisherman	Flymaker
Gardener	Gas fitter	Gloveress
Hawker	Horse breaker	Imprisoned
Joiner	Labourer	Malt maker
Mason	Mason's labourer	Miller
Millwright	Nailer	Needlewoman
Ostler	Papermaker	Plasterer
Policeman	Saddler	Sawyer
Scavenger	Sempstress	Servant
Shoemaker	Spinner	Stocking knitter
Sweep	Stones castrator (deformed)	
Taylor	Tinman	Trader
Traveller	Travelling fiddler	Washerwoman

Labourers, servants, shoemakers and repairers were the most numerous categories, the last probably being indicative of the straitened circumstances of the poor – being literally 'down on their uppers'!

It is important to recognise that to some of those who would not normally expect to be poor, a sudden change in circumstances could bring destitution. Applicants of this type include:

Richard Taylor (38), a cooper, with a wife and five month old child. The wife was ill and they were allowed 2s 6d and a Medical order.

Edward Breeze, blacksmith, married with four children, was badly burned and applied for a Medical Order.

William Fox (37), policeman, supporting a wife and five children on 14s weekly and living in the yard of the King's Arms, applied for a Medical Order.

Richard Francis (58), cabinetmaker living in Corve Street with a wife and two children. Unable to work with "swelled legs and bad breath", he received 10s from his club, and asked for a Medical Order.

Richard Griffiths (42), a miller, with wife, Hannah (39), and two children, John (9) and

Elizabeth (2½) occupying one furnished room in Lower Gaolford for which they paid 1s 10d rent weekly. In July 1842 Richard was ill and, noting that he had a pension of 5s 10d weekly, probably from a Friendly Society, the Guardians awarded him a single payment of 9s. In September he applied again and was granted 2s 10d weekly for one month. Accompanying a further application in November, the Relieving Officer noted that "this man is so ill he must have a bed to himself", and "the boy is almost naked". It was ordered that a rug, blankets and sheets should be loaned, and 15s given for the boy. Nothing more is entered until the following February when Richard was dead and Hannah was allowed the usual funeral expenses. She was also allowed 3s temporary relief and 2s weekly. A little later she is entered in the Application Book in her own right as a widow at the same address, occupation "sempstress" continuing to receive 2s weekly, and applying for 2s for the boy's shoes to be repaired. Her regular relief would pay the rent with 2d over, with the bulk of their living expenses being the responsibility of mother and son who – at 9 years – would be regarded as an earner. Hence the need for his shoe repairs.

In general, the paupers lived in the southern and eastern parts of the town: 39 in Upper and Lower Gaolford; 23 in Old Gate and Holdgate Fee; 17 in Frog Lane and Lower Broad St, and smaller contingents in Corve Street, Temeside, and Rock Lane.

Characteristic of Ludlow's smaller yards was that of the King's Arms, in the Bull Ring. The photograph shows the yard in 1916, with John Fury, a Boer War veteran, helping to enlist recruits for World War I; but its appearance was much the same as it had been in the Victorian period. William Fox, aged 37, a police-man, lived here in 1843 and received 14s a week out relief to help support his wife and five children.

St John's Lane, sloping southwards towards Temeside, photographed in the 1960s, prior to redevelopment of the area left of the lane. In the 19th century this was one of the poorer parts of the town, with the families of labourers and other manual workers often receiving poor relief.

In 1849/50 the cost to the Union of in-maintenance was £604, and of out relief, £4,232 – a factor of seven. This was contrary to the expectations of the Poor Law Board and the intention of the 1834 Act. In 1860/61, the comparable costs were £555 and £3,836. Most of the recipients of out relief were elderly, and widows with infant children. In all, in 1860/61 there were nearly 900 paupers getting out relief from a district population of approximately 8,500.

The year 1860/61 was a hard one for the poor of the town. Of the 60 applications for out relief in the first (April – June) quarter by Common Fund paupers, 54 included a request for a Medical Order. The summer months passed quietly, but as winter approached 74 applications included Medical Orders. In some families measles was diagnosed. During the year payments were made for 32 funerals, 21 of them being for children. Towards the end of January and into February 1861, contrary to the exhortations of the authorities, there were 15 occasions when out relief was awarded to able-bodied men with families who were simply entered as "out of work"; four were in St Laurence parish and eleven in the Common Fund. The ages of the latter group ranged from 24 to 49, and overall they had 28 children; relief varied from 2s 6d to 5s 6d weekly. However, not all were so lucky. Richard Everall (24) with a wife and 2 children was offered the House.

The amount of out relief awarded continued to rise for another five or six years, but that was about to change. Pressure to reduce the amount of out relief awarded continued to be applied to the Unions by the Poor Law Board, and this was expressed locally by the Revd Dr Bowles, Guardian for Stanton Lacy. His interventions became increasingly acrimonious and resulted in him being appointed to chair a committee "to investigate, consider and report on the administration of relief and the general mode of government of the Ludlow Union". The report was tabled on 5 April 1866 and includes the following observations and recommendations regarding out relief:

This was taken about 1900 by Jane Green, an amateur photographer with an unusual interest in social issues. It shows the cottages and passage behind 139 Corve Street. Many of those who received out relief lived in such places.

"...expenditure of the Union has greatly increased in recent years due to the large amount given in out relief, which has risen from £3,951 in the year ended March 1859 to £4,589 in the year ended March 1865. The amount of out relief in the Ludlow Union far exceeds (with one exception) that of any other Union in Shropshire in proportion to the population. The extent to which out relief is given in the Ludlow union tends to stimulate imposture and generate and encourage pauperism. The Committee recommends the Board to carry out far more strictly than has hitherto been done the orders of the Poor Law Board ...in some instances incautious orders have been given for meat and wine with a direct tendency to encourage

Medical and General Pauperism. Guardians should attend as often as possible the different pay stations when the poor are paid by the Relieving Officers to understand the wants of the poor…"

The result of the committee report was that from 1865 the cost of out relief fell over two years from almost £4,500 to just below £3,500 *per annum* before steadying for a further two years as if the Guardians needed to draw breath and take stock. However, continuing pressure on expenditure is reflected in a recommendation of a Board meeting of April 1869, that "all applications for relief, including casual (temporary) relief and particularly extra diet recommended by Medical Officers should be carefully considered. By a careful consideration of each application, due regard being had as well to economy as to the absolute wants and necessities of the poor, the interests of the ratepayers will be observed and good ground for hoping that the poor rates may not be increased but decreased."

The Local Government Board through its inspectorate continued to apply pressure on the Unions and in 1871 a general circular said "… out relief is in many cases granted by the Guardians too easily".[11] Englander has written, "The downward squeeze was only limited by the legal requirement that the poor law authorities intervene to prevent the destitute dying of starvation. Negligent authorities exposed their Relieving Officers to a charge of murder…Rising costs prompted reform … women who accounted for the bulk of recipients of out relief became one of the principal targets. Out relief was denied to mothers with one dependant child. Deserted wives were denied relief for the first twelve months of desertion. Guardians knew applicants required assistance but the screw could always withstand another turn. Out relief became dependent upon character and conduct and was denied to those whose habits were intemperate, immoral or insanitary."[12] The Ludlow Board had always tried to adhere to this principle. In January 1868, however, Mr Kilvert, one of the Ludlow Guardians, successfully moved that the Board's practice of automatically refusing out relief to deserted wives should be rescinded; it was agreed unanimously that each case should be considered on its merits.

By far the greatest expenditure being on regular relief, this was where most economies had to be sought. But as most of the recipients were old and infirm there was not much scope except in keeping a sharp eye on their circumstances. Eventually a new column headed "Observations" appeared in the Application Books requiring Relieving Officers to record "the names of relations liable by law to relieve the applicant, distinguishing those apparently capable of assisting the applicant." Relieving Officers were also instructed to find out if there were family members, particularly sons, capable of helping with relief and who could by law be summoned to contribute. Further, they were asked to investigate thoroughly the circumstances of female applicants, looking out for associated men friends and liaisons. The money involved was thought to be sufficient for the Union to appoint a Collecting Officer. In September 1866 the Clerk reported various orders made by the Justices, and similar orders appeared nearly every month thereafter. Examples are:

John Clee, of Peaton Strand, given 14 days hard labour for disobeying a maintenance order;

Sam Beddoes, ordered to pay 1s 6d weekly to maintain his father and mother;

Thomas Sankey, given 28 days hard labour for deserting his wife;

John Gittins, given 28 days hard labour for neglecting to maintain his children now in the workhouse.

Over the following nine years to 1878 out relief was reduced by a further £2,300, and then steadied at around £1,100. It was not all saving, for to achieve this result the Guardians had to offer the workhouse to applicants who may previously have remained on or been given out relief. Consequently the cost of in-maintenance rose over the same period by about £500 to approximately £1,500. In 1877 they were level at approximately £1,400, after which, for the first time ever in the Ludlow Union, the cost of in-maintenance exceeded that of out relief.

For the first six months of the year 1880/81, the Ludlow Regular Review list had fallen to 61 recipients with 18 dependants at a cost of £170. Only nine were under 60yrs of age, and 32 were widows. An example was Fanny Williams (40), living in Frog Lane with eight children. She was paid 7s 0d weekly (£9 2s 0d for the half-year). In the second half of the year the list fell further to 40 names with 16 dependants, costing £120. Missing from the first list were three widows and four widowers who went to the workhouse, and one widow who had died. Fanny Williams was now listed with seven children. Another widow common to both lists was Jane Sankey (92), of Dinham, receiving 2s 6d weekly, two or three pence above the average. There was a marked shift in the allotment of temporary relief from couples with children to the elderly.

During the year 60 Workhouse Orders were issued; 16 of them being in January. It is apparent from the Relieving Officer's Relief Book that at this time all temporary relief was given in kind, usually bread at 5d per loaf, or mutton at 5½d per pound. Groceries and arrowroot also appear, more rarely, coal, and even more rarely, wine. Quite often the Relieving Officer records that a particular kind of relief has been awarded on the recommendation of the Medical Officer, usually because the pauper was ill and needed nourishment.

Relief continued to decrease over the next five years and then stabilised at around £1,000 for in-maintenance and £600 for out relief. Tighter control was exercised, by the paupers' circumstances being reviewed at intervals of 4 to 24 weeks rather than at six months. By 1889/90 the number of regular paupers in the District was 67, 46 in St Laurence parish, at a cost of £231. Fanny Williams continued to be listed, now aged 48, described as a laundress, and

receiving 2s 0d weekly for two of her children, aged 9 and 11 and still at home. Fanny (23), a daughter, was said to have bad health and to be at home; Thomas (22) was "at Ludlow"; Sarah and Ellen were at service; Martha (15) and Richard (13) were "out days". It is apparent that the Guardians had reverted to six monthly reviews of the regular list. Temporary paupers numbered 63 and received a total of £35.

It was not just severe scrutiny of applications for relief that brought about this reduction. Ludlow itself was changing, leading to a decline in the number of applications for relief. There were improvements in public health, medical care was more widely available, child labour laws reduced the exploitation of children, compulsory schooling brought them under the eye of authority, vaccination became obligatory, purchased food less adulterated, Factory Acts were introduced, living standards were improving. The coming of the railway brought fresh employment opportunities as well as enabling local people more easily to move further afield in search of work.

In the last years of the 19th century the public conscience began to be aroused to the appalling state in which the urban poor lived. The Royal Commission on the Aged Poor reported in 1895. While not advocating major changes, it recommended that out relief should be adequate, and conditions in workhouses improved. The Local Government Board urged Boards of Guardians to give adequate relief and, within the workhouse, to improve comforts and increase privileges.

These social and political pressures arrested the decline in the amount of out relief paid in the Ludlow Union and, by the end of the century, out relief payments showed a significant rise. By 1899/1900, although the cost of in-maintenance was little changed, the amount disbursed in out relief, at £1,400, was twice what it had been ten years previously. In the Ludlow District the amounts given in both temporary and regular relief had doubled, the total being once again higher than that of in-maintenance. At 3s 1d per week, there was a slight increase in the average paid to regular paupers, with just over one third of them receiving extra temporary relief. During the year 22 Ludlow paupers were given Workhouse Orders, five being over 80 years of age, five in their 70s, and three in their 60s. Five of them were conveyed to the House at the Union's expense.

A more sympathetic attitude towards the sick also became apparent. During the year £18 13s was allowed for nursing attendance on 13 paupers, usually at 5s 0d per week. On two occasions the allowance was for the confinement of young single women. Three men had the benefit of male attendance which seems to have been twice as expensive at 10s 0d weekly. Almost all the temporary relief was given in kind on the recommendation of the Medical Officer. Bread, milk, and most commonly, mutton, were awarded, with occasionally linseed meal and medication.

Charles Hodges (42) of Dinham Bank, with a wife and three children, paid a rent of 2s 7d. He was said to be wholly disabled with an abscess on the lung, and allowed 5s 0d weekly temporary relief and 1s 9d for Tenax (some kind of surgical dressing). This continued from April to September when he was put on regular relief

at the same rate. The payments for Tenax continued with occasionally a little additional temporary relief.

Ellen Bromley (30), a widow with three children, suffered from acute asthma and received 4s 0d regular relief. During the year she received nursing attendance on 26 occasions at 5s 0d weekly, and occasionally a payment of 3s 6d for Kutnows Asthmatic Powder. She once received a shot of whisky at 10d!

Smellie has written "the old Poor Law System which had been so firmly planted in 1834 had within it the germ of a comprehensive medical service for the whole population."[13] In these final years of the nineteenth century we see this claim beginning to come to pass.

Moreover, as the Queen's reign drew to its end the aged poor came to be regarded as the most deserving amongst the recipients of out relief. Those in Ludlow and East Hamlet in receipt of regular relief were well worthy of the title "aged poor". Of the 78 listed recipients, with spouses added, 25 were in their 60s, 41 in their 70s, and 14 were over 80. In February the Guardians took the unprecedented step of awarding all the regular paupers an additional 6d per week. Some would live to collect their non-contributory old age pensions.

ENDNOTES

1   In 1847 the Poor Law Commission was succeeded by the Poor Law Board. In 1871, in another reorganisation, the Poor Law Board became a department of the Local Government Board.
2   Rose, M.E., *The English Poor Law*, 1780-1930 (1971), p.160.
3   Crowther, M.A., *The Workhouse system 1834-1929* (1981).
4   The main source of information on the poor law in Ludlow & district after 1834 is the PL9 (Ludlow Poor Law Union) collection housed in the Shropshire Archive Centre, Shrewsbury. In this chapter, the principal sources for reference are the Guardians' Minute Books (PL9/2/1) and the Application & Report Books of the Relieving Officers (PL9/24/1et seq.).
5   Laski, H.J., *A Century of Municipal Progress 1835-1935* (1935), p.348.

6   The Poor Law Commission and its successors employed a number of highly paid, peripatetic Inspectors, each of whom was expected to become familiar with the problems and circumstances of the Unions to which they were attached, and to advise their Boards on aspects of poor law policy and practice.
7   Williams, D., *The Ludlow Guardians*. SAHS Transactions (anticipated).
8   Laski, op.cit., p.357.
9   Ibid., p.15.
10 Webb, S & B, *English Poor Law History*, Pt II, Vol.1, p.424.
11 Englander D., *Poverty and Poor Law reform in 19th century Britain 1834-1914* (1998), p.106.
12 Ibid., p.19.
13 Smellie, K.B., *A History of local government* (1946).

CHAPTER 9

SCHOOLS AND SCHOOLCHILDREN

DAVID LLOYD

Fig. 1: A detail from a painting of the Reader's House by Henry Ziegler, probably in the early 1830s.
Groups of children are gathered informally on the edge of the churchyard.
Improvements in the way such children were educated are a central theme of this chapter.

"Open wide the gates of knowledge, needing not the golden key"

These words come from the poem "Jubilee Ode", written in New Zealand in 1897 when the diamond jubilee of Queen Victoria's accession was celebrated throughout the British Empire.[1] The author was William Jukes Steward (1841-1912), then Speaker of the House of Representatives, who was to be knighted five years later for his service as a journalist and as a member of the New Zealand Parliament for 38 years.[2]

Though born in Berkshire, Steward grew up in Ludlow, where his father was a King Street draper. He attended the Grammar School, where he was a regular annual prize winner, taking the "Examiner's prize" in 1855.[3] Yet he was unable to proceed to university: partly because his family were Congregationalists, for whom advancement was still difficult, and partly because his family, with other children to support, lacked "the golden key". He found fulfilment in other ways, emigrating to New Zealand in 1862, becoming a journalist, then a

Fig. 2: Sir William Jukes Steward.

Member of Parliament.[4] He wrote poems for recreation, some of which reflect his yearning for Ludlow.

This chapter examines the ways in which education in Ludlow during Victoria's reign moved towards the kind of opportunities for all that Steward craved. It was not always a smooth passage, but if Steward had grown up in the 1890s the options available to him would have been wider.

WHAT THE COMMISSIONER FOUND

Late in 1832 or early in 1833, a few months after the Great Reform Bill received its royal assent, a government commissioner visited Ludlow. He was one of a team of civil servants sent to all parts of the country to gather information on education for a Parliamentary paper to the House of Commons.[5] It was an early, cautious step in the process by which the State took responsibility for the welfare of its citizens.

As shown in chapter 1, the Commissioner found a town of about 5,500 people.[6] Using analysis of the 1841 census as a guide, it seems that just over a thousand of these were between the ages of five and thirteen. To cater for them, and for a few that were older and younger, the Borough had 21 educational establishments. There was an ancient Grammar School, managed by the Corporation, which had taken over from the dissolved Palmers Guild in 1552.[7] There were day schools and Sunday schools for children of the poor, provided voluntarily by church organisations and heavily dependent on local subscriptions. Greatest provision came from the Church of England National Society, founded in 1811 "for Promoting the Education of the Poor", but the non-conformist churches had two well supported Sunday schools. There were 15 private schools of diverse character, which were maintained by fees, with profit to the proprietor. The medieval apprenticeship system was still in place for some trades and crafts. Nothing came from the state and even a passionate advocate of education, Henry Brougham (M.P. and later Lord Chancellor), affirmed that legislative interference is "in many respects to be either altogether avoided or very cautiously employed".[8]

The Commissioner's figures are in Fig. 3. They show that the number of day pupils at the endowed and voluntary schools together – 275 – coincidently matched the estimated number of

	1833 enrolment numbers	1851 enrolment numbers	1851 attendance numbers	1851 attendance %
Fig. 3: Enrolment and attendance at Ludlow Schools, 1833 and 1851				
Day schools				
National	250	456	323	69
GS	25	12	12	
Private (not boarders)	275	222	202	91
TOTAL	550	690	537	
Sunday schools	200	196	149	76

day pupils at the private schools. Of an estimated 1,037 Ludlow children aged between five and 13, 550 – 53% – were receiving some week day schooling. The children at school were just over a tenth of the town's population, a figure better than the 1 in 15 which Brougham had calculated as a national average from earlier statistics; and close to the 1 in 8 which he urged as the ideal.[9] Lack of competition from paid employment probably made it easier for Ludlow's schools to attract pupils. In 1812 the number of men, women and children in glove making in Ludlow had amounted to "several hundreds", but numbers had declined after 1815.[10]

Fig. 4: The Grammar School before alterations in 1800, when the Headmaster's house on the left was rebuilt. The hall of the medieval house, left of the doorway, was used as the main schoolroom, where the Headmaster taught the older boys. The younger boys were taught by the Usher in the former service end, right of the entrance. The roof was raised and the dormer windows inserted in 1686.

If the Commissioner concluded that Ludlow was better served than most places, he should not have been complacent. Arrangements for education were fragmented and uncoordinated. At any one time nearly 300 children of school age were not being educated. There had been some improvement in basic literacy since the National Schools opened in 1813, but in the 1830s 20% of grooms and 36% of brides married at St Laurence's could not sign their name. Most classrooms were small, badly heated and grossly over-crowded. Discipline was harsh, one Grammar School Headmaster writing that "fear of the birch rather than the desire of excelling I have ever found to be the greatest spur to exertion".[11]

THE EARLY VICTORIAN YEARS:
UNCOORDINATED COMPONENTS

The Grammar School

Since 1527 the Grammar School had been accommodated in a fourteenth century house in Mill Street. From 1816 to 1838 the Headmaster was the Revd John Hinde, "the very model of a Regency gentleman", who had been Headmaster of the King's School, Peterborough, and may have come to Ludlow under the patronage of the Earl of Powis.[12] Under him the school had about 25 day boys, to whom the classics were taught free of charge, and up to 40 boarders, from whose fees he supplemented his salary of £100 a year.[13] A former pupil later wrote:

"….in the years between 1820 and 1835 Ludlow.....was more successful than any in the adjacent counties in training boys for good places in such schools as Rugby, Repton, Shrewsbury and the Military Colleges".[14]

Under his successor, however, fortunes declined. This was Revd Arthur Willis, formerly 11th classic at Cambridge, and then a master at Shrewsbury School. "A small nervous man of high principle but lacking in tact and grace", Willis was a zealous teacher; but he quickly became a protagonist in the Great Law Suit and it is difficult not to detect self interest in some of his actions.[15] Numbers declined, with only five boarders and twelve day boys in 1851.[16] A

Fig. 5: A silhouette of the Revd John Hinde, who was Vicar of Ludford and Preacher of Ludlow, as well as Headmaster of the Grammar School. He delivered "a fine sermon" when the Duchess of Kent and Princess Victoria attended morning service on 22 November 1832.

When a vacancy occurred in 1817, Hinde reported that there was no boy at Ludlow "sufficiently qualified", so the award went to a Shrewsbury School pupil. Only three town boys went direct from the Grammar School to Oxford or Cambridge between 1821 and 1843, but during the Great Law Suit Willis pleaded passionately for more exhibitions.

Private schools: the superior kind

The need for a modern curriculum, geared to commerce and business, was met by the better kind of private school, usually listed in trade directories. That of William Price in the Bull Ring taught Latin and a range of modern subjects. William Tinson called his Old Street school "a Commercial Academy". It was "to instruct youth in reading, writing, English Grammar, arithmetic, book keeping and mensuration", for a fee of 10s 6d a term.[19] By 1841 Tinson had moved to 22 Mill Street, into premises occupied in 1835 by T.R. Revis and grandly called "Gordon Academy".[20] A long lasting school was that of Horatio Russell, who sought to meet all needs at 2 Mill Street, advertised in 1838 as a "Classical, Mathematical

dispute with usher John Williams worsened his cause, especially when the boys of the two masters came to "feuds and fisticuffs", the older boys hanging an effigy of the Usher, "significantly fashioned and labelled", above his desk, and greeting his entry with "uproarious jibes and jeers".[17]

The unpopularity of the school was not entirely due to such incidents. The dominance of the classics deterred many parents. Although mathematics, modern languages and dancing were available for fees, Dr John Harley, one of Willis's pupils, declared in later life:

"Ours was a Grammar School, pure and simple, quite unsophisticated. Chemistry! Carpentry! Of all things in the world! Degrading.....Our atmosphere was a "learned one". The affairs of Plantagenets, Tudors, Stuarts and the like questionable characters never occurred to us. We contested with Romulus and Remus, and discoursed with Numa Pompilius and Tullius Hortilius..."[18]

The school had first claim on "two valuable exhibitions" to Balliol College, Oxford, which had been awarded 22 times between 1760 and 1813, but most had gone to boarders, their availability helping to attract boys to the school.

Fig. 6: No. 22 Mill Street, which accommodated private schools in the mid nineteenth century. The first proprietor of Gordon Academy was T.R. Revis, who operated a lending library higher up Mill Street and was active in local politics - "in the Conservative interest".

Fig. 7: No. 2 Mill Street, where there was a boys' school from the 1820s into the twentieth century.

and Commercial Academy".[21]

Girls' schools offered general education with emphasis on "accomplishments". Earlier, Miss Valentine, "at a large and convenient house in Castle Square", had promised "unremitting attention to the Health, Morals and Education of her pupils".[22] In 1840 the Misses Clewers advertised their Old Street Establishment, where "young ladies are genteely boarded and carefully instructed in the English Language, History, etc.", with 18 guineas a year for boarding and instruction.[23]

Devoid of control or regulation, private schools varied greatly. Charlotte Bronte, famously, experienced both the horrors of Cowan Bridge and the refinements of Roe Head. The status of the teachers is a useful indicator. Horatio Russell and William Tinson were men of standing, serving as Borough Councillors.[24] Rebecca Acton, who ran a "ladies boarding school" at St Leonard's House, Linney, was the widow of a surgeon, obliged, one suspects, to sustain her large family. Eliza Powell, who had a similar establishment in Castle Street, was the sister of a prosperous brick maker. The only personalised account of one of these schools is that of Henry Peach Robinson, son of the Master of the Boys' National School, who described his seven years at "Mr Russell's Academy" as

"verily the happiest days I shall ever spend".[25]

Apprenticeships

Sometimes described as "the Englishman's school", the apprenticeship system, with the trade guilds, had been superseded in some occupations before the Victorian period, especially in places of mass production.[26] In Ludlow, however, though the last guilds had ceased operation in the early nineteenth century, 72 apprentices were recorded in the 1841 census, involving 26 trades and occupations, as shown in Fig. 8.[27] Drapers had the most apprentices, followed by grocers and chemists. Many of the 1841 apprentices

class	group	number	class number
Fig. 8: Apprentices in 1841			
1 The land	gardeners	1	**1**
3 Building	builders	4	
	carpenters	1	
	joiners	1	
	masons	1	
	plumbers/glaziers	4	**11**
5 Manufacturing			
	gun-makers	1	
	blacksmiths	1	
	tinmen	1	
	whitesmiths	3	
	saddlers	1	
	dressmakers	3	
	milliners	2	
	shoemakers	7	
	tailors	1	
	bakers	5	
	watchmakers	1	**26**
7 Dealers	drapers	9	
	butchers	3	
	grocers	6	
	booksellers	1	
	ironmongers	3	
	mercers	1	**23**
9 Professional	chemists	6	**6**
11 Services	chimney sweeps	2	
	hairdressers	3	**5**
TOTAL			**72**

disappear from local records and presumably left the town, but others acquired their own businesses. Edwin Morgan, a tailor's apprentice in 1841, was a tailor and shopkeeper in Castle Street in 1861, while James Evans, a draper's apprentice in 1841, was a linen and woollen draper in King Street.[28]

Apprentices received preliminary education elsewhere. Henry Peach Robinson spent seven years at "Mr Russell's Academy" in Mill Street. He then went "to Mr Jones to learn the printing", being bound for five years on his fourteenth birthday.[29] John Harley, whose mother was an innkeeper's widow, attended the Grammar School, before being apprenticed to George Cocking, chemist, in 1847. The indenture for this apprenticeship shows that he was to be "taught and instructed in the trade and business of a Chemist and Druggist" for five years. His mother paid £40 immediately and another £40 after two years. In return Cocking would provide "the said John Harley with suitable and sufficient diet and lodgings in the house of the said George Cocking in a like and equal manner with the rest of his family".[30] In this case apprenticeship was the passport to a fine career, for on completion in 1852 John Harley became a chemist's assistant in London,

The Market Cross.

Fig. 10: The woodcut of the Butter Cross, published in "History of Ludlow", by Thomas Wright, senior, 1824.

later taking a degree in medicine and becoming a consultant physician.

Day Schools for the Poor

Voluntary effort had provided limited education for poor children in Ludlow since 1714, when a small Blue Coat Charity School was opened. This moved to the Butter Cross, with invested funds that supported 30 boys and 15 girls. In 1813 it was absorbed into the new National Schools, the Boys' School taking over the Butter Cross room, with new premises for the girls in Brand Lane.[31] Both schools were taught on the monitorial system of Dr Bell, whereby one teacher taught the older children, styled monitors, who in turn taught the rest. In 1833 there were six monitors for the boys and five for the girls. As a means of instructing hordes of children with minimum resources, the system was praised by contemporaries, Samuel Taylor Coleridge, eager to inculcate good behaviour among the lower classes, calling it "a vast moral steam engine".[32] The educational content, however, was limited, relying on "the impartation of facts and their

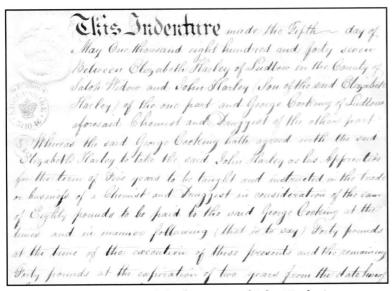

Fig. 9: A copy of the first page of John Harley's apprenticeship indenture, 1847.

Fig. 11: Children in rows in the 1820s, under the supervision of monitors.

memorisation by constant repetition, drilling and testing". The illustration shows the regimentation which must have occurred. The boys had an average of five square feet each and the girls four square feet, but the area for each child was less, to allow for the teacher's desk and access.[33]

The Ludlow National Schools were well served by their teachers. From 1827 to 1855 the boys' Master was John Robinson, son of a Ludlow glover. There is no record of training before he took charge of the school at the age of 21, though he may have been a monitor. He was "a devoted student of Shakespeare"; his wife Eliza (nee Peach) was a person "of artistic knowledge and sensitivity"; and their eldest son, Henry Peach Robinson, became a celebrated pioneer of artistic photography.[34] By 1841 Robinson could employ a servant, and he commissioned portraits of himself and Eliza. Nothing is known about Rosetta Simmons, Girls' Mistress in 1835, but by 1841 she had been succeeded by Charlotte Baker, then twenty. Her work must have been satisfactory, for when given notice in 1855 due to ill health, she was awarded a pension of £20 16s a year (£973 in modern terms).[35]

Sunday Schools

Started in the 1780s, Sunday schools had a rapid success, the historian J.R. Green calling them "the beginning of popular education".[36] The earliest in Ludlow was that of the Independents, who had a small

Figs. 12 and 13: John and Eliza Robinson, photographed by their son, Henry Peach Robinson, from unattributed watercolours.

church in lower Corve Street. Enthused by a new minister, Revd David Francis, "a man of piety, talent and energy", a Sunday school was established here soon after 1800. John Evans, a Ludlow bookseller, "was a pupil when writing and arithmetic were taught there on the Sabbath".[37] Later, the National Society supplemented its day schools with a Sunday School, which had 80 pupils in 1818.[38] This school was held in the Guildhall and was taught by volunteers, as described in a contemporary poem:

"On Sunday there's taught a large children's school,
By all the good ladies, who make it a rule,
To send them to church their maker to praise,
May they all go there the rest of their days".[39]

In 1833 only eight pupils at this school did not also attend the National Society day schools but there were 110 pupils at the Independents' school, and another 82 at the Wesleyan Sunday school, held in Lower Broad Street.

The movement thrived. The Primitive Methodists opened a chapel in Ludlow in 1836 and then started a Sunday School, which had 40 scholars in 1842.[40] By 1851, the National Society Sunday School was moribund, but when the Ecclesiastical Census was taken on 30 March, 1851, there were 163 pupils at the three non-conformist schools, with another 50 attending the Primitive Methodist school in the afternoon.[41] In 1855 the Independents built a new schoolroom at the front of their site in Old Street, to which they had moved in 1835.[42]

The Mechanics Institute

On 25 October, 1841, a Mechanics Institute was opened in Ludlow in a room over the Market Hall. Originating in Glasgow, but reaching London in 1822, such institutes aimed "to instruct artisans in .... arts and manufactures", though basic literacy and numeracy were often added.[43] Institutes mushroomed in manufacturing districts, but there were a few in rural locations.

The committee, on which Dr C. Brice – a newcomer to Ludlow – was a driving force, provided a library, regular classes and fortnightly lectures. The library was for "apprentices, artisans and others". Classes were to be "speedily formed", to enable adults, whose "education had been imperfect, to improve themselves in reading and writing." Lectures were to be provided, and invitations had been addressed to several gentlemen, though "a feeling of diffidence had caused some to decline".

By 1851 there were 96 members, 90 of whom were male; the Library had 260 volumes; and lectures were given fortnightly, some in conjunction with the Ludlow Natural History Society - then the focus of much intellectual activity.[44] The classes, however, are not mentioned and perhaps were not functioning. The Institute is not referred to in the Robinson diary, though Henry and his friends, one of whom was John Harley, had their own Corresponding Society, taking it in turn to give lectures. It can be inferred, then, that the Institute catered for the less well educated, for whom, indeed, it was intended.[45]

An Infants' School

The Ludlow National schools, like the Charity School before them, admitted children aged seven and over, most staying until they were ten or eleven. There was no attempt to extend this range until 1846, when a sub-committee was set up to "establish an infant school".[46] The realisation that very young children could benefit from education had started before 1820, largely due to the efforts of Robert Owen. Born at Newtown, thirty miles from Ludlow, his lasting work was in Scotland, where he opened an infants' school for employees' children at his model factory in New Lanark.[47]

Inspired from afar, it was again local initiative that brought the infants' school into being. The sub-committee was chaired by the Revd Robert Meyricke, Reader of Ludlow from 1824 to 1881. In 1847 an Inquiry recorded that "arrangements have been made for an Infants' School in Ludlow and subscriptions are raised".[48] The school was open by 1848, when the Mistress was Miss Owen, the daughter of a Bitterley labourer.[49] Its location is uncertain, but an entry in the 1851 census returns suggests it was in Upper Gaolford, possibly east of the Tower, on the site later occupied by the Police Station.

Private schools: the inferior kind (Dame Schools)

Low in the educational hierarchy were private schools that were not in directories, and where the persons in charge had humble social status. Such schools were often called Dame Schools, though at least one in Ludlow was kept by a man. Only rudiments of literacy and numeracy were taught, often in over-crowded rooms. In 1810 the poet George Crabbe had described the worst of these schools, which were little more than child minding establishments:

Yet one there is, that small regard to rule,
Or study pays, and still is deemed a school;
That where a deaf, poor, patient widow sits
And awes some thirty infants as she knits –
Infants of humble, busy wives, who pay
Some trifling price for freedom through the day.[50]

Six such schools have been identified in the 1841 census, all with low house values. They were in the poorer parts of the town, two of them in yards where there was gross over-crowding. A characteristic "Dame" was Mary Wilkes, aged 60, who lived in a small house in Lower Gaolford. She had been a pupil at the Blue Coat Charity School in the 1790s, leaving as a pauper apprentice to a mantua-maker.

THE NEW NATIONAL SCHOOLS, 1855

"To improve and extend"

The first impetus for improvement came from the Hereford Diocesan Board of Education, founded in 1849 "to improve and extend elementary education throughout the diocese ….. in strict accordance with the teaching of the church".[51] In February 1852 the Board held a meeting at Ludlow Assembly Rooms, which was attended by Anna Maria Fay. She described the Bishop, Dr Renn Hampden – a notable scholar – as "a little man in breeches and gaiters" and condemned him as "a very uninteresting speaker". The Earl of Powis, on the other hand, "was in the highest degree elegant and gentlemanly, but every word told". "The audience", she added, "was cold and the room colder".[52]

In spite of this alleged lack of enthusiasm, plans for a new National Society building went ahead, with the Rector, Revd John Phillips, as the motivator. "Although", it was later said, "old Ludlow shook its head at the Quixotism of the scheme", planning and building were completed in five years, the new school opening in February 1857.[53] The cost was nearly £3,000, over half raised by public subscription, helped by the Rector's "ample patrimony".[54] Substantial sums came from the Diocesan Board and the National Society, and from the sale of the Girls' School in Brand Lane, but the balance was provided by a £900 grant from the Committee in Council (Privy Council), acting for the government. This was the first serious input of national funds into Ludlow for education, but to achieve it the school had to submit to annual inspections.

The building

An acre of ground was purchased in Lower Gaolford, the conveyance deed specifying the purpose of the school: "…. for the education of children of the labouring, manufacturing and other poorer classes in the parish of Ludlow, and for no other purpose."[55] Plans were made for a school of 500 pupils – 150 boys, 150 girls and 200 infants, only a slight increase on existing numbers but housed in a single building. The design was by Thomas Nicholson, diocesan architect, and exhibited many of the characteristics decreed by the Committee in Council as "suitable for elementary schools".[56] The layout was almost exactly symmetrical, the Infants' hall, porch and yard forming a central axis with the Boys' and Girls' Schools on either

Fig. 14: The National Schools in Ludlow, from Partridge's undated "Views of Ludlow".

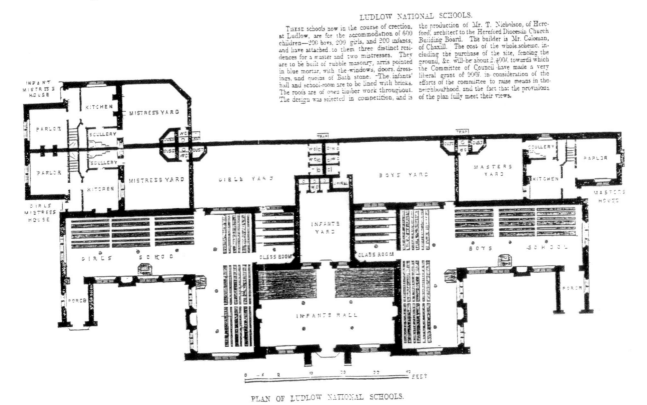

LUDLOW NATIONAL SCHOOLS.

These schools now in the course of erection, at Ludlow, are for the accommodation of 600 children—200 boys, 200 girls, and 200 infants; and have attached to them three distinct residences for a master and two mistresses. They are to be built of rubble masonry, arris pointed in blue mortar, with the windows, doors, dressings, and quoins of Bath stone. The infants' hall and school-room are to be lined with bricks. The roofs are of open timber work throughout. The design was selected in competition, and is the production of Mr. T. Nicholson, of Hereford, architect to the Hereford Diocesan Church Building Board. The builder is Mr. Coleman, of Chaxill. The cost of the whole scheme, including the purchase of the site, fencing the ground, &c. will be about 2,400l. towards which the Committee of Council have made a very liberal grant of 900l. in consideration of the efforts of the committee to raise means in the neighbourhood, and the fact that the provisions of the plan fully meet their views.

PLAN OF LUDLOW NATIONAL SCHOOLS.

Fig. 15: The plan of the Ludlow National Schools, from "The Builder".

side. Each of these had an L-shaped hall, a small rectangular schoolroom, porch and yard. Houses for the Master and Mistresses completed the pattern, though the house for the Infants' Mistress, abutting on the left hand side, was an asymmetrical element in the design. The building was a prestigious one and was included in Partridge's Views of Ludlow (undated).

Both Boys' and Girls' Schools had an average floor space of over ten square feet per pupil. The infants, however, had only just over four square feet. They were seated on long benches tiered to form a gallery. This allowed little movement, but facilitated the instruction of many children by a single mistress helped by young assistants. Heating was by fires behind protective rails, producing several chimney stacks. An elegant spire and weather vane gave an ecclesiastical finish.

Teachers, pupil teachers and pupils

With the new buildings came new teachers. The first Master of the Boys' School was Frederick Cox, from Battersea Training College, which had opened in 1840. It aimed to reconcile "the simplicity of life of the humble classes" with "proficiency in intellectual attainments" and "skill in the art of teaching", to produce "efficient masters of elementary schools".[57] Cox was a fine ambassador for the College, giving good service at Ludlow for 36 years, and becoming a much respected figure in the town. When he died in 1894 his obituary spoke of "earnestness, high ideal of duty, integrity of purpose, love of work" and "thoroughness".[58] The Girls' School had four Mistresses between 1855 and 1876 and the Infants' School two, but the second of these, Elizabeth Cantrell, who started in January 1868, was to remain for a remarkable 46 years.[59]

The Master and Mistresses were assisted by pupil teachers, who served an apprenticeship for five years from the age of thirteen. Like their monitor predecessors, they taught groups of children but received instruction themselves for seven and a half hours a week, before or after school. If successful in examinations, they could attend a teacher training college.[60] The first to be indentured, in November, 1856, were Cornelius Felton and Henry Child, both proceeding to Saltley College, Birmingham, in January 1861.[61] The names of 25 others are known from the log books, kept from 1863. Some, like Emma Bathurst in 1875, gave up and "left for service"; several became un-certificated teachers, including Sarah Pivor, who went in 1876 "to take charge at Burrington"; but a few gained Queen's Scholarships to Training Colleges. The latter included John Palmer in 1874, who went to Saltley. He taught English and "junior" mathematics at the Grammar School, and was Mayor of Ludlow a record five times, from 1925 to 1930.

The new buildings did not generate a dramatic rise in numbers. In 1860 average attendances were 116 at the Boys' School, 96 at the Girls' and 120 at the Infants', almost exactly the same as the 335 total in 1851. By 1868 the figure was still only 348. Comments in the Boys' School Log show that absenteeism was a problem. On 26 October 1863 it was very wet, with the school "very considerably thinned in attendance". In June 1864 "Sanger's Circus was in town, with numbers down to 40". A year later, "attendance has been very much reduced by smallpox". On one occasion punishment was threatened "for poor Friday afternoon attendance". The problem persisted at both schools, Sarah Hall, the new Girls' Mistress, writing despairingly in 1876: "Irregularity of attendance is the bane of this school".

The log books give instances of poverty and hardship. In 1871 one girl was "so ragged", that her mother "didn't like to send her". Another mother sent word that her child was needed "to carry water", but when the teacher called she found "the truth of the matter was her boots were old". In 1872 girls were sharply rebuked for laughing at Eliza Robinson "a motherless, neglected child with her head shaven". Later, however, it was recorded approvingly that "an older girl had brought little Eliza a jacket and scarf".

An inspector calls

The ogre of annual inspection loomed heavily over schools from the 1860s. Seen originally as benign visitors who gave advice and encouragement, inspectors took on a more sinister role after the Newcastle Commission into Popular Education reported in 1861. In pursuance of the recommendation that elementary education should be "sound and cheap", a Revised Code now enacted that annual grants to schools and to pupil teachers should be related to results. "If it is not cheap it shall be efficient; if it is not efficient it shall be cheap" boasted Robert Lowe, the Government minister in charge.[62]

The reports, copied into the log books, have a number of criticisms in the early years especially for the Girls' School, but the tone becomes more favourable by the late 1860s. In 1864 the attainments of the boys were "fair", but the "order was faulty in some points". In 1865 there were "few failures except in writing and spelling in the fourth standard". By 1867, however, the spelling was "very good", while in 1868 the boys passed "an exceedingly successful examination in the elementary subjects", though "general knowledge should be better in a town this size".

The early reports on the Girls' School were worse. In 1865 there had been "only moderate progress during the last year". In 1866 it was grimly reported: "My lords have ordered a reduction of a tenth to be made from the Grant to the Girls' School on account of the defects of instruction".

In 1867 needlework was taught "with care and success", but in other points the school was "very backward". Religious Knowledge was "imperfect except in the first class"; spelling was "very moderate"; and in arithmetic "the failure was almost complete". In 1868, however, there was "decided improvement in the elementary subjects", though the little children were "rather inclined to chatter".

Funding streams

As shown in Fig. 16, the annual revenue of the National Schools derived from several sources. About a quarter of the income came from investments, some of them the legacy of the pre-1813 Blue Coat Charity School. In 1863 the Government grant was only £20 17s, but by 1869, as the Revised Code became operational, it rose to over £110, 22% of total income.[63] About a sixth of the total came from "school pence", introduced in voluntary schools to establish the principle of parental contribution.

Fig. 16: Simplified accounts of Ludlow National Schools, 1863 (1)

National Schools	£	s	d	Infants Schools	£	s	d
Receipts				Receipts			
Balance from 1862	22	4	1	Balance from 1862	3	4	6
Investments (1)	83	13	1	Investments	15	12	0
Subscriptions	65	15	6	Subscriptions	36	6	0
Weekly payments: boys(2)	33	0	5	Weekly payments	22	17	9
Weekly payments: girls	19	13	5				
Attendance Grant (3)	20	17	0				
Church collection	39	13	3				
TOTAL	**284**	**16**	**9**	**TOTAL**	**78**	**0**	**3**
Payments				Payments			
Property and repairs	12	15	6	Property	2	8	9
Costs of sermon	1	5	0				
Salary to Mr Cox	80	0	0	Salary to Miss Hodnet	40	0	0
Boys school expenses	26	3	8	Expenses	9	15	0
Salary to Miss Pitson	50	0	0				
Girls' school expenses	25	7	6				
Books	15	2	0	Books & apparatus	9	10	8
Coals and wood	17	17	6	Coals and wood	9	4	3
Payments for night school	5	16	2			37	8
TOTAL	**234**	**7**	**4**	**TOTAL**	**70**	**18**	**8**
Balance in Savings Banks	50	9	0	Balance in Savings Bank	7	1	7

1. Report for the Year 1863 on Ludlow Charities (12 listed), 1864, pp.3,5

Although a very small amount – the equivalent of 23p today – this was widely resented. In the Girls' Log it is recorded that on 1 October 1873: "the father of a scholar entered the room in the middle of the first lesson (Scripture) and in a rude manner demanded instantly 19s 11d change for a sovereign which he offered in payment of his child's penny".

The remaining income – 37% for the Boys' and Girls' Schools, 46% for the Infants' – came from voluntary effort. An established event was the annual sermon on the first Sunday of the Mayoral year, the collection of which was traditionally given to "the Charity Schools". Anna Maria Fay gives an account in 1851, when Aunt Catherine, "a distinguished stranger", was asked to stand by the Mayor as the collection was taken "at the door".[64]

The sermon raised more than £30 a year, but three times that amount came from subscribers, whose names, with donations, were in the annual Charities Report. There were three lists – for "the National Schools", "the Infants School" and "the Sunday schools "– which have been collated for 1863 to produce the figures and graph below. There were 147 subscribers, 15 of whom are on three lists, with 43 on two and the remaining 89 on just one.

For most subscribers, this was not impulse giving, but a graded response to social status. The National Schools list is headed by the Earl of Powis, who gave £5 5s, followed by his relatives the Windsor Clives of Oakly Park, four of whom also gave 5 guineas or £5. Taking the three lists together, the most bountiful was the Hon. George Windsor Clive, M.P., who gave £9 9s, followed by his fellow M.P., Sir William Fraser. The contributions of the aristocracy accounted for a third of all giving, with gentry contributing another sixth. Of the rest, half came from the professions, headed by the Rector, who gave £5 4s 6d. Subscribers from the business sector accounted for an eighth of the total, most of them giving 10s 6d, 5s or less.

Teachers' salaries accounted for just over half of all expenditure, though small payments to Pupil Teachers were not shown here. Even with rent free accommodation, the salaries were meagre, Cox's £80 being equivalent to £4,322 today, and the £50 and £40 of his colleagues to £2,707 and £2,166 respectively. For most of the 19th century school mistresses in the Ludlow workhouse school earned about £20 a year. Books and apparatus cost £25, 8% of

Fig. 17: Voluntary subscriptions to the National Schools, 1863.

	number of subscribers	amount subscribed	average subscribed
		£ s d	£ s d
The National Schools (boys and girls)	42	65 15 08	1 11 04
The Infant School	99	36 06 00	7 04
The Sunday schools	50	22 10 06	5 00

Fig. 18: Proportion of subscribed funds contributed by social and occupational groups, 1863

Group	Total subscribed (pence)	Number of subscribers	Average subscription £ s d	%
building	270	5	4 06	1
manufacturing	1566	20	6 06	5
dealers	2070	31	5 07	7
finance	386	3	10 09	1
professions	7676	43	15 00	26
aristocracy	10332	7	6 03 00	35
gentry	5388	17	1 06 05	18
unidentified	2256	21	8 11	8
TOTAL	**29944**	**147**		

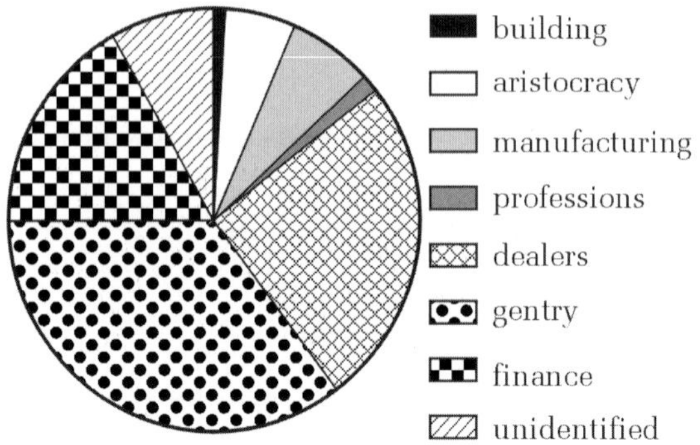

building
aristocracy
manufacturing
professions
dealers
gentry
finance
unidentified

expenditure, while heating was a little more. An interesting entry is the payment for night schools, probably the evening classes in literacy which were held in the late 1860s.[65]

MID-VICTORIAN GOVERNMENT INITIATIVES

The 1870 Education Act

Driven by economic need, and the belief that greater literacy would improve morality and facilitate social control, "universal education" was high on the political agenda in the 1860s. The aim was agreed by all, the method aroused passionate debate. The churches wanted to expand sectarian or voluntary provision. Others, including the vociferous Education League of Birmingham, wanted non-sectarian education, financed by local rates.

The 1870 Education Act, promoted by the new Liberal Government, was a compromise. Where sectarian bodies were able and willing, as at Ludlow, they were helped by Government grants to provide places for all children of school age in their areas. Elsewhere secular school boards would be elected by ratepayers to "fill up the gaps", – the phrase of W. E. Forster, the blunt speaking M.P. for Bradford who was "the man behind the Act".[66] A frenzy of school building followed, though attendance did not become compulsory until 1880.[67] The Rector, Revd E. Clayton, claimed that "there is a very wholesome repugnance to a School Board at Ludlow", though he admitted that a section of the parish had "endeavoured to secure a School Board, aided by the Birmingham League".[68]

New buildings for elementary schools

The first Ludlow response was a non-Conformist school in Old Street, which opened in 1871, occupying former premises of the Primitive Methodists, who had moved to a new chapel.[69] The old chapel had been consecrated in 1836, with schoolrooms provided later.[70] The school had more than 150 pupils, with boys', girls' and infants' departments,[71], and was linked with the Gospel Hall, having been "helped" by a

Fig. 19: The Primitive Methodist Chapel and School, photographed in the 1960s.

Mr Miller of Bristol.[72] In 1880 the Wesleyan Minister alleged that the school was "insufficiently taught", though he may have been prejudiced by his desire to promote a new Methodist School.

Perhaps spurred on by this development, a new building for "an Intermediate School" was proposed as an addition to the Lower Gaolford National Schools. Clayton claimed that "our parish has the credit of inaugurating a scheme which may prove to be a very important improvement in our National School system", arguing that "the younger classes" required "a somewhat different treatment, training and teaching from the higher classes".[73] The new department opened on 25 March, 1874, in a building praised by Clayton as "good and

Fig. 20: The Intermediate School, a reconstruction drawing by Ivan Hall.

substantial but quite plain", with Susanna Cox, wife of Frederick, in charge.[74]

The next Anglican church venture was a new school at East Hamlet, built to serve the expanding suburbs. East Hamlet was in Stanton Lacy parish, where the incumbent, the elderly Dr Bowles, was "pre-occupied with his own village school".[75] Clayton was again the driving force, with Sir Charles Rouse Boughton of Downton Hall chairman of the supervising committee. The building, with an infants' school, a mixed school and a smaller classroom, opened on 26 June 1876, with Clayton saying prayers and addressing parents on "the importance of sending their children regularly and on time". The cost was £1,498 0s 8d, of which over £1,100 were subscriptions and collections. The balance came from the Government, the Diocesan Board and the National Society, though the latter's grant was cut "on account of the omission of a teacher's residence". This was added in 1885, similar in plan to the houses in Lower Gaolford, but more attractively designed.

The Grammar School, the Schools Inquiry Commission and the 1876 scheme

Though the Charity Commission had been established in 1853, to whom the Ludlow Municipal Charity Trustees were accountable, state action was more tentative in secondary education than in elementary. In 1864, however, a Schools Inquiry Commission was set up, with one of the commissioners, James Bryce – later a Government minister – visiting Ludlow in 1866.

Under the headmasterships of James Banks and Sampson Kingsford, both distinguished classicists, the work of the school had been sound.[76] Though Latin and Greek were prominent in the curriculum, a range of other subjects had been introduced, and there was a regular class in science as early as 1855. But Bryce found the buildings "old and gloomy", and noted that numbers remained under 50. A handful of boys had gone to university, but several of these were boarders. Bryce noted that only "tradesmen and professional men" patronised the school, "the latter being neither numerous nor wealthy, the former, as always in

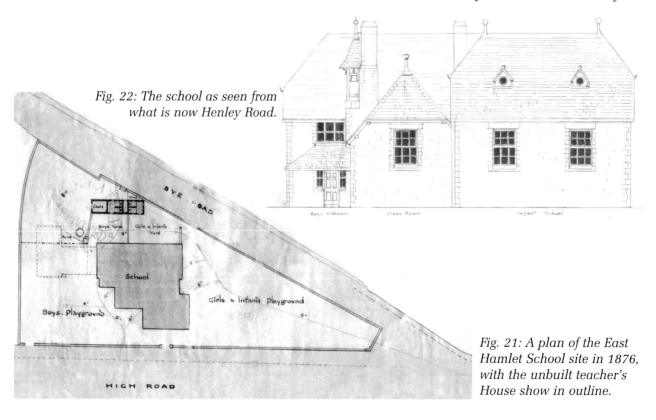

Fig. 22: The school as seen from what is now Henley Road.

Fig. 21: A plan of the East Hamlet School site in 1876, with the unbuilt teacher's House show in outline.

country towns, un-ambitious". Bryce advocated inducements to farmers, a policy pursued by the next Headmaster, Dr W. Sparrow, from Trinity College, Dublin. Winning paeans of praise from Trustees, inspectors, parents and boys, Sparrow quickly raised the school's profile, numbers reaching 120 in 1871, though they later declined.

The Commission's report, named after its Chairman, Lord Taunton, was published in 1868. Its most radical proposal, for County Education Authorities, was postponed, but other measures formed the Endowed Schools Act of 1869.[77] This decreed the formulation of new schemes for grammar schools. That for Ludlow, published in 1876, separated a portion of the King Edward VI estates for the school, to be regulated by a Board of Governors. More contentious was the status of the school. The commissioners had recommended that there should be three types of secondary schools, with leaving ages of 19, 16 and 14. Grade 1 schools would retain Greek and Latin, and would prepare boys for university, but Grade 2

schools would have Latin only, catering for "boys wishing to enter the professions and requiring early specialised training". It was suggested that Ludlow should be Grade 2, a view supported by some people in the town, including Humphrey Salwey, solicitor, who argued "if this school be made a first class one it would be highly injurious to the interests of the general inhabitants of the Borough".[78] Predictably Dr Sparrow and most Trustees pleaded for Grade 1, and won a compromise, by which the official leaving age would be 17, with boys allowed to remain with Governors' permission. Greek was still to be taught, but only for £3 extra a year.

THE 1877 SCHOOL ATTENDANCE CENSUS

The census

All over Ludlow on weekday mornings in 1877, children made their way to school – some eagerly, others reluctantly, a few late-comers running before the bell stopped ringing. The six

Fig. 23: The boys and masters of Ludlow Grammar School, gathered outside the school in the early 1870s. The front of the Headmaster's house, rebuilt in 1802, can be seen on the far left. Dr Sparrow, the Headmaster, stands without his mortar board a few places left of the doorway into the schoolroom.

children of Charles Farmer, a journeyman carpenter, would have left their stone cottage in Lower Mill Street. The oldest, William and Charles, aged 9 and 8, attended the Boys' National School. The next two, Mary and Edith, 7 and 6, were at the Girls' School. Emma and Matilda, both under five, were in the Infants' Department. It is likely that they went via Silk Mill Lane, through the Broad Gate, along St John's Lane, over busy Old Street, and up Friars' Walk: the latter well worn by generations of children "going to the National".

This information, and much more, is available from a School Census in the Borough archives, one sheet of which is shown on Fig. 27. With adequate school places, the concern was to fill them by improving attendances. In 1876 the government, now Conservative, set up school attendance committees in areas without school boards, and brought in measures obliging parents to ensure their children received instruction "in reading, writing and arithmetic". Attendance did not become compulsory until 1880, but employment under ten was banned, and could not be undertaken under 14 unless specified attainments had been reached.[79]

The Council set up its Attendance Committee in October 1876, and appointed Josiah Smith, bookseller, as Attendance Officer.[80] It was probably he who compiled the census, using a standardised form from the Education Department, reproduced as Fig. 27.[81] The census can often be correlated with the

Fig. 24: This pleasing sketch of Ludlow, the frontispiece of Gissing's "Ludlow and Stokesay" (1895), shows the house at the top of Lower Mill Street where the Farmer family lived in 1877.

Fig. 25: The view in 2004 along Friars' Walk, with the road rising in the far distance before bending left to give access to the National Schools.

1881 national census to give the names of children. The head of household is given on the left, then postal number and occupation. The next four columns list numbers of children, followed by enrolments at private and "public schools", i.e. the Grammar School and the sectarian schools. Then the school is named, followed by information about non-attendance. However, there are defects. First, there are cases when it is not possible to allocate children to a school. Mrs Shepherd, grocer, the fifth name on Fig. 27, had six children, but it is not known how many went to each of the three named schools. Reasoned guesses have to be made, therefore, to calculate school totals. Secondly, the census only covers Ludlow Borough, so that the new suburbs in Stanton Lacy and Ludford are omitted. Nevertheless, the census affords a rare snapshot of the schools attended by Ludlow children in 1877.

The figures in Fig. 26 show that there were 713 children between the ages of five and 13 in Ludlow, all but 43 of whom were attending school or, in a few cases, receiving home tuition. Though the figures are not directly comparable, this is much better than the 53% attained in 1833.[82] There were also 69 children under the age of five attending schools, out of 210 such children on the census.

Schools and occupational groups

The bar graphs illustrate the dominance of the sectarian schools. Of 713 Ludlow children attending school, 591 – 83% – went to the National Schools in Lower Gaolford or East Hamlet, or to the Old Street school. Many parents chose a school for religious affiliation, but this was not binding, as shown by the mother who defended her daughter's poor attendance at the Girls' National School in 1871: "She wasn't going to be bothered by the Governors or the teacher. Bless their hearts, if they bothered her, she would send her to another school".[83] Only 96 (13%) of Ludlow children went to private schools in 1877, compared with the estimated 275 in 1833; 24 received home tuition; and 12 went to village schools. This left 43 (5.5%) children between 5 and 13 not attending school at all.

Fig. 28 shows the schooling received by children from occupational and social status groups. Predictably, all labourers and transport workers – carters, hauliers, and railwaymen – sent their children to the sectarian schools. So did nearly all building operatives, nailers, sawyers and shoemakers. Many pupils came from the poorer parts of the town, such as Holdgate Fee and Lower Gaolford, and from slums such as Sims Yard[84] in Lower Broad Street. It is a mark of the rising status of these schools, however, that they now recruited also from families of business men. Pupils at the National Schools included those of John Bytheway, butcher; Thomas Lowe, fishmonger; the landlords of four inns; and two coal dealers, William Blake and John Pardoe. The parents of the Old Street pupils included George Williams, butcher; Daniel Crundell, a High Street draper; John Harper, furniture dealer; and three grocers.

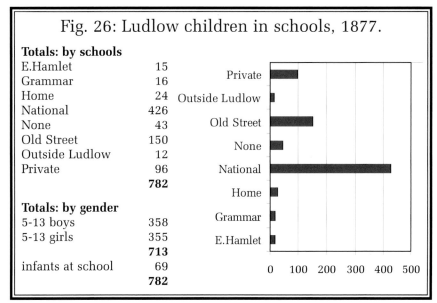

Fig. 26: Ludlow children in schools, 1877.

Totals: by schools

E.Hamlet	15
Grammar	16
Home	24
National	426
None	43
Old Street	150
Outside Ludlow	12
Private	96
	782

Totals: by gender

5-13 boys	358
5-13 girls	355
	713
infants at school	69
	782

Old Street.

(School Board 12 G.)—London : KNIGHT & Co., 90 Fleet Street.

NAME.	No. of House.	OCCUPATION.	No. of Children from 3 to 5.		No of Children from 5 to 13.		No. at Private School.	
			Boys.	Girls.	Boys.	Girls.	Boys.	Girls.
Powell Mrs	78	Widow	.		1	1		1
Bethell John	76	Painter			1			∓
Thomas Mrs	72					1		
Jones John	75	Bricklayer	1	1				
Shepherd Mrs		Grocer		1	2	3	1	4
Jones Eliz		Widow			1			
Humphreys Mrs	4?	Telegraph Clerk	∓	∓	1	3		2
Peacock John	5?	Cashier at Bank	1			2		2
Liles John	63	Soda Water Maker			1	1		1
Ross W.	59	Cabinet Maker		1				
Rickards Wm	55	Blacksmith		1	2			
Turner Thos	48	Builder	.		1	3	1	3
Higgins Thos	46	Policeman	1		1	1		
Rose H.	45	Schoolmaster			1	1	1	1
Morris Benjn	42	Carpenter			1			
Pearce Wm	38	Labourer			3			
Preece John	28	do		1	2	1		
Felton Edward	31	Shoemaker		1		2		
Hughes Wm	27	Tailor	1		1	1		
Morse John	23	Labourer				1		
Brought over			1?	21	70	69	16	19

~ 176 ~

Fig. 27, this page and previous: Page 8 of the 1877 census of children of school age in Ludlow.

No. at Public School.		NAME OF SCHOOL.	No. of Children from 5 to 13 not attending any efficient School.		How many under 13 have left School and can read well.		How many at work.		REMARKS.
Boys.	Girls.		Boys.	Girls.	Boys.	Girls.	Boys.	Girls.	
1		Natnl & Bitterley Schl							
1		Natnl							
	1	Old St Schl							
			1	1			1 ^{10gm}		Nephew
1		at work Miss Brown & written at home							
1		Natrinal do &							Grandchild
1	1	Miss Baldwin							Parents dead lives with their Sister (Breeze)
1		Miss Powell Gr School & Mrs Mathre							
2	1	Natnl							
2	1	Mr Reed's & Miss Powell Old St Sch.							
1		Miss Russell Sandpits Old St Sch							To go to the National Schl
2	2	Old St Schl							
	3	Natnl							
2	1	Old St Schl							Old a
	1	Old St Schl							
65	59		3	3	2	1	2		

	Total		National		E.Hamlet		Old Street		Grammar		Private		Home		None		Outside	
	No.	Dir.	No.	Dir.	No.	Dir.	No.	Dir.	No.	Dir.	No.	Dir.	No.	Dir.	No.	Dir.	No.	Dir.
Agriculture	14	7	7	6			5				2	1						
Extraction	11	0	3				2				5				1			
Building	73	4	53				14				3	1	3	3				
Manufacturing	188	33	108	9	2	1	45	7	3	3	22	13			6		2	
Transport	56	0	38				15								3			
Dealers	140	112	31	22	1	1	31	22	9	9	49	45	6	6	6		7	7
Finance	10	6	4	2							3	1	3	3				
Labour	175	0	129		9		20								17			
Administration	24	0	15				4				2		3					
Professional	19	15							3	3	3	1	9	8	2	2	2	1
Services	10	4	5				4	4							1			
Unidentified	62	0	33		3		10		1		7				7		1	
Total	**782**	**181**	**426**	**39**	**15**	**2**	**150**	**33**	**16**	**15**	**96**	**62**	**24**	**20**	**43**	**2**	**12**	**8**

Fig. 28: Children, groups and schools, 1877.

No.: number of children

Dir.: number of children of parents listed in Mercer and Crocker, Directory of Shropshire, 1877, pp.55 to 59.

A number of the National School boys in the 1880 photograph of the parish church choir (Fig. 31) were from this kind of background and appear as smartly dressed as their Grammar School companions.

Nevertheless, a majority of dealers and substantial manufacturers, with the few professional families, chose the Grammar School or a private school, or opted for home tuition. There were 76 boys at the Grammar School in 1877, but only 16 were town boys under 13, the rest being older town boys, country boys or boarders. The private schools showed a wide range, from small establishments such as that of Mrs Molyneaux, to those that took boarders. John Reed, formerly English Master at the Grammar School, had taken over the school at 3 Mill Street in 1876, advertising as "The Commercial School, to prepare boys for an ordinary life of business". In 1877 there were only 8 day boys in the under 13 age group, but by 1890 there were 70 pupils, including 20 boarders.[85] The most refined girls' school was that of Mrs Crawford Watson, "for ladies" at Castle Lodge. She had 15 boarders, aged from 12 to 18 in 1881, but in 1877 took 13 girls from the town, including daughters of Francis Calver,

seeds-man, Herbert Evans surveyor, and John Liles, soda water manufacturer. Mixed schools drew younger children, e.g. Fanny Brown, at 28 Broad Street, taught five boys and two girls, among them James, aged five, second son of Heber Rickards, ironmonger.

Fig. 29: Teachers and pupils from Mrs Crawford Watson's "School for Ladies". The bows show that the girls took part in archery, a fashionable sport in mid-Victorian Ludlow.

Home tuition.

Some parents taught their children themselves, among them James Lang, draper, who was a passionate natural scientist.[86] In 1877 the eldest son, Ernest, was at the Grammar School, but girls aged ten and six and a boy of four were instructed at home. Others who taught children at home included a chemist, a solicitor, a revenue officer and Arthur Price, a pianoforte tutor who styled himself "Professor of Music".

Those disinclined to teach themselves employed governesses or tutors. The children of Revd Charles Kent, Vicar of Ludford, who lived at 9 Dinham, had a tutor. Later, Revd Clayton, Rector of Ludlow, who had four children born between 1875 and 1880, engaged a series of governesses, one of whom was Margaret McMillan (1860-1931). Born in Scotland,

Fig. 30: Margaret McMillan (1860- 1931), C.B., as portrayed at the Rachel McMillan Teachers' Training College, which she helped to found in honour of her sister, her lifelong collaborator.

Margaret and her sister Rachel became Christian Socialists active in British politics, campaigning particularly for nursery education, and writing a number of books, such as *Early Childhood* (1900).[87] Margaret's biographer attests that Ludlow was the setting for "the influence", a spiritual experience which shaped her life.[88]

Those not at school

The total number of children between five and 13 who were not at school was 43. Of these, 20 were the children of labourers or transport workers, and seven of widows. A few were already at work. The ten year old son of William Bishop, a Lower Broad Street labourer, was "carrying bark". Another, the twelve year son of Matthew Husk, a Frog Lane chimney sweep, was "helping father" – an echo of "The Water Babies", published 14 years before. Others, especially girls, looked after relatives, including the five year old daughter of James Everall of Corve Street, railway porter, whose wife was ill. Further cases are instanced in the log books, as in August 1873, when boys attended part-time, "being employed in the brick works". Some absentees went back to school, as in 1880, when Arthur Higgins "returned after three months work". Some defaulters pleaded poverty or poor health. Emma Mantle, widow, of 86 Corve Street, could not afford school pence. The four children of Job Hall, butcher's assistant, of 111 Lower Gaolford, had scarlatina. Thomas Reynolds, labourer, living in one of the yards off Lower Gaolford, had smallpox and was off work, so there were no clothes for his son and daughter, aged 6 and 8.

The authorities campaigned vigorously for better attendance, Clayton writing in May 1877: "It may be necessary to make an example of one or two in the first instance".[89] This proved over-optimistic, for in 1882 the Attendance Committee reported that "44 summonses have been sent out", most of which "led to school orders", though a few "to penalties".[90] Bad cases were highlighted in the press, such as that of Eliza Price of Sandpits, who was charged in

1885 for not sending her son Charles to school, the Attendance Officer reporting that he had made "only 2 attendances out of 401".[91]

A photograph three years after the census

School photographs from the time of the census are extremely rare but that reproduced as Fig. 31 is a precious survival. It comes from an album of Ludlow photographs presented by members of the choir of St Laurence's to a curate, Revd W. Pinckney, when he left Ludlow in 1880.[92] The photograph shows the choir boys with their names given below, most of which can be correlated with census details. The inset, from a photograph of the mens' choir, shows the National School Master, Frederick Cox, who no doubt played a part in enrolling boys who were past or present pupils at his school.

Four of the boys were from the Grammar School, readily identifiable by their mortar boards. The tallest, in the back row, is Bartholmew, a son of the church organist. Further along is Tillett, son of a Broad Street grocer, while in the front row, from the left, are Hoare, son of a ship's clerk, and Crosse, son of a tailor. Crosse and Tillett both held elementary scholarships and were former National School pupils. Except for James Davies, a baker's son from Lower Broad Street, who is sitting on the far left and who attended Miss Copner's school, the others were

Fig. 31: The boys' choir of St Laurence's, photographed in the castle, apparently on a choir outing. The inset shows a few members of the mens' choir, among them Frederick Cox, the National School Master, who is perhaps turning sideways to keep a careful watch on his pupils. Sitting in front of him is Samuel Herbert Valentine, later Mayor and Church Warden.

Holt, Watkins, Newman i, Bartholomew, Harmer, Reynolds, Tillett ii, Tillett i, Maund, Davies, Harmer, Hoare, Crosse, Page, Steele, Newman ii, Banks, Jones.

from the National School. Some were the sons of tradesmen, including the two Harmers – one right of Bartholomew, the other right of Davies – whose father was a grocer at 76 Lower Broad Street. The saddest circumstances were those of Thomas Reynolds, sixth from the left on the back row, who lived in a yard in Lower Gaolford, and whose father, according to the census, had smallpox.

LADDERS OF OPPORTUNITIES

Additions and amendments

When the Methodists – "with a maximum of faith and a minimum of cash"[93] – built a new chapel in Broad Street in 1879 and acquired a manse in Old Street, their Lower Broad Street chapel became a Wesleyan school, which soon caused the closure of the earlier non-conformist school in Old Street.[94] By 1885 the Wesleyans had 150 pupils, with John Barker, from Westminster Training College, as Master. A prospectus shows that the curriculum was wider than at most elementary schools :

Fig. 32: The Wesleyan Methodist chapel in Lower Broad Street (extreme left), seen from Whitcliffe. It opened as a chapel in 1800. Characteristically, the chapel was discreetly located at the back of a burgage plot, just outside the walled town.

Reading,	*Spelling,*	*Writing,*	*Drawing,*
Mapping,	*Arithmetic,*	*Grammar,*	*English,*
Literature.	*Recitation,*	*Singing,*	*Geography,*
History,	*Composition,*	*French (if required),*	
Needlework (girls).[95]			

In 1898 the Trustees placed what was clearly a thriving school under the auspices of the British and Foreign School Society, the non-conformist equivalent of the National Society. A new school – affectionately known as "the British" – was then built at the Old Street site, the manse becoming the schoolmaster's house.

The Grammar School experienced some difficulties responding to external ordinances. After losing a Government grant for teaching agriculture and science because of inadequate

Fig. 33: The British School in Old Street, with a twentieth century two storey extension at the rear. The date on the slab of the right gable, now obscured by recent building, is 1898.

buildings in 1887, the Grammar School governors acquired an eleven acre site at Burway for a new school; but the cost proved prohibitive, leaving development of the Mill Street site as the only option. The forceful Revd F.H. Hastings became Headmaster in 1894, and some adaptations to the buildings were undertaken in 1897, yet in 1900 there were only 58 boys on roll.

Elementary scholarships

Since the early seventeenth century there had been four Langfordian scholarships for boys between the ages of 9 and 16, endowed by Charles Langford (d.1607), a Ludlow boy who became Dean of Hereford.[96] Though for boys who were "poor and towardly for learning", they went in the mid-Victorian period to the sons of Ludlow tradesmen, such as W.H. (1868-73) and C.B. Marston (1870-77), sons of William Marston, corn merchant, later partners in Marston Brothers. The 1876 Scheme, which applied not less than £50 yearly for boys from elementary schools, increased the availability of scholarships, so that 71 were awarded to Ludlow boys between 1877 and 1901 (Fig. 34).[97]

The social range was wide but not complete. There were no sons of labourers, menial manufacturers or transport workers, but there were three sons of servants, and a handful of manual workers, one of whom was Henry Blackmore (1884), son of the Rectory gardener. Many fathers held managerial positions, among them James Elliott, manager of the Gas Works, three of whose sons won scholarships (1879, 1884, 1889). Almost a third of the boys were sons of tradesmen. There were four sons of ironmongers, five of grocers, and three of drapers, one of the latter, Frank Goodall (1886), being described as the son of an assistant. A quarter of the boys came from professional backgrounds, including sons of Thomas Jones, photographer (1880), S.R. Chubb, non-

Fig. 34, right and next page: Elementary scholarships to Ludlow Grammer School, 1877-1901.

A: Social background of scholarship boys[1]

Occupational class	Occupational group	No.	Total
1 Agriculture	cattle dealer	1	
	farm bailiff	1	
	farmer	1	
	gardener	1	4
4 Building	builder	4	
	painter	2	
	plumber	1	7
5 Manufacturing	blacksmith	1	
	currier	1	
	cabinet maker	3	
	shoemaker	1	
	confectioner	2	
	watchmaker	1	
	compositor	1	10
6 Transport	railway manager	1	
	station master	1	2
7 Dealing	coal merchant	3	
	draper's assistant	3	
	grocer	5	
	butcher	1	
	barman	1	
	wine merchant	1	
	bookseller	1	
	music dealer	2	
	ironmonger	4	
	trader	1	22
8 Finance	bank manager	1	
	bank clerk	1	2
10 Public service professional	attendance officer	1	
	gas works manager	4	
	rate collector	1	
	sea officer	2	
	police constable	1	
	lawyer's clerk	1	
	chemist	1	
	photographer	3	
	schoomaster	3	
	clergyman (non-conformist)	1	18
11 Service	hotel servant	2	
	servant	1	
	hairdresser	1	4
13 Dependent	orphan	1	1
99 Unidentified	widow	1	1
TOTAL		**71**	**71**

[1] (previous page)

B: Length of tenure [2]

Years	Boys		
1 year or less	3		
2 years	21		
3 years	12		
4 years	11		
5 years		Clee	business
		Everall	GPO (Birmingham)
		Hobbs	GPO (Birmingham)
		Jones	business
		Nickson	business
		Powell	journalism/degree
		Roberts	business
6 years	0		
7 years		Pool	elementary teacher
		Sharp	unknown
		Stephens	technical teacher
		Tillett	inland revenue
8 years		Bright	business
9 years		Ashton	Teachers T.C.
		Palmer	Cambridge degree

[1] (previous page) Data from Ludlow Grammar School Register, 1866-1913 (at Ludlow College). See n.4, chapter 1, for occupational classification.
[2] (this page) Ibid.

Fig. 34 continued.

conformist minister (1890) and F.K. Stevens (1895), bank manager.

It was disappointing that of 54 boys whose dates of leaving are recorded, 24 stayed for two years or less. A few left through illness – one boy with "severe ringworm" – and some left the area. Several leaving after four years became pupil teachers, including P.S. Reed (1891), son of the private school master. A few left to enter family businesses, such as C.W. Roberts (1890), son of an ironmonger. A handful stayed for seven years or more, seeking places at training colleges or Universities.

University exhibitions

Though about forty Grammar School boys went to university during Victoria's reign, only twelve came from the town, two of them sons of Dr Sparrow. As shown in Fig. 35, eight were from professional backgrounds, with only two – Harley Jones and Harding – coming "from trade". The most brilliant school career was that of John Palmer, son of the former National School pupil teacher, who won an Open Exhibition in Mathematics to St John's College, Cambridge. Seven of the 12 became clergymen, a traditional

Fig. 35: University Scholars and Exhibitioners from Ludlow Grammar School (Town boys only).

date	surname	first name	father's occupation	university	exhibition	career
1843	Acton	William	surgeon	Oxford	Greaves	clergyman
1861	Meyricke	Robert	clergyman	Cambridge	Town	barrister
1861	Sanders	Samuel	clergyman (non-conformist)	Cambridge	Town	clergyman (Anglican)
1866	Harley-Jones	Thomas	draper	Cambridge	Town	solicitor
1867	Sparrow	William	schoolmaster	Durham	Town	clergyman
1869	Sparrow	James	schoolmaster	Oxford	Town	clergyman
1882	Meredith	William Chubb	clergyman (non-conformist)	London	Town	schoolmaster
1888	Smith	Edward	chemist	Oxford	Town	clergyman
1889	Harding	William	draper		Town	clergyman
1890	Montford	John	solicitor	Oxford	Greaves	clergyman
1894	Warren	Charles	excise officer	Oxford	Town	solicitor
1900	Palmer	John	schoolmaster	Cambridge	Open/County	schoolmaster

career path for graduates, two became schoolmasters and three were lawyers.

There were, however, other routes to eminence, such as that taken by Ellis Powell, a fine example of advancement from modest origins. The son of a painter and decorator in Lower Gaolford, he attended the National School and then won a Grammar School scholarship. Leaving after five years, he became a London journalist and eventually Editor of The Financial News. He showed remarkable capacity for part-time study, qualifying as a barrister and obtaining degrees in economics: first a Bachelor's, then a Doctorate. He finally became a lecturer at the London School of Economics.

Fig. 36: Dr Ellis Powell (1869-1942), a scholarship boy who 'made good'.

Opportunities for girls

When the inspector, Revd Bonner, presented his report on the Girls' National School in 1870 he wrote: "From girls, of course, I do not expect so much and they very rightly spend much time in needlework". Such an attitude underlay the Industrial School for Girls, started by the Rector in 1870, at which girls who had left the National School "were regularly employed in all kinds of house-work", including supplying dinners "for the sick poor".[98] Service in private employment was the route taken by many school leavers, including the most able, Miss Greathurst recording sadly in April 1864: "One of the oldest and best pupils was withdrawn to go to service. Felt her loss very much". Teaching training offered an alternative for some girls, such as Emma Wall, a pupil teacher, who went to Fishponds, Bristol, in 1878.

There were initiatives in London and elsewhere, to promote secondary education for girls, ripples of which reached Ludlow. In 1885 six pupils of Mrs Crawford Watson attained passes from the College of Preceptors, which had been founded in 1846 to provide qualifications by written papers.[99] Late in the century, girls at Miss Courtney's School were able to take "French, German, mathematics, geography. History, Latin, drawing and botany", a few aspiring to take the same Cambridge Locals as their brothers did at the Grammar School.[100]

The end of the reign

When the Queen died in January, 1901, a major restructuring of education was under discussion, following the recommendation by the Bryce commission in 1895 that County Councils, newly constituted in 1889, should be responsible for secondary schools. This included an obligation to provide girls' schools, leading to the opening of Ludlow Girls' High School in 1910, with staff and girls from Miss Courtney's school incorporated. Tentacles from Shrewsbury had already reached Ludlow, one of them the receipt of an annual £50 for science teaching from 1898. In 1902 the newly returned

Conservative Government went further than Bryce, and made County Councils responsible for all levels of education, though preserving rights and responsibilities for endowed schools and sectarian schools, such as those at Ludlow.

The "Gates of Knowledge" were not yet fully open, and "the golden key" not totally put aside, but during the Queen's reign the educational system in Ludlow had been transformed. To a degree, this had been in response to outside forces and pressures, but local instigators and teachers had played their part. The development of its schools was not the least of the achievements of Victorian Ludlow.

ENDNOTES

1   Steward, W.J., *The Vision of Aorangi and other poems*, Timaur, 1906, p.12.
2   *The Times*, 2 November 1912.
3   LMCT minutes, various entries, 1852-55.
4   Schofield (Ed.), *New Zealand Dictionary of Biography*, 1940.
5   House of Commons Papers: Education. Abstract of the Answers and Reports made pursuant to an Address to the House of Commons, Vol.11, 1833, p.777.
6   The total given for Ludlow for the 1831 census was 5,253; the number living in adjoining parts of Ludford and Stanton Lacy is unknown, but is likely to be a little less than the 387 calculated from the 1841 census returns.
7   Lloyd, D.J., *Country Grammar School*, 1977, p.39.
8   Cited in Midwinter, E., *Nineteenth Century Education*, 1970, p.4.
9   Barnard, H.C., *A Short History of English Education*, 1947, pp.77-79.
10 Felton, W., *Guide Book to Ludlow*, p.40.
11 Carless, W.T., *A Short History of Hereford School*, 1923, p.54. Revd Charles Taylor, Headmaster at Ludlow 1801 to 1807, was subsequently Headmaster at Hereford.
12 Lloyd, op.cit., pp.85, 88.
13 *The Ludlow Elections*, 1837, p.5; House of Commons Papers: Education. Abstract of Answers and Returns made pursuant to an Address to the House of Commons, Vol.11, 1833, p.777.
14 PRO 27/3957.
15 Oldham, J.B., *A History of Shrewsbury School, 1552-1952* (1952), pp.187-88.
16 1851 census; LMTC minutes, 1848-77, p.14.
17 Brice, C., *Ludlow Grammar School as it is and was*, Ludlow, 1850, pp.6-7.
18 *The Ludlovian*, 1918, Recollections of Dr John Harley.
19 Griffiths scrapbook.
20 1835 Wood map of Ludlow; 1841 census.
21 *Shropshire Journal*, 24 Jan., 1838, p.3.
22 Felton, op.cit., p.12.
23 *Shropshire Journal*, 15 Jan., 1840, p.3.
24 SA DA3/100/2.
25 Robinson diary, p.1.
26 Midwinter, op.cit., pp.17-18.
27 e.g. there are no entries in the minute book the Guild of Stitchmen after 18 Sept.1832 (LB 17/3).
28 1841 census; Harrison, Harrod & Co., 1861, pp.709,710.
29 Robinson diary, pp.1-2.
30 Indenture in the Old Ludlovians archive, Ludlow library.
31 Lloyd, D.J., *Popular Education and Society in Ludlow, 1711-1861*, 1974, pp.38-39.
32 Midwinter, op.cit., p.29.
33 Wright,T., *The History and Antiquities of the Town of Ludlow*, 1826, p.186.
34 Harker, M.F., *Henry Peach Robinson: Master of Photographic Art 1830-1901*, 1988, p2.
35 Charity School Minutes, iii (1806-63), p.38.
36 *Short History of the English People*, 1874, cited by Barnard, op.cit., p.11.
37 Evans, J., *Handbook to Ludlow*, 1865, p.97.
38 Nat.Society Annual Report, 1818, p.153.
39 Bullock, J., *The Beauties of Ludlow*, Herefordshire Tracts, 1818.
40 *Primitive Methodist Magazine*, 1842, p.96.
41 see p.159.
42 Congregational Church minute book.
43 Barnard, op.cit., pp.105-107.
44 Parliamentary Accounts and Papers, 1852-53, Vol.XL, p.235.
45 Robinson diary, p.6.
46 Ibid., p.42.
47 Lawson, J. and Silver, H., *A Social History of Education in England*, 1973, pp.246-47.
48 Result of Returns to the General Inquiry made by the National Society into the State and Progress of Schools for the Education of the Poor, 1846-47, p.101.
49 Infant Schools Accounts, in possession of the author; 1851 census.
50 Crabbe, G., *The Borough*, 1810, letter xiv.
51 1st Annual Report of the Hereford Diocesan Board of Education, 1850, p.1.
52 Southern diary, p.66; Fay, *Victorian Days in England*, p.132.
53 Packer papers: undated obituary of Rev. John Phillips.

54 National Society., Ludlow file: balance sheet sent to Society, 4 Oct.1856.
55 National Society, Ludlow file.
56 Minutes of the Committee of Council, 1839-40, pp.2,11,52, archives of St Laurence's Church.
57 Barnard, op.cit., p.118.
58 *Ludlow Parish Magazine*, Feb. 1894.
59 School log books.
60 Barnard, op.cit., p.122.
61 Admissions Register, Saltley Training College, Birmingham.
62 Barnard, op.cit., p.130.
63 Report for the Year 1869 on Ludlow Charities.
64 Fay, op.cit., pp.26-27.
65 *Parish Magazine*, Dec. 1868.
66 Jeffreys, M.V.C., *The Man Behind the 1870 Act*, review in The Birmingham Post, 11 April 1970.
67 Barnard, op.cit., p.198.
68 National Society files, application form for grant of East Hamlet School, Feb. 1875.
69 *Parish Magazine*, July, 1871, ref. to inspection of Nonconformist school in Old Street.
70 *Primitive Methodist Magazine*, 1837, pp.69-70; SA 5411/131/8.
71 Kelly, 1879, p.348.
72 PRO: Ed.21/14844.
73 *Parish Magazine* April 1874.
74 Ibid., Nov. 1873.
75 National Society files.
76 This and the next paragraph based on Lloyd, 1977, chapter 7.
77 Barnard, op.cit., p.149.
78 P.R.O. Ed.2/3957.
79 Barnard, op.cit., p.198.
80 Town Council Minutes, 5 Oct 1876, p.189.
81 His name is the first of the list, which begins at the top of Mill Street.
82 See p.159-60.
83 Girls' National School Log, 19 May 1871.
84 Later Taylor's Yard.
85 P.R.O. Ed.27/3964.
86 Lloyd, D., *The History of Ludlow Museum, 1833-1983*, 1984, p.14.
87 Internet: University of Greenwich, AIM 25.
88 Steedman, C., *Childhood, Culture and Class in Britain: Margaret McMillan, 1860-1931*, Virago, 1990, pp.20-21.
89 *Parish Magazine*, May 1877.
90 Town Council Minutes, p.394.
91 *Ludlow Advertiser*, 28 Feb. 1885.
92 The album is now among the records of St Laurence's Church.
93 *Methodist Recorder*, 16 Nov. 1899, p.11.
94 PRO Ed/21/14844.
95 Ludlow Museum.
96 Lloyd, D., 1977, pp.48, 148.
97 Ludlow Grammar School Register, 1866-1913.
98 *Parish Magazine* March 1870.
99 *Ludlow Advertiser* 24 Jan. 1885.
100 Interview with the late Mrs V. Packer, reported in Burns, R. and Lloyd, D., *Century of Change, 1900-2000*, 2000, pp.20-21.

CHAPTER 10

GLIMPSES OF MID-CENTURY LIFE

MARGARET TEAGUE, GILLIAN SHARPE, ROY COLES, JO BRISTOW

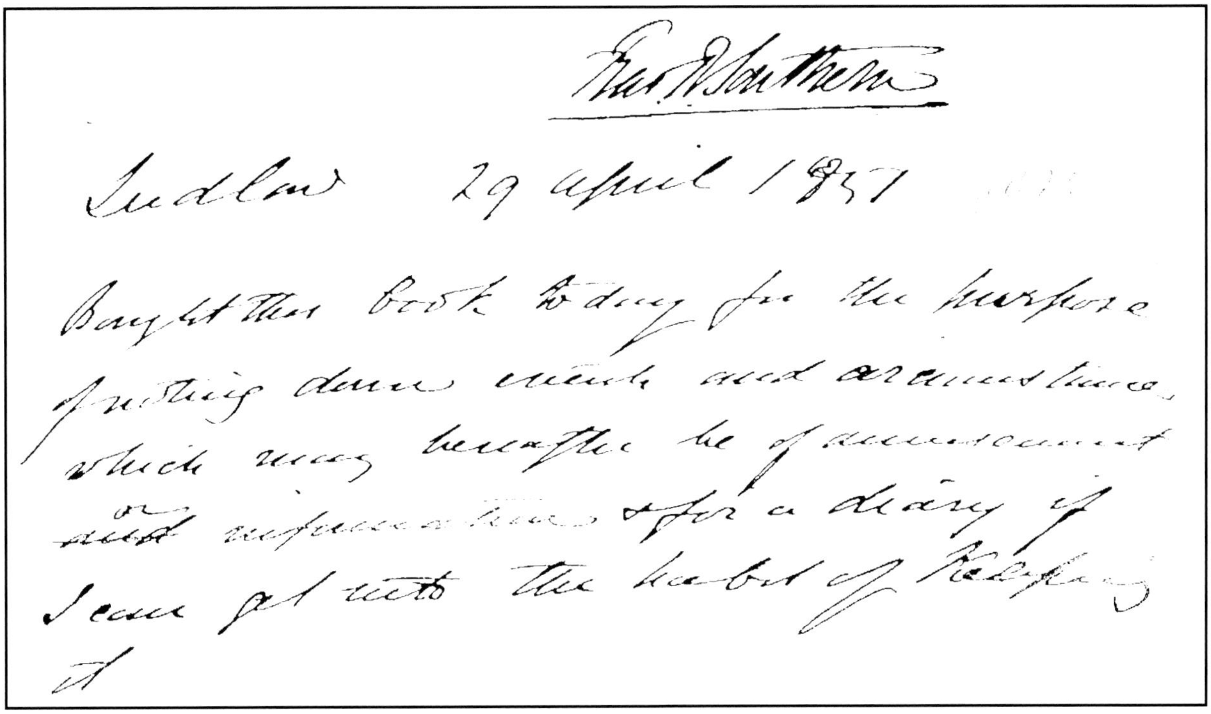

Fig. 1: The opening entry in the Southern diary.

The principal source for this chapter, used by all contributors, is the remarkably detailed diary of Francis Richard Southern, a young Ludlow solicitor who later became a Borough Councillor. The diary, covering the years 1851 and 1852, was transcribed by Southern's great grand-daughter, Rachel Millard, who lives in Buckinghamshire. We thank her for generously making the text available to us.[1] A second diary, started on New Year's Day 1849 and continuing to November 1851, is that of Henry Peach Robinson. The son of the National School Master, he was a bookseller's apprentice who later became a pioneer of artistic photography, practising in Tunbridge Wells.[2] The now well known letters of Anna Maria Fay are a third

contemporary source. She was a young American woman who stayed at Moor Park just outside Ludlow for twelve months from November 1851 and again briefly in 1864. Her letters were published in 1923 under the title *Victorian Days in England*, which has been recently reprinted by a local publisher.[3]

Diaries and letters are among the most vivid of historical sources, giving contemporary descriptions of events that are often fresh and spontaneous. They are also one of the most biased, reflecting the circumstances, opinions and prejudices of the writer. This is well illustrated here, for the three writers focus on a comparatively short period – principally 1851 and 1852 – and sometimes describe the same events. The contributors to this chapter, though drawing liberally from the diaries and letters, have sought to balance them with other kinds of evidence, such as census returns, trade directories and newspaper reports.

1: FRANCIS RICHARD SOUTHERN
FAMILY AND FRIENDS

Francis Southern's diary commenced on 29 April 1851 when he bought a book "for the purpose of noting down events and circumstances which may hereafter be of amusement or information and for a diary if I can get into the habit of keeping it". His habit in fact lasted for just nineteen months but during much of that time his entries were regular, informative and occasionally spiced with a touch of gossip. They provide a picture of the life of a young and up-and-coming professional man in a busy rural market town, and in particular describe the kinship and social networks to which he belonged and upon which he built his own social and professional life.

Francis Richard Southern was born on 15 March 1823 at Lydbury North, a large rural parish fifteen miles north west of Ludlow. In the early 1850s he lived in Mill Street and was making his way as a lawyer. His parents were Francis Richard Southern of Lydbury North and Mary, the eldest daughter of Richard Watters of Little Brampton and then Longnor. In 1846 the Tithe apportionment showed the family farming nearly 300 acres, mostly rented from the Plowden estate.[4] By 1851 Francis's father was dead and his mother was living at Condover with her sister. Francis junior was most attentive to them, making frequent visits, especially after the railway came in 1852. He had two brothers: John, living at The Lyth near Shrewsbury, upon whom he called when he went to Condover, and Will, farming at Lydbury. His paternal grandfather, also Francis Southern of Lydbury North, had married Clara, daughter of Richard Wollaston, a surgeon of Bishop's Castle, whose wife, Mary, was a daughter of John Acton, also a surgeon of Bishop's Castle, and his wife, Mary Sandford. He was related therefore to well known south Shropshire professional and farming families.[5]

Fig. 2: The Southern and Lloyd families (simplified).

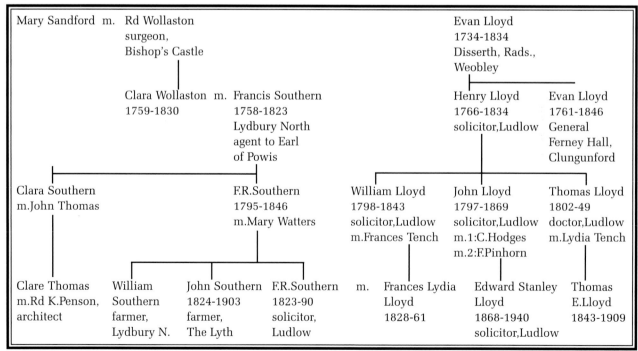

In Ludlow he moved in the upper levels of society, having the support and friendship of his aunt, Mrs Thomas (his mother's sister) of Dinham House. On Sundays he records sitting in the Dinham House pew in church and when his mother and her sister came to stay in Ludlow in August 1851 they also sat there, the seat having been "fitted out afresh in 1831 or 1832 when the Duchess of Kent and her present Majesty, then Princess Victoria, were at Oakley [sic] Park. They both attended Ludlow church on Sunday and sat in this seat and the scarlet cloth, etc. with which the seat was lined for the occasion still remains."

His cousin John, a surgeon living at 50 Broad Street, and John's sister, Mary Ann, were his constant companions and hosts for dinner. Through them came close links with their brother, Frank, who farmed at Kempton in the Clun Valley close to Lydbury North. The diary records frequent visits to Kempton, sometimes with his cousin John to go fishing, and often combined with a call on brother Will, at Lydbury. News of Will is regularly reported. In September 1851 he and his wife had their first child, a daughter, Francis commenting that this was "his first shot at being an uncle". The following June Will had an accident when a struggling sheep knocked the shears out of the hands of the shearer and in doing so they stuck in Will's leg, causing him to be "still lame" three weeks later. Frank and Will would be entertained when they came into Ludlow for the market or the sheep and cattle fairs in September. When Will attended the large Christmas Poultry Market in Ludlow on 22 December 1851 ("said to be more turkeys and geese here than for many years"), he brought Francis a turkey.

Francis and his Ludlow cousins were fellow guests at social events, as on 8 October 1851, when they visited the Reverend George Pinhorn at Brimfield. A party of twelve enjoyed an evening of music and singing, though John Southern, the surgeon, was "called away shortly after dinner to see Mr Massey of Ludlow" (probably Francis Massey, the Bull Ring wine merchant). There were also Pic Nic parties further afield, for example in September 1852 at the Compton's of Kinsham near Presteigne to which he went with Jim Davies, one of his Ludlow friends: "Dined at the house then walked about, then tea and afterwards dancing till supper and dancing again until nearly 5 o'clock the next morning. J. Davies drove me back, he rather Queer, a little too much to drink."

Another Ludlow family with whom he often dined were the Tenches of Springfield House in Lower Gaolford, where their niece, Fanny Lloyd, lived with her uncle. Her father, William Lloyd, a Ludlow solicitor, had married Francis (Fanny Tench), daughter of Robert Tench, a Bromfield land agent.[6] He first mentions Fanny when he has supper with the Tenches after church on 7 May 1851, during a spell of unseasonably cold weather, when the Long Mynd and Titterstone Clee Hill were covered with snow. On Friday 6 June he spent an evening at Dinham House, noting that "Miss Fanny Lloyd also there and walked home with her at night". The encounters continued. Both Francis and Fanny were among the guests at a large gathering on Tuesday 4 November at the Mill Street home of another Ludlow solicitor, Rodney Anderson. On Sunday 7 December, again after church, Francis went to supper at the Tenches, remarking that he sat "with Mrs Lloyd and Miss Lloyd"; and he was there again on 13 December for an evening of musical entertainment. Fanny attended a large party held at Dinham House on 10 January 1852 with Francis also present (it was cousin John Southern's 34th birthday; but "he was not at the party through some misunderstanding"). On 1 February, the first of the five Sundays in February, it being a Leap Year, a curiosity upon which he comments, he walked with Miss Lloyd and her brother, and afterwards had dinner at the Tenches.

As a coming professional man with good social connections, now aged 28, Francis must have been one of Ludlow's most eligible bachelors. It is not surprising, therefore, that in

Fig.3: Some of the Ludlow houses of Francis Richard Southern and his Ludlow relatives and friends.

Top: The elevation of Dinham House, as drawn about 1850. It was owned by the Earl of Powis, and tenanted from 1842 by John Thomas Esq., and his wife Clare, aunt of Francis Southern. As the eighteenth century town residence of the Johnes of Croft Castle, where Lucien Bonaparte was held on parole in 1811, Dinham House had great cachet in early Victorian Ludlow, and may have been the model for The Town House in Stanley Weyman's novel, The New Rector (1891).

Centre: Springfield House, Lower Gaolford, which from 1841 or earlier was the home of the Tench family, "highly respectable land stewards" (Hereford Journal, 12 June 1844). The business, started by Robert Tench of Bromfield, was continued by his sons Richard (1813-95) and John (1812-96).

Bottom: This photograph of part of Broad Street was taken in the 1860s. Behind the spreading tree, it shows the spacious house over Broad Gate which was acquired by Henry Lloyd, solicitor, in 1815, remaining in the possession of his heirs until 1940. The first house visible left of the tree is No. 31, an elegant five bay Georgian house which became the home of Francis and Fanny Southern in 1858.

1852 he received three Valentines, arriving on 14, 15 and 16 February, though he noted that he did "not recollect having one for several years". Meetings with Fanny Lloyd and her family continued, but there was a long gap during the second half of 1852 before what is one of the last entries in the diary on 7 December 1852, when he once more "dined at Tench's" adding "Fanny Lloyd at home again after a long visit at Bradford in Wiltshire [where she had relatives]". What this comment reveals about his feelings towards her is a matter of speculation, but the fact that he took the trouble so often to mention her presence on social occasions, though never in romantic terms, suggests that he may already have been thinking of her as his future wife. But whatever his feelings were at this time, he did not marry Fanny until 1858, when he was 35 and she was 30. Long courtships and long engagements, of course, were not uncommon at this time, one of the most notable, although the circumstances were scarcely comparable, being that of Lord Alfred Tennyson and Emily Sellwood, which lasted seventeen years.[7] An earlier entry, on 21 February 1852, suggests an aversion to marrying below oneself rather than to matrimony itself: "Heard Mr W Acton of Corve Street was married at Munslow on Thursday to his servant. He, I am told, is 61 years of age. Verification of the old adage, of all fools an old fool is the worst".

The amount of time Francis gave to socialising and other pleasures was substantial, but many diary entries do relate to his work as a solicitor. On 13 April 1851, for example, he "went to Knighton with Mr Gibbons on business", meeting a fellow solicitor from Rhayader, while on 9 September he "attended before the Commissioners for Assessed Taxes to appeal for two parties". Many of his diary entries refer to legal work undertaken for his family. On 29 August he "went to Eardisland and Leominster by hired gig" on behalf of his uncle, Mr Thomas of Dinham House, while later in the week the same business took him to Stafford. On 13 October he attended Birmingham Bankruptcy Court on behalf of his uncle, and then took the opportunity to travel on to Lichfield to search the will indexes for members of his family. He lists eleven wills which he found, among them that of Francis Southern of Harley, one of many Shropshire parishes in the Lichfield Diocese. This and other entries show that he was a keen and capable genealogist. More immediate family concerns included the collection of rents for his mother on land at Moat Hill, Bishop's Castle left to her by Grandfather Watters, which was to be inherited by Francis on her death; and a meeting with cousin Frank to discuss the settlement on his impending marriage to a Miss Danford of Bishop's Castle. His lucrative legal practice was the partnership of Southern, Appleton and Lloyd, the Lloyd partner being Fanny's brother Robert. The firm had its offices at 9 Castle Street.

Business and pleasure were also combined on his visits to London, where the family had connections. One of the earliest entries in the diary is to a letter written to his Aunt Thomas from his cousin William Seabrook, who was House Steward to the Duchess of Kent at Frogmore House, Windsor. The letter offered a juicy piece of Ludlow gossip, giving news of a Mr Andrews, brother of Mrs Meyricke, wife of the Reverend Robert Meyricke, Reader of Ludlow. Andrews, a surgeon at Windsor had absconded the previous Sunday "with about £60,000", and had forged a Power of Attorney to enable him to transfer stock "from Mr Meyricke of Windsor, an uncle of the Reverend". In June 1851, whilst on a fortnight's visit to London, Francis called at Clarence House, St James's, the town residence of the Duchess of Kent, and saw William Seabrook and Caroline Southern, another relative, who was the Duchess's cook, and the same day he called on Caroline's sister, Harriet, a lady's maid at a no doubt smart house in South Audley Street. His mother and aunt were also in London on this occasion, staying at Great Marlborough Street, where Francis "took up quarters". Together they called on the Watters family, his mother's cousins, who lived in New Road, Commercial Road East and the following day they went to see his aunt and uncle Thomas from Dinham House who together with other cousins up from Shropshire were staying at Russell Place, Fitzroy Square. On his mother's birthday on 18 June they went to the Lyceum Theatre and saw King Charming, in which Madam Vestris performed.

The following day he "went by myself to the Great Exhibition of All Nations. Paid admission 1 shilling. It is an immense building and has a very imposing appearance and is quite as wonderful as the exhibitions within it. Covered 18 acres of ground. The interior is very beautiful and is altogether a grand sight but rather confusing there are so many things to be seen. Remained there about 4 hours and met with my mother and party who had come in and paid for a strawberry ice in the building 1 shilling. Believe there were about 60,000 people there."

In London again on family business in November 1852 Francis's diary entry for Thursday 18 November records "Up at 6, breakfasted and then to 391 Strand, where I took my seat [he had booked it the previous day for one guinea in order to watch the Duke of Wellington's funeral procession] soon after half past 7. The streets already very full of people. There were about 30 persons in this shop. The carriageway eventually cleared by the police but foot passengers allowed on the pavement. About 10 minutes past 10 the procession began to move past and went slowly and gradually on until 20 minutes to 12 when it ended. Altogether very imposing affair. Was most struck with the Chelsea Pensioners and the Duke's horse, led by a groom, with the boots reversed in the stirrups. Almost everyone in black with band round the hat. Soon after procession was passed left my seat and walked among the crowd nearly to Temple Bar. But

Fig. 4: A view of Crystal Palace, in Hyde Park, London, where Francis Southern saw "The Great Exhibition of All Nations" in 1851. The exhibition aroused great enthusiasm and national pride, causing one visitor to observe: "with steam and the Bible, the English traverse the globe".

there found it so thick that I went no further."

The diary also records Francis's growing involvement in the official life of the Town. When it began he was already a member of the Board of Guardians of the Poor for St Laurence, Ludlow and his attendance at meetings is carefully recorded. His social and professional standing and contacts clearly stood him in good stead, for on Thursday 13 November 1851 he records "met Mr J. Williams Junior, Town Clerk, who told me I had that morning been elected a Councillor for the Borough in the room of Thomas Jones, elected on 1 November but who had failed to qualify within the required time." On Sunday 16 November he wrote "Sat of right now in the Corporation seat." For the rest of the

Fig. 5: Detail of a lithograph of the interior of St Laurence's, published in the 1830s by Richard Jones, bookseller. The Council pews, with red baize headrests, can be seen in front of the pulpit, a position they continued to occupy until 1985. Francis Southern sat there "of right" after his election as a Borough Councillor in November 1851. The organ and screen were omitted in this illustration.

diary he mentions his involvement as a Councillor in many of the lively issues of the day in Ludlow – the sale of Corporation land, the preparation for the opening of the railway, and the proposed building of a cattle market. He became Mayor in 1855 and 1865, and Alderman from 1866, remaining on the Council until a few years before his death.

After their marriage the Southerns made their home at 31 Broad Street, a large Georgian house close to the Lloyd's residence at the Broad Gate, but Fanny died in 1861 leaving no children and Francis did not marry again. He himself died on 12 November 1890, having remained at 31 Broad Street as a widower.[8]

2: FAITH AND WORSHIP

The diarists give revealing glimpses of the religious life of Ludlow, but most of these refer to the parish church. This is in spite of the fact that, as shown in Fig. 6, 87% of all church attendances recorded by the Ecclesiastical Census of 30 March 1851 were at the town's four independent churches. Because some people would have attended twice or even three times, the total number of people involved is less than the total number of attendances, which was 2,010. It may have been about 1,600, just over a third of the town's population, which would allow for about 400 people attending twice.

Anna Maria Fay visited St Laurence's on 9 November 1851. In one of her letters home she described the service as "very grand and solemn, the congregation so devout and the responses so full."[9] She praised the organ as "large and really fine: not over-powerful, but the tones round and full". She added, however, that the organist, who was Adam Rea, "did not do it justice", though his obituary, five years later, described him as "the eminent organist" of Ludlow.[10] She was equally critical of the singing: "The Te Deum was chanted to a rather ordinary double chant....while the words of the Jubilate and the Gloria were miserably divided, some gabbled and others drawled out".

Church	Informant	morning			afternoon			evening			total	
		no.	SS	total	no.	SS	total	no.	SS	total	no.	%
parish church	John Phillips, Rector	210		210	51		51				**261**	13
Independent church - Old Street	Theophilus Davies	100	60	160	108		108	120		120	**388**	19
Christadelphians - Brand Lane	Henry Meymott	42		42				27		27	**69**	3
Wesleyan - Lower Broad Street	Ralph Stoll	137	63	200	78		78	344		344	**622**	31
Primitive Methodists - Old Street	Joseph Middleton	120	40	160	160	50	210	300		300	**670**	33
		609	**163**	**772**	**397**	**50**	**447**	**791**		**791**	**2010**	

Fig. 6: Church attendances in Ludlow, 30 March, 1851.

Source: PRO: HO 129/352.

Her most severe censure, however, was reserved for the Rector, the Reverend John Phillips: "The Rector is a miserably low churchman – indeed they say he is a very bad man, and his face justifies the report. He is so unpopular that the Dissenting chapels and the alehouses are filled on Sunday". The extent to which such criticism was deserved is difficult to assess, but it must be taken within the context of local politics, for Phillips was a Whig in a town of predominantly Tory opinion. His obituary, written after his death on 22 September, 1866, develops this point: "He was a Whig whose liberal political views aroused some hostility......He was viewed with suspicion and coldness by well to do parishioners who were mainly Tory, but they grew to appreciate his excellent qualities".[11]

Other comments by Anna Maria Fay give a clear picture of the parish church a few years before the major restoration that began in 1859. "Nothing could exceed the solemnity of the scene, the antique roof, the vaulted arches above us, the stained glass windows of some chapel behind the organ, the rich screens dividing this portion of the church from the choir and chapels". She paints a moving picture of "the devout poor seated on the benches in the middle aisle – old men and decrepit old women leaning on their sticks and looking up so reverently to the clergyman and helping to follow the clerk with their quavering voices in their full responses which seem to roll through the church". In contrast, she also described the pews reserved for the Borough Council: "under the pulpit are four pews lined with red, in which sit the Mayor and Corporation in blue silk gowns trimmed with fur".

A week later she and her relatives were back for the first Sunday after the election of the

Fig. 7: The interior of St Laurence's as shown in a painting in the 1830s. The artist was Edward Hodson the younger son of Edward Hodson, a Broad Street bookseller. The picture shows the benches in the middle for "the devout poor", and the Snetzler organ in its original position on a gallery in front of the rood screen.

Borough Council, when Francis Southern, a newly elected member, was one of those occupying the Council pews. He wrote in his diary on 16 November 1851: "Went in procession with the Mayor and Corporation to church in the morning. It seems to be the custom to attend the Mayor at church the first Sunday and the last in his year of office and then after church to return to the Council Chambers to take cake and wine with the Mayor".

Francis Southern was a regular churchgoer. Very early in the diary, on 11 May 1851, he records going to church "in morning and again after tea", a pattern followed at other times. Occasionally he remained "for the sacrament", as on 1 June 1851. The following Sunday he heard the Bishop of Hereford, Renn Dickson Hampden, preach from "19th Acts, second verse", Southern sitting, he tells us proudly, "in the Dinham House pew".[12] In the afternoon he was in church again for a confirmation: "about 180 confirmed, many more girls than boys".

The discovery of a hidden altar piece in the church during this period caused great excitement. It was the youthful Henry Peach Robinson, with a maturing interest in art, who reported the find in a letter to The Hereford Times on 25 February, 1849. The removal of "the oak screen of Corinthian columns" had revealed the original medieval reredos, though many of the figures were worn and often badly mutilated. Robinson also sent a drawing of the reredos to the Ludlow-born historian, Thomas Wright, and recorded in his diary that he had received a letter in reply, "the contents of which were much better than I had anticipated".[13] The find helped to stimulate a growing awareness of the need for restoration at St Laurence's, the Bishop of Hereford on 3 June 1849 preaching a sermon on "repairs and restoration, particularly the altar piece". Robinson's interest was supported by the architect Richard Kyrke Penson, in 1849 a tenant at Dinham House, though soon to have a practice in Chester and to succeed his father as County Surveyor of Montgomeryshire.[14] Robinson wrote in his diary

Fig. 8: The restored medieval reredos, photographed about 1858 by Ludlow's first professional photographer, Thomas Jones. The sixteenth century altar rail was later moved to St John's chapel.

on 9 June 1849: "I called at Dinham House this morning and saw Mr Penson", who said "that he would get Lord Dungannon to use his influence on my behalf". In fact, Robinson's career progressed in a different direction, but it was probably due to Penson's influence that Lord Dungannon, a member of the Welsh border families of Trevor and Hill, later met most of the cost of restoring the reredos.[15] Work on the reredos was part of the momentum towards the Gilbert Scott restoration of St Laurence's in 1859-60. On 22 August, 1852, for example, Francis Southern recorded that the collection at the morning's service had been "in aid of the Society for Building Churches". During this service the Rector made the surprising statement that "a gentleman unconnected with the district had offered to build another church in Ludlow"; and it is tempting to wonder if this was Lord Dungannon.

It is unfortunate that the diarists do not give this kind of detail for the town's non-conformist churches, in spite of the much greater numbers in their congregations. The oldest of these were the Independents. They had built a small place of worship in lower Corve Street in 1736, moving to a larger, newly built chapel in Old Street in 1830.[16] Entries in the church minute book record the lows and highs of the 16 year ministry of the Reverend Theophilus Davies, Minister from 1835 to 1852.[17] There had been 29 members in 1836 but these had increased to 70 by 1841. In succeeding years there were a number of defections, five to the Plymouth Brethren, two to the Mormons, and one with "Armenian views", while another was "solemnly expelled from this fellowship for intoxication", though with "earnest prayer for his repentance and conversion". After "a disappointing year" in 1846, numbers rose again to 77 by the end of 1847, but in 1851 Davies complained of "the low state of the cause generally". One of the Deacons of the Independent Church was the Bull Ring chemist and Borough Councillor, George Cocking (1808-1888).[18] His wife, Elizabeth (nee Harding), converted to the church as a young woman, was

Fig. 9: The choir of the Old Street Primitive Methodist Church, photographed in 1873, the year when their new chapel was opened. The builder of the chapel, William Russell, seen on the left at the back, was a passionate Methodist. His eldest son Henry, third from the left in the front row, succeeded him in the business. Another son, John, became a Methodist Minister, first in Durham, then in Blackburn.

a member for over fifty years, being described in her obituary as "a valued friend of the poor". Their daughter, Mary Ellen, married Theophilus Davies' son, who later became a missionary in Honolulu. It is a remarkable fact that there is a memorial to Mary Ellen Davies and to her parents inside St Laurence's parish church, affirming that the west front of the church was restored in 1912 in her memory and "to the glory of God". No narrow sectarianism here!

Francis Southern did make some references to the non-conformists, grouping them together as "dissenters". On Good Friday, 9 April, 1852, he noted that there had been "A great tea drinking (Dissenters) over the Market Hall at night", where there were "said to be 600 to 800 people present". An entry on 1 January of the same year noted that after Southern himself had seen the New Year in at the Angel, coming home with his friend Hoggis, a veterinary surgeon, he "fell in with people singing hymns, to celebrate the commencement of the new year". His comment is a testimony to non-conformist zeal in early Victorian Ludlow: "They are Dissenters (I know not what class) and it is their custom to pray in their chapel the last day of each year commencing late in the evening and remaining till the new year begins when they sally out and sing through the streets. I should think there were more than 100 persons singing this morning. I have heard them in previous years here".

3: THE COMING OF THE RAILWAY

On Tuesday, 20 April, 1852 Ludlow changed forever, for it was on this day that the railway arrived. Contemporary accounts show that it was a great occasion with celebrations both at the station and throughout the town. Anna Maria Fay described it as "a great day in the annals of Ludlow".[19] There was a dinner at the Assembly Rooms, sports in the outer bailey of the castle and the whole town was decorated for the occasion with flowers and banners.

The Shrewsbury and Hereford Railway (S&H) was not in the first wave of railway building but it was conceived as a link joining Shrewsbury with Hereford and on via Abergavenny and Pontypool to Newport, giving access to the ports in South Wales. The line from Chester to Shrewsbury was opened on 12 October 1848 and that from Shrewsbury to Wolverhampton had been completed on 12 April 1849. By this time the "Railway Mania" of the mid-1840s had led to many bankruptcies and the S&H was only saved by the combined efforts of Henry Robertson, its engineer, W. Ormsby-Gore, a local MP, and others who had already paid out £25,000 for their share of the joint station at Shrewsbury and were therefore reluctant to forfeit their investment. They engaged Mr Thomas Brassey to build the line. He was well known in the area as a contractor, for he had already built the line between

Fig. 10: The railway line on its embankment, seen from Corve bridge. Straight ahead is the Queen's Arms, which opened in 1850. Before the railway was built the New Road turnpike up to Gravel Hill passed to the right of the inn and the road to Fishmore went to the left; but to save expense only the latter was bridged, so that a detour had to be made to reach New Road. By Ludlow artist William Gwynn (1782 to c.1860).

Shrewsbury and Chester.[20]

Work began on the S&H at the end of 1850 and progress was rapid over the route. It had no major engineering works except the viaduct just to the south of Shrewsbury station to cross the river Rea which is some 700ft long. Difficulties with the construction of the tunnel at Dinmore held up the completion of the line to Hereford for over a year but it was opened to Ludlow in April 1852.

In early April plans were being laid for a celebration to mark the opening. Francis Southern records on Wednesday 7 April: "Attended meeting of the Corporation to devise a plan of rejoicing on the opening of the Railway on the 20th. Ball Committee appointed, also subscriptions to be opened, etc. Rural sports to be got up". The poster imploring Ludlow businessmen to support the opening appropriately is shown as Fig. 12.

The actual construction must have provided quite a spectacle. Southern writes that he twice visited the works, at Felton on Sunday 10 August 1851 and again at a place described as "Corve", two days later. Previously, on Sunday, 20 July, he had visited Felton and the Old Field "to see the railway progress". The sight of the navvies constructing the earthworks, embankments and cuttings ready for the laying of the tracks was on a scale which had never been seen in the area before.

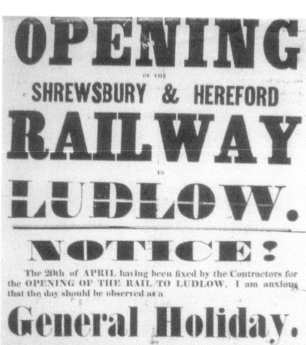

Fig. 12: A poster printed in 1852, by means of which the Mayor – Benjamin Urwick, tanner – sought to persuade Ludlow businessmen and women to close their shops and workshops in celebration of the coming of the railway.

Fig. 11: The earliest known illustration of a steam train at Ludlow. A steam locomotive with a trailing plume of smoke is pulling a line of open carriages, with easily recognisable Ludlow buildings in the background; but the engine shed is shown on the wrong side of the track. By Ludlow artist William Gwynn (1782 to c.1860).

There are two very full descriptions of the opening ceremonies on 20 April 1852. Anna Maria Fay wrote: "We got in town too late to see the train arrive but we were told that all the fields around the station were a sea of people........We went into town under a laurel arch. The Angel's Inn was decorated with greens and flowers and the Town Hall was resplendent with verdant trimmings. At the station was another arch upon which was lettered, "Welcome to Ludlow, Success to Brassy (*sic*)". She goes on to describe the dress of "all sorts of people (who) thronged the street" and gives a list of the sports in the outer bailey of the castle. Not everyone, it appears, thought the sports appropriate: "the Methodist minister .....denounced these sports as degrading and demoralizing, particularly the race on the part of the women"!

Francis Southern described the day as follows. "The town decorated very smartly with flags, evergreen arches etc. Great numbers of people flocking in. Went to the station (as one of the Corporation) to meet the Directors etc. The people about and on the opposite sides of the rails on the bank in great force. First passenger train, consisting of about 25 carriages and two engines, arrived in Ludlow about half past 1 pm bringing the Directors and a full load of passengers. The people cheered heartily, and besides the church bells were ringing and cannon were fired. Altogether it was a very exciting scene........We arrived in the Ballroom where was laid out a luncheon

.....given by Mr Brassey, the contractor........365 were there by invitation tickets and others got in who had no business there.........Then to the Castle Green where there were 'Rural Sports' going on and dancing on the Green. I assisted in getting up this last. The Green was crowded with people. Afterwards to the Railway Station to see the train off again." Later he went to the Ball which was held at the Assembly Rooms. "About 245 present at the Ball. The supper (a horrid affair) in the newsroom. Did not leave until nearly 4am the Wednesday morning. Ladies' tickets 5 shillings, gentlemen 7s and 6d".

It is difficult to appreciate what it must have been like to travel before the coming of the railways. Turn-piking had improved the roads but travel by coach was still slow and expensive. There is a good description of coach travel by George Griffiths, a corn merchant, when he journeyed from Bewdley to Ludlow in June 1837. The coach left the Wheat Sheaf Inn in Load Street at about 6am having already travelled from Birmingham that morning. Because of the extended journey times it appears that passengers were prepared to put up with travelling during unsocial hours in order to reach their destination as quickly as possible. "The journey to Ludlow was the pleasantest I

Fig. 13: This picture of a London coach outside The Feathers Inn was painted some years after the coaching era. Both the coach and the richly decorated inn – "a prime image of Olde England" (New York Times, 9 Oct. 1983) – were portrayed as romantic symbols of the past, regardless of the fact that The Feathers was never a major coaching inn. Scenes such as this, however, were commonplace in Broad Street, where the leading coaching inns were located: The Crown, Kent and Victoria and The Angel, the latter being a stopping place for Anna Maria Fay in 1851.

ever travelled.....We were on the top of the Clee Hill, 1200 feet above the valley and on a fine summer's morning the view from it was very imposing........[on arrival at] the Rose and Crown at Ludlow, the coachman and I were waited upon like lords, and at the same time were charged very moderately. In the season, too, the landlord always took care to give us a dish of fresh trout, just caught; fancy that! just caught in the river Teme – oh! that I could go on that old journey again!"[21]

Another vivid description of coach travel comes from Anna Maria Fay, who arrived in England in late 1851 and travelled south to Ludlow from Liverpool by coach. Her journey through Shropshire began before daybreak. "....it was some time before there was light enough to see anything but the hedges by the side of the road. Finally, however, the light came and with it such scenes! Every cottage a picture, every landscape a poem! For twenty miles we drove through what appeared to us Paradise. .....such was the country through which we approached the Moor Park.....at last we reached Ludlow, yet more antique if possible than anything we have seen, and the coach put us down before the Angel Inn..."[22]

The timetable reproduced as Fig. 14 shows the train times and fares from the opening day in 1852. The journey time was about one hour and 20 minutes between Ludlow and Shrewsbury compared with over three hours by coach. The return 1st class fare was 8s 9d.[23] There were three trains in each direction each day, one being the *Parliamentary*, the train required by Gladstone's

Railway Act of 1844 to cost only 1d per mile travelled. Contemporary accounts give the fare by coach between Ludlow and Hereford as five shillings single and the timetable shows the journey took three hours.[24]

Such was the success of the railway that the *Engineer* coach ceased to run between Ludlow and Shrewsbury the same day as the railway opened. Following the opening of the line Francis Southern took advantage of it to go to Shrewsbury. In his entry for Saturday 23 April 1852 he wrote: "Went for the first time by the new train. Left here at 8am (however, the proper time for the train to have started was that hour but we did not get away until about 8.45) and arrived at Shrewsbury in 1 hour and about 10 minutes. The line runs very smoothly and is a great contrast to my last journey by the coach. I took a day ticket which first class cost eight shillings and nine pence, enabling me to return by any train up to and on the following Monday."

The *Rover* continued to ply between Ludlow and Hereford until the line through Dinmore tunnel was opened at the end of 1853. People were quick to realise the potential of using the

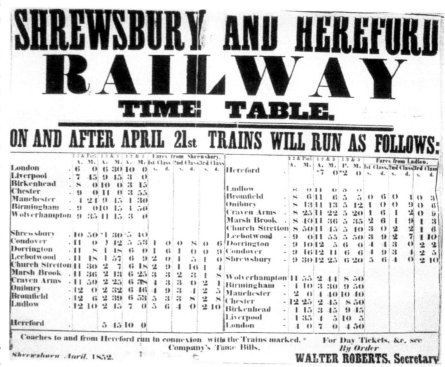

Fig. 14: The first timetable, showing train times and fares.

Fig. 15: A locomotive of the Shrewsbury and Hereford Railway, 1853.

railway for travel to otherwise previously inaccessible places. A few years after the opening, the Ludlow Wesleyan Methodist Sunday School hired a whole train for a day trip to Llandrindod. The train was to take them down the Central Wales line from Craven Arms but they had to travel from Ludlow on the ordinary train for the first stage of the journey. Having been advised that there would be an hour's wait for the special at Craven Arms, most of the 200 excursionists decided to go into the town and even as far as Stokesay. However the plan was changed "and so when the consideration of the Railway Co for our convenience and their own prompted them to put on a 'special' (saloon train), swift boy messengers were pressed into service and put on their trail. They got on the scent of most of the stragglers and ran them back to the station". One wonders if they were found in the Temperance Hotel or further down the road at the Craven Arms! A "Mr Bessell......had taken a short cut to Stokesay, and it was not until the luncheon hour at Llandrindod that his relations and friends could breathe freely again by dismissing the fear that he had been engulphed (*sic*) in some secret passage of the old ruin". He had missed the special train and had had to follow by the ordinary service. He is later recorded as having photographed the party at Llandrindod.[25]

4: ENTERTAINMENTS

"And what shall we do for pastimes?" The lively society of mid-nineteenth century Ludlow had many answers. Letters and diaries reflect the leisure pursuits of those with time, money and education, and there are accounts of days when the whole town came together to join in the festivities.

The May Fair, originally a commercial fair with its roots in the twelfth century, was a great day for people of all walks of life. It was still at this time an annual holiday for servants and country people. Francis Southern tells of a menagerie, "Wombwell's Wild Beasts", which came each year.[26] There were fortune tellers where "every young man might see his future wife and every young woman her future husband". You could "shoot for nuts at one stall or visit a sideshow depicting horrid murders". Street entertainers sang ballads, and children, fantastically dressed, danced in the muddy streets, afterwards collecting half pennies.[27] On May Day also, as described in another contemporary source, there was dancing round the maypole at Holdgate Fee, the southern part of Old Street.[28] Here there might be as many as twenty fiddlers, with dancing couples reaching the whole length of the street.

Shrove Tuesday was eagerly anticipated by

Francis Southern and Henry Peach Robinson, for this was rope pulling day. The tug of war was a custom from time immemorial, thought to have begun as a commemoration of some remarkable happening in the past, possibly an event at the time of the Wars of the Roses.[29] On the day of the pull huge crowds gathered outside the Market Hall. At exactly four o'clock the Mayor, from the Market Hall window, handed out a rope. This was three inches thick and 36 yards long, with a blue knob at one end and the red knob at the other – the colours of York and Lancaster! It was quickly taken by the contestants, those from Castle and Broad Street wards at one end, those from Old Street and Corve Street wards at the other. If the red knob team was able to pull its opponents down Mill Street it was declared to have won. For blue to win they must pull the other side to the Bull Ring. The winners of two pulls were the victors. However, excitement and enthusiasm were so great as to be a danger to life and limb and a few years later this "heathenish and barbarous custom" was abolished.[30]

The diarists make little mention of other sports. But Francis Southern recorded on 7 April 1852 in connection with the preparation for the celebrations for the opening of the railway: "Rural sports to be held" and he continues "Walked

Fig. 16: A painting in the 1840s by Edmund Gill, a local artist. (In 1841, Gill, aged 20, was lodging with William his younger brother in the household of William Ingram, tailor, at No. 15 Mill Street.)
The picture shows Ludford Bridge, with the Lower Broad Street weir in the foreground.

with Robert Lloyd to the Cricket Ground, only four there." The Ludlow Cricket Club had moved in 1848 to the Linney Fields on the banks of the Teme (the earliest known match having taken place in 1833 on the Old Racecourse), where a Southern was a member of the Ludlow team in the first recorded game. Whether this was Francis Southern or his cousin John is not known.[31]

Magic and mystery are often crowd pullers and there was always a good house when Mr Bernard Eagles came to the Assembly Rooms as conjuror and hypnotist. On Saturday, 20

December, 1851, Francis Southern wrote in his diary: "He did several good ones this evening including the ring trick and producing out of one bottle rum, whisky, brandy and port wine one after the other as the audience called for and they were allowed to drink it." The circus too was popular. On 14 May 1851 Francis Southern recorded a performance of Cookes Circus in a tent in a field in Holdgate Fee, when there were "a great many people there: I should think as many as 1500". There had been a midday performance commencing at 2p.m. "at which I was told one man threw 62 somersaults without stopping".

Fig. 17: This illustration of a "provincial theatre" in 1842 by the painter Theodore Lane shows the kind of three level seating available at Ludlow: pit, dress circle and gallery.

There were other pursuits, more limited in appeal, that were followed keenly by some people from all classes, as recorded by the sculptor Adrian Jones. "There was bare knuckle fighting, not legal, so taking place outside the town and for a purse".[32] He also described ratting, where terriers were matched against each other to kill the largest number of rats in the shortest time, and there was also cock fighting, cocks being "especially trained and prepared, fitted as a rule with steel spurs which they aimed at the breast of the opponent".[33] There was a well established tradition of angling at Ludlow and the serving of trout at a Ludlow Inn has been cited above.[34]

The Ludlow Theatre was in Mill Street, where Nos 23 and 23A now stand. It had been built in 1806, replacing an earlier theatre.[35] Opinions of the architecture varied, but the interior met with general approval. Anna Maria Fay wrote of "a square room divided into pit, dress circle and gallery, lined with striped paper, the walls hung with matting made of rushes, the whole lighted with gas-burners without shades".[36] She told of coming from three nights at the opera in London to the plays at Ludlow which she called "rustic". Some of the plays she saw were *The Used Up Man*, *Uncle Jerry* and *A Screaming Farce*. She found them "exceedingly entertaining" and describes how, on occasions, the performers would interrupt their colloquy to keep the audience in order. An instance of this was when a Mr Ponsford, playing Sir Charles Coldstream, addressed someone in the gallery: "You, sir, if you cannot stop talking, please depart, and you will find your money at the door; otherwise I shall call the police". The man replied that "I am not the person you allude to", but silence did ensue, ensuring that there was "no need of further parley". Three violins and a violoncello played in the interval, but did not win the approval of Miss Fay. They were, she wrote, "disdainful of a vulgar prejudice in favour of harmony, following each his own fancy rather than that of the composer". This, she continued, was done "to the accompaniment of much hissing from the Ludlow audience objecting to hearing their favourite waltzes murdered".

Great play was made of lavish provision for the poor at times of grand public and social occasions. Francis Southern described the events of October, 1852, when Robert Clive, M.P. for Ludlow, married Lady Mary Bridgeman, daughter of the Earl of Bradford. The wedding was at Weston-under-Lizard, near the bride's home at Weston Hall, but Ludlow celebrated in style, with "guns firing, bells ringing and a band parading the town", the first tune played, at 9 a.m., being Haste to the Bride". An ox had been roasted the day before, so on the day itself "from 800 to 1000 dined", the joints having been cooked at the houses of the Committee and subscribers "and the puddings made by them at their own expense also", though "each diner brought a knife and fork". After this "the Castle Green was thrown open and dancing went on". Meanwhile, Southern "went at 4 to a dinner at the Feathers", where "nearly 50 were present". The event lasted "till about ten", Southern himself proposing two toasts and singing a song.

The town's elite had other means of entertainment. There were the Winter Assemblies held at the Assembly Rooms fortnightly from October to March. All the diarists write of them enthusiastically. They are described in the language of the times as "under distinguished patronage with lustre, grandeur and aristocratic beauty".[37] Here was the chance to widen one's acquaintance, to converse, to flirt, to gossip, to dance, to play at cards and to enjoy the great pleasure of seeing and being seen in the best social circles.

The Assembly Rooms were the natural rendezvous for grand occasions. One of the most handsome was Race Ball in Races Week. There were balls for charities, to celebrate royal occasions and the coming of age or marriage of the local aristocracy. Anna Maria Fay wrote of a January Ball in 1851. She was met "in the kindest and most cordial manner" by the Clives and went on to dance the Lancers, the Valse a Deux Temps, the Gallop, the Quadrille and the Polka. The hall itself was "high and large with a capital floor and the band was good". She saw "none but ladies and gentlemen there", finding it "curious to see a Public Ball so select".[38]

Amongst the town's "bon ton" there were those with wider interests. The same young men who danced at the Assemblies and applauded at the theatre were at this time forming new societies and joining older ones to

Fig. 18: An early view of the Assembly Rooms, which opened in 1840 after £6,000 had been raised by public subscription. The architect was Matthew Stead, with his brother Samuel Stead as contractor. The ballroom was on the first floor of the nearer building.

Fig. 19: A ball in the County Assembly Rooms, Lincoln, in 1850. There were similar gatherings in the ballroom at Ludlow, many of them in aid of local charities.

learn more and to appreciate more of the world around them. Henry Peach Robinson and Francis Southern write of meetings of the Ludlow Agricultural Society, the Natural History Society and the nationally known Cambrian Archaeological Society. Robinson brought together a group of friends to form a Chess and Reading Club. They met each Friday from eight o'clock until ten. "Each member in turn shall buy a book paid for out of the funds; after it has been read by each one (who has it for a week) it shall belong to the orderer."[39] A Ludlow Corresponding Society had its first meeting at this time. Lots were drawn as to who would give a lecture and a librarian was elected. Robinson himself was to draw diagrams to illustrate the lectures. Titles were given as they

took place over the year, among them The Barometer Explained, The History of Printing, Bees, Heat and Optics.

The sports, pastimes and entertainments which the mid-century diarists describe had perhaps been much the same over the preceding fifty or more years. One thing was to alter that, the coming of the railway. Only a fortnight after its opening Francis Southern reported "This morning before breakfast walked to the station to see the first train 8.15 off, being the "Chester Cup" day and the Railway Company having advertised to take parties there and back today for 15 shillings first class, 10 shillings second class. Long train started and a good many people went, most second classes." The world of entertainment was already widening.

ENDNOTES

1 A photocopy of the Southern diary and a transcription are held by the Ludlow Historical Research Group (L.H.R.G.). All dated references are from this source, unless stated otherwise.

2 The diary is often cited by Harker, M.F., *Henry Peach Robinson: Master of Photographic Art, 1830-1901*, 1986. She acknowledges the help of the late Joan Rider, a member of L.H.R.G. The group has a transcription of the diary.

3 Anna Maria Fay, *Victorian days in England: Letters home by an American girl*, Boston, 1923; reprinted Ludlow, 2002, by Dog Rose Press.

4 Tithe map IK/29/29/209.

5 Family details supplied by Rachel Millard.

6 Lloyd, M.E., *The Lloyds: A Brief Family History*, p.21.

7 *Oxford Companion to English Literature*, 1967, p.808.

8 Memorial inscription, St Leonard's Churchyard.

9 Fay, op. cit., pp.20-21.

10 Francis, R. and Klein, P. *The Organs and Organists of Ludlow Parish Church*, Ludlow, 1982, p.46.

11 Packer scrapbook.

12 Aylmer, G. and Tiller, T., *Hereford Cathedral: A History*, 2000, p.160.

13 15 April, 1849 (Robinson diary, p.18).

14 Haslam, R., *The Buildings of Wales: Powys*, 1979, p.59; Colvin, H., *A Biographical Dictionary of British Architects, 1600-1840*, 1995, p.749.

15 Shepherd, F.G., *The Parish Church of Ludlow*, 1944, p.32.

16 Elliot, E.A., *A History of Congregationalism in Shropshire*, 1898, pp.97-104.

17 The minute book was seen in 1870, when it was in the possession of the late Mrs Dorothy Beagley.

18 Davies, A.W., *The Cockings of Ludlow*, 1959, p.10.

19 Fay, op. cit., p.1.

20 Morris, R.K., *Railways of Shropshire*, Shropshire Libraries, 1983, p.12.

21 Griffiths, G., *Going to Markets and Grammar Schools*, Vol.1, pp.108-110.

22 Fay, op. cit., p.8.

23 Southern transcript, p.79.

24 Ibid., p.121.

25 From The Ludlow Circuit Wesleyan Methodist Church Record.

26 Southern transcript, p.80.

27 Fay, op. cit., p.178.

28 Burne, C.S., *Shropshire Folklore*, 1883, p.360.

29 Ibid., p.219.

30 Evans, J., *A Ludlow Handbook*, 1861, pp.344-345.

31 Information from Ludlow and South Shropshire Cricket Club, via Mr J.Hearne.

32 Jones, A., *Memoirs of a Soldier Artist*, 1933, p.21.

33 Ibid., pp.21-22, 24.

34 Ibid., p.11.

35 SJ, 30 April, 1806, p.3, col.2.

36 Fay, op. cit., pp.227-229.

37 Evans, op. cit., p.33.

38 Fay, op. cit., pp.87-89.

39 Robinson, op. cit., p.19.

CHAPTER 11

THE ANGLICAN CHURCH IN LUDLOW 1867 ~ 1907

CHRISTOPHER TRAIN

EVEN SO FAITH, IF IT HATH NOT WORKS, IS DEAD, BEING ALONE. JAMES II. 17.

St Laurence's Church, Ludlow.

On Wednesday 13 March, 1867 the Reader at the Evening Service at St Laurence's, Ludlow was the new Rector, the Reverend Edward ffarington Clayton.[1] On the next Sunday he preached his first sermon, to the text, from the Second Epistle to the Corinthians, "Who is sufficient for these things?" In this he committed himself to his ministry in Ludlow: "Gladly therefore will I, by God's help, spend and be spent at the post to which he has called me."[2] It was a ministry that was to last for the rest of his life. He died on 24 November 1907, after an incumbency second in length at St Laurence's only to that of the Reverend Thomas Roche in the eighteenth century.

Clayton was born in September 1830, so he was 36 when he came to Ludlow. He was the second son of a banker from Preston, William Clayton of Lostock Hall. The Claytons were a well established and well connected County family. His paternal grandmother's (Dorothy Clayton's) son by her first marriage, Sir Robert Barrie, became Rear Admiral of the Blue and her brother was Admiral Lord Gardner. It was from this side of the family that Edward got his second name, ffarington.[3] He was educated at Sedbergh School, arriving in August 1843 and leaving in June 1849.[4] He was, to judge from the school records of his final year, no more than an average pupil, but he went on to St John's

College, Cambridge, being supported by the generosity of his uncle, Thomas Gorst, since his father had by now lost all his money in the failure of the bank.[5] Clayton matriculated in 1849, and obtained an ordinary B.A. in 1853, becoming M.A. in 1858.

He was ordained deacon to the curacy of Stapleton in Bristol by the Bishop of Gloucester and Bristol in 1854 and priest in the following year. He held a series of curacies before leaving Putney in 1867 to be instituted as Rector of Ludlow on 4 March that year, having been recommended by Bishop Claughton, the Bishop of Rochester, to Lady Mary Windsor Clive, then patroness of the living.[6] Still a bachelor, he first lived at 52 Broad Street (his predecessor, the Reverend John Phillips, had also resided in Broad Street), moving sometime in 1870 to 22½ Brand Lane, where the 1871 Census recorded him together with his elder sister, Mary, and three domestic servants.

It was not long, however, before his links with the Windsor Clive family, which had been close from the beginning of his incumbency, were further strengthened. The Parish Magazine of May 1874 contained the following letter to the Rector signed by 128 parishioners: "We the undersigned.......tender you our hearty congratulations on your approaching marriage with the Hon. Victoria Alexandrina Windsor Clive, and wishing to mark our sense of the pleasure the occasion affords us, and understanding that a gift to the Parish Church of Ludlow will be more agreeable to you than any token of a personal character, we desire to make known to you that in honour and commemoration of the event, we have taken the necessary measures for carrying out the restoration of the East Window of St John's

High Hall, Castle Square.
The residence of the Reverend
and the Hon. Mrs Clayton.

Chapel. We trust you may be pleased to consider this work an acceptable form of demonstrating to you the sincerity of our regard and our appreciation of the energetic and faithful manner in which you have discharged the duties of the important office you hold amongst us." Victoria Windsor Clive, at 33, was ten years younger than her husband, and the youngest daughter of Lady Harriet Clive (Baroness Windsor) and Robert Henry Clive (the second son of the Earl of Powis), and sister-in-law of Clayton's patron, Lady Mary Windsor Clive. Queen Victoria had stood sponsor for her at her christening.

The Claytons moved into the house now called High Hall in Castle Square, where they are to be found in the 1881 Census, already with four children (a son, Edward and three daughters, Margaret, Mildred and Agnes) and a substantial domestic household - a butler, cook, nurse, two nursemaids, a house maid and a kitchen maid. Although his sister, Mary, writing to Victoria, shortly after Clayton's death, surmised that Clayton's income when he came to Ludlow was not more than £130 a year from his family resources (about £6,000 in modern terms)[7], and the net annual value of the Ludlow incumbency was in 1880 about £360, it is clear that his private means later became substantial. He left £42,907 10s 5d on his death (about £2.5

million in modern terms).[8] It was a marriage, then, of advantage to the Rector not only in social and other ways, but also for the furtherance of his ministry to the parish – "his ripe judgment giving him great influence with his relatives of the Clive family and the Earl of Plymouth".[9]

Clayton's spiritual and pastoral inheritance on his arrival was not rich. "Coming here at a period of ecclesiastical unrest, when old methods of Church work were proving obsolete and new ideals were taking their place, he found a parish as yet hardly touched by the wave of fresh vigour and enthusiasm which was spreading over the religious life of England" wrote his obituarist in the Parish Magazine. David Lloyd in the *Concise History of Ludlow* quotes the letters of Anna Maria Fay in 1851, which called the Reverend John Phillips, the Rector from 1841, "a miserable low churchman, who is so unpopular that the Dissenting chapels and the alehouses are full on Sundays."

The numbers attending services before Clayton came cannot be determined, since the surviving Church Register begins with his arrival, and even when it was introduced it recorded only the numbers of those who took Communion.[10] But the table below gives some indication of the growth in church membership during the first half of his ministry and of

continuing health thereafter, even allowing for growth in the population of the churches' catchment area over the period. (The increase in the number of churches in the parish is described below.)

The largest number of Easter communicants in any one year in this period was 833 in 1904. This was also the year in which St Laurence's had its largest number: 547. 1907 saw St John's largest number (174); 1890 St Stephen's (142); and 1906 St Leonard's (83).

Two complementary elements lay at the heart of this revitalisation of the Anglican church in Ludlow during Clayton's time – the spiritual and the pastoral. His obituary in the Parish Magazine describes his spiritual ministry: "Quietly and cautiously, laying the foundations deep like a wise master-builder....Mr Clayton raised the tone of Christian faith and practice among his parishioners; and, utilising all that was of lasting value in the old regime, he set up that sober standard of feeling in matters of practical religion which Keble has taught us comes next in value to a sound rule of faith." The note of his death in the Shrewsbury Chronicle gives a more practical edge to this: "On his appointment to Ludlow he adhered to the custom of the parish for a time, preaching, for instance, in a black gown, but he gradually introduced alterations in the services of the

Year	Number of Communicants				
	St Laurence's	St Stephen's	Gravel Hill/St John's	St Leonard's	Total
1867	174	-	-	-	174
1872	252	-	-	-	252
1877	321	36	20	-	377
1882	502	-	64	-	566
1887	508	75	60	18	661
1892	444	101	145	20	710
1897	482	68	154	38	742
1902	519	65	153	35	772
1907	510	not given	174	49	733

Table I: Number of Easter Communicants at five yearly intervals 1867 – 1907

church, one of the first in June 1867 being the use of 'Hymns Ancient and Modern', which replaced the old 'Mitre Hymn Book' with which the parishioners had been familiar for a long time. Some time after, the black gown was discarded and the surplice remained the only vestment for the clergy during his long tenure of office. He was a devoted and consistent adherent to the old High Church School of thought."

The parish magazine, begun in June 1867, brought the church and its congregation into a closer relationship, and the November edition, reporting the introduction of a full service with sermon on a Sunday afternoon, indicates one of his earliest steps to broaden the appeal of the church. "At this service many of the seats in the Church will be open for the use of those who wish to occupy them. There are hundreds in the Parish who seldom or never enter the doors of God's House; and many of these, when told of the sin of neglecting Public Worship, answer that there is no room for them in the free seats. But this excuse can no longer be made." The renting of pews continued through Clayton's time, and indeed was one of the church's main sources of revenue[11], but it went on causing concern that poorer people were thereby kept away from church. So, in March 1879 the magazine reported that "At a meeting of seat holders....it was unanimously resolved by those present...that all seats, whether rented as pews or not, shall be absolutely free when the big bell ceases ringing, five minutes before the time of commencing Divine Service."

However, Clayton had well before 1879 been tackling the problem of those "who seldom or never enter the doors of God's House" by other more substantial means. In 1871 a purpose built chapel, St Leonard's, replaced a Mission Chapel in lower Corve Street (which had been opened in December 1853[12]), and so took "its place among the daughters of St Laurence, the Mother Church of Ludlow". St

Leonard's was revisiting an ancient place of worship.

Two years before the Rector had broken entirely new ground by opening St Stephen's Mission Chapel in Gaolford – the poorest and most populous part of the town. The Parish Magazine of June 1869 reported "[The] Mission Church has been opened in Upper Gaolford....Services will be held on Sundays at 10 o'clock in the morning and at 6.30 in the evening." Clayton was following a practice which had been developed in many working class parishes of the cities of England over the past thirty years. It was based on the assumption that, since the Church of England was largely the province of the middle and upper classes[13], if working class people could be offered a place of worship in their own locality, where seats were free and where they would not stand out from their fellow worshippers because of their poorer clothing, they would come more readily to church.[14]

St Leonard's Chapel, opened in 1871.

Clayton and his colleagues had to work hard to attract a congregation, as the following letter of July 1871 to the "WORKING MEN of LUDLOW and THEIR FAMILIES" shows. "St Stephen's Mission Chapel was opened two years ago in order to give you more opportunities than you enjoyed before of giving the Lord the honour due to His Name....While Evening Service shews a fair attendance, and gives us encouragement to persevere....few are found to avail themselves of the short Morning Service at Ten o'clock, though specially intended for you.....The Service is short....We try to make it simple, hearty, and plain, and yet you do not come. Men! Husbands! Fathers! Will you not make a fresh effort to devote part of your Sunday mornings to the glory of God....Women! Wives! Mothers! Will you not do your best that either your husbands or yourselves shall worship with us, sometimes, in the mornings as well as the evenings of the Lord's Day?"

The chapel did not fail. In October 1878 the building was given up; "not we are very thankful

St Stephen's Chapel, opened in 1907, replacing the earlier iron Mission chapel.

to say that it has been a failure....It is about to move into a larger building....the congregation demanded it (silently indeed but pointedly) by having sometimes to remain, in the persons of late comers, either in the Vestry or on the doorstep....At one time fewer than at first start seemed to come to its services....but now again a congregation has poured in from what we hope is fresh ground." At its opening on 6 October 300 packed into evening service and many were turned away. That was not the end of the matter and again it was the growth of the congregation which caused the development. This was a purpose built iron building close by, with seating for some 400 people. It opened in July 1880 and Harvest Festival in October that year saw 630 people crushed into the building. The iron church flourished for some twenty five years, until, in June 1906, it was found to be unsafe for use, and the decision was taken to replace it with a brick built church. Services resumed there in May 1907.

The increase in the number of worshippers at the Mission Chapel during the 1870s may be partly attributable to the growth of the town on its eastern side. By 1875 the population had reached the point where a new school had to be provided specifically for the children of the area. Although its site in Gravel Hill lay in Stanton Lacy, Clayton was also closely involved, and when it was ready, in conjunction with the Rector and church wardens of Stanton Lacy[15], he took the opportunity to provide a local place of worship. The school was adapted for services, which were held there from July 1876. That was, however, only a temporary expedient.

Early in July 1880 the Hon. Mrs Clayton laid the foundation stone of a new church in Gravel Hill, the cost of the church being paid for out of a legacy left by her sister, the Hon. Miss Mary Windsor Clive, who had died in 1873. The site was also in Stanton Lacy, but at the end of June 1880 it was brought into Ludlow ecclesiastical parish[16] and on Friday 3 June 1881 the Bishop of Hereford dedicated the church of St John the Evangelist, Gravel Hill for worship.

St Stephen's and St John's were looked after by a specific member of Clayton's team, while St Leonard's was looked after by the Headmaster of the Grammar School, who had the chaplaincy of the adjacent Foxe's Almshouses. When Clayton arrived in 1867 there were two other clergy to support him, the Revd R. Meyricke, the Reader, who had been at Ludlow since 1824 and who was to die in office in 1881, and the Lecturer, the Revd R.W. Russell. During Clayton's incumbency the number of assistant clergy was doubled, largely at Clayton's own expense. A list of Ludlow clergy from 1867 to 1907 is given in Appendix I.

The establishment of the new chapels and the accompanying increase in clergy brought the Anglican Church and its ministry into closer touch with the whole of Ludlow. Places of worship were available for all, regardless of location and class. This had been the purpose of

St John's, Gravel Hill, opened in 1881.

the mission service and mission chapel movement in other parts of the country. But if the numbers going to church were to increase beyond those who had not gone previously solely because of their location and class, additional action was required. Here again, Clayton followed initiatives developed elsewhere.

In February 1879 a Mission was held in Ludlow. Launching it, Clayton wrote in the Magazine "A Mission is a series of Services in which an especial effort is made by Prayer, Preaching and Instruction, under the guidance of the Holy Spirit, to lead sinners to Jesus Christ, to stir up the faithful to greater devotion and diligence, and to unite all of us in love to Jesus Christ and in the fellowship of the Holy Ghost....Try and arrange beforehand that you may have the week of the Mission....as free as possible. Do not have any work or business fixed for that week which can be fixed for another time. Do not have any amusements fixed for that week. There will be Special Services for Children, it would be well that parents see that their children go to them. There will be Special Services for Servants, it would be well if masters and mistresses would enable the servants to attend them."

The March Magazine carried a long report. "'It was very wonderful' will have been the repeated exclamation from the lips of hundreds, who had the great privilege of attending the Services in our dear old Parish Church during the Mission.....It was very wonderful to see men and women of all classes so busily and earnestly employed in bringing people to the various services." 1,200 people attended the first weekday evening service on the Monday, and on the final Sunday evening for the Thanksgiving Service the congregation numbered some 3,500. All the special services, in the Market, for children, for servants, for women, for men, were well attended (the last attracting over 500 on each occasion). "We do not hesitate to say that great good has been done; whether it will be lasting, how widespread it may be, or how far commensurate with our expectations, and with the extent of the means used, we cannot tell – the Great Day will tell us that."

The Magazine was similarly guarded in assessing the impact of a second Mission to Ludlow in 1892. "What we often call success, God, who looks into the hearts of men, may call very differently. Yet so far as human eyes can judge, the continuous prayers and the self denying labours of many were answered and rewarded by crowded and attentive congregations, and an undoubted deepening of interest in spiritual things throughout the parish."

Of a very different kind was the lay mission in 1899 for the workers taking the water main from mid-Wales to Birmingham. The Rector gave the room over the Butter Cross for the use of the men each evening as a Club, where games, books and papers were available. Thursday evenings were devoted to Temperance meetings, and readings, recitations and various entertainments were provided. Every Sunday night there was a service conducted by the Lay Missioner with an address.

This juxtaposition of the temporal and the spiritual – the provision of wholesome entertainment, which would keep the men from the alehouses and the corruption of drunkenness, accompanied by and as an instrument for active evangelism – was characteristic of the Victorian church.[17] It was also characteristic of Clayton's ministry in Ludlow, a text for whose life in Ludlow could have been taken from the General Epistle of James: "Even so faith, if it hath not works, is dead, being alone." It is to this pastoral side of his incumbency that we now turn.

When Clayton arrived in 1867, he found the church involved in most aspects of what may broadly be termed community welfare – education, health care and charitable relief. There had been a Church of England National School since 1813 and an Anglican Sunday School was established in 1844. A Dispensary, sponsored by the church on public subscription, was in existence by the late 1820s. A Winter Clothing Club was founded in 1829 – again run by the church – and there was a long-standing District Visiting Society, offering both spiritual sustenance through the distribution of tracts and material support through a savings club supported by charitable subscription. Over the next twenty years, under Clayton's leadership, this work was broadened in its

The Reverend Clayton and his ministerial team about 1889. Clayton is seated centre between, on his right, the Reverend J.C.E. Besant, and, on his left, the Reverend G.W. Turner. Standing on Clayton's right is the Reverend J.C. Gray, and, on his left, the Reverend L.C. Wilkinson.

scope and deepened in its impact on the community.

The development of education in Ludlow over these years is described in Chapter 9, but some points about the part played by the church should be made here. The Rector used the Parish Magazine throughout the period to keep the life of the National Schools in the minds of its readers. These were years, beginning with the Forster Education Act of 1870, when universal, compulsory and finally free education was introduced to the country and the Magazine chronicled these innovations. It argued the merits of the voluntary Church of England system over the Board School system; it urged parents to send their children to school; it commended the introduction of the School Attendance Committee; it described the extension of the buildings in Lower Gaolford and the opening of the Intermediate School there; from 1877 it frequently set out the Inspector's Annual reports; and it encouraged financial support for the Schools through the voluntary school rate[18] and through dedicated church collections.[19]

As befitted Schools, whose Managing Committee, chaired by the Rector, and teachers were required to be members of the Church of England, and whose "religious and moral instruction were under the superintendence of the Minister" the School Log Books confirm that there was close involvement of the clergy in the running of the Schools. These also recorded the attendance of the children at the Church during term time for services on Ash Wednesday, Ascension Day and Harvest Festival. The great celebration of the union of church and school occurred, usually in August, with the Annual Festival of the National and Sunday Schools. The first report of one of these is in the September Magazine of 1870, when on 16 August "Upwards of 700 children, headed by Mr Cox and Mr Wigmore, with the Drum and Fife band, marched to Church for Service at 2.30p.m." They then processed into Castle Green, where the Infant School to the number of 200 were already seated, "looking somewhat wistfully at their empty cups, and the huge baskets piled up with cakes and buns, from which some keen eyed wasps were already taking toll. Six hundred pounds weight of cake and nine hundred buns did certainly succeed in satisfying the claims made upon the caterers by the 936 hungry children". After the meal, "the little army betook themselves to the Green, and, the weather being most enjoyable, spent an afternoon in a variety of games, races, etc., ending with the sending off, very successfully, of four fire balloons..."

The provision of Sunday Schools had started in the late eighteenth century, one of their principal functions being to give basic schooling to children who were working during the week, and it was only after Forster's Education Act 1870 that they developed into institutions whose central role was to offer denominational moral and religious teaching. As already noted, the Church of England Sunday School was established in Ludlow in 1844. Detailed statistics of the numbers on the books of the Sunday Schools are available only from towards the end of Clayton's incumbency, but it seems likely that there were about 400 scholars in 1870 – the girls at the old Market Hall and the boys at the National School and the Butter Cross. In 1899 there were 273 boys – at the Butter Cross, Brand Lane and East Hamlet –, 311 girls – at the Market Hall and East Hamlet –, and 148 infants – at the Market Hall and East Hamlet, that is 732 in all with an average attendance of just over 500. They were taught by 73 teachers[20] who were predominantly unmarried ladies.[21]

Nor was the spiritual education of adults neglected. The March 1880 edition of the Magazine listed: Confirmation Class, Men's Church Society, Women's Church Society, Young Men's Church Society, Church Society (B) Branch – another young men's group –, Devotional Reading Class, and Sunday School Teachers' Lecture. All of these were devoted to spiritual instruction and had been in existence for some years. The church had also given attention to secular studies for adults, for as early as October 1867 it was announced that "A Night School for Men and Boys will be held at the National Schools every Tuesday, Wednesday and Thursday during the winter at 7.30 o'clock" Instruction in those classes was in reading, writing, arithmetic and Holy Scripture. The clergy were involved in the teaching as were other lay members of the Parish. By 1882 there was a Night School for girls. Access to this was by recommendation of one of the Clergy or a District Visitor.

The Manse, 8 Julian Road.
The Industrial School for Girls was here in 1881.

A different kind of further education for girls was the Industrial School or Home for Girls opened in 1870. This provided residential training for girls in Domestic Service – housework, plain cooking and baking, washing and ironing, and, a later addition when an infant day nursery was introduced, nursing and managing little children. A house was taken in Dinham, where eleven or twelve girls could be boarded and instructed for a period of two years. "The benefits which have resulted from institutions of the kind in different parts of the Country give every ground for hope that, by God's Blessing, similar good effects may be brought about by this School. It will be the aim of the Founders of the School not only to train the girls in every branch of household work but also to give them such moral and religious training as may make them reliable, as well as useful, servants." The home was sustained by an annual subscription for its working expenses, and by sponsoring a girl's expenses during the two years of her residence. Miss Jessie Overend was the first matron and in 1871, as the Census reveals, there were eight girls in residence, five local and one each from Birmingham, Liverpool and Warwick. The home had a number of locations, being in Corve Street for a while in the 1870s, in Julian Road when the 1881 census was taken, before finally settling into the Old Rectory in College Street in 1884.

Also caring for working class girls was the Girls' Friendly Society. A branch was launched in Ludlow and the surrounding district in 1878. Girls from the age of 12 could be members, paying one shilling monthly. The Magazine in August 1889 described the Society as follows: "A society to promote purity of life and faithfulness in duty....It is for the help of girls, who, starting in life either in service or in business have many temptations and difficulties, and who are often far from home and friends. [The Society's branches have] Lady Associates, who admit members, look after them, and on their leaving the Parish commend them to the care of the Associate in the place to which they are going....There are Lodges and Homes of Rest in various places for Members out of place or ill....classes for instruction in religious and useful knowledge, wholesome amusements, bonuses on savings, premiums for good service, etc." The principal event of the Society's year in Ludlow was the annual summer festival. By the 1890s upwards of 150 members attended, the substantial majority from the Ludlow and Gravel Hill branches. Tea and wholesome entertainment were provided, usually in the Rectory garden. There would be an address urging the girls to remember and live by the objects of the Society. "Many noble societies there are, working for the rescue of the fallen (all honour to them), but the object of this society is to prevent girls falling.....No girl shall be admitted who does not bear a virtuous character, and if a member should lose her character she must at once leave the society." Premiums and cards of merit for good and long service were awarded, and bonuses on Post Office Bank savings.

Another innovation of Clayton's earliest time was a Literary Institute, held in the Market Hall. "We are glad to find that this Institution has met with a large amount of support since its establishment. The Institute comprises a Reading Room and a Library; the former supplied with four daily papers, together with the local papers; Punch, Fun, Illustrated London News and a number of periodicals; the latter is in conjunction with Mudie's Select Library. The Reading Room is open daily... and the Library on Tuesday and Friday evenings, and on Wednesday mornings" reported the Magazine in August 1867. But the Literary Institute faltered and was closed in September 1869 through lack of support from the young men of the town. It was replaced by two institutions – the Parish Library and the Evening Club.

The former started in July, 1868. It was originally in the Market Hall, but by 1869 it was in the room over the Butter Cross. To begin with anyone connected with the Parochial Schools could take out books free of charge; for others the subscription was a half-penny per volume or an annual subscription of 5/-. By 1873 the rules were as follows: the library to be open every Wednesday, from 12 to 1 o'clock, for the giving and exchange of books; books lent out at one penny a volume; subscribers of 5s a year were entitled to one volume a week; no book to be kept longer than three weeks; and "Persons

not residing in the parishes of Ludlow or Ludford or the Gravel Hill District of Stanton Lacy are to be charged double the local subscription." The library was sustained by subscriptions, lending charges and an occasional fund raising event. Its contents were regularly listed in the Magazine.

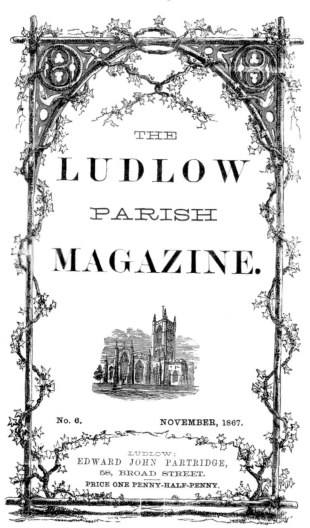

Cover of Ludlow Parish Magazine for November 1867.

The Evening Club "was opened on Monday October 18th [1869], at the Room over the Butter Market.... At the general request of those who use the Room, coffee and other refreshments are provided. The amusements supplied in the Room are very popular and many have found interest in the books in the

Public Library." The room was hired by the Rector from the Corporation, and he was the Club's President. The Club was open during the winter months, and was sustained by the sale of season tickets (at 3s 6d), weekly tickets (2d) and visitors (1d) and by providing entertainments, usually in the Market Hall. The Club flourished for some twenty years, with the occasional dip in popularity, which drew exhortations not to let this "most useful Parish institution" fail. The following table shows the pattern of attendance and support.

Table II: Ludlow Evening Club Statistics 1880 to 1886							
Ticket type	**1880**	**1881**	**1882**	**1883**	**1884**	**1885**	**1886**
Season	70	67	75	105	87	97	102
Weekly	1027	698	522	564	779	696	958
Visitors	166	115	148	153	239	191	397

And then in the late 1880s counter attractions were reported (in 1888 the Conservative Club "by its more extensive premises has drawn away many supporters, who cannot afford to subscribe to two clubs", and in 1889 "numerous theatrical companies offered greater attractions than the evening club could afford"). After that year reports of it disappeared from the Magazine until in September 1903 when "[w]e are glad to say that it has been thought well to re-establish the old Evening Club which has been in abeyance during the last nine years." The Club was established to attract working class men. In 1882 the Magazine observed: "After a hard day's work there is often a desire to spend an hour or so in society and in hearing and discussing the news of the day. A large airy room, well warmed and lighted, with papers, books and games scattered hither and thither, is a great boon to our younger generation who desire to spend their evenings in innocent and profitable recreation; may we not add in cheap recreation also?" The announcement of the Club in

October 1885 read "If our working men are to make intelligent use of the 'franchise' we cannot help thinking that they ought to avail themselves of the opportunity of reading the various Daily Papers which they can do at the Evening Club." The Club certainly fulfilled an educational, social and recreational role in the life of Ludlow's men. But the words 'innocent', 'profitable' and 'cheap recreation' reveal another purpose. It was also to be an alternative attraction to the ale houses of the town.

An institution with this as its primary and explicit purpose was the Ludlow Coffee Tavern. This was opened in the Bull Ring in October 1879, "[its] object being to provide a counter-attraction to the Public House, where all the comforts and conveniences of a Public House may be obtained without the temptations of the 'drink'; and which may enable anyone to prove by experience that he can be better in every respect by taking good, wholesome and cheap Coffee, Cocoa and non-intoxicants, instead of the usual Beer, Cider and other drinks now so universal." Ludlow was following a precedent set by "other towns in this part of the country, as well as throughout England." A Limited Company was established with twelve Directors, one being a member of the clergy, with an issue of 500 £1 shares. The Tavern got off to a shaky start; in April 1880 it was reported to be now in the hands of "a new and promising manager, who with his wife will endeavour to restore the good name of the place, which an unlucky chapter of accidents has sadly tarnished. We hope that many of our working class friends will now give it another trial." It appears in the 1885 edition of Kelly's Directory at 19 Bull Ring under the management of W. Meredith, and in 1891, managed by J. Prince, but not thereafter.

By 1879 the Church temperance movement had been established in Ludlow for three years. The movement had begun nationally in the

1830s and in 1862 the Church of England Temperance Society was founded, but it was only after 1875 when Queen Victoria agreed to become its patron that it gained a prominent station among the social agencies of the Anglican Church.[22] Drunkenness was certainly a major social problem in the Victorian period, being associated particularly with the poorer classes.[23] The extent to which drunkenness was a problem in Ludlow is difficult to say, but whatever its actual level and whatever the social and family hardships it caused, it was certainly seen by the church as such in the town, as the language used to report the local work of the Society in the Magazine indicates: "The evil of intemperance is...deeply rooted and....terribly prevalent"; "the miserable sin of drunkenness, so rife among us." "A sad increase of drunkards among women. This is most deplorable, as, in looking to the future generation, we must remember that men are what women make them".

The Ludlow Branch of the Church of England Temperance Society was launched in September 1876 "at the request of the Young Men's Church Society". One of the curates of the time, the Reverend A.C. Lee, is described as "its originator". There were two branches – senior and juvenile – the latter being for total abstainers only, the Senior branch admitting non-abstainers, either on the pledge of abstinence except at meal times, or on the general pledge of temperance. Meetings were fortnightly. The Juvenile Branch had a Fife and Drum Band under the management of Mr George Meyrick, "who is heart and soul in the work or he could never have persevered as he has done." In 1881 there were 170 members in all; 115 seniors, of whom 45 were total abstainers, and 55 juveniles (aged 9 to 19). In that year it was proposed that a Girls' Branch (ages 9 or 10 to 15) should be added, but nothing came of it and by the end of 1882 the Society was moribund. At a public meeting in the Market Hall in November the Reverend W.J. Pinckney announced that "the Church of

England Temperance Society, having broken down and almost died out in this parish, it was thought advisable to start afresh and reorganize it anew." Once it was revived it ran for the rest of Clayton's time, being joined in 1885 first by a Girls' Branch and then by a Children's Branch, the Band of Hope. The final addition was a Women's Union in 1888.

Junior Branch teas and outings got substantial coverage in the Magazine and bring out the importance of these institutions in providing relaxation and entertainment for their members. On the 3 August 1886 "[a]bout 80 [members of the Junior Branch of the Temperance Society]....left for Hereford by the 8.12 train arriving at 9.20. They marched to the tunes of their own excellent band to the Cathedral; after duly inspecting it they dispersed and walked around the city until 11am, when... they marched to Lugwardine, a short three miles away. There the Rector of Lugwardine, the Rev A.C. Lee, met them and....conducted them to a large Barn where was laid out a capital dinner which was greatly appreciated by the youthful excursionists. After dinner, cricket, football and other games filled the afternoon until tea was announced at 5.30.....From 6 to 6.30 they went to the Church for a short service, at the end of which the Rev A.C. Lee gave them a few words of council [sic] and encouragement.....The walk back to Hereford was a merry one, and they arrived just in time to catch the mail train. The band played in a most energetic way all up Corve Street as if it were the beginning rather than the ending of the day."

Alongside these new organisations which looked in one way or another to the interests of the working class lay a number of church administered institutions which catered for the poor and had, in some cases, a much longer history. With the passage of the Poor Law Amendment Act 1834 and the development of the administrative machinery surrounding it the clergy had lost their central and ancient role in the formal arrangements for relieving the destitute. But one of the effects of the new system was to give prominence to the clergy's place in the informal and charitable systems of relief.[24]

In Ludlow the longest standing of these institutions was the Winter Clothing Club, established in 1829. It was a so-called 'penny' club, each member paying in a penny a week (later this became a minimum) and, originally, receiving a bonus of four shillings and four pence at the end of the year, that is an amount equal to his own contribution. This went to the purchase of winter clothing. In 1877 the bonus was reduced to two shillings and sixpence, "so as to admit more to the benefits which the Club offers". The bonus was paid out of subscriptions from other members of the Parish, and the Magazine regularly each autumn solicited further subscribers. "We are sorry to say that of late while the number of depositors has immensely increased the number of subscribers has deplorably decreased. The way to help is to take tickets (2s 6d each); each ticket gives power to nominate a depositor....A good many people are still applying for tickets and still remain to be supplied with them because of the lack of subscribers." Between 1885 and 1905 subscriptions reported in the Magazine varied between £46 and £51 a year from some 60 subscribers, with a town membership starting in 1881 at 282 and climbing to over 400 during the 1890s. There were also members at the town National Schools and Sunday Schools, and at East Hamlet. The accounts of the Club for 1903/4 give subscriptions of £54 and deposits of £600, which, with other income, made a total of receipts of £767. This was spent on £700 worth of clothing, boots and shoes, the largest amounts for clothing being at Bodenhams (£232) and E.W. Harding (£107) and for boots at Webbs (£54).

Started in the 1850s[25] a women's sewing class offered "a cheerful afternoon once a week, but with good warm clothes against winter necessities" for hard working mothers. They could join only on the written recommendation of a District Visitor, met weekly during the summer and autumn in the Parish Rooms in Brand Lane, and were given assistance with their sewing. They paid a small fee and this together with subscriptions paid for the costs of materials. In the 1881 season "Fifty nine mothers have [been] since last Easter – average attendance, twenty six. Four hundred and thirty well made garments have been taken away and paid for."

The last of this kind of institution was the District Visiting Society. These societies had started in the late eighteenth century.[26] When a scheme was established in Ludlow is unclear and there is no mention of its introduction in Clayton's time. The Visitors had three main functions: to act as a link between the church and all members of the parish, to distribute and maintain the 'tracts' which offered religious and moral instruction to parishioners, and to collect the weekly savings which were paid into club funds and repaid with a small bonus, provided from subscriptions, at the end of the year. An appeal for subscriptions in July 1900 describes how the scheme worked. "£251/7/11 has been collected by the District Visitors in their weekly rounds throughout the year 1899. This means that more than £251 has been saved, and instead of having been spent in the public-houses, or in trifles which bring no real good to the spenders, it has been used for coal, household necessaries or warm clothing. The bonus on the money thus saved (1d in every 1/- [later corrected to 1d in every 1/- up to £1]) is derived from the subscriptions given to the District Visiting Society." The subscriptions for that year were £10 11s 6d and there were twenty eight District Visitors, all of them ladies.

The District Visitors were, to some extent, the eyes and ears of the clergy in a large and populous parish, but they did not necessarily hear of every case of need, as this entry in the Magazine for January 1880 reveals. "It is earnestly requested that in cases of sickness where the visits of the Parish Clergy are desired information may be sent to them. Sometimes sick people are surprised that they are overlooked and no call is made, the simple reason being that the clergy are wholly unaware of their particular case." This reference to the role of the clergy in ministering to the sick introduces the final element of Clayton's ministry in Ludlow.

Under the heading "Nurses for the Poor" the Magazine of October 1870 reported: "The Rector three years ago was called upon to visit a person dying from a painful and lingering disease, one which requires constant and considerable nursing. The sufferer however had only been able to obtain occasional and irregular assistance from a neighbour, and besides was only provided with coarse woollen rags.... Deeply impressed by the sight of suffering which it was impossible to alleviate adequately, the Rector determined to use every effort to procure efficient nursing for the sick poor. One of the chief difficulties in obtaining it has at length been removed and a trained nurse has, during the last three months, been at work in the Parish to the great advantage of many sufferers. She will in a few days be succeeded by two Ladies who have had long experience in nursing. With so many claims on the charitable at this particular time we hesitate to ask for help, never the less we feel sure there are some who may think it a privilege to share with the Rector the burden of expenses incurred with such an object." The first two nurses were Miss Martin and Miss Pierrepoint, whose salaries were paid by the Honourable Mary Windsor Clive, the costs of equipment being found from donations.

There was already in Ludlow a church sponsored charity which provided for the sick poor. This was the Ludlow Dispensary started in the 1820s.[27] It was supported by subscriptions and by periodic collections at the Ludlow churches and those in neighbouring parishes. Subscribers were enabled to buy Dispensary tickets, which they gave to poor members of the community. The funds also maintained a dispenser[28] and a housekeeper for the dispensary. One or more of the local doctors gave their services to the dispensary; sometimes this was free and sometimes an *ex gratia* payment was voted by the Committee. In 1885, when some 350 patients were treated, income from subscriptions was £112 and the main disbursements were on drugs (£60), dispenser's salary (£20), with £25 being voted to Dr Southern, one of the two medical officers.

The provision by Mary Windsor Clive, with the Rector's support, of a nursing service for the poor was but the first stage of a greater ambition, signalled in February 1871 by this note on Cottage Hospitals "Oswestry contains we believe one of the best of the smaller hospitals in the Island, and there are at Tenbury and Bromyard nearer home two Cottage Hospitals which seem to accomplish all that their benevolent promoters desired in their establishment. The question of a hospital of this character in Ludlow has been mooted, and we shall very much rejoice if the difficulties which naturally stand in the way of its being successfully founded should be removed." It was to take thirteen years for this ambition to be fulfilled.

In June 1873 Mary Windsor Clive died, leaving in trust £7,000, the interest of which was to go towards continuing the work of nursing and providing relief for the sick poor of

Ludlow Cottage Hospital in College Street, opened in 1884.

Ludlow which she had begun. Describing what followed the Magazine in November 1884 continued: "It seemed to the Trustees that it would be most desirable to provide a small hospital as soon as a suitable building could be found, in which such cases might be treated as could not receive sufficient care and attention at home." And so in that year the Rector and his wife took advantage of an offer of the Old College Buildings, at the bottom of College Street, buying them for £625, which included the cost of repairs. They made the buildings over to the Trustees at a rent of £22 a year. The Trustees altered the buildings at a cost of £884 "so that on the site there now stands a good Cottage Hospital, ready for use." Drs Southern, Brooks and Long undertook to provide medical supervision free of charge. The first matron of the Hospital was Miss Fitzmaurice, for the last twelve years the Lady Nurse. The Rules of the Hospital are set out in Appendix II.

From 1884 onwards the development of and support for the Cottage Hospital became a regular feature in the Magazine. Support came in kind, from subscriptions, from donations by individuals, businesses and societies, from Ludlow and district church collections, from fund raising and bequests. From 1895 the Magazine published the accounts annually. Typically receipts ran at between £500 and £600, more than half of that coming from dividends and interest on investments, while the largest elements of expenditure were on provisions, salaries and wages, and heating, lighting and house necessities. Part of the expenditure (usually some £60) went on outdoor nursing and relief; in February 1895 it was reported that: "During the month of January the Out-door Relief Fund of the Hospital has been distributed as follows: 118 Dinner tickets, 476 pints of milk, 55 hot dinners with vegetables, 78 pints of broth or

soup, as well as brandy, whisky, Port wine, stout, Cod Liver Oil, Linseed meal, etc. The Loan Fund is also in active work: blankets, sheets, nightgowns, flannel jackets and other sick room necessaries being constantly applied for. Between 40 and 50 families have been visited and aided in sickness in their homes." This was for the relief of what the Hospital Rules called "the industrious poor", who were not in habitual receipt of poor relief.

The following Table taken from the accounts published in the Magazine gives the numbers of in-patients dealt with by the Hospital in the ten years 1895-1904.

Table III: Ludlow Cottage Hospital Statistics 1895-1904				
Year	Admitted	Relieved	Cured	Died	Average stay in days
1895	33	18	14	1	n/a
1896	37	18	18	1	n/a
1897	48	15	30	3	32
1898	32	9	23	0	35
1899	46	18	28	0	26
1900	50	14	30	6	27
1901	43	10	31	2	24
1902	50	13	31	6	21
1903	61	12	41	8	20
1904	104	40	63	1	12½

The Cottage Hospital was to remain open until 1982, so serving the people of Ludlow for almost one hundred years.

These were the temporal contributions which Clayton and his clerical colleagues made to the welfare of Ludlow during the forty years of his incumbency. But they did not do it alone. The contribution made by the lay members of the church warrants a study of its own, but one point is worth bringing out here. Clayton certainly owed a great deal to his connections with and the generosity of the Windsor Clives, and other local gentry and upper middle class families were prominent in their support for the church. Sir

Charles Rouse Boughton of Downton Hall, Mr A. Boughton Knight of Downton Castle, Mr Alfred Salwey of Overton, and the Pensons of Dinham House all appear regularly in the lists of subscribers to church causes, great and small. But support for the church was not solely an upper class prerogative. The list of church wardens at Appendix III shows the part played by Ludlow shopkeepers and tradesmen in the running of the church in Clayton's time and they feature largely among those paying the voluntary church rate and pew rents. The report of the annual church workers service and entertainment at the Rectory in 1878 broadens that base still further: "We cannot refrain from remarking upon a very noticeable feature in meetings such as these, viz. the union between class and class brought about by the church. Here were assembled at one table [there were over 100 guests] people belonging to every rank of society, who were all interested in and working harmoniously together for one object..... It would be hard to find such another common meeting ground, as the Church affords, where people laying aside all class feeling not only work for one end but what is the surest test of real union can heartily enjoy and enter into a social gathering."

In his *Country Grammar School* David Lloyd cites two references to Clayton's style and manner: one in 1876 speaks of his "immense influence [which] it is difficult to oppose", the other in 1883 comments on "the domination of the [Grammar] School by the Rector", who was "very unpopular", partly on account of his fairly high churchmanship.[29] McLeod remarks of the nineteenth century church and clergy "Not only in small market towns such as Ludlow, Warwick or Oakham...but in modern places like Birmingham and Leeds, the parish church was a formidable presence. Similarly with the position of the clergy in the social landscape: in most villages the vicar was the most powerful individual....in the town the vicar was part of a much larger and more variegated elite, but still enjoyed a great deal of prestige and influence."[30] In Clayton's case we may add the fact that he had married into one of the great families of the land, let alone the locality. In the circumstances it would be surprising if there were not some in the town who found their Rector autocratic, especially so as his churchmanship was described in his obituary as "grave" and the disciplines of his character as a Christian "stern". But against this should be set the achievements of his ministry and the fact that these were not and could not have been achieved by him alone. Only a person who had the respect, the trust and, indeed, the affection of those to whom he ministered, with whom he worked and whom he led could have achieved what he did. His character and his achievement are caught by his obituarist: "Thenceforth, through evil report and good report, by love unfeigned, by the Word of Truth, by the power of God, Mr Clayton commended himself and his Creed to every man's conscience; for of him, it could be truly said, 'he lived what he preached.'"

Edward ffarington Clayton,
Rector of Ludlow 1867-1907.

LUDLOW CLERGY 1867 - 1907

Name	Date of arrival	Office	Date of departure
E. ff. Clayton	March 1867	RECTOR	Nov 1907
R. Meyricke	1824	Reader* from 1825	Sept 1881
R. V. Russell	c. 1854	Lecturer† and Chaplain to Ludlow Union	April 1874
P. F. Hamond	1869	St Stephen's	Sept 1870
W. J. Pinckney (1)	1869	August 1874 Lecturer	June 1880
E. S. Lowndes	1870	St Stephen's	Sept 1877
A. C. Lee	Sept 1874		Jan 1881
C. L. V. Baker	1876	Gravel Hill and St. John's	Sept 1882
T. J. F. Bennett	1877	St Stephen's Lecturer 1880 – 81	1881
G. W. Turner	1880	Reader 1882 Lecturer 1886	Oct 1896
C. U. Manning	1881		1883
W. Humphreys	1882	St Stephen's Lecturer 1882	1886
W. J. Pinckney (2)	Oct 1882	St John's	1884
J. C. Grey	June 1883		Dec 1890
A. Wight	1884	St John's	1886
J. C. E. Besant	1886	St Stephen's Reader 1891 – 93	1893
H. F. Grove	1886	St John's	June 1888
L. C. Wilkinson	June 1888	St John's	1892
H. J. Drake	July 1890		Dec 1893
L. H. Nicholl	1892	St John's Chaplain to Ludlow Union 1895	Oct 1902
J. H. D. Creighton	1893	St Stephen's Reader	Dec 1894
R. A. Lyne	1893	Reader 1895	Sept 1901
J. S. Munn	Jan 1894	St Stephen's	March 1901
S. H. Cubitt (1)	1895		1898
J. N. Gill	June 1898		1901
W. I. Wolfenden	1899	Reader Chaplain to Ludlow Union 1902 St John's 1903	
J. J. Antrobus	1901		May 1904
S. H. Cubitt (2)	1901	St Stephen's	Oct 1905
F. O. Poole	1902	Lecturer	Sept 1906
J. E. Fyffe	May 1904		1907
W. J. Clarke	Oct 1905	St Stephen's	Oct 1906
G. R. Peak	Sept 1906	Lecturer	
V. A. Cresswell	1906		
T. L. Carpenter	July 1907		

* When Revd G. W. Turner was appointed Reader in 1882 the February Magazine reported his appointment as "Assistant to the Rector", adding "sometimes miscalled 'Reader'".

† The same Magazine remarked, on the appointment of Revd W. Humphreys to be Lecturer, that this office was also known as "Preacher to the Town".

RULES OF LUDLOW COTTAGE HOSPITAL 1884

The Hospital is designed for the reception of persons suffering from accidents and from diseases of a probably temporary character, which cannot be adequately treated at the house of the patient; and especially for the relief of the industrious poor who are not habitual recipients of relief under the Poor Law Act.

Persons resident within the existing Parliamentary Borough of Ludlow will be admitted without payment. Should admission be sought for others, a payment of 1/6 a day must be guaranteed.

The Honorary Medical Officers will take charge of the patients for a week at a time in rotation, but each patient will, so long as he or she remains in the hospital, continue to be under the care of the same medical officer.

The Hospital will be under the superintendence of the Lady Nurse and her assistants.

Presents of linen, wine, fruit and other necessaries for the use of patients will be gladly received at any time by the resident Lady Nurse.

No case of fever, mania, epilepsy, nor any which does not offer hope of relief within a reasonable period, nor any of a contagious or infectious nature, nor any woman within five months of her confinement will be admitted.

No patient will be permitted to go out of the Hospital grounds without the permission of the Medical Officer in charge.

Profane, abusive, or immoral language or behaviour will not be permitted, and if persisted in, will be followed by dismissal from the Hospital.

Male patients will not be permitted to go into the Women's, nor Female patients into the Men's ward.

Patients will not be allowed to smoke, nor play at cards or any gambling game.

Patients will not be allowed to waste or damage the smallest thing belonging to the Institution.

Patients will be required to assist in housework, needlework, washing, gardening, etc. subject to the permission of the Medical Officer in charge.

The friends of patients will be allowed to visit them between the hours of two and four on Wednesdays and Sundays, but not more than two friends of any one patient can be admitted at the same time.

Nothing of any sort whatsoever may be conveyed in to a patient except with the consent of the Medical Officer in charge. Any one breaking this rule will be liable to be refused admission on any subsequent occasion.

Patients will be received into the Hospital for not more than six weeks, unless on consultation the Medical Officers agree that a longer course of treatment is requisite.

ST LAURENCE, CHURCH WARDENS 1870 - 1907

1870 H. Johnson*, draper, High St
     H. Rickards*, ironmonger, Bull Ring
1871 W. Powell, jeweller, High St
     H. Rickards
1872 W. Powell
     E. Leake, draper, Castle Square
1873 C. Harper, post office, Castle Square
     W. Cooke*, cabinet maker, Bull Ring
1874 H. Gatehouse, wine & spirits, Market St
     W. Cooke
1875 H. Gatehouse
     W. Cooke
1876 Herbert Evans, architect, Corve St
     E. Partridge, printer, bookseller, Broad St
1877 E. Partridge
     C. F. Keysell*, wine & spirits, Bull Ring
1878 G. Woolley, printer, bookseller, Bull Ring
     C. F. Keysell
1879 G. Woolley
     H. T. Weyman*, solicitor, Mill St
1880 H. T. Weyman
     E. Leake, Castle Square
1881 T. Williams, draper, Broad St
     W. Holyoake, china warehouse, King St
1882 T. Williams
     W. Holyoake
1883 H. Gray, 40 Mill Street
     G. H. Woodhouse, chemist, Bull Ring
1884 H. Gray
     G. H. Woodhouse
1885 H. Gray
     G. H. Woodhouse
1886 H. Gray
     G. H. Woodhouse
1887 H. Gray
     G. H. Woodhouse
1888 H. Gray
     G. H. Woodhouse
1889 G. H. Woodhouse
     T. W. Lowe, fishmonger, Broad St

1890 G. H. Woodhouse
     T. W. Lowe
1891 G. H. Woodhouse
     T. W. Lowe
1892 G. H. Woodhouse
     T. W. Lowe
1893 G. Woolley*, printer, Bull Ring
     T. W. Lowe
1894 G. Woolley
     T. W. Lowe
1895 G. Woolley
     T. W. Lowe
1896 G. Woolley
     T. W. Lowe
1897 G. Woolley
     T. W. Lowe
1898 G. Woolley
     T. W. Lowe
1899 R. Marston*, solicitor, The Castle
     E. S. Lloyd, solicitor, Broad St
1900 R. Marston
     E. S. Lloyd
1901 R. Marston
     G. France, bank manager, Broad St
1902 R. Marston
     G. France
1903 H. T. Weyman, solicitor, Mill St
     S. H. Valentine, grocer, Broad St
1904 H. T. Weyman
     S. H. Valentine
1905 H. T. Weyman
     S. H. Valentine
1906 S. H. Valentine
     R. Sweetman, chemist, The Cross
1907 S. H. Valentine
     R. Sweetman

* These men were all on the Town Council at some time or other during the period.

ENDNOTES

1. This and other information about church services at St Laurence's comes from the Church Register of Preachers, Readers, Services, Collections, etc. for the year concerned. (SA) P176/A/7/1 - 6.

2. One of Clayton's earliest innovations was the establishment of a Parish Magazine, the first edition of which appeared in June 1867. This provides the principal source for this chapter and quotations, unless otherwise cited, are taken from a contemporary Magazine. The series of Ludlow Parish Magazines is held at St Laurence Church House. The magazine started in a small way so far as local information was concerned, the inside front cover giving the church calendar for the month and a list of the Sunday and other services at the Parish Church, and the then Mission Church in Corve Street. There were also brief notes of significance for the Parish, including remarks on important events in the Church Calendar or on matters of spiritual note, for example the importance of daily worship. The bulk of the magazine was syndicated material of an uplifting nature, either fictional or factual. The cast and tone of the entries, as they grow in length and relevance to parish life, suggest that the editor was Clayton himself. The magazine was printed locally by Edward Partridge of 58 Broad Street, and cost a penny halfpenny (roughly ½p in modern terms). This reference is from Clayton's obituary in December 1907.

3. Diaries and Memoranda of Dolly Clayton, wife of George Clayton, of Lostock Hall, Preston. Lancashire Record Office DDX 510.

4. From information provided by Mrs M. E. Griffiths, Archivist and Librarian, Sedbergh School.

5. From a private communication from Mr David Clayton, the Reverend Clayton's grandson.

6. Lady Mary Windsor Clive was the youngest daughter of the 2nd Earl of Bradford. Her brother the Hon. and Reverend George Bridgeman was the Rector of Wigan (see *Burke's Peerage, Baronetage and Knightage* 1888, p. 167). He was the preacher at the first Harvest Thanksgiving of Clayton's Ministry in September 1867. It is tempting to think that he may have been previously acquainted with the Clayton family in Lancashire and that this might also have been a factor in commending Clayton to the patroness of the Ludlow living.

7. Private communication from Mr David Clayton. The conversion to modern terms is for illustrative purposes only, and has throughout been done on the basis of John J. McKusker's "Comparing the Purchasing Power of Money in Great Britain from 1264 to any other year, including the present" Economic History Services 2001, URL, Copyright © 2004 EH.Net.

8. Probate. London 16 January 1908.

9. *Shrewsbury Chronicle* 29 November 1907.

10. "In spite of the requirement [to take communion at Easter] there were large numbers of Anglicans in the nineteenth century who attended church regularly but seldom or never received communion." Hugh McLeod, *Religion and Society in England 1850 - 1914*, MacMillan 1996, p. 175. In Ludlow this is borne out by the numbers of communicants at St Stephen's recorded in the St Laurence register in the late 1870s (an average in the low 20s) compared with the sizes of the congregations reported in the Magazine when the new Iron Church was being planned "[the old chapel] being crowded Sunday after Sunday by a congregation almost double the number it was intended to hold [about 200]".

11. For example, income from kneelings, as they were called, produced £202 10s. out of a total income of just over £419 in 1891/2. The Pew Rental Accounts, which run from 1861 to 1893, show that about 130 people rented one or more pews in the church (at prices from 5/- to £1) in the years 1888 - 1893 (SA P176/2881/2/9a).

12. The Bishop of Hereford's licence for Divine Service at 10 o'clock every Sunday, with a sermon, had been given because "inhabitants of a district...situate in and adjacent to Corve Street...., being in want of greater church accommodation, have procured the use of a building situate in Corve Street and fitted up the same in a fit and appropriate manner for the performance of divine service." SA P176/2881/8/1. T. Curley's map of the Geological Sections of Ludlow made in 1862 showed a 'Chapel of Ease' at the rear of a building in lower Corve Street backing onto the River Corve close to what is now the Merchant House Restaurant. As this is listed in the Key immediately after St Laurence Church and before the Non-Conformist Chapels it seems a reasonable supposition that this may have been the Corve Street Mission Chapel. It subsequently became a Non-Conformist Chapel.

13. K. Hylson-Smith, *The Churches in England Vol. III 1833-1998*, SCM Press, 1998, p.15: "[The middle classes were] the men and women who formed the nucleus and driving force of the churches."

14. E. R. Norman, *Church and Society in England 1770 – 1970*, Oxford, 1976, p.126. "The Church of England seemed to most working-class men, an institution for the well-to-do."

15. The licence to use the school for divine service was applied for by the Stanton Lacy vestry and was granted on 11 September 1876. HD 10/41 Diocesan Record Annual Box 1876 (2). The HD series is at the Hereford Record Office.

16. Order in Council 28 June 1880 annexing East Hamlet, Rock, Henley and some other southern parts of Stanton Lacy into the Parish of St Laurence, Ludlow. HD 10/48 Diocesan Records Annual Box 1880(1).

17. "No distinction should be made between what was 'sacred' and what was 'secular'; all human life was God's concern, and concern for human beings included a concern for their bodies, their minds and their souls - any work which limited itself to one part of the human

18. personality was incomplete." McLeod, op. cit., p.144.

18. The Magazine published a list of subscribers and the Schools' accounts from the early 1890s until 1903, when the arrangements for financing Church schools were changed

19. The accounts for this period reveal the extent to which the Schools were supported by the Church. The 1894/5 accounts, published in August 1895, show that nearly 20% of the schools' income of about £900 came from Voluntary Contributions and Collections in Church. There were 113 voluntary contributions. The church collections came from the annual Mayor's Sunday in November and, for the infant school, at the Harvest Thanksgiving.

20. Report for the Year 1899 of the Ludlow Parochial Statistics and Institutions. (SA) P176/10/1/03.

21. In 1870 out of 43 teachers, 29 were unmarried ladies, 5 were married and there were 9 men. The expenses of running the Sunday Schools were of the order of £50, which came partly from subscriptions and partly from the church collections on one day in the summer each year.

22. E. R. Norman, op. cit., pp.123ff.

23. See, for example, Donald Read, *England 1868-1914*. Volume 10 of A History of England in Eleven Volumes, Longman, 1979 p. 109.

24. "The parochial clergyman in the 1840s and 1850s found himself as the only charitable agent between the pauper and the workhouse. Thus the typical clergyman put himself at the head of a wide variety of provident institutions and clubs designed to help the labourer to help himself, and keep him from the workhouse." Anthony Russell, *The Clerical Profession*, London,

SPCK, 1980, p.177.

25. It is referred to in 1891 as having existed for more than thirty years.

26. In 1828 the General Society for the Promotion of District Visiting was formed and by the mid-1830s they were widespread. Russell, op. cit., pp.119ff..

27. The surviving Committee minutes begin in October 1828. Minutes of Ludlow Dispensary Committee 1828-1846 (SA) P176/3036/5/1. The Oswestry Provident Dispensary opened in the same year, and that at Wellington in 1834. Kelly's Directory for Shropshire 1891, p.381 and p.456.

28. For thirty or more years John Nixon, chemist and druggist of 56 Broad Street. See Kelly's Directories for Shropshire 1870 onwards.

29. D. Lloyd *Country Grammar School*, Birmingham, 1977, p.130 and p.133, citing respectively a letter from H. Salwey (PRO Ed 27/3957) and a Charity Commission enquiry (PRO Ed 27/3964).

30. McLeod, op. cit., pp.13 and 14.

31. The sources for this are Crockford's Clerical Directory, the Ludlow Parish Magazine and the Church Calendars for the Diocese of Hereford (to be found at the Hereford Cathedral Library, the continuous run starts in 1870)

32. This was printed in the Parish Magazine of November 1884.

33. This list is compiled from the Church Calendars of the Diocese of Hereford, and from the relevant editions of Kelly's Directories of Shropshire. It is supplemented from 1897, when the Parish Magazine periodically reported the election of Wardens. It is reasonable to infer from this that the first named were the Rector's Wardens and the second the People's Wardens.

The End of the Era

Queen Victoria died at 6.40pm on Monday, 22 January 1901. In Ludlow that evening crowds gathered in Castle Square to await a public announcement, though the Mayor, Councillor William Chubb, felt obliged to delay until the news was verified. The first official reaction came, in fact, from the Rector, who ordered the tenor bell at St Laurence's to start tolling at 8.40pm. On the next day the town was in mourning: shops were closed, blinds were drawn, and the flags on the Butter Cross and the Castle were at half mast. Many of those in the streets wore black. Four days later, before a crowd of about 2,000 in Castle Square, the Mayor read the proclamation of Edward VII from a special platform built over the entrance to the Market Hall. He and the Corporation then moved on, with a police escort, to the Butter Cross to repeat the ceremony in the presence of an even larger crowd.

Very few in that assembly would have remembered the Ludlow which Victoria had visited as a young Princess back in 1832 – the visit with which this book began. Indeed the great majority would not have known a time when Victoria was not on the throne. They no doubt accepted as the natural order of things many of the changes in Ludlow during the Queen's reign. The principal features of these have been described or touched upon in the preceding chapters – the re-assertion of Ludlow's historic role as a market town; the coming of the railway; the physical growth of the town beyond its age-old boundaries; the gradual extension of the franchise with its implications for national and representative local government; the arrangements for dealing with the indigent or 'undeserving' poor; the introduction of universal and compulsory education; and, latterly and not without resistance, improvements in public health provision, notably a clean water supply and a sewerage system.

The Memorial Service for the Queen took place, like many others across the Empire, on Friday, 2 February, the day of her funeral. At the heart of the procession to St Laurence's came the Borough Council, then at the peak of its local power and dignity, and comprised predominantly of tradesmen representing the core of the town's modern economy. But the presence of the public services – the Police and the Fire Brigade – the full range of the educational establishment, the Board of Guardians and the Overseers of the Poor, all created or substantially developed in the Victorian period, signal their present importance in the town's life. The order of the procession catches in a striking way many of the principal strands which, woven together, make up the history of Victorian Ludlow and have provided the themes of this book.

FUNERAL

Of Her (late) Most Gracious Majesty

QUEEN VICTORIA,

Memorial Service

IN THE

PARISH CHURCH, LUDLOW.

2nd FEBRUARY, 1901.

Order of the Procession.

1   Fire Brigade
2   Band of the Shropshire Yeomanry
3   Ludlow Squadron of the Shropshire Yeomanry
4   The "G" Company 1st (Vol.) King's Shropshire Light Infantry
5   The Police
6   The Town Crier and Mace Bearers
7   His Worship the Mayor, the Aldermen, Borough Magistrates, and Councillors, with the Officials.
8   The County Magistrates
9   The Charity Trustees
10   The Governors of the Ludlow Grammar School ; the Masters of that School ; the Committee and Masters of the National Schools; the Committee and Masters of the British Schools; with the Local Committee under the Technical Instruction Acts
11   The Ludlow Natural History Society
12   The Board of Guardians and the Overseers of the Poor
13   The Ludlow Agricultural Society
14   The Freemasons and the Friendly Societies.

CRUNDELL, Caxton Press.

Abbreviations used in endnotes

HJ   Hereford Journal
HRO   Hereford Record Office
LA   Ludlow Advertiser
LHN   Ludlow Heritage News
LLH   Ludlow & Leominster Herald
LMCT   Ludlow Municipal Charity Trustees
LS   Ludlow Standard
MI   Memorial Inscriptions

PRO   Public Record Office
SAHS   Shropshire Archaeological and Historical Society
SA   Shropshire Archives
SC   Shrewsbury Chronicle
SJ   Salopian Journal
TSAS   Transactions of the Shropshire Archaeological Society

Index